DATE DUE

DEMCO 128-5046

SOMETHING ABOUT THE AUTHOR®

Something about
the Author *was named
an* **"Outstanding
Reference Source"**
*the highest honor given
by the American
Library Association
Reference and Adult
Services Division.*

ISSN 0276-816X

SOMETHING ABOUT THE AUTHOR®

**Facts and Pictures about Authors
and Illustrators of Books for Young People**

EDITED BY
KEVIN S. HILE

VOLUME 87

GALE

DETROIT · NEW YORK · TORONTO · LONDON

STAFF

Editor: Kevin S. Hile
Managing Editor: Joyce Nakamura
Publisher: Hal May
Contributing Editor: Alan Hedblad
Assistant Editor: Marilyn O'Connell Allen

Sketchwriters/Copyeditors: Linda R. Andres, Shelly Andrews, Joanna Brod,
Ronie-Richele Garcia-Johnson, Mary Gillis, Janet L. Hile, Laurie Hillstrom,
Motoko Fujishiro Huthwaite, David Johnson, J. Sydney Jones, Julie Karmazin,
Sharyn Kolberg, Thomas F. McMahon, Pamela J. Nealon-LaBreck, Susan Reicha,
Gerard J. Senick, Pamela L. Shelton, Diane Telgen, and Michaela Swart Wilson

Research Manager: Victoria B. Cariappa
Project Coordinator: Cheryl L. Warnock
Research Specialist: Gary J. Oudersluys
Research Associates: Michelle Lee, Michele P. Pica, and Norma Sawaya

Permissions Manager: Marlene S. Hurst
Permissions Specialists: Margaret A. Chamberlain and Maria Franklin
Permissions Associate: Margaret McAvoy-Amato

Production Director: Mary Beth Trimper
Production Assistant: Deborah Milliken

Image Database Supervisor: Randy Bassett
Macintosh Artist: Sherrell Hobbs
Imaging Specialist: Robert Duncan
Photography Coordinator: Pamela A. Hayes

Library of Congress Catalog Card Number 72-27107

ISBN 0-8103-9373-5 ISSN 0276-816X

Printed in the United States of America

10 9 8 7 6 5 4 3 2 1

Contents

A

B

C

D

E-F

G

H

V-W

Authors in Forthcoming Volumes

Below are some of the authors and illustrators that will be featured in upcoming volumes of *SATA*. These include new entries on the swiftly-rising stars of the field, as well as completely revised and updated entries (indicated with *) on some of the most notable and best-loved creators of books for children.

*Nathan Aaseng: A winner of numerous awards for his nonfiction works for young readers, Aaseng is especially noted for his sports books, such as his "Sports Heroes" and "You Are the Coach" series.

Anthea Bell: Bell, the winner of four prestigious Mildred L. Batchelder awards, among many other honors, is a noted translator and adapter of German, French, and Danish stories for young readers of English, including fables, picture books, novels, and comic books.

*Ann Cameron: Best known for her stories featuring the creative and energetic character Julian Corsaro, including *The Stories Julian Tells* and *Julian, Secret Agent,* Cameron especially enjoys writing about children from different cultures and ethnic backgrounds.

*Michael Crichton: The acknowledged pioneer of the "techno-thriller," Crichton is the author of huge bestsellers like *Sphere, Jurassic Park,* and *Congo,* some of which he has adapted for the screen.

Elzbieta: Elzbieta is the award-winning Polish-born author and illustrator who now lives in France, where she has penned works featuring such colorful characters as Little Mops and Dikou.

Sheila Gordon: This South African author won the Jane Addams Children's Book Award in 1988 for *Waiting for the Rain,* a story of apartheid seen through the eyes of two children, one white and one black.

Eileen Goudge: Known for her young adult romance novels, Goudge has written over thirty books since the early 1980s that have found a large audience with teen readers.

*Tanith Lee: Lee is the author of both fantasy and science fiction novels and short stories that explore such themes as destiny versus free will and the search for personal identity.

Tololwa M. Mollel: Tanzanian-born Canadian author Mollel has received much attention in recent years for such picturebooks as *The Orphan Boy* that acquaint readers with the life and culture of the Maasai people.

Richard and Wendy Pini: The Pinis are the husband-and-wife team responsible for the popular "Elfquest" fantasy comic book series that has been honored with a Balrog Award, among other prizes.

Philip Ridley: Well known in his native Britain for his stage and screen writings for adults, Ridley is also the author of quirky children's books like *Dakota of the White Flats* and *Krindlekrax.*

*Nicole St. John: St. John, who often writes under the name Norma Johnston, has been highly praised for her young adult historical novels like the "Keeping Days" series, though she also writes for other audiences and in other genres.

*Aranka Siegal: Siegal's books *Upon the Head of a Goat* and *Grace in the Wilderness* are fictionalized accounts of the author's horrifying experiences as a Jew living in Hungary under the Nazis.

Helen Hughes Vick: The author of the "Walker" trilogy, Vick has created a time-travel adventure about a modern Hopi boy who journeys back 750 years to help save his ancestral tribe.

Introduction

Something about the Author (SATA) is an ongoing reference series that deals with the lives and works of authors and illustrators of children's books. *SATA* includes not only well-known authors and illustrators whose books are widely read, but also those less prominent people whose works are just coming to be recognized. This series is often the only readily available information source on emerging writers and artists. You'll find *SATA* informative and entertaining, whether you are a student, a librarian, an English teacher, a parent, or simply an adult who enjoys children's literature for its own sake.

What's Inside SATA

SATA provides detailed information about authors and illustrators who span the full time range of children's literature, from early figures like John Newbery and L. Frank Baum to contemporary figures like Judy Blume and Richard Peck. Authors in the series represent primarily English-speaking countries, particularly the United States, Canada, and the United Kingdom. Also included, however, are authors from around the world whose works are available in English translation. The writings represented in *SATA* include those created intentionally for children and young adults as well as those written for a general audience and known to interest younger readers. These writings cover the entire spectrum of children's literature, including picture books, humor, folk and fairy tales, animal stories, mystery and adventure, science fiction and fantasy, historical fiction, poetry and nonsense verse, drama, biography, and nonfiction.

Obituaries are also included in *SATA* and are intended not only as death notices but also as concise overviews of people's lives and work. Additionally, each edition features newly revised and updated entries for a selection of *SATA* listees who remain of interest to today's readers and who have been active enough to require extensive revisions of their earlier biographies.

Two Convenient Indexes

In response to suggestions from librarians, *SATA* indexes no longer appear in every volume but are included in alternate (odd-numbered) volumes of the series, beginning with Volume 57.

SATA continues to include two indexes that cumulate with each alternate volume: the Illustrations Index, arranged by the name of the illustrator, gives the number of the volume and page where the illustrator's work appears in the current volume as well as all preceding volumes in the series; the Author Index gives the number of the volume in which a person's Biographical Sketch or Obituary appears in the current volume as well as all preceding volumes in the series.

These indexes also include references to authors and illustrators who appear in Gale's *Yesterday's Authors of Books for Children, Children's Literature Review,* and the *Something about the Author Autobiography Series.*

Easy-to-Use Entry Format

Whether you're already familiar with the *SATA* series or just getting acquainted, you will want to be aware of the kind of information that an entry provides. In every *SATA* entry the editors attempt to give as complete a picture of the person's life and work as possible. A typical entry in *SATA* includes the following clearly labeled information sections:

- *PERSONAL:* date and place of birth and death, parents' names and occupations, name of spouse, date of marriage, names of children, educational institutions attended, degrees received, religious and political affiliations, hobbies and other interests.

- *ADDRESSES:* complete home, office, electronic mail, and agent addresses, whenever available.

- *CAREER:* name of employer, position, and dates for each career post; art exhibitions; military service; memberships and offices held in professional and civic organizations.

- *AWARDS, HONORS:* literary and professional awards received.

- *WRITINGS:* title-by-title chronological bibliography of books written and/or illustrated, listed by genre when known; lists of other notable publications, such as plays, screenplays, and periodical contributions.

- *ADAPTATIONS:* a list of films, television programs, plays, CD-ROMs, recordings, and other media presentations that have been adapted from the author's work.

- *WORK IN PROGRESS:* description of projects in progress.

- *SIDELIGHTS:* a biographical portrait of the author or illustrator's development, either directly from the biographee—and often written specifically for the *SATA* entry—or gathered from diaries, letters, interviews, or other published sources.

- *FOR MORE INFORMATION SEE:* references for further reading.

- *EXTENSIVE ILLUSTRATIONS:* photographs, movie stills, book illustrations, and other interesting visual materials supplement the text.

How a SATA Entry Is Compiled

A *SATA* entry progresses through a series of steps. If the biographee is living, the *SATA* editors try to secure information directly from him or her through a questionnaire. From the information that the biographee supplies, the editors prepare an entry, filling in any essential missing details with research and/or telephone interviews. If possible, the author or illustrator is sent a copy of the entry to check for accuracy and completeness.

If the biographee is deceased or cannot be reached by questionnaire, the *SATA* editors examine a wide variety of published sources to gather information for an entry. Biographical and bibliographic sources are consulted, as are book reviews, feature articles, published interviews, and material sometimes obtained from the biographee's family, publishers, agent, or other associates.

Entries that have not been verified by the biographees or their representatives are marked with an asterisk (*).

Contact the Editor

We encourage our readers to examine the entire *SATA* series. Please write and tell us if we can make *SATA* even more helpful to you. Give your comments and suggestions to the editor:

BY MAIL: The Editor, *Something about the Author,* Gale Research, 835 Penobscot Bldg., 645 Griswold St., Detroit, MI 48226-4094.

BY TELEPHONE: (800) 347-GALE

BY FAX: (313) 961-6599

BY E-MAIL: CYA@Gale.com@Galesmtp

Acknowledgments

Grateful acknowledgment is made to the following publishers, authors, and artists whose works appear in this volume.

JAMES ALDRIDGE. Jacket illustration by Alun Hood from *The Broken Saddle*. By James Aldridge. Julia MacRae Books, 1982. Copyright © James Aldridge. Reproduced by permission of Walker Books, Ltd. / Portrait of James Aldridge. Reproduced by permission of Walker Books Ltd. / From a scene from *Ride a Wild Pony*. Copyright © Walt Disney Productions. World rights reserved. Reproduced by permission.

PRUDENCE ANDREW. From a jacket of *Una and the Heaven Baby*. Thomas Nelson, Inc., Publishers, 1972. Copyright © 1972 by Prudence Andrew. Reproduced with permission. / Jacket illustration by Hal Siegel from *Close within my own Circle*. By Prudence Andrew. Elsevier/Nelson Books, 1978. All rights reserved. Used by permission of the publisher, E. P. Dutton, an imprint of New American Library, a division of Penguin Books USA, Inc.

SUSAN C. ANTHONY. Portrait of Susan C. Anthony. Reproduced by permission.

DEBBY ATWELL. Portrait of Debby Atwell. Reproduced by permission.

ALLAN BAILLIE. Portrait of Allan Baillie. Reproduced by permission. / Cover illustration by Jane Tanner from *Drac and the Gremlin*. By Allan Baillie. Dial Books for Young Readers, 1988. Pictures copyright © 1988 by Jane Tanner. Reproduced by permission of Dial Books for Young Readers, a division of Penguin Books USA, Inc. / Jacket illustration by Todd Doney from *Little Brother*. By Allan Baillie. Viking Penguin, 1985. Jacket illustration copyright © Todd Doney, 1992. Reproduced by permission of Viking Penguin, a division of Penguin Books USA, Inc.

ETHEL BARRETT. From a cover of *The Man Struck Down by Light*. Regal Books, 1987. Copyright © 1979, 1987 by GL Publications. All rights reserved. Reproduced by permission of the publisher.

JAY BENNETT. Portrait of Jay Bennett courtesy of the author. / Jacket illustration by Cris Cocozza from *Coverup: A Novel*. By Jay Bennett. Franklin Watts, 1991. All rights reserved. Reprinted by permission of the publisher. / Jacket illustration by Walter Harper from *The Dangling Witness*. By Jay Bennett. Delacorte Press, 1974. All rights reserved. Reprinted by permission of Delacorte Press, a division of Bantam Doubleday Dell Publishing Group, Inc.

NATALIE S. BOBER. Portrait of Natalie S. Bober by Lawrence H. Bober. / Illustration by Vera Rosenberry from *Marc Chagall: Painter of Dreams*. By Natalie S. Bober. The Jewish Publication Society, 1991. All rights reserved. Used through the courtesy of The Jewish Publication Society. / "The Declaration of Independence," painting by John Trumbull. Courtesy of Yale University Art Gallery. From a cover of *Thomas Jefferson: Man on a Mountain*. By Natalie S. Bober. Collier Books, 1993. All rights reserved. Reproduced by permission of the publisher. / Portrait of Abigail Adams by Benjamin Blyth, and engraving, "Boston Massacre" by J. H. Bufford. Courtesy of Massachusetts Historical Society. From a cover of *Abigail Adams*. By Natalie S. Bober. Atheneum, 1995. All rights reserved. Reproduced by permission of Massachusetts Historical Society.

RUSKIN BOND. Portrait of Ruskin Bond from a jacket of *Binya's Blue Umbrella*. By Ruskin Bond. Caroline House, 1995. All rights reserved. Reprinted by permission of the publisher. / Illustration by Vera Rosenberry from *Binya's Blue Umbrella*. By Ruskin Bond. Caroline House, 1995. Illustration copyright © 1995 by Vera Rosenberry. All rights reserved. Reprinted by permission of the author. / From an illustration in *Angry River*. By Ruskin Bond. Hamish Hamilton, 1972. Reprinted by permission of the author. / Illustration by Sally Scott from *Tales and Legends from India*. By Ruskin Bond. Franklin Watts, 1982. Illustrations copyright © 1982 by Sally Scott. Reprinted by permission of the publisher.

JIM BRANDENBURG. Portrait of Jim Brandenburg by Steve Durst. / Photograph by Jim Brandenburg from *White Wolf: Living with an Arctic Legend*. By Jim Brandenburg. Northwood Press, Inc., 1988. Copyright © 1988 by Jim Brandenburg. All rights reserved. Reproduced by permission of Jim Brandenburg.

JANET MITSUI BROWN. Portrait of Janet Mitsui Brown. Reproduced by permission.

MICHAEL CADNUM. Portrait of Michael Cadnum by Dave Thomas. / Cover illustration by Bill Binger from *Ghostwright*. By Michael Cadnum. Carroll & Graf, 1992. All rights reserved. Reprinted by permission of the publisher.

JUDITH CASELEY. Portrait of Judith Caseley by Neil Curtis. / Jacket illustration by Ellen Thompson from *Harry and Arney*. By Judith Caseley. Greenwillow Books, 1994. Jacket art copyright © by Ellen Thompson. All rights reserved. Reprinted by permission of the publisher. / From an illustration in *Dear Annie*. By Judith Casely. Greenwillow Books, 1991. All rights reserved. Reprinted by permission of the publisher.

JILL CHANEY. Cover illustration by Catherine Leeming from *Woffle, R. A.* By Jill Chaney. Dobson Books, Ltd., 1976. Illustrations copyright © 1976 Dobson Books Ltd. All rights reserved. Reprinted by permission of the publisher.

JOSEPH E. CHIPPERFIELD. Portrait of Joseph E. Chipperfield. Courtesy of International Portrait Gallery. / Illustration by Helen Torrey from *Storm of Dancerwood.* By Joseph E. Chipperfield. David McKay Company, Inc., 1949. All rights reserved. Reprinted by permission of Random House, Inc.

CHRIS CLAREMONT. Portrait of Chris Claremont. Copyright © by M. C. Valada. Reproduced by permission.

FRANK E. COOKE. Portrait of Frank E. Cooke. Reproduced by permission.

RUTH CRAFT. Jacket illustration by Erik Blegvad from *The Winter Bear.* By Ruth Craft. Atheneum, 1975. Illustrations copyright © 1974 by Erik Blegvad. All rights reserved. Reprinted by permission of Margaret K. McElderry Books, an imprint of Simon & Schuster. / Illustration by Irene Haas from *Carrie Hepple's Garden.* By Ruth Craft. Atheneum, 1979. Illustrations copyright © 1979 by Irene Haas. All rights reserved. Reprinted by permission of Margaret K. McElderry Books, an imprint of Simon & Schuster.

MARJORIE SHEILA DARKE. Portrait of Marjorie Darke.

LIONEL DAVIDSON. Portrait of Lionel Davidson. Copyright © Jerry Bauer. Reproduced by permission. / Jacket illustration by Laurie Schmidt from *Screaming High.* By David Line. Little, Brown and Company, 1985. Copyright © 1985 by David Line. Reproduced by permission of Little, Brown and Company. / From the cover of *The Menorah Men.* By Lionel Davidson. Copyright © 1966 by Lionel Davidson. Reproduced by permission.

ROBIN W. DAVIS. Portrait of Robin Works Davis. Reproduced by permission of Highsmith Press.

PLEASANT DeSPAIN. Portrait of Pleasant DeSpain by Jason L. Tyler.

MARY ALICE DOWNIE. Portrait of Mary Alice Downie by Jocelyn Downie. / From a cover of *How the Devil Got His Cat.* By Mary Alice Downie. Quarry Press. Reprinted by permission of the publisher. / From a cover of *The Buffalo Boy and the Weaver Girl.* By Mary Alice Downie. Quarry Press. Reprinted by permission of the publisher.

AGNES M. R. DUNLOP. Jacket illustration by Milton Glaser from *The Swedish Nightingale: Jenny Lind.* By Elisabeth Kyle. Holt, Rinehart and Winston, 1964. Copyright © 1964 by Elisabeth Kyle. Reproduced with permission of Henry Holt and Company, Inc. / Jacket illustration by Ellen Raskin from *Duet.* By Elisabeth Kyle. Holt, Rinehart & Winston, 1968. Copyright © 1968 by Elisabeth Kyle. Reproduced by permission of Henry Holt and Company, Inc.

KIM ENGELMANN. Cover illustration by Dan Craig from *Journey to Joona.* By Kim V. Engelmann. Navpress, 1995. Copyright © 1995 by Kim V. Engelmann. All rights reserved. Reproduced by permission of the publisher.

KATHLEEN FIDLER. Illustration by Victor Ambrus from *Haki the Shetland Pony.* By Kathleen Fidler. Rand McNally & Company, 1970. Copyright © 1968 by Kathleen A. Goldie. Reproduced by permission.

DIANE E. FILDERMAN. Portrait of Diane Filderman. Reproduced by permission of David M. Blecman Studio.

ANNE FRANK. From *Anne Frank: The Diary of a Young Girl.* Translated by B. M. Moyaart. ANNE FRANK-Fonds, Basel, Switzerland. Cover photo copyright © 1986 by ANNE FRANK-Fonds, Basel, Switzerland. / Photograph of Anne Frank (with S. Ledermann). From *The Diary of Anne Frank: The Critical Edition.* By Anne Frank. Doubleday, 1967. Copyright © 1986 by ANNE FRANK-Fonds, Basel/Switzerland, for all texts of Anne Frank. Used by permission of Doubleday, a division of Bantam Doubleday Dell Publishing Group, Inc. / Portrait of Otto Frank. From *The Diary of Anne Frank: The Critical Edition.* By Anne Frank. Doubleday, 1967. Copyright © 1986 by ANNE FRANK-Fonds, Basel/Switzerland, for all texts of Anne Frank. Used by permission of Doubleday, a division of Bantam Doubleday Dell Publishing Group, Inc. / From *Anne Frank's Tales from the Secret Annex.* Translated by Michel Mok and Ralph Manheim. AFF/AFS Amsterdam, The Netherlands. Cover art copyright © 1994 by AFF/AFS Amsterdam, The Netherlands.

ROY FULLER. Jacket illustration by Craig Dodd from *Stares.* By Roy Fuller. Sinclair-Stevenson Ltd. Copyright © 1990 by Roy Fuller. Reproduced by permission of the publisher. / Portrait of Roy Broadbent Fuller by Jerry Bauer. Copyright © Jerry Bauer.

ADELE GERAS. Portrait of Adele Geras. Copyright © Peter Walsh. Reproduced by permission. / Jacket illustration by Douglas Hall from *The Girls in the Velvet Frame.* By Adele Geras. Atheneum, 1979. Copyright © 1978 by Adele Geras. All rights reserved. Reproduced by permission of the publisher. / From a jacket of *Golden Windows.* Willa Perlman Books, 1993. Copyright © 1993 by Adele Geras. Reproduced by permission of the publisher. / Jacket illustration by S. M. Saelig from *Watching the Roses.* By Adele Geras. Harcourt Brace Jovanovich, 1992. Copyright © 1992, 1991 by Adele Geras. All rights reserved. Reproduced by permission of the publisher.

KATE GILMORE. Jacket illustration by Mike Dooling from *Jason and the Bard.* By Kate Gilmore. Houghton Mifflin Company, 1993. Copyright © 1993 by Kate Gilmore. Reproduced by permission of Houghton Mifflin Company. / From a cover of *Enter Three Witches.* Scholastic Inc., 1990. Copyright © 1990 by Kate Gilmore. All rights reserved. Reproduced by permission of the publisher.

CATHERINE TROXELL GONZALEZ. Cover illustration by Don Ivan Punchatz by *Cherub in Stone.* By Catherine Gonzalez. Texas Christian University Press, 1995. Reproduced by permission.

MARGARET GREAVES. Illustration by Teresa O'Brien from *Henry's Wild Morning.* By Margaret Greaves. Dial Book for Young Readers, 1991. Pictures copyright © 1990 by Teresa O'Brien. Reproduced by permission of Penguin USA. / Jacket illustration by

GERALDINE McCAUGHREAN. Portrait of Geraldine McCaughrean. / Illustration by Victor Ambrus from *The Canterbury Tales*. By Geraldine McCaughrean. Rand McNally & Company, 1985. Illustration copyright © by Victor Ambrus 1984. Reproduced by permission. / Jacket illustration by Robina Green from *A Pack of Lies*. By Geraldine McCaughrean. Copyright © by Geraldine McCaughrean, 1988. Reproduced by permission of Oxford University Press. / From an illustration in *One Thousand One Arabian Nights*. By Geraldine Jones. Oxford University Press, 1982. Reprinted by permission of Oxford University Press.

KATE McMULLAN. Portrait of Kate and Jim McMullan. Reproduced by Star Black. / Jacket illustration by Emma Chichester Clark from *Good Night, Stella*. By Kate and Jim McMullan. Candlewick Press, 1994. Jacket illustration copyright © 1994 by Emma Chichester Clark. Reproduced by permission. / Cover art by James McMullan from *Hey, Pipsqueak!* By Kate and Jim McMullan. HarperCollins Publishers, 1995. Reproduced by permission of Kate and Jim McMullan. / Jacket illustration by Diane de Groat from *The Great Eggspectations of Lila Fenwick*. By Kate and Jim McMullan. Farrar, Straus and Giroux, 1991. Reproduced by permission of Farrar, Straus and Giroux.

JANET McNEILL. Portrait of Janet McNeill by Derek Balmer. Courtesy of International Portrait Gallery. / Illustration by Ingrid Fetz from *A Monster Too Many*. By Janet McNeill. Little, Brown and Company, 1972. Illustration copyright © 1972 by Ingrid Fetz. All rights reserved. Reprinted by permission of Little, Brown and Company. / Illustration by Mary Russon from *The Battle of St. George Without*. By Janet McNeill. Little, Brown and Company, 1966. All rights reserved. Reprinted by permission of Little, Brown and Company.

VIRGINIA MEACHUM. Portrait of Virginia Meachum. Courtesy of Virginia Meachum.

ELLANITA MILLER. Portrait of Ellanita Miller. Reproduced by permission.

GORDON MORRISON. Portrait of Gordon Morrison. / From a cover of *Endangered Wildlife*. By Richard K. Walton and Gordon Morrison. Houghton Mifflin Company, 1991. Illustrations copyright © 1991 by Gordon Morrison. All rights reserved. Reprinted by permission of Houghton Mifflin Company.

ROBERT NEWMAN. From *The Case of the Baker Street Irregular*. Aladdin Books, 1978. Copyright © 1978 by Robert Newman. Reproduced by permission of Simon & Schuster, Inc. / Illustration by Paul Sagsoorian from *The Boy Who Could Fly*. By Robert Newman. Atheneum, 1967. Copyright © 1967 by Robert Newman. Reproduced by permission of Atheneum, a division of Simon & Schuster, Inc. / Jacket illustration by David L. Stone from *The Case of the Vanishing Corpse*. By Robert Newman. Atheneum, 1981. Jacket illustration copyright © 1980 by David L. Stone. Reproduced by permission of Atheneum, a division of Simon & Schuster, Inc. / From *Merlin's Mistake*. Atheneum, 1970. Reproduced by permission of Atheneum, a division of Simon & Schuster, Inc.

HELEN NICOLL. Illustration by Jan Pienkowski from *Meg and Mog*. By Helen Nicoll. Picture Puffins, 1975. Reproduced by permission of Reed Books Service Ltd. / Illustration by Jan Pienkowski from *Meg on the Moon*. By Helen Nicoll. Picture Puffins, 1976. Reproduced by permission of Reed Books Service Ltd.

JENNY NIMMO. Jacket illustration by Forest Rogers from *Rainbow and Mr. Zed*. By Jenny Nimmo. Dutton Children's Books, 1992. Jacket illustration copyright © by Forest Rogers, 1994. Reproduced by permission. / From a cover of *The Snow Spider*. By Jenny Nimmo. Troll Associates, 1986. All rights reserved. Reproduced by permission of the publisher.

MORGAN NYBERG. Cover illustration by VictoR GAD from *Galahad Schwartz and the Cockroach Army*. By Morgan Nyberg. Douglas & McIntyre, 1987. Copyright © 1987 Morgan Nyberg. Reproduced by permission.

PAT O'SHEA. Portrait of Pat O'Shea. Reproduced by permission. / Illustration by Stephen Lavis from *Finn MacCool and the Small Men of Deeds*. By Pat O'Shea. Oxford University Press, 1987. Reprinted by permission of Oxford University Press. / Jacket illustration by Stephen Lavis from *The Hounds of the Morrigan*. By Pat O'Shea. Holiday House, 1986. Copyright © by Pat O'Shea, 1985. Reprinted by permission of the publisher.

PENELOPE COLVILLE PAINE. Portrait of Penelope C. Paine by Deborah Samuel. Reproduced by permission.

DENNIS PERNU. Portrait of Dennis Pernu. Reproduced by permission.

JAMES POLESE. Portrait of James Polese. Reproduced by permission.

KRISTIN JOY PRATT. Portrait of Kristin Pratt. Reproduced by permission.

MARY RAYNER. Portrait of Mary Rayner by Eleanor MacDonald. Courtesy of Mary Rayner. / From *Mr. and Mrs. Pig's Evening Out*. Atheneum, 1976. Copyright © 1976 by Mary Rayner. Reproduced by permission of Atheneum, a division of Simon & Schuster, Inc. / From a jacket of *Marathon and Steve*. E. P. Dutton, 1989. Copyright © 1989 by Mary Rayner. Reproduced by permission of E. P. Dutton, a division of Penguin Books USA, Inc.

JOHN MORRIS REEVES. Cover illustration by Joan Kiddell-Monroe from *English Fables and Fairy Stories*. Retold by James Reeves. Oxford University Press, 1954. All rights reserved. Reprinted by permission of Oxford University Press. / Illustration by Quentin Blake from *Mr. Horrox and the Gratch*. By James Reeves. Wellington Publishing, 1991. Illustrations copyright © 1969 by Quentin Blake. All rights reserved. Reproduced by permission of A. P. Watt Ltd. on behalf of Quentin Blake. / Illustration by Edward Ardizzone from *Rhyming Will*. By James Reeves. McGraw-Hill Book Company, 1968. Illustrations © Edward Ardizzone, 1967. All rights reserved. Reproduced with permission.

SOMETHING ABOUT THE AUTHOR®

ABBOTT, R(obert) Tucker 1919-1995

OBITUARY NOTICE—See index for *SATA* sketch: Born September 28, 1919, in Watertown, MA; died of a stroke, November 3, 1995, on Sanibel Island, FL. Zoologist, curator, author. Abbott is remembered for his work in the field of malacology (the study of mollusks), which included numerous books on seashells. He is credited with identifying around one thousand species of mollusks (oysters, clams, snails, conchs, squids, etc.). More than one hundred thousand species are known to exist. Developing an interest in shells as a child, Abbott established a science museum in his family's home when he was just a teenager. He pursued his interest in college and later became the assistant curator in the division of mollusks at the U.S. National Museum (Smithsonian) in 1946. Earlier, during World War II, he had set up a malacology research facility on Guam. Through his work at the station, he helped stop the spread of a disease linked to parasites in snails. In 1954, Abbott joined the staff at the Academy of Natural Sciences of Philadelphia as research scientist and the Pilsbry Chair from 1954 to 1969. After nine years as assistant director of malacology at the Delaware Museum of Natural History, he established American Malacologists Inc., a publishing company. Abbott had already earned a reputation as a writer of books about mollusks after his *American Seashells* was published in 1954. Abbott was also director of the Bailey-Matthews Shell Museum on Sanibel Island, which opened in 1995. It contains some two million seashells from about 20,000 mollusk species. Other books by Abbott include *Sea Shells of the World, Seashells of North America: A Guide to Field Identification, Collectible Florida Shells,* and *Seashells of Southeast Asia.*

OBITUARIES AND OTHER SOURCES

BOOKS

Who's Who in America, Marquis, 1995.

PERIODICALS

New York Times, November 9, 1995, p. B18.

* * *

ADLER, Irene
See STORR, Catherine (Cole)

* * *

ALDRIDGE, (Harold Edward) James 1918-

■ **Personal**

Born July 10, 1918, in White Hills, Victoria, Australia; son of William Thomas (a newspaper publisher) and Edith (Quayle) Aldridge; married Dina Mitchnik, 1942; children: two sons. *Education:* Attended London School of Economics and Political Science; attended Oxford University, 1939. *Hobbies and other interests:* Trout-fishing.

■ Addresses

Home—21 Kersley St., London SW11, England. *Agent*—Curtis Brown, Ltd., 162-68 Regent St., London W1R 5TB, England.

■ Career

Writer. *Sun,* Melbourne, Australia, office boy and file clerk, 1934-37, reporter, 1937-38; *Herald,* Melbourne, reporter, 1937-38; *Daily Sketch* and *Sunday Dispatch,* London, England, feature writer, 1939; freelance war correspondent for Australian Newspaper Service and North American Newspaper Alliance in Finland, Norway, Greece, the Middle East, and the Soviet Union, 1939-44; *Time* and *Life* correspondent in Teheran, Iran, 1944. *Member:* British Sub-Aqua Club.

■ Awards, Honors

Rhys Memorial Prize, 1945; International Organization of Journalists Prize, 1967; Lenin Memorial Peace Prize, 1972; Australian Children's Book Council Book of the Year Award, 1985; *Guardian* Children's Fiction Prize, 1987, for *The True Story of Spit MacPhee;* World Peace Council Gold Medal.

■ Writings

FICTION FOR YOUNG ADULTS

The Flying Nineteen, Hamish Hamilton, 1966.
My Brother Tom, Hamish Hamilton, 1966, published as *My Brother Tom: A Love Story,* Little, Brown, 1967.
A Sporting Proposition, Little, Brown, 1973, published as *Ride a Wild Pony,* Penguin, 1976.
The Marvelous Mongolian, Little, Brown, 1974.
The Broken Saddle, MacRae Books, 1983.
The True Story of Lilli Stubeck, Hyland House, 1984, Penguin, 1986.
The True Story of Spit MacPhee, Viking, 1986.
The True Story of Lola MacKellar, Viking, 1992.

FICTION FOR ADULTS

Signed with Their Honour, Little, Brown, 1942.
The Sea Eagle, Little, Brown, 1944.
Of Many Men, Little, Brown, 1946.
The 49th State (play), first produced in London, England, 1946.
The Diplomat, Bodley Head, 1949, Little, Brown, 1950.
The Hunter, Little, Brown, 1951.
Heroes of the Empty View, Knopf, 1954.
I Wish He Would Not Die, Doubleday, 1958.
Gold and Sand (short stories), Bodley Head, 1960.
The Last Exile, Doubleday, 1961.
A Captive in the Land, Hamish Hamilton, 1962.
The Statesman's Game, Doubleday, 1966.
Mockery in Arms, M. Joseph, 1974, Little, Brown, 1975.
The Untouchable Juli, Little, Brown, 1975.
One Last Glimpse (play; first produced in Prague, Czechoslovakia, 1981), Little, Brown, 1977.
Flying, Pan Books, 1979.
Goodbye Un-America, M. Joseph, 1979, Little, Brown, 1979.

JAMES ALDRIDGE

OTHER

Underwater Hunting for the Inexperienced Englishman, Allen & Unwin, 1955.
Cairo: Biography of a City (travel), Little, Brown, 1969.
(With Paul Strand) *Living Egypt* (travel), Horizon Press, 1969.

Also contributor to the anthology *Winter's Tales 15,* edited by A. D. Maclean, Macmillan, 1969, St. Martin's, 1970. Author of scripts for *Robin Hood* television series, and articles in *Playboy.*

■ Adaptations

Ride a Wild Pony was filmed by Disney in the late 1970s.

■ Sidelights

After spending ten years as a journalist and twenty-five years as a writer of international suspense novels for adults, Australian author James Aldridge began writing fiction for young adults in 1966. Most of his young adult novels take place in the fictional town of St. Helen, Australia, which closely resembles the real town of Swan Hill on the banks of the Murray River near where he was born. Though he has lived most of his life outside his native land, Aldridge told Michael Stone in *Twenti-eth-Century Young Adult Writers* that he revisits his childhood home in his novels because "I can't escape Australia, and I don't want to."

Three of Aldridge's publications for young adults—*A Sporting Proposition* (also published as *Ride a Wild Pony*), *The Marvelous Mongolian,* and *The Broken Saddle*—are "considered among the finest horse stories written by an Australian," according to Stone. *A Sporting Proposition* takes place during the Great Depression. It tells the story of thirteen-year-old Scott Pirie, the poor son of Scotch immigrants whose main joy in life is his Welsh pony, Taff. Scott loses Taff, and he soon learns that the pony has been adopted by Josie, the handicapped daughter of a wealthy family, who has renamed the horse Bo. The whole town takes sides during their ensuing fight over ownership of the pony. They take the matter to court, but it is finally resolved when Scott's lawyer devises a "sporting proposition" that everyone can agree to. In a review for *Library Journal,* Margaret Wimsatt called *A Sporting Proposition* "an atmospheric tale, professionally told." The story was later adapted for a Disney movie in the 1970s.

The Marvelous Mongolian, Aldridge's next book for young adults, also describes the love two young people share for a horse. Tachi, a wild Mongolian stallion, is taken from his home in the mountains to a game preserve in England, where scientists hope he will help establish new herds of wild horses. Although he becomes attached to a Welsh pony mare named Peep, Tachi is unhappy in captivity. He finally escapes from the game preserve with Peep and makes his way back to Mongolia, enduring numerous dangers along the way. His incredible journey is followed anxiously by Kitty Jamieson, an English girl whose grandfather is in charge of the game preserve, and Baryut Mingha, a Mongolian boy who saw Tachi in the wild. They write letters to each other whenever they receive word about Tachi's whereabouts. A *Publishers Weekly* reviewer praised the book as "a remarkable and charming animal story for young and old alike."

Like *The Sporting Proposition,* Aldridge's third horse story, *The Broken Saddle,* is also set in Australia during the Great Depression. Eric Thompson comes from a poor family. His father was forced to move far away to get a job driving cattle, and Eric must perform odd jobs for neighbors in order to help put food on the table. On one return visit, his father brings Eric a pony. At first Eric and the willful pony are inseparable, but as they become involved in more formal activities like saddle-riding and performing in gymkhanas, their relationship begins to grow more distant. After Eric breaks his leg in a riding accident, his mother sells the pony to pay for food. Although he is sad when he sees his now docile

Thirteen-year-old Scott Pirie races his Welsh pony against a train in this 1975 screen adaptation of Aldridge's novel, *Ride a Wild Pony.*

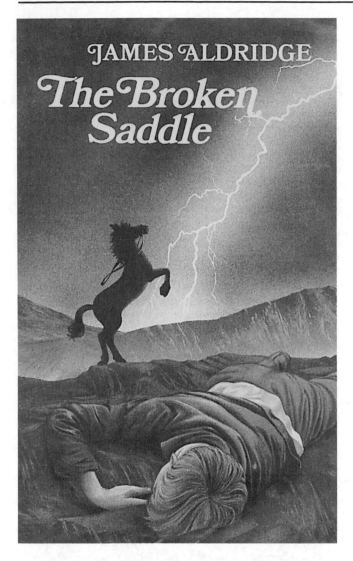

Aldridge's young adult novel captures the special bond between an Australian boy and his horse during the Great Depression. (Cover illustration by Alun Hood.)

pony being ridden by a wealthy girl, Eric learns from the experience. A reviewer for *Junior Bookshelf* praised Aldridge for avoiding sentimentality, calling *The Broken Saddle* "a powerful story ... written with such skill as to make it compulsive reading."

Aldridge's next three books for young adults tell the "true story" of a series of unusual and sometimes mysterious characters. *The True Story of Lilli Stubeck,* set during the Great Depression, describes the life of a girl who arrives in St. Helen with her disreputable family at the age of seven. When the family leaves town, they sell Lilli to a wealthy old lady, Miss Dalgleish, as a servant. Miss Dalgleish decides to turn Lilli into a civilized young woman, and outwardly she improves her appearance and manners. When her ill mother returns with her younger brother, Lilli begins to revert back to her old ways. In the end, she manages to establish her own identity and leave a distinct impression on the town. A reviewer for *Growing Point* called Aldridge's work "a remarkable tale which calls upon the reader for

close attention and sympathy and will reward this kind of approach handsomely."

Aldridge received the *Guardian* Children's Fiction Award for his next book, *The True Story of Spit MacPhee.* It follows the adventures of an eleven-year-old orphan boy, Spit, who lives with his mentally ill grandfather along the banks of the Murray River. Although his grandfather is sometimes prone to violent fits, the two manage to build a satisfying, independent life for themselves. When his grandfather finally burns down their home and is taken away to die, two families from town fight to decide what happens to Spit. Betty Arbuckle, an Evangelical Christian, wants to send Spit to the Bendingo Boys' Home, where he can be civilized and turned into a proper boy. Meanwhile, Grace Tree, the Catholic mother of one of Spit's friends, wants to adopt Spit and take care of him. During the ensuing court battle, the entire town is divided along religious lines. "Work of this quality is rare indeed," according to one *Junior Bookshelf* reviewer. "Aldridge has given us a very fine story, tough, penetrating, and profoundly honest."

Aldridge's 1992 book, *The True Story of Lola MacKellar,* slowly unravels the mystery of Lola's background. The story begins when the wealthy Eyre family brings five-year-old Lola to their estate, but then leaves her in the care of their hired hands, the Scobies. The Eyres pay for Lola's room and board, but they also tell the Scobies to keep her far away from their house and their young daughter, Josie. Several years later, the two girls meet and become friends anyway, and Lola helps Josie recover from polio. The mystery reaches its peak when Lola's biological mother suddenly appears at the estate, accompanied by Lola's twin sister, and asks her to leave the only home she has known and return with them to Germany. A *Junior Bookshelf* reviewer called the novel "story-telling at its best," noting that "the secrets of Lola's background are divulged at tantalizing intervals holding the reader's attention up to the final revelation of her true past and the settling of her future."

Summing up Aldridge's work for young adults, Stone commented: "Through his novels James Aldridge seeks to answer age-old questions that have concerned humanity since Plato and Aristotle: how people ought to live in communities and how best to organize their political and social life. Aldridge is concerned with the betterment of life through the search for moral and religious understandings."

■ Works Cited

Review of *The Broken Saddle, Junior Bookshelf,* February 1983, p. 36.

Review of *The Marvelous Mongolian, Publishers Weekly,* March 25, 1974, p. 49.

Stone, Michael, "James Aldridge," *Twentieth-Century Young Adult Writers,* 1st edition, edited by Laura Standley Berger, St. James Press, 1994, p. 11.

Review of *The True Story of Lilli Stubeck, Growing Point,* September 1986.

In her 1984 book, *The Other Side of the Park,* Andrew presents a teenager who is struggling to understand and accept her family. Fifteen-year-old Judy suffers the loss of her beloved great-grandmother, who had become somewhat senile but was very supportive of Judy's talent for ventriloquism. Her great-grandmother had fallen down a flight of stairs, but as Judy notices how materialistic her father and sister have become, she begins to suspect them of playing a role in her death. She works through her questions and doubts about her family with the help of her ventriloquist's dummy, Tatty 'Ead, and her sensible, working-class boyfriend. In the process, Judy grows up and becomes more independent. In a review for the *Times Educational Supplement,* Neil Philip states that "teenage girls may well identify with her, though they may also resent the too easy ending." A *Junior Bookshelf* reviewer declares that Andrew's "characterization is first rate," adding that *The Other Side of the Park* contains "much to be recommended."

■ Works Cited

Fisher, Margery, review of *Robinson Daniel Crusoe, Growing Point,* March, 1979, p. 3483.

Review of *Mister O'Brien,* "Problems of Pain," *Times Literary Supplement,* April 28, 1972, p. 5660.

Review of *The Other Side of the Park, Junior Bookshelf,* October, 1984, p. 213.

Philip, Neil, review of *The Other Side of the Park, Times Educational Supplement,* January 4, 1985, p. 20.

Ray, Sheila G., "Prudence Andrew," *Twentieth-Century Children's Writers,* 4th edition, edited by Laura Standley Berger, St. James Press, 1995, pp. 26-27.

Review of *Robinson Daniel Crusoe, Junior Bookshelf,* June, 1979, p. 164.

Williams, Gladys, "Forward into Space," *Books and Bookmen,* May, 1973, p. XIII.

■ For More Information See

PERIODICALS

Booklist, May 15, 1973, p. 903.

Bulletin of the Center for Children's Books, May, 1976; July-August, 1980.

Growing Point, October, 1975, pp. 2721-22; September, 1977, p. 3176; September, 1987, p. 4873.

Horn Book, August, 1980, pp. 412-13.

Kirkus Reviews, July 1, 1973, p. 684.

Library Journal, April 15, 1973, p. 1384.

School Library Journal, March, 1976, p. 109; February, 1980, p. 63.

Times Literary Supplement, November 24, 1966, p. 1085; July 11, 1975, p. 770.*

*   *   *

ANTHONY, Susan C(arol) 1953-

■ Personal

Born April 20, 1953; daughter of Norman French (a contractor) and Beverly (a secretary; maiden name, Mayfield) Wheeler; married Dennis Henry Weston (a

SUSAN C. ANTHONY

teacher), November 21, 1992. *Education:* University of Northern Colorado, B.A. (elementary education), 1976. *Politics:* Republican. *Religion:* Protestant. *Hobbies and other interests:* Flying, international travel, wilderness adventures, skiing, hiking, boating, singing, and Christian apologetics.

■ Addresses

Home—17300 Golden View Dr., Anchorage, AK 99516. *Office*—Instructional Resources Company, P.O. Box 111704, Anchorage, AK 99511-1704.

■ Career

Weld County School District, Greeley, CO, teacher, 1978-79; Tom Thumb Montessori, Anchorage, AK, teacher, 1979; Anchorage School District, Anchorage, teacher, 1980-92; Houghton Mifflin Company, Boston, MA, consultant, 1985-86; Instructional Resources Company, Anchorage, writer and publisher, 1990—. Has also worked as a consultant and workshop leader for teachers and home school parents. *Member:* International Association of Independent Publishers (COSMEP), National Geographic Society.

■ Awards, Honors

Facts Plus: An Almanac of Essential Information was selected as a recommended reference book, *School Library Journal,* 1992; Distinguished Teaching Achievement Award, National Council for Geographic Education, 1992.

■ Writings

ALL PUBLISHED BY INSTRUCTIONAL RESOURCES COMPANY

Encyclopedia Activity for Use with the World Book, 1994.
Facts Plus: An Almanac of Essential Information (for children), 1991, new edition, 1995.
Facts Plus Activity Book (for teachers), 1995.
Spelling Plus: Spelling for Success in Kindergarten-6th Grade (for teachers), 1995.
Homophones Resource Book (for teachers), 1995.
Dictation Resource Book (for teachers), 1995.
Addition Facts in 5 Minutes a Day (for teachers), 1995.
Subtraction Facts in 5 Minutes a Day (for teachers), 1995.
Multiplication Facts in 5 Minutes a Day (for teachers), 1995.
Division Facts in 5 Minutes a Day (for teachers), 1995.
Casting Nines, 1995.

■ Work in Progress

Videotape on methods for teaching reference, spelling, and math. Researching evolution/creation and the English language.

■ Sidelights

Susan Anthony told *SATA,* "I still remember my first school assignment using reference books. I was in seventh grade in a small school in the Rocky Mountains in Colorado. Our little library was housed in a closet. My English teacher had written a set of questions which required us to use the indexes in a variety of reference books to locate specific facts. About the time I located the name of the seventeenth pope, a light went on for me. I realized that the answer to *any* question I could think of, whether important or trivial, could be found in a book if I knew where to look. I felt powerful! The world was at my fingertips, even in my small mountain community.

"I enjoyed doing reports and research projects throughout school, and that interest carried into my own teaching. My sixth grade students each had almanacs in their desks, which were used during discussions and to satisfy their curiosity whenever questions came to mind. I developed activities to use the almanacs in studying current events, science, social studies, and even math. When I was assigned to teach fifth grade, however, the students were frustrated with the small type, abbreviations, and confusing data in adult almanacs. I was frustrated because I wanted them to *enjoy* and look forward to reference work. On a particularly bad day,

September 14, 1984, the idea for a kid's almanac came, the idea which led to *Facts Plus.* I was surprised that I couldn't find such a book in the bookstores! I had more ideas than time, and my first priority while teaching was my students. The first edition of *Facts Plus* wasn't published for seven years, during which time we lived in a small Quonset hut in the mountains outside of Anchorage which was heated by a wood stove.

"I do a lot of my writing at our homestead in the Alaskan wilderness. We have a cabin on a lake just south of the Alaska Range. In the winter, we ride snowmobiles twenty miles to get to the cabin. I carry my PowerBook portable computer in a pack on my back. We often see caribou, moose, ptarmigan, fox, otter, and bald eagles. Occasionally we see grizzly bears or wolves. There is no telephone communication there, so we listen to 'Caribou Clatters,' personal messages read over the local radio station, which broadcasts from a small town about seventy miles away. With the PowerBook, I can write anywhere and anytime. I did most of one book for teachers while traveling up the Alaska Highway, and worked more on it during a trip up the Inside Passage in a twenty-one foot cabin cruiser from Prince Rupert, British Columbia, to Haines, Alaska. I still have more ideas than time, and hope to write many more books, for both kids and teachers, in the future."

■ For More Information See

PERIODICALS

Booklist, June 1, 1991, p. 1899.
School Library Journal, May, 1992, p. 26.

* * *

ASHE, Arthur (Robert, Jr.) 1943-1993

OBITUARY NOTICE—See index for *SATA* sketch: Born July 10, 1943, in Richmond, VA; died of pneumonia as a complication of AIDS, February 6, 1993, in Richmond, VA. Professional tennis player and author. The first African American to win at Wimbledon and the first to be inducted into the International Tennis Hall of Fame, Ashe was a renowned tennis player who broke racial barriers and became a role model for many Americans. As an amateur player in high school and college, he encountered several obstacles to his aspiration of becoming a professional, including being barred from tennis clubs across the country. Nevertheless, exhibiting admirable grace under pressure, he became one of the top-ranked players in the United States. His career as a competitor ended in 1979 when, as a member of the Davis Cup team, he suffered a heart attack and had to undergo quadruple bypass surgery. Although he survived his illness, he could no longer actively play tennis and became captain of his team. His heart problems, which were inherited, would eventually prove fatal, though in an unexpectedly tragic way. After being operated on a second time in 1983, Ashe contracted the HIV virus from a blood transfusion. At first insisting on his right to privacy, the tennis star eventually gave in to media pressure to announce on April 7, 1992, that he had the virus. One reason for the announcement was to help the public become more aware that AIDS can be contracted through means other than sexual intercourse. He later recorded his feelings about his illness—as well as racism and many other issues—in his 1993 autobiography, *Days of Grace: A Memoir*. In addition to this work, Ashe had published many other books during his lifetime, including the autobiographies *Advantage Ashe* (1967), *Arthur Ashe: Portrait in Motion* (1975), and *Off the Court* (1981), and books about tennis and sports, including *Getting Started in Tennis* (1977), *Mastering Your Tennis Strokes* (1978), *Arthur Ashe's Tennis Clinic* (1981), and the critically praised, three-volume work, *A Hard Road to Glory: A History of the African-American Athlete* (1987).

OBITUARIES AND OTHER SOURCES:

BOOKS

Ashe, Arthur, and Arnold Rampersad, *Days of Grace: A Memoir*, Knopf, 1993.
Contemporary Black Biography: Profiles from the International Black Community, Volume 1, Gale, 1992.
Robinson, Louie, Jr., *Arthur Ashe: Tennis Champion*, Doubleday, 1970.

PERIODICALS

New York Times, June 10, 1993, p. B2.

Time, February 15, 1993, p. 70.

* * *

ATWELL, Debby 1953-

■ Personal

Born May 28, 1953, in Providence, RI; daughter of Peter Butler II (a businessman) and Frances (a teacher; maiden name, Swift) Olney; married David Lewis Atwell (a carpenter); children: Nathanael, Olney, Tegan. *Education:* University of New Hampshire, B.F.A., 1976. *Politics:* Democrat. *Religion:* Christian.

■ Addresses

Home—81 Pleasant St., Rockland, ME 04841.

■ Career

Children's book writer and illustrator; iconographer.

■ Illustrator

David Lewis Atwell, *The Day Hans Got His Way*, Houghton Mifflin, 1992.
David Lewis Atwell, *Sleeping Moon*, Houghton Mifflin, 1994.

DEBBY ATWELL

■ Work in Progress

Writing and illustrating *Barn,* a children's book due.

■ Sidelights

Debby Atwell told *SATA:* "There are so many talented children's artists and authors that it is difficult to carve a niche truly one's own in the world. My aim is to intrigue the child's mind with a story they can't predict, and do my best to make pictures that hold their attention. All the intangibles, I just hope for."

B

ALLAN BAILLIE

BAILLIE, Allan (Stuart) 1943-

■ Personal

Born January 29, 1943, in Prestwick, Scotland; son of Alistair (a teller) and Anne (a hotel manager; maiden name, McEwan) Baillie; married Ngan Yeok (a librarian), January 14, 1972; children: Lynne, Peter. *Education:* Attended University of Melbourne, 1962-63. *Politics:* Australian Labour Party. *Religion:* None.

■ Addresses

Home—197 Riverview Rd., Clareville, New South Wales 2107, Australia.

■ Career

Full-time writer, 1987—. *Herald/Sun,* Melbourne, Australia, reporter and subeditor, 1961-64; *Middlesex Advertiser,* London, England, subeditor, 1966-67; Australian Associated Press, Sydney, Australia, subeditor, 1968-69; freelance writer, Cambodia and Laos, 1969; *Sunday Telegraph,* Sydney, subeditor, 1970-73; *Daily Telegraph,* Sydney, subeditor, 1973-74; Australian Broadcasting Commission, Sydney, subeditor, 1974-78; *Women's Weekly,* Sydney, subeditor, 1978-80; *Sun,* Sydney, subeditor, 1980-87. *Member:* Australian Society of Authors.

■ Awards, Honors

Captain Cook Literature Award, 1970, for short story "Chuck's Town"; Warana Short Story Award, 1973, for "Empty House"; Kathleen Fidler Award, National Book League, 1982, for *The Pirate's Last Voyage* (published as *Adrift*); Arts Council Special Purpose Grants, 1983, for *Riverman,* and 1984, for *Eagle Island;* Australian Children's Book Award, Book of the Year Highly Commended citation, 1986, for *Little Brother;* Arts Council Fellowship, 1988, for *The China Coin;* International Board on Books for Young People Honour Diploma, 1988, for *Riverman;* CBCA Picture Book of the Year, 1989, for *Drac and the Gremlin;* Peace and Friendship Prize for Children's Literature of the World, *Children's Literary Monthly* (Beijing), 1990, for "The Sorcerers"; Multicultural Children's Book Award, 1992, for *The China Coin;* Diabetes Australia Alan Marshall Prize for children's literature, for *Songman.*

■ Writings

FICTION FOR YOUNG ADULTS

Adrift, Viking, 1983.
Little Brother, Viking, 1985.
Riverman, Blackie, 1986.
Eagle Island, Blackie, 1987.
Drac and the Gremlin, illustrated by Jane Tanner, Dial, 1988, Nelson (Melbourne, Australia), 1988.
Megan's Star, Blackie, 1988.
Mates, Omnibus (Adelaide, Australia), 1989.
Hero, Blackie, 1990.
(With Chun-Chan Yeh) *Bawshou Rescues the Sun: A Han Folktale,* illustrated by Michelle Powell, Scholastic, 1991.
The China Coin, Blackie, 1991.
Little Monster, illustrated by David Cox, Omnibus, 1991.
The Boss, illustrated by Fiona O'Bierne, Scholastic, 1992.
The Bad Boys, Scholastic, 1993, published in Australia as *The Bad Guys,* illustrated by David Cox, Omnibus, 1993.
Magician, Viking O'Neil (Melbourne, Australia), 1993.

In the aftermath of the Vietnam War, eleven-year-old Vithy flees Khmer Rouge soldiers and learns how to survive alone in the jungles of Cambodia. (Cover illustration by Todd Doney.)

Rebel!, illustrated by Di Wu, Ticknor & Fields, 1994, Ashton, 1994.
Songman, Viking O'Neil, 1994.
Dream Catcher, Omnibus/Scholastic (Sydney, Australia), 1995.
Old Magic, illustrated by Di Wu, Random, in press.
Last Dragon, illustrated by Wayne Harris, Scholastic, in press.
Archie Wolf, illustrated by Jonathan Bentley, Random, in press.
Walden Rising, Viking O'Neil, in press.

FICTION FOR ADULTS

Mask Maker, Macmillan (London), 1975.

OTHER

Contributor of short stories to anthologies (including *Under Twenty-Five, Transition,* and *Bad Deeds Gang*) and magazines (including *Child Life, Pursuit, School Magazine,* and *Meanjin*) in Australia, Britain, the United States, and China. A number of Baillie's books are available in Braille or on audio tape; some have also been published in Japan, South Africa, and several European countries.

■ Sidelights

Two elements inspired Allan Baillie to write: displacement caused by being born in Scotland, adopting an English accent in London, and then being raised in Australia, and an accident that occurred when he and a friend engaged in a mock sword fight. "He lunged, I parried, and his foil hit me between the left eye and bridge of the nose. I remember falling and seeing blood on the grass ...," Baillie wrote in his *Something about the Author Autobiography Series* (*SAAS*) entry. "After eleven months the hospital decided they could not do anything more with me. Basically I was left with a limp, a very clumsy right hand, and a slow way with words. That shows up as a stammer as I fish for the word I want to use .... But something had happened to me since the accident. The most obvious part of that was an obsession with pushing out my personal envelope, the hell with anything else. I learned to drive my way, to swim, to write."

Baillie spent many years travelling the world as a journalist before he turned to writing young adult fiction. As a result, most of his novels center around actual world events—such as the Tiananmen Square uprising in Beijing, China, in 1989—and feature young characters who have fictional adventures related to those events. "The event, perhaps a disaster, will bring out special qualities in a character," Baillie admitted to Agnes Nieuwenhuizen in *Magpies.* "All my books have that same element. Give 'em hell." Assessing his career in *Twentieth-Century Young Adult Writers,* Alf Mappin called Baillie "a significant and important writer for young adults," noting that he "gives his YA readers a sense of the values of humanity in today's world, wherein individuals must come to grips with a sense of themselves against the larger problems of survival in a sometimes difficult modern world."

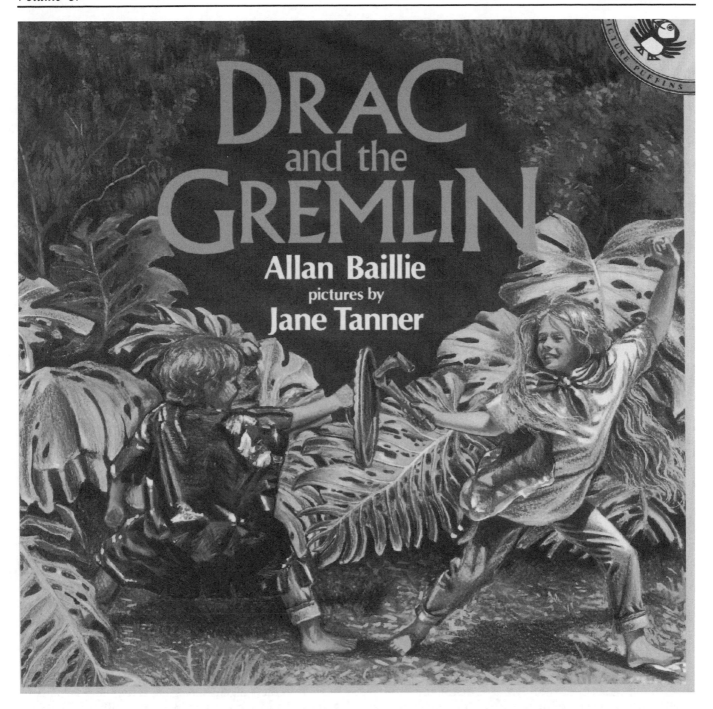

DRAC
and the
GREMLIN

Allan Baillie
pictures by
Jane Tanner

Jane Tanner illustrated Baillie's first picture book, which was named a 1989 Children's Book Council of Australia Picture Book of the Year.

In a profile of the author in *Books for Keeps,* Valerie Bierman noted that Baillie "toyed with the idea of writing an adult novel for years, then realised that perhaps the horrors of war could best be conveyed through the eyes of a child—to give a child's innocent view which often has a clarity and understanding lacking in adults." Baillie based the heroine of *Adrift* on his daughter. "Why not put Lynne, age five now, on the crate?" he wrote in *SAAS*. "She was giving me no end of trouble, including a demand that she be given a new name, Sally. So Sally is going to be stuck on a crate in the Pacific—with her arrogant and irksome black cat." The first version of this story was called *The Pirate's*

Last Voyage, and it won the Kathleen Fidler Award in Scotland. At a publisher's suggestion, he examined his characters and increased the story's length. "On this rewrite I realised that I was writing as hard as I had done with the adult novels—harder," he remembered in *SAAS*. "Characterisation, atmosphere, theme, plot, tension, humour, emotion—they were all there." The rewrite was called *Adrift.*

Baillie got the idea for his award-winning 1985 book, *Little Brother,* while he was a freelance journalist in Cambodia. He based the main character, Vuthy, on a boy he met in a Thai refugee camp. Baillie commented further in *SAAS*: "There were limitations in writing a novel about Cambodia for children, fences I could not climb, but these fences actually helped. With a children's story I couldn't tell the full horror. If I wrote about the obscenity of the plastic bag executions, the image would stay with the child at night. But if I stepped back a little, the truth and the tragedy would still be there. I would have only reduced the horror to a shadow. But the child reader would see enough."

"*I could write Cambodia's story through a boy's eyes.* This boy's eyes, Vuthy's eyes," Baillie realized. "Vuthy had been a slave-labourer on a Big Paddy as the Khmer Rouge whittled his family from him. He was actually marched into the forest to be executed, but gunfire distracted the soldiers and he was able to bolt. He wandered into an almost deserted Phnom Penh and loaded rice trucks for the North Vietnamese. Eventually he hid in one of the trucks and reached Battambang. Using a little hidden gold, he moved on with a cyclopousse (a bike-powered rickshaw), then a buffalo cart, and entered a forest loaded with mines and armed men at war. Finally he crossed the Thai border and became an orderly-interpreter at the comparative safety of the Khao-I-Dang camp hospital." The resulting story was called *Little Brother.*

In *Little Brother,* eleven-year-old Vithy (his name changed slightly from Vuthy) and his older brother, Mang, escape from a prison camp and a life of forced labor in the rice paddies and flee toward Thailand. The boys become separated along the way when Mang acts as a decoy to lure some Khmer Rouge troops away from his brother. "Dodging the Khmer Rouge, terrorized by the unfamiliar forest environment, and basically struggling for survival, Vithy perseveres in his arduous journey" to reach safety in Thailand and locate Mang, writes Karen Jameyson in a review in *Horn Book.* In the end, Vithy is adopted by a kind Australian doctor and has a triumphant reunion with his brother. In her review in *Books for Keeps* Bierman calls *Little Brother* "a gem which deserves to become a classic, if only to demonstrate to children the futility and cruelty of war."

Baillie's 1990 book, *Hero,* chronicles the disastrous flood that hit the suburbs of Sydney, Australia, in 1986. It follows the struggles of three very different children as they are forced to work together to survive the catastrophe. Wealthy and snobbish Pam, angry and rebellious Darcy, and serious-minded Barney take turns telling about the dangers they face during the flood, and the three narrators also reveal their personalities and the problems they face at home. Jameyson claimed that Baillie's descriptions are so vivid that "the penetrating wetness practically oozes through the pages," and his characterizations so skillful that "the climactic scene simply swells with poignancy." In a review for *Growing Point,* Margery Fisher called *Hero* Baillie's "most powerful tale so far."

"A Melbourne artist, Jane Tanner, suggested I have a go at writing the script for a picture book," Baillie wrote in *SAAS*. "I watched Lynne and Peter play at being

monsters and remembered my days as Tarzan in Portarlington and before, when everything could be anything you wanted it to be. So Jane and I did *Drac and the Gremlin,* where I wrote about a 'terrible-tongued dragon' and Jane had to draw the dog the dragon really was. She growled that I was having all the fun."

A visit to China in 1989—during the time when hundreds of student protesters were massacred by government troops at Tiananmen Square in Beijing—compelled Baillie to write *The China Coin.* It tells the story of Leah Waters, a half-Chinese, half-Australian girl who travels to China with her mother following the death of her father. Bringing along half of a Chinese coin that had belonged to Leah's grandfather, the two embark on a search for information about their heritage. They encounter a number of interesting characters along the way, and they experience firsthand the extreme political tension in China at that time. "The entire experience turns out to be an amazing emotional hodgepodge in a country creaking and swaying under the weight of student demonstrations," Jameyson stated. Their quest finally leads them to Tiananmen Square at the time of the massacre. A reviewer in *Reading Time* called *The China Coin* "a gripping novel well up to the high standards of this much respected author."

After writing about Cambodian and Chinese characters, Baillie decided in 1995 to write about Aboriginal Australians in *Songman.* "I believed I should have a go at writing about our people," he explained to Nieuwenhuizen. "I was spurred on by hearing politicians and judges saying that there was no civilisation in Australia before Captain Cook. Not quite fair is it?" *Songman* "seems to be a culmination of my moving about and the books I have done," Baillie also remarked in *SAAS*. "I stumbled across a little known chapter of Australia's history, the trade between the Aborigines and the Macassans way before Captain Cook. A chapter as intriguing as the Vikings contacting the Indians in Newfoundland. I wanted to write about this period, including the Dutch empire in Indonesia, through the eyes of an Aborigine around 1720. To do that I had to get all the help possible.

"I went to the Yolgnu Aboriginal settlement Yirrkala in Arnhem Land and was taught a way of life for six weeks. Mind you, I *was* an oafish pupil, and there was a mutter about feeding me to the crocodiles. And then of course I had to go to Sulawesi to get the Macassan side of the story. Sailing ancient prahus, swimming in coral reefs—Oh, I do *love* to do research." The result was what Nieuwenhuizen called "a deeply felt, beautifully written testament to the civilisation, culture, and lifestyle that flourished in just one part of Australia before the white man came." Set in 1720, *Songman* tells the story of the Yolngu people of Arnhem Land in Australia, who traded and interacted with the people of neighboring Madagascar for hundreds of years before Australia was discovered by the rest of the world. Yukuwa, a sensitive and vulnerable young man, and Dawu, his unhappy adopted father, travel across the sea to the home of their Macassan trading partners. Dawu decides to stay and become a boat builder, while Yukuwa returns home and discovers his talents as a "songman," recording the experiences of his tribe.

Summing up Baillie's career as a young-adult novelist, Bierman declared in *Books for Keeps,* "Here is a first-class writer with the power to stretch children's imaginations and make them think." Baillie told Jameyson that his purpose in writing is a simple one: "The centrepin of all my books is simply to get read, to construct a book like a trap in an attempt to grab the reader, shake him, and—just maybe—never let him go."

■ Works Cited

Baillie, Allan, essay in *Something about the Author Autobiography Series,* Volume 21, Gale, 1995, pp. 1-22.

Bierman, Valerie, "May We Recommend: Allan Baillie," *Books for Keeps,* July, 1988, p. 17.

Review of *The China Coin, Reading Time,* Volume 36, number 1, 1991, p. 28.

Fisher, Margery, "Motives for Action," *Growing Point,* July, 1990, pp. 5365-70.

Jameyson, Karen, "News from Down Under," *Horn Book,* July/August, 1991, pp. 493-95.

Mappin, Alf, "Allan Baillie," *Twentieth-Century Young Adult Writers,* 1st edition, edited by Laura Standley Berger, St. James Press, 1994, pp. 44-45.

Nieuwenhuizen, Agnes, "Know the Author: Allan Baillie," *Magpies,* March, 1995, pp. 16-18.

■ For More Information See

PERIODICALS

Bulletin of the Center for Children's Books, September, 1992, pp. 5-6.

Horn Book, March/April, 1992, pp. 201-2; September/ October, 1992, p. 584.

Junior Bookshelf, June, 1987, p. 129; June, 1990, p. 139; December, 1993, p. 238; August, 1995, pp. 141-42.

Kirkus Reviews, January 15, 1989, p. 119.

Magpies, March, 1995, p. 30.

Publishers Weekly, January 24, 1994.

School Librarian, February, 1992, p. 30; November, 1993, p. 164; August, 1995, p. 116.

School Library Journal, August, 1989, p. 114.

Voice of Youth Advocates, August, 1992, p. 166.

*   *   *

BARRETT, Ethel

■ Personal

Married; children: two sons.

■ Addresses

Home—Arizona. *Office*—c/o Regal Books, 2300 Knoll Dr., Ventura, CA 93003.

The stories in Ethel Barrett's 1987 collection capture the drama and suspense found in the Bible.

■ Career

Writer and inspirational speaker. Has appeared on television and radio programs and at numerous conferences; has recorded more than thirty albums.

■ Writings

Storytelling—It's Easy!, Zondervan, 1960.

"Sometimes I Feel Like a Blob," Regal Books, 1965.

It Didn't Just Happen, and Other Talk-About Bible Stories, Regal Books, 1967.

Don't Look Now, Regal Books, 1968.

Ethel Barrett's Holy War, with Apologies to John Bunyan (adaptation of Bunyan's *Holy War*), Regal Books, 1969, 2nd edition published as *The Great Conflict,* 1969, 3rd edition published as *Chronicles of Mansoul: A John Bunyan Classic,* 1980.

The Strangest Thing Happened, Regal Books, 1969.

Which Way to Nineveh?, Regal Books, 1969.

Will the Real Phony Please Stand Up?, Regal Books, 1969, 2nd revised edition (with Peggy Parker), 1984.

The People Who Couldn't Be Stopped, Regal Books, 1970.

The Secret Sign, Regal Books, 1970.

If I Had a Wish ..., Regal Books, 1974.

I'm No Hero, Regal Books, 1974.

Rules, Who Needs Them?, Regal Books, 1974.

God and a Boy Named Joe, Regal Books, 1975.

God, Have You Got It All Together?, Regal Books, 1977.

Barrett: A Street Cop Who Cared, Fleming Revell, 1978.

Blister Lamb, Regal Books, 1978.

Buzz Bee, Regal Books, 1978.

Ethel Barrett Tells Favorite Bible Stories, three volumes, Regal Books, 1978, Volume 2 published separately as *Ethel Barrett Tells Bible Stories to Children.*

Gregory the Grub, Regal Books, 1978.

Quacky and Wacky, Regal Books, 1978.

Cracker, the Horse Who Lost His Temper: Communicating Christian Values to Children, Regal Books, 1979.

Master of Mystery and Dreams: Daniel, Regal Books, 1979.

Men of Mystery and Miracles: Elijah and Elisha, Regal Books, 1979.

Joseph, Regal Books, 1979.

Joshua, Regal Books, 1979.

Ice, Water, and Snow, Regal Books, 1980.

John Welch: The Man Who Couldn't Be Stopped, Zondervan, 1980.

Peace and Quiet and Other Hazards, Fleming Revell, 1980.

Ruth, Regal Books, 1980.

Sylvester the Three-Spined Stickleback, Regal Books, 1980.

Paul: One Man's Extraordinary Adventures, Regal Books, 1981.

Abraham: God's Faithful Pilgrim, Regal Books, 1982.

David: The Giant Slayer, Regal Books, 1982.

Moses: Mission Impossible!, Regal Books, 1982.

Peter: The Story of a Deserter Who Became a Forceful Leader, Regal Books, 1982.

Fanny Crosby, Regal Books, 1984.

Steve Paxon: Can't Lose for Winning, Regal Books, 1985.

The Disappearing Prophets and Other Stories about Elijah and Elisha, Regal Books, 1987.

Doomed or Delivered and Other Stories about Daniel, Regal Books, 1987.

Journey into the Unknown and Other Stories about Joshua, Regal Books, 1987.

The Man Struck Down by Light and Other Stories about Paul, Regal Books, 1987.

Jasper the Jealous Dog Learns the Value of True Friendship, Regal Books, 1989.

Puff the Uppity Ant, edited by Frances Blankenbaker, Regal Books, 1989.

Smarty the Adventurous Fly, edited by Blankenbaker, Regal Books, 1989.

Sunny the Greedy Goat Learns the Value of Self-Control, edited by Blankenbaker, Regal Books, 1989.

Also author, with Blankenbaker, of *Our Family's First Bible Story Book.* Many of Barrett's works have been translated into Spanish.*

*   *   *

BB
See WATKINS-PITCHFORD, Denys James

JAY BENNETT

BENNETT, Jay 1912-

■ Personal

Born December 24, 1912, in New York, NY; son of Pincus Shapiro (a businessman) and Estelle Bennett; married Sally Stern, February 2, 1937; children: Steven Cullen, Randy Elliot. *Education:* Attended New York University. *Religion:* Jewish. *Hobbies and other interests:* Music, art, ballet, travel, and sports.

■ Addresses

Home—64 Greensward Ln., Cherry Hill, NJ 08002.

■ Career

Writer, 1930—. Has worked variously as a farmhand, factory worker, lifeguard, mailman, and salesman. Scriptwriter for radio and television dramas, during the 1940s and 1950s. Grolier Education Corp., New York City, senior editor of encyclopedias, c. 1960. *Wartime service:* U.S. Office of War Information, English features writer and editor, 1942-45. *Member:* Mystery Writers of America, Authors League of America, Writers Guild, Dramatists Guild (life member).

■ Awards, Honors

Edgar Allan Poe Award for best juvenile mystery novel, Mystery Writers of America, 1974, for *The Long Black Coat,* and 1975, for *The Dangling Witness; Variety* award for television script for *Monodrama Theatre;*

Shakespeare Society award for television adaptation of *Hamlet*.

■ Writings

Catacombs, Abelard-Schuman, 1959.
Murder Money, Fawcett, 1963.
Death Is a Silent Room, Abelard-Schuman, 1965.
Shadows Offstage, Nelson, 1974.

MYSTERIES FOR YOUNG ADULTS

Deathman, Do Not Follow Me, Meredith Press, 1968.
The Deadly Gift, Meredith Press, 1969.
Masks: A Love Story, F. Watts, 1971.
The Killing Tree, F. Watts, 1972.
The Long Black Coat, Delacorte, 1973.
The Dangling Witness, Delacorte, 1974.
Say Hello to the Hit Man, Delacorte, 1976.
The Birthday Murderer, Delacorte, 1977.
The Pigeon, Methuen, 1980.
The Executioner, Avon, 1982.
Slowly, Slowly I Raise the Gun, Avon, 1983.
I Never Said I Loved You, Avon, 1984.
To Be a Killer, Scholastic Inc., 1985.
The Skeleton Man, F. Watts, 1986.
The Haunted One, Avon, 1987.
The Dark Corridor, F. Watts, 1988.
Sing Me a Death Song, F. Watts, 1990.
Coverup, F. Watts, 1991.
Skinhead, F. Watts, 1991.
The Hooded Man, Fawcett-Juniper, 1993.
Death Grip, Fawcett-Juniper, 1993.

PLAYS

No Hiding Place (three-act), first produced in New York, 1949.
Lions after Slumber (three-act), first produced in London, 1951.

Also author of numerous radio plays, including *Miracle before Christmas* and *The Wind and Stars Are Witness;* author of television plays for *Alfred Hitchcock Presents, Harlem Detective, Crime Syndicated, Wide, Wide World, Cameo Theater,* and *Monodrama Theater.*

OTHER

The Guiccoli Miniature (short stories), Scholastic, 1991.

■ Adaptations

One of Bennett's novels for adults was adapted as a film produced by Warner Brothers.

■ Work in Progress

Another young adult suspense novel.

■ Sidelights

Jay Bennett is the author of many popular suspense novels for young readers. With his work translated into over fifteen languages and twice honored with the coveted Edgar Allan Poe Award, Bennett has been called

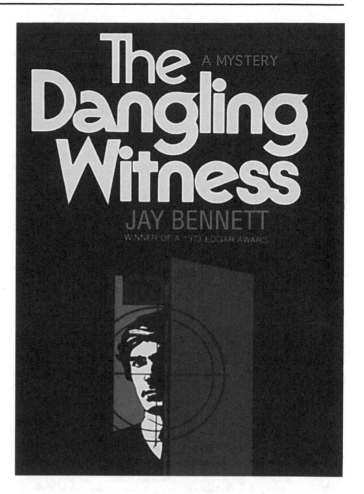

Matthew Garth, the only witness to a murder in a Brooklyn movie theater, fears the Syndicate will take revenge on him if he tells the police.

"the master of short sentences" by Judie Porter in *School Library Journal.* His stories of suspense, written in his characteristic succinct, lean style, appeal to teen readers who can relate to the stresses endured by his young characters. As Bennett's youthful male protagonists battle radical racist supremacists, murderous members of crime syndicates, and other menacing adults who draw them into life-threatening situations, they are also forced to come to terms with the psychological traumas that such events bring forth.

"I deal with the loner in our society," Bennett once told *Something about the Author* (*SATA*), "and show that it is possible to survive alone." His protagonists, like Matthew Garth in the Edgar Allan Poe Award-winning *The Dangling Witness,* find themselves in threatening situations that demand this capability and draw upon each young man's inner strength. In Matthew's case, as a witness to a murder he must confront his own abhorrence of violence in order to right a wrong for the good of society. "One must come to a decision, the decision to relate to the rest of humanity," noted Bennett. "The reader identifies with my 'loner' characters and enjoys the crisis of decision and at the same time finds his sensibilities opened up. The reader thinks and feels as he enjoys, and whether or not he knows it consciously, he has learned something about the world he is living in."

Bennett was born on December 24, 1912, in the borough of Manhattan. His father was a Jew who had emigrated from Russia to escape a sentence in the Russian Army, an institution noted for its rampant anti-Semitism. Growing up in Brooklyn would inspire many of the settings for Bennett's later fiction—especially the urban ethnic neighborhoods with their rows of brownstone houses, street lamps, the ever present sounds of city life, and the sometimes real, sometimes imagined threat of violence. Bennett received his elementary education at a Hebrew school where he gained an enduring love for the writings of the great Hebrew prophets of the Old Testament, as well as for Shakespeare. "Shakespeare taught me an awful lot about writing," he noted in the *Something about the Author Autobiography Series* (*SAAS*). "He knew how to create mood, atmosphere, character, and action better than any writer I've ever read.... Every writer should study Old William. Particularly suspense writers."

Unable to remember the events of last night's party, Brad cannot escape the nagging suspicion that, while driving home drunk, his best friend may have killed a homeless pedestrian. (Cover illustration by Cris Cocozza.)

After high school Bennett enrolled at New York University, but the circumstances of the Great Depression eroded his desire for study. After his father joined the ranks of so many other Americans in the lines of the unemployed, Jay left school and tried to find work. Discouraged after several months with no luck, he hopped a freight train and spent the next several months wandering the country amid the swelling ranks of indigents and vagrants that inhabited trainyards, flophouses, soup kitchens, and even the county jail. Finally, he had had enough; he returned to New York City and the relative security that a succession of odd jobs provided both him and his new wife, Sally.

Bennett also returned to a dream he had held on to since he was a child: to become a writer. For the next fourteen years, he worked steadily at his craft part time; when he lost still another job, his wife decided to support the two of them on her salary as a beautician while Bennett pursued writing full time. Just when things had begun to look their bleakest—she had lost her job and had gone home to stay with her mother—he got what turned out to be his big break. A friend told him that a national network radio show was in the market for scripts, so, as Bennett recalled in *SAAS*, "I sat by the radio for ten hours a day, listening to the dramas and soaps and whatever else was on that I could learn from." Once he learned the technique of radio writing, he cranked out twenty-eight radio scripts and sent them along to the producer. The phone call that followed asking for more was the beginning of Bennett's long association with both radio and television as a script writer.

Bennett followed his initial success in radio by writing several novels for adults: *Catacombs, Murder Money,* and *Death Is a Silent Room,* as well as several plays. In fact, drama had been the first form that Bennett's early desire to be a writer had taken. When he was sixteen, he had authored his first three-act play about the adjustments that a soldier wounded in battle in World War I has to make upon returning home. But, as Bennett admitted in *SAAS,* "I quickly found out that I had no deep sense of stagecraft. No true life experience to draw upon and no staying power as a playwright." By the late 1940s that had changed: between 1949 and 1951 two of his plays were produced, one in New York City and one in London.

By the end of the 1950s, Bennett had accumulated enough life experience to have scripted many plays for radio and television. But despite his success, he was becoming more and more distracted from his work in the media by the plight of the younger generation. It was because of that concern that he switched his focus to the young adult novel. "When I was young," he recalled, "one had to grow up arithmetically. You did that and you were able to make some sense out of life. But today with the world—a pretty sick and chaotic one at that—hovering on the edge of extinction, the young have to grow up geometrically. Their perceptions must be deeper and quicker. Their grasp of essential knowledge swift and sure. Their search for truth pure and inviolate. In a word, they must grow up fast."

Bennett's first novel for young adult readers was *Death-man, Do Not Follow Me,* published in 1968. It features the format that Bennett would follow in his later stories: the young, introspective, nonconformist hero, almost into his twenties, who is drawn into dangerous circumstances by people and events over which he is powerless. In *Deathman,* for example, young Danny Morgan fears for his life and yet is unable to confide in anyone when a priceless painting disappears from the Brooklyn Museum and he is drawn in to the crime. Phil Brant is on his own in his efforts to outwit his brother's army buddies when they come to town in search of stolen money in the award-winning *The Long Black Coat.* And Jason Ross in 1990's *Sing Me a Death Song* knows he has to go it alone in uncovering the truth about a murder that his mother is scheduled to be executed for—in less than a week. A compelling argument against the use of the death sentence, Bennett's story was praised by Randy Brough in *Voice of Youth Advocates* as a "taut, spare, poignant" mystery sure to appeal to young adult readers.

But often Bennett's protagonists are fearful of their own unresolved psychological turmoils, as well as the threat of violence from outside sources. Gil realizes that he is half-owner of a winning lottery ticket in *The Death Ticket.* But author Bennett scatters obstacles along his protagonist's path, like the young hero's confused love-hate relationship with his dwarfed older brother, Gareth, as well as a nasty group of thugs who will stop at nothing to acquire Gil's winnings. And a priceless violin hangs in the balance in *Death Grip,* Bennett's 1993 mystery, as young violinist Shane Lockwood finds himself coerced into smuggling diamonds from Europe through customs into the United States in order to get back his prized instrument. Shane's problems are compounded when he begins to suspect that Laurie, his new love interest, may be involved in the crime.

During his many visits to young readers in schools and libraries, Bennett has often been asked where he gets the ideas for his books. "Well, let me cite one example," he once told *SATA.* "I wrote a book, *The Deadly Gift,* which has as its central character a young Mohawk Indian, the son of steelworkers who have a community in Brooklyn. I should say had a community, because I understand that most of the Indian community has been thinned out. I always thought the idea and central character of the book came to me intuitively one morning as I sat at the typewriter. I distinctly remember the character and central situation just kind of bursting into life. It was almost like automatic writing. And I thought it all must have come from my walking around the neighborhood and talking to some of the Mohawk steelworkers. But now I know that it was not that at all. I know the very experience from which the book emerged. I know because one night, for no reason at all, sitting alone, it came back to me, vivid and very forceful. I remember it all.

"Many years ago I was riding a freight train from Kansas to Colorado. Sitting with me in the empty boxcar was a young Navaho. He had hopped on just as the train was clearing Junction City and starting its slow climb to Denver. We sat and talked a good way through the night. And then the train stopped dead and a big guy with a club and a gun came along and threw us out into the rain. There was a look on the Navaho's face. A hard, hopeless look. He never said another word to me as we walked along the tracks. I saw his eyes, the hat, the dungarees tight and wet on his legs. I never saw him again. But I now know that I never forgot him and all he said to me in the boxcar, and all he said when we walked to the dawn, and he didn't speak a word. I know now how I came to write *The Deadly Gift,* and why I feel the way I do about Indians. You see, I went back to New York and became a writer. And he went on to nowhere."

■ Works Cited

Bennett, Jay, essay in *Something about the Author Autobiography Series,* Volume 4, Gale, 1987, pp. 75-90.
Brough, Randy, review of *Sing Me a Death Song, Voice of Youth Advocates,* August, 1990, p. 158.
Porter, Judie, review of *Coverup, School Library Journal,* August, 1991, p. 195.

■ For More Information See

BOOKS

Contemporary Literary Criticism, Volume 35, Gale, 1985, pp. 42-46.
Donelson, Kenneth L., and Alleen Pace Nilsen, *Literature for Today's Young Adults,* HarperCollins, 1995, pp. 68-69, 195.

PERIODICALS

Best Sellers, January, 1981, p. 349.
Booklist, November 15, 1985, p. 481.
English Journal, February, 1969, pp. 295-96; April, 1970, p. 591.
New York Times Book Review, August 22, 1965; July 7, 1968, p. 16; November 1, 1974, pp. 8, 10; May 2, 1976, p. 38.
Publishers Weekly, May 7, 1973, p. 65; June 3, 1974, p. 157; August 12, 1974, p. 58; August 22, 1977, p. 66; July 1, 1983, p. 103; September 27, 1985, p. 97; October 28, 1988, p. 83.
School Library Journal, May, 1970, p. 92; May, 1974, p. 69; May, 1976, p. 77; May, 1980, p. 86; May, 1982, p. 84; December, 1983, p. 84; August, 1984, p. 80; October, 1986, pp. 185-86; November, 1987, p. 112; April, 1990, p. 139; May, 1991, p. 108.
Times Literary Supplement, August 19, 1988, p. 917.
Voice of Youth Advocates, August, 1982, p. 28; February, 1984, p. 337; August, 1984, p. 143; April, 1987, p. 28; February, 1988, p. 277; April, 1991, p. 26; October, 1991, p. 222; June, 1993, p. 80.
Washington Post Book World, October 7, 1979, p. 15.

NATALIE S. BOBER

BOBER, Natalie S. 1930-

■ Personal

Born December 27, 1930, in New York, NY; daughter of Samuel (in real estate) and Dolly (an editor, researcher, and indexer; maiden name, Goodman) Birnbaum; married Lawrence H. Bober (a banker), August 27, 1950; children: Stephen, Marc, Elizabeth Polivy. *Education:* Hunter College, B.A., 1951; Hofstra University, M.S., 1966; additional graduate studies. *Religion:* Jewish.

■ Addresses

Home and office—7 Westfield Ln., White Plains, NY 10605.

■ Career

Educator and consultant at junior high school and college level; author of biographies for children and young adults. Co-owner of children's bookstore, Once Upon a Time, with daughter, Elizabeth Bober Polivy, 1985-93.

■ Awards, Honors

William Wordsworth: The Wandering Poet was named one of the Best Books of the Year, Child Study Association, 1975; *Boston Globe-Horn Book* Award for nonfiction, 1995, for *Abigail Adams: Witness to a Revolution; A Restless Spirit: The Story of Robert Frost, Breaking Tradition: The Story of Louise Nevelson,* and *Thomas Jefferson: Man on a Mountain* appeared on New York Public Library lists for Children's Books, Books for the Teen Age, and Best Books in the Field of Social Studies; *A Restless Spirit* appeared on the Doro-

thy Canfield Fisher list; *School Library Journal* Best Books of 1995 selection, *Booklist* 1995 Editor's Choice selection, *Boston Globe-Horn Book* Award for nonfiction, 1995, Golden Kite Award for Nonfiction, Society of Children's Authors, 1995, all for *Abigail Adams: Witness to a Revolution.*

■ Writings

William Wordsworth: The Wandering Poet, Thomas Nelson, 1975.
A Restless Spirit: The Story of Robert Frost, Atheneum, 1981.
Breaking Tradition: The Story of Louise Nevelson, Atheneum, 1984.
(Compiler) *Let's Pretend: Poems of Flight and Fancy,* illustrated by Bill Bell, Viking, 1986.
Thomas Jefferson: Man on a Mountain, Atheneum, 1988.
Marc Chagall: Painter of Dreams, illustrated by Vera Rosenberry, Jewish Publication Society, 1991.
Abigail Adams: Witness to a Revolution, Atheneum, 1995.

Contributor to *The Lion and the Unicorn.*

■ Sidelights

Award-winning biographer Natalie S. Bober told *SATA:* "A lifelong interest in the creative arts, a strong background in the humanities, and many years of teaching have prompted me to tell the stories of men and women whose achievements might serve as an inspiration for junior and senior high school students. There is a strong need today for role models relevant to this age group who can inspire young people to find the greatness within themselves. It is important for them to recognize that all great people were once young, with the same fears, doubts and concerns that they have. Yet they achieved. But they achieved by faith in themselves, persistence, and hard work."

Bober also told *SATA* the following story: "Now let me tell you how my first book came to be. While recovering from a problem with a leg that kept me off my feet and away from my job as a reading teacher for a long time, I chanced upon a magazine article about writing biographies for young people. My husband challenged me to try. 'You've always wanted to write,' he said. 'Besides, it will keep you sane.' Never one to ignore a challenge, I decided to take him up on it. I *had* always wanted to write, but I'd never had the nerve to try. I never thought I was good enough.

"Now I began to think about the love of England that I had absorbed from my English grandmother, about the English poet William Wordsworth, and how much I loved his poetry, and about the trip we had just taken to Wordsworth country in England. I thought, too, about how much one of my sons resembled Wordsworth: he was a rebel—but a rebel and a gentleman at the same time. And I knew that during William's last summer vacation while he was at Cambridge University, when

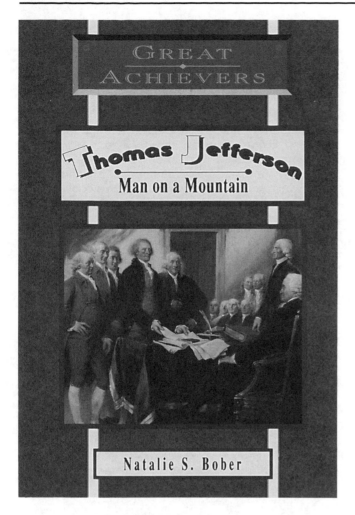

In her award-winning biography of Thomas Jefferson, Bober details the life of the man who wrote the *Declaration of Independence* and later became the third president of the United States.

he should have been studying for his approaching exams, he and a friend decided instead to take a three-month walking tour of France and Switzerland to see the Alps. Here was my perfect character.

"My mother and a friend brought me books from the library, I wrote to publishing houses to order books, I re-read the poetry I had in my home, and so the research began. When I was finally able to walk a bit, my husband all but drove me up the steps of the library so I could do some looking on my own. Eventually I started to write. And I sent query letters, then proposals, outlines and sample chapters to publishing houses. Twenty-one houses responded: 'No thank you.' They all told me, kindly, that it was a great idea, well written, but it wouldn't sell. Young people today just don't read William Wordsworth, they said.

"I was devastated. But I continued to send it around—one publishing house at a time. The *twenty-second* editor who read the manuscript was an Anglophile—she loved all things English—and she was willing to take a chance. *But*—she wanted a complete manuscript before she would give me a contract, *and* she wanted a new

beginning. She got them both. When the book was finally published, after twenty-one rejections and four years of research and writing, *William Wordsworth: The Wandering Poet* was named by the Child Study Association to its list, 'Best Biographies of the Year,' and I was off and running—literally and figuratively. And that's the definition of the word *persistence.*"

Bober's biographies for young people have been widely praised as clearly written and interesting accounts of the lives of important figures in the arts, literature, and history. Critics often emphasize the author's ability to show the human side of her larger-than-life subjects by including details that do not always flatter them. While some critics found her early prose uninspired, many recommend her biographies to teachers and librarians with students looking for role models.

In *William Wordsworth: The Wandering Poet* Bober recounts the life of one of England's most revered nineteenth-century poets, beginning with his early loss of both parents and his lifelong attachment to his sister Dorothy, and ending with his adult success and friendship with other important literary figures like Samuel Coleridge. Several reviewers praised Bober's literate text and sensitive handling of her subject. A reviewer for *School Library Journal,* for example, called *William Wordsworth* "well-researched" and "very readable." According to a critic in *Publishers Weekly,* the author provides an informative and "well-written" account of the poet's life.

A Restless Spirit: The Story of Robert Frost, a biography of the important twentieth-century American poet, followed Bober's book on Wordsworth. In this work, which appeared in a revised edition that added numerous photographs and more than forty complete poems by Frost, Bober "successfully portrays the four-time Pulitzer Prize winner as a very human schoolboy, husband, father, farmer, and teacher," according to Pat Katka in the *School Library Journal.* A *Horn Book* reviewer emphasized the author's "straightforward yet detailed" approach to Frost's emotionally turbulent life, and in a review in the *Washington Post Book World* Mary Jo Salter similarly claimed that Bober meets the challenge of showing both sides—the "escapist" and the man of "courage"—of her "self-contradictory" subject. Salter averred that in reading *A Restless Spirit,* "one rediscovers how perfectly [Frost] may serve as a model for children of eventual accomplishment." Bober's writing style was also commended. A *Booklist* contributor hailed Bober's "gracefully written, at times even dramatic narrative."

With *Breaking Tradition: The Story of Louise Nevelson,* Bober turned to chronicling the life of a twentieth-century sculptor. Louise Nevelson emigrated to the east coast of the United States from Russia with her family in 1905 and spent her life exploring a variety of outlets for her creativity. Zena Sutherland remarked in a *Bulletin of the Center for Children's Books* review that *Breaking Tradition* illustrates "how an individual artist moves toward a form of expression in which ... there is

Bober depicts the vibrant life and career of a world renowned artist in _Marc Chagall: Painter of Dreams._ (Illustration by Vera Rosenberry.)

integrity and a personal voice." _Voice of Youth Advocates_ contributor Beth E. Andersen found the details of Nevelson's life recounted in _Breaking Tradition_ "fascinating" and praised Bober's "spellbinding account of a woman who has been heralded as 'the finest living American artist of our time.'"

Bober's next publication was an anthology of poetry for children, entitled _Let's Pretend: Poems of Flight and Fancy,_ a collection that emphasizes the imaginative life of children. Barbara Chatton's review in _School Library Journal_ stressed Bober's careful selection of material, found the book's focus "unique," and concluded that educators looking "to encourage imaginative writing and speculative thinking ... will find this to be a useful collection." Although a _Publishers Weekly_ reviewer complained that "the quality of the verse varies greatly," Christine Boutross dubbed _Let's Pretend_ a "delightful" and "wonderful" anthology in her critique in _Children's Book Review Service._

Bober's next publication, _Thomas Jefferson: Man on a Mountain,_ revived her reputation as a biographer capable of putting forward the human side of her subjects while highlighting those qualities that brought them success in their chosen fields. The third president of the United States and author of the _Declaration of Indepen-_

dence, as well as a scientist and plantation owner, Jefferson was about as important a figure in history that Bober could choose to write about. However, a reviewer in _Booklist_ claimed that Jefferson "remains a distant figure" in Bober's biography, despite her inclusion of personal documents and Jefferson family stories, because the author follows a chronology rather than focusing on his "inner life." But Shirley Wilton, writing in _School Library Journal,_ called _Thomas Jefferson_ "a marvelously readable and informative biography that breathes life into an 'American hero.'" "This biography is one which shows just how well written a book about a giant can be," asserted _Voice of Youth Advocates_ reviewer John Lord.

Bober's next biography, _Marc Chagall: Painter of Dreams,_ "celebrates Chagall's Jewish heritage as well as his creative life," in the words of a reviewer in _Publishers Weekly._ Chagall became a successful artist of international renown, overcoming his early struggles with his father over his artistic leanings and persecution by government officials because of his religion, which forced him to move frequently throughout Europe before emigrating to France. Although Deborah Stevenson complained in the _Bulletin of the Center for Chil-_

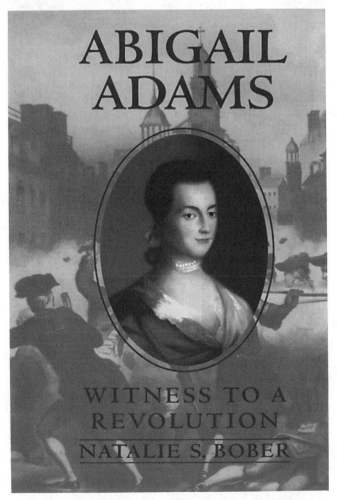

Through excerpts from Abigail Adams' remarkable personal correspondence, Bober offers readers insight into the lives of women in colonial America.

dren's Books that Bober's "writing style tends to be pedestrian," she also noted that young people in particular find Chagall's art attractive. Other critics complained of the paucity of reproductions of the artist's work in *Marc Chagall*, but the critic for *Publishers Weekly* concluded that the "sympathetic and vivacious biography" could interest readers to seek out the works of this important artist.

In 1995 Bober received the *Boston Globe-Horn Book* Award for nonfiction for her work *Abigail Adams: Witness to a Revolution*. Abigail, husband of John Adams, the second president of the United States, and mother of John Quincy Adams, the nation's sixth president, lived from 1744 to 1818. Through this work, which combines selections from Abigail's personal letters with findings from Bober's own research, the author "nudges readers to look beyond their twentieth-century expectations and become absorbed in another age," according to *Booklist* contributor Carolyn Phelan. Stephanie Loer, writing in the *Boston Globe*, stated that the work "is a sensitive portrayal of an intelligent and independent woman" who "expresses the importance of education and equal legal status for women" in her letters. Maura Bresnahan, writing in *Voice of Youth Advocates*, found *Abigail Adams* to be a "richly-crafted tribute" to its subject, noting that Adams's "own voice is heard through the beautifully balanced use of quotations" from her correspondences.

"My books," Bober concluded for *SATA*, "describe the milieu from which my subjects sprang—the forces that shaped their lives—and show how their accomplishments were an outgrowth of the lives they lived. They attempt to make readers feel that they are living at the same time or moving in the same circle of friends and family as the hero or heroine. My aim is to 'ungrave' my subjects, to bring them alive for young people, and to enable the reader to identify with them."

■ Works Cited

Andersen, Beth E., review of *Breaking Tradition: The Story of Louise Nevelson, Voice of Youth Advocates,* February, 1985, p. 342.

Boutross, Christine, review of *Let's Pretend: Poems of Flight and Fancy, Children's Book Review Service,* February, 1987.

Bresnahan, Maura, review of *Abigail Adams: Witness to a Revolution, Voice of Youth Advocates,* October, 1995.

Chatton, Barbara, review of *Let's Pretend: Poems of Flight and Fancy, School Library Journal,* January, 1987, p. 58.

Katka, Pat, review of *A Restless Spirit: The Story of Robert Frost, School Library Journal,* December, 1991.

Review of *Let's Pretend: Poems of Flight and Fancy, Publishers Weekly,* December 12, 1986, p. 53.

Loer, Stephanie, "Writers, Artist to Be Honored for Excellence in Publishing," *Boston Globe,* October 1, 1995.

Lord, John, review of *Thomas Jefferson: Man on a Mountain, Voice of Youth Advocates,* October, 1988, pp. 197-98.

Review of *Marc Chagall: Painter of Dreams, Publishers Weekly,* November 22, 1991.

Phelan, Carolyn, review of *Abigail Adams: Witness to a Revolution, Booklist,* April 15, 1995, p. 1498.

Review of *A Restless Spirit: The Story of Robert Frost, Booklist,* April 1, 1981.

Review of *A Restless Spirit: The Story of Robert Frost, Horn Book,* August, 1981.

Salter, Mary Jo, "Robert Frost: Life with Poetry," *Washington Post Book World,* September 13, 1981, p. 8.

Stevenson, Deborah, review of *Marc Chagall: Painter of Dreams, Bulletin of the Center for Children's Books,* March, 1992, p. 175.

Sutherland, Zena, review of *Breaking Tradition: The Story of Louise Nevelson, Bulletin of the Center for Children's Books,* May, 1984, p. 161.

Review of *Thomas Jefferson: Man on a Mountain, Booklist,* January 15, 1989.

Review of *William Wordsworth: The Wandering Poet, Publishers Weekly,* June 2, 1975, p. 54.

Review of *William Wordsworth: The Wandering Poet, School Library Journal,* September, 1975.

Wilton, Shirley, review of *Thomas Jefferson: Man on a Mountain, School Library Journal,* November 1, 1988.

■ For More Information See

PERIODICALS

Booklist, November 15, 1991.
Language Arts, March, 1982.
School Library Journal, January, 1992.

—*Sketch by Mary Gillis*

*   *   *

BOND, Ruskin 1934-

■ Personal

Born May 19, 1934, in Kasauli, Himachal, India; son of Aubrey Alexander (in the Royal Air Force) and Edith (Clerke) Bond. *Education:* Attended Bishop Cotton School, Simla, India, 1943-50. *Hobbies and other interests:* Folk songs, American operetta (favorite singers include Nelson Eddy and Jeannette MacDonald), and ghost stories.

■ Addresses

Home—Ivy Cottage, Landour Cantt, Mussoorie, Uttar Pradesh 2481279, India.

■ Career

Freelance writer since 1956; managing editor, *Imprint* magazine, 1975-79; has worked for Cooperative for American Relief Everywhere (CARE).

RUSKIN BOND

■ **Awards, Honors**

John Llewellyn Rhys Memorial Prize, 1957, for *The Room on the Roof;* Sahitya Academy award for English writing in India, 1992.

■ **Writings**

FOR CHILDREN

The Hidden Pool, illustrated by Arup Das, Children's Book Trust (New Delhi), 1966.

Grandfather's Private Zoo, illustrated by Mario Miranda, India Book House (Bombay), 1967.

The Wonderful World of Insects, Trees, and Wild Flowers (nonfiction), illustrated by Kamal Kishore, India Book House, 1968.

Panther's Moon, illustrated by Tom Feelings, Random House, 1969.

Tales Told at Twilight (folktales), illustrated by Madhu Powle, India Book House, 1970.

The Last Tiger, Government of Indian Publications (New Delhi), 1971.

Angry River, illustrated by Trevor Stubley, Hamish Hamilton, 1972.

The Blue Umbrella, illustrated by Trevor Stubley, Hamish Hamilton, 1974.

World of Trees (nonfiction), illustrated by Siddhartha Banerjee, National Book Trust (New Delhi), 1974.

Who's Who at the Zoo (nonfiction), photographs by Raghu Rai, National Book Trust, 1974.

Once upon a Monsoon Time (autobiography), Orient Longman, 1974.

Man of Destiny: A Biography of Jawaharlal Nehru, Orient Longman, 1976.

Night of the Leopard, illustrated by Eileen Green, Hamish Hamilton, 1979.

Big Business, illustrated by Valerie Littlewood, Hamish Hamilton, 1979.

The Cherry Tree, illustrated by Valerie Littlewood, Hamish Hamilton, 1980, illustrated by Allan Eitzen, Boyds Mills Press, 1991.

Flames in the Forest, illustrated by Valerie Littlewood, MacRae, 1981.

The Adventures of Rusty, illustrated by Imtiaz Dharker, Thompson (New Delhi), 1981.

A Garland of Memories (essays), Mukul Prakashan (New Delhi), 1982.

Tales and Legend of India, illustrated by Sally Scott, MacRae and F. Watts, 1982.

Tigers Forever, illustrated by Valerie Littlewood, MacRae/F. Watts (New York), 1983.

To Live in Magic (poetry), Thompson, 1983.

Earthquake, illustrated by Valerie Littlewood, MacRae, 1984.

Getting Granny's Glasses, illustrated by Barbara Walker, MacRae, 1985.

Cricket for the Crocodile, illustrated by Barbara Walker, MacRae, 1986.

The Adventures of Rama and Sita, illustrated by Valerie Littlewood, MacRae, 1987.

The Eyes of the Eagle, illustrated by Valerie Littlewood, MacRae, 1987.

Ghost Trouble, MacRae, 1989.

Dust on the Mountain, MacRae, 1990.

Snake Trouble, illustrated by Mickey Patel, MacRae, 1990.

An Island of Trees: Nature Stories and Poems, illustrated by Basu, Ratna Sagar (Delhi), 1992.

Tiger Roars, Eagle Soars, Walker, 1994.

(Editor) *The Green Book,* Roli (New Delhi), 1995.

Binya's Blue Umbrella, illustrated by Vera Rosenberry, Boyds Mills Press, 1995.

SHORT STORIES FOR CHILDREN

The Road to the Bazaar, illustrated by Valerie Littlewood, MacRae, 1980.

Panther's Moon, and Other Stories, illustrated by Suddhasattwa Basu, Puffin (New Delhi), 1990.

Ruskin Bond Children's Omnibus, Rupa (New Delhi), 1994.

Quakes and Flames, illustrated by Subir Roy, National Book Trust, 1994.

NOVELS FOR ADULTS

The Room on the Roof, Deutsch (London), 1956, Coward McCann, 1957.

An Axe for the Rani, Hind (Delhi), 1972.

Love Is a Sad Song, Orient Longman, 1975.

A Flight of Pigeons, India Book House, 1980.

The Young Vagrants, India Book House, 1981.

SHORT STORIES FOR ADULTS

The Neighbour's Wife, and Other Stories, Higginbothams (Madras), 1967.

My First Love, and Other Stories, Pearl (Bombay), 1968.

The Man-Eater of Manjari, Sterling (New Delhi), 1974.

A Girl from Copenhagen, India Paperbacks, 1977.

Ghosts of a Hill Station, India Book House, 1983.

The Night Train at Deoli, and Other Stories, Penguin India (New Delhi), 1988.

Time Stops at Shamli, and Other Stories, Penguin
    (London), 1990.
Our Trees Still Grow in Dehra, Penguin India, 1991.
Delhi Is Not Far: The Best of Bond, Penguin India, 1995.

POETRY FOR ADULTS

It Isn't Time That's Passing: Poem 1970-1971, Writers
    Workshop (Calcutta), 1972.
Lone Fox Dancing: Lyric Poems, Writers Workshop,
    1975.

OTHER

Strange Men, Strange Places, Pearl, 1969.
Beautiful Garhwal, English Book Depot (Dehra Dun),
    1988.
Ganga Descends, English Book Depot, 1992.
Mussoorie and Landour: Days of Wine and Roses,
    illustrated by Ganesh Saili, Lustre Press (New
    Delhi), 1992.
Rain in the Mountains: Notes from the Himalayas,
    Viking (New Delhi), 1993.
(Editor) *Penguin Book of Indian Ghost Stories,* Penguin
    India, 1993.
(Editor) *Penguin Book of Indian Railway Stories,* Pen-
    guin India, 1994.

Also contributor of short stories to numerous antholo-
gies and periodicals, including *Blackwood's, Christian
Science Monitor, Cricket, Highlights for Children, New
Renaissance, Reader's Digest, School,* and *Short Story
International.* Several of Bond's books have been trans-
lated into French, German, Danish, Dutch, and Span-
ish. The author's manuscripts are housed at the Mugar
Memorial Library, Boston University.

■ Adaptations

A Flight of Pigeons was adapted into the Hindi film
Junoon.

■ Sidelights

Born in India of British parents, Ruskin Bond paints
sensitive, colorful portraits of life in his native country
to capture the imaginations of his readers, both young
and old. One of India's most noted children's authors,
he depicts the many facets of that country's natural and
social landscape through his simple stories—from a
temple near a quiet, rural village or a bazaar in a small
provincial town to a narrow city street brimming over
with buses, bicycles, and the clamor of people. As Bond
noted in his *Rain in the Mountains: Notes from the
Himalayas,* "I have been writing in order to sustain the
sort of life I like to lead—unhurried, even-paced,
sensual, in step with the natural world, most at home
with humble people."

Bond was born in Kasauli, Himachal, India, on May 19,
1934. The son of an Englishman who served in the
Royal Air Force and as tutor-guardian to the royal
children in Jamnagar, Bond was nonetheless raised as
an Indian, spending many quiet days at the home of his
grandparents in Dehra Dun, a village near the base of

the Himalayan Mountains. While a student, he was
inspired by the works of novelists Charles Dickens and
William Saroyan and the poetry of Indian philosopher
Sir Rabindranath Tagore. After leaving high school,
Bond worked for a short time for the Cooperative for
American Relief Everywhere (CARE), but he soon
returned to writing. Although he would leave India for
England when British colonial rule of India finally came
to an end in 1948, Bond returned to the country of his
youth after only five years and has remained there ever
since, among a large family of adopted children. A
naturally gifted storyteller, Bond found that his talent
enabled him to make a living away from the more highly
industrialized, congested areas of the country. Following
the philosophy he outlined in "What's Your Dream?,"
an autobiographical essay from 1982's *A Garland of
Memories,* Bond has found "a room of his own" at Ivy
Cottage, a house 7,500 feet from the foothills of the
Himalayan Mountains, and has pursued his single
dream by dedicating his life to being a storyteller.

Bond had his first success as a writer very early in his
career. In fact, he was not even twenty when he
published *The Room on the Roof,* a novel that dealt with
growing up in a changing India. Although he believes
himself to be of British blood, Rusty, the tale's orphaned
protagonist, finds himself strangely attracted to the
colorful crafts, the spicy scent of Indian foods, and the
energetic hubbub of the local bazaar. After he discovers
that he is of mixed Indian-English heritage and is beaten
by his overly strict English guardian, Rusty leaves to
make his own way in the town of Dehra Dun; he gets a
job as a tutor and makes new Indian friends. Tragedy
strikes, however, when his naive romantic relationship
with the mother of his young charge is discovered by her
alcoholic husband. Rusty is forced to leave the life he
has made for himself and move to another city to find a
new place in society. Although Helen W. Coonley sensed
the author's youth—Bond was seventeen when he wrote
the novel—and noted in *Kliatt* that *The Room on the
Roof* incorporated a somewhat immature outlook, she
went on to say that "though awkward in parts, the book
is still fresh and likable." *The Room on the Roof* was the
winner of the John Llewellyn Rhys Memorial Prize in
1957, an annual award given to a quality work of fiction
written by a resident of the British Commonwealth
(which then included India) under the age of thirty.

The Room on the Roof made its author something of a
celebrity in India, not only because of his young age but
also because he was able to capture the spirit of the land
and its people so sensitively through his fiction.
Throughout his twenties Bond continued to write adult
novels about his childhood, not turning to writing for
children until he had reached his thirties. Since then, he
has written numerous stories and poems that capture his
nostalgia for the days of his boyhood: the natural beauty
and tranquility of his grandparent's home and the close,
secure, loving relationships that he experienced with
friends and family.

"Bond illustrates his vision of childhood as a carefree
age of mischief and joy where the only worries are

associated with cricket matches, beetle races, and parental anger at bad report cards," explained Meena Khorana in *Twentieth-Century Children's Writers.* "In this comfortable and familiar world, there is a sense of security in friendship and the love and guidance of adults." In books such as *The Cherry Tree, The Adventures of Rusty,* and *Getting Granny's Glasses,* relationships among friends and family are warmly illustrated through incidents in the lives of each of Bond's youthful characters. A young girl is the focus of *The Cherry Tree,* Bond's heartwarming story of six-year-old Rakhi's attempt to grow a cherry tree from a seed, which was praised by a *Publishers Weekly* reviewer as "abound[ing] with quiet wisdom and love of life."

Several of Bond's books offer drama and suspense. In *Flames in the Forest,* for example, young Romi rides his new bicycle home from the village after school, only to find himself suddenly caught in a forest fire in an area that has no fire engine. He and another boy travelling the same road must help each other race to the river in time to escape the smoke and flames, along with frightened birds and animals—even an elephant herd. The determined Romi and his partner manage to survive the tragedy in a story that Ellen D. Warwick described in *School Library Journal* as full of "action, suspense, local color, even a bit of humor." A young

Ten-year-old Binya trades her leopard-claw necklace for a bright blue umbrella and becomes the envy of her rural Indian village in Bond's *Binya's Blue Umbrella.* (Illustration by Vera Rosenberry.)

Left alone by her grandfather on her island home, Sita is miraculously saved from the thundering flood waters by a boy in a boat in Bond's *Angry River.* (Illustration by Trevor Stubley.)

boy's trip through the forest again provides the focus in *Night of the Leopard,* as twelve-year-old Raki is stalked by a leopard that has been forced by the midsummer heat to come down from the mountains in search of food and water. Terrorizing the local mountain villages, the wild cat captures Raki's dog and injures one of his friends. The boy finally decides to fight back when the leopard follows him home from school; through Raki's quick wits and determination, he and his neighbors rid themselves of the beast.

A more recent work, *Binya's Blue Umbrella,* was inspired by a child Bond had seen roaming the hillsides near his home, grazing her family's cattle. The story's main character, ten-year-old Binya, comes upon a bright blue umbrella while following her cows. The umbrella's owner, a wealthy woman from a neighboring town, agrees to trade it for a leopard-claw necklace that Binya wears, and soon the girl is the talk of the village. Now she must deal with the envy of her neighbors, especially that of the crafty store owner Ram Bharosa, who never owned such a wonderful thing and plots to steal it. Bond's *Angry River* features a young girl who has been left alone on her island home while her grandfather takes his dying wife to the hospital. As the river surrounding her island rises, Sita climbs a tree to safety; after the tree is washed downriver by the raging water, she is rescued by the providential appearance of a boy in a boat. "The power and size of the river, the fear and the danger are all present," stated a *Times Literary Supplement* reviewer, "as is the sense of smallness in a vast world .... This really is India you feel."

The Indian landscape serves as one of the main characters in each of Bond's books, and his concern over its future is a theme that runs through several of his stories. *The Last Tiger,* a children's novel published in 1971, concerns the disappearance of wildlife in India. Featuring a similar theme, *Dust on the Mountain* "strongly expresses" Bond's concern for the degradation of the environment in the Himalayas. After twelve-year-old Bisnu leaves his mountain-farm home to find work in a nearby town and help his family, he is shocked by the devastation of the land—especially the native walnut and chestnut trees and their lush undergrowth—both by the growing city and at a quarry where he gets a job driving a truck. Almost killed in an accident on a winding road, the boy is saved by a lone tree left on the scarred mountainside, which saves his truck's fall. His renewed love and respect for nature prompts Bisnu to return home to work the family farm, hoping to save it from a similar destruction.

Bond has also adapted many of the traditional tales of India into books for learning readers. *The Adventures of Rama and Sita* is based on the epic Sanskrit poem *The Ramayana.* In nine short stories, Bond translates the ancient verses that spin the tale of the Indian Prince Rama and his wife, the beautiful Sita, as they do battle with evil forces. And in *Tales and Legend of India,* the oral traditions of India are mixed with other epics and Jakata Buddhist stories. From "Beautiful and Brave," a tale of a youthful prince who learns self-reliance, to the homespun "The Ghost and the Idiot," a fable with a curious ending, Bond's collection was praised by critics for his sensitive rendering of time and place.

"At the heart of [Bond's] writings is the value placed on simplicity and a selfless attitude toward life," explained Khorana. "Although the stories deal with the pleasures of humble people, their lives are enriched by meaningful experiences and a profound insight into life." Bond himself gains much of his inspiration from his surroundings and develops many of his ideas for children's books on the long walks he takes on the mountains near where he lives. "My interests (mountains, animals, trees, wild flowers) are embodied in these and other writings," Bond once told *SATA.* "I live in the foothills of the Himalayas and my window opens out on the forest and the distant snow-peaks—the highest mountains in the world .... I sit here and, inspired by the life of the hill people and the presence of birds and trees, write my stories and poems." Of his preoccupation with the landscape that features so prominently in his work, Bond once explained, "Once you have lived in the mountains, you belong to them and must come back again and again. There is no escape."

In his retelling of Indian folklore and religious tales, Bond celebrates the diversity of Indian culture, landscape, and people in *Tales and Legends from India.* (Illustration by Sally Scott.)

■ Works Cited

Review of *Angry River, Times Literary Supplement,* July 14, 1972, p. 804.

Bond, Ruskin, *Rain in the Mountains: Notes from the Himalayas,* Viking, 1993.

Coonley, Helen W., review of *The Room on the Roof, Kliatt,* September, 1989, p. 4.

Review of *Cherry Tree, Publishers Weekly,* November 15, 1991, p. 71.

Khorana, Meena, "Ruskin Bond," in *Twentieth-Century Children's Writers,* 4th edition, edited by Laura Standley Berger, St. James Press, 1995, pp. 123-26.

Warwick, Ellen D., review of *Flames in the Forest, School Library Journal,* August, 1981, p. 53.

■ For More Information See

PERIODICALS

Booklist, March 15, 1995, p. 1327.

Growing Point, July, 1982, p. 3923; November, 1987, p. 4876; September, 1990, p. 5408.

Junior Bookshelf, June, 1980, p. 125; June, 1985, p. 125; February, 1991, p. 29.

School Librarian, September, 1980, p. 262; December, 1985, p. 234; February, 1991, p. 21; November, 1992, p. 149.

School Library Journal, May, 1969, p. 83; August, 1981,
    p. 63; March, 1992, p. 208.
Times Literary Supplement, July 5, 1974, p. 722.*

* * *

BRANDENBURG, Jim 1945-

■ Personal

Born November 23, 1945, in Luverne, MN; son of
Edward Henry and Olga (Aanenson) Brandenburg;
married Judy D. Frederiksen (in management); children: Heidi K., Anthony James. *Education:* Attended
Worthington Community College; graduate, University
of Minnesota Duluth.

■ Addresses

Office—1715 Meadow Woods Trail, Long Lake, MN
55356-9311.

■ Career

Worked as a picture editor, *Daily Globe,* Worthington,
MN, during the 1970s; *National Geographic,* Washington, DC, contract photographer, 1978—. Board member
emeritus, Wolf Ridge Environmental Learning Center.
Commissioned by U.S. Postal Service to photograph
and design ten stamps, released May 14, 1981. Co-
producer, director, and cinematographer of documentary film, *White Wolf,* National Geographic/BBC TV,
1988. *Exhibits:* "Graphic Design in America," United
States and England, 1990; "The Photography of Jim
Brandenburg," North American and European cities.
Member: American Society of Magazine Photographers,
Sierra Club, Nature Conservancy, Defenders of Wildlife
(member of board of directors).

■ Awards, Honors

Magazine Photographer of the Year, National Press
Photographer's Association, 1981, 1983; World
Achievement Award, United Nations Environmental
Programme, 1991, for "using nature photography to
raise public awareness for the environment"; Kodak
Wildlife Photographer of the Year, National History
Museum—London/*BBC Wildlife,* 1988.

■ Writings

(And photographer) *White Wolf: Living with an Arctic
    Legend,* NorthWord Press, 1988.
(And photographer) *Brother Wolf: A Forgotten Promise,*
    NorthWord Press, 1993.
(And photographer) *To the Top of the World: Adventures
    with Arctic Wolves* (for children), Walker, 1993.
(And photographer) *Sand and Fog: Adventures in South-
    ern Africa* (for children), Walker, 1994.
(And photographer) *An American Safari: Adventures on
    the North American Prairie,* Walker, 1995.

Brandenburg's photographs have appeared in *Minnesota: Images of Home,* Blandin Foundation, 1990, *Discovering Britain and Ireland, Alaska's Magnificent Park-
lands, Our Threatened Inheritance, The Wonder of
Birds, Journey into China,* and *The Curious Naturalist,*
National Geographic Society, and *The World's Best
Photographs 1980-1990,* Time/Life; photographs have
also appeared in numerous periodicals, including *Audubon, BBC Wildlife, Geo, Life, Modern Maturity, National Geographic, National Wildlife, Natural History,
Smithsonian,* and *World.*

■ Work in Progress

An untitled work that will present "one shot a day for an
entire Autumn season."

■ Sidelights

Esteemed for his many photographic essays for *National
Geographic* magazine, award-winning photographer Jim
Brandenburg has travelled the world capturing the
vastness of the natural landscape on film. The author of
several books featuring his photographs, Brandenburg
has compiled three works for children—*Sand and Fog:
Adventures in Southern Africa; An American Safari:
Adventures on the North American Prairie;* and *To the
Top of the World: Adventures with Arctic Wolves*—that
allow curious young minds an intimate look at the grand
variety of wildlife in the world.

After graduating from the University of Minnesota with
a major in studio art, Brandenburg was hired by the
Worthington, Minnesota, *Daily Globe* as picture editor.
In 1978, he received an assignment for *National Geographic,* the first of many that have since taken him
around the globe for that magazine. His work in
Manchuria was featured in *Journey into China,* and his
trek through the Scottish Highlands was recorded in
Discovering Britain and Ireland, also a National Geo-
graphic publication. Exhibited around the country,
Brandenburg's work came to the attention of the United
States Postal Service, which commissioned him to
design and photograph a set of ten wildlife stamps that
were released in 1981 and included in the exhibit
"Graphic Design in America" that toured the United
States and England in 1990.

It has been the wolves of the northern Arctic regions,
however, that have most often captured the photographer's interest. After a story for *National Geographic*
took him to the Arctic to photograph a wolf pack in
1986, Brandenburg arranged 160 of the resulting color
photographs and laced them together with textual
commentary on his observations and experiences among
the wolves. Published in 1988 as *White Wolf: Living
with an Arctic Legend,* Brandenburg's volume was the
first book of photographs ever published about wolves
living in the wilderness.

Brandenburg again ventured to the frozen north in 1987
and 1988, where he spent the summers near a pack of
white wolves living close to the Arctic Circle. *To the Top*

of the World: Adventures with Arctic Wolves and the National Geographic television show *White Wolf* were the results of these additional trips to the high Arctic. Amid the remote landscape of Ellesmere Island, Brandenburg was quickly accepted by the wolves, which had as yet not acquired the fear of humans that develops through hunting or other violent interaction with mankind. Studying the day-to-day habits of the wolves as an anthropologist might, he was able to photograph the animals in a relaxed, natural state, capturing on film such things as five-week-old wolf pups leaving the safety of their den for the first time and playing in the snow, and adult wolves satisfying their hunger with a meal of musk ox that they had isolated from its herd and killed. At one point, Brandenburg witnessed the entire wolf pack engaging in a "howlalong" under the Arctic moon and described the cacophony: "Every wolf avoided hitting the same note," he wrote, explaining that when two animals accidentally howled the same tone in unison "one of the voices would frantically shuffle about until discord could be achieved once again."

At the end of his visit, as Brandenburg was preparing to board the plane and depart, the pack of white wolves that had come to accept his presence in their midst appeared alongside the runway to watch him leave. Brandenburg's full-color photographs, arranged in pictorial vignettes, portray the intelligence, pride, and unique personality of each of these animals, and his accompanying text offers numerous insights into animal behavior while stressing the dangers of anthropomorphizing—giving human feelings to an animal's actions. From the brash young wolf he named "Scruffy" to "Buster," the alpha male—or top-dog of the wolf pack—"Brandenburg's respect and awe are apparent in every paragraph of text," notes Denia Hester in *Booklist*. Hester adds that *To the Top of the World* convinces the reader to reevaluate his fear of wolves as misplaced.

From the desolate, icy reaches of the Arctic, Brandenburg travelled south with his camera to Namibia, South Africa, to provide photographic coverage of the fight for colonial independence. While there, he captured breathtaking views of life on the arid Namib Desert, collected in *Sand and Fog: Adventures in Southern Africa.* From elephants gathering around the local watering-hole or a group of flamingos crowding atop a sandy peak, to giraffes, ostriches, and the rare horned oryx in their natural desert habitats, the photographs in *Sand and Fog* are set within the tale of their making: what combination of light and shadow Brandenburg the photographer was inspired by, and what Brandenburg the man was thinking and feeling at the moment the shutter clicked. The book's short texts reveal the author's great dedication to his work, his love of nature, the hardships that he had to face in working in the

JIM BRANDENBURG

Brandenburg received numerous awards for the compelling wildlife photographs in his 1988 work, *White Wolf: Living with an Arctic Legend.*

desert heat, and, as a contributor in *Kirkus Reviews* notes, "the ability to bring a sense of wonder, joy, and discovery" to that forbidding land.

Not only African wildlife but the tribal customs of the Himba and Herero peoples, natives of the Skeleton Coast, are distilled through the photographer's lens: from a group baptism, where the priest spits water on those gathered before him to purify them, to a Herero woman, her brightly patterned skirt dancing about her, walking down the road under the weight of the Singer sewing machine balanced on her head. Although he does include some human subjects, Brandenburg primarily captures the natural side of Africa and allows the reader to discover the beauty and life that can exist in a seemingly dead environment. As with other books by Brandenburg, *Sand and Fog* is recommended for its spectacular photography, "for browsing and incidental reading rather than research," according to Susan Giffard in *School Library Journal.*

■ Works Cited

Brandenburg, Jim, *To the Top of the World: Adventures with Arctic Wolves,* Walker, 1993.

Giffard, Susan, review of *Sand and Fog: Adventures in Southern Africa, School Library Journal,* May, 1994.

Hester, Denia, review of *To the Top of the World: Adventures with Arctic Wolves, Booklist,* January 1, 1994.

Review of *Sand and Fog: Adventures in Southern Africa, Kirkus Reviews,* March 15, 1994.

■ For More Information See

PERIODICALS

Booklist, December 15, 1988; March 1, 1994.
Publishers Weekly, October 11, 1993; April 14, 1994.
School Library Journal, December, 1993.

*   *   *

BRONSON, Lynn
See LAMPMAN, Evelyn Sibley

JANET MITSUI BROWN

BROWN, Janet Mitsui

■ Personal

Born in Los Angeles, CA; daughter of Satoru (a manager) and Akiko (a library assistant; maiden name Sakamoto) Mitsui; married Roger Brown (an actor), July 4, 1987; children: Tani. *Education:* University of California at Los Angeles, B.A., 1970.

■ Addresses

Office—c/o Publicity Director, Polychrome Publishing Corp., 4509 North Francisco Ave., Chicago, IL 60525-3808.

■ Career

East West Players, Los Angeles, CA, administrator, 1980-86.

■ Writings

(And illustrator) *Thanksgiving at Obaachan's,* Polychrome Publishing, 1994.

■ Work in Progress

Oshogatsu at Obaachan's, 1996; *Obon for Obaachan,* 1997.

■ Sidelights

Janet Mitsui Brown has been writing since she was in elementary school and has always wanted to write children's stories. She told *SATA,* "I believe it's because I have always been an avid reader and I loved becoming engrossed in other people's lives and experiencing new kinds of journeys. As I grew older I wanted to share my life adventures with others." Brown said that she was motivated to write *Thanksgiving at Obaachan's* because she "wanted to pass on the custom of Thanksgiving in a Japanese-American household." She chose Thanksgiving for the holiday because "it was a particularly special holiday for me and my family; fate dictated that it was also a day of a particular tragedy, so this day is filled with bittersweet memories. It is still a special holiday to me, and I'm glad I've preserved this day for future generations."

Thanksgiving at Obaachan's is a story about a Japanese-American girl, who can't speak Japanese, and the Thanksgiving day she spends with her grandmother, who can't speak English. "The tale centers on their efforts at communication," said *School Library Journal* critic Margaret A. Chang. "I wanted to convey that love can be communicated in many ways other than language." Brown told *SATA,* "My favorite part of the book is when the little girl's hand gets stuck to the paper napkin, and she and her grandmother laugh about it together. It shows how they share an incident without speaking the same language, and laugh together to seal the bond. This book comes from my heart and I hope the reader can sense this as they experience the journey with me. I want young readers to share these moments with me, and in the process recall some special time of their own."

■ Works Cited

Chang, Margaret A., review of *Thanksgiving at Obachaan's, School Library Journal,* August, 1994, p. 126.

■ For More Information See

PERIODICALS
Publishers Weekly, May 30, 1994, p. 55.

C

CADNUM, Michael 1949-

■ Personal

Born May 3, 1949, in Orange, CA; married; wife's name, Sherina.

■ Addresses

Home—Albany, CA. *Agents*—Katharine Kidde, Kidde, Hoyt & Picard, 335 East 51st St., New York, NY 10022; and Michael Thomas, A. M. Heath & Co., 79 St. Martin's Ln., London WC2N 4AA.

■ Career

Poet and novelist.

■ Awards, Honors

Creative Writing Fellowship; National Endowment for the Arts; *Poetry Northwest*'s Helen Bullis Prize; Owl Creek Book Award.

■ Writings

MYSTERY AND HORROR NOVELS

Nightlight, St. Martin's, 1990.
Sleepwalker, St. Martin's, 1991.
Saint Peter's Wolf (for young adults), Carroll & Graf, 1991.
Calling Home (for young adults), Viking, 1991.
Ghostwright, Carroll & Graf, 1992.
Breaking the Fall (for young adults), Viking, 1992.
The Horses of the Night, Carroll & Graf, 1993.
Skyscape, Carroll & Graf, 1994.
Taking It (for young adults), Viking, 1995.

POETRY

The Morning of the Massacre (chapbook), Bieler Press, 1982.
Wrecking the Cactus (chapbook), Salt Lick Press, 1985.
Invisible Mirror (chapbook), Ommation Press, 1986.
Foreign Springs (chapbook), Amelia Press, 1987.

By Evening, Owl Creek Press, 1992.
The Cities We Will Never See, Singular Speech Press, 1993.
The Judas Glass, Carroll & Graf, 1996.
Zero at the Bone, Viking, 1996.

OTHER

Author of short essays, including "The Ghost and the Panda," in *Mystery Writer's Annual*, "Dreams with Teeth," in *Mystery Scene*, and a commentary to his poem "Sunbathing in Winter," in *Poet & Critic*. Has also contributed to numerous periodicals, including *America, Antioch Review, Beloit Fiction Journal, Beloit Poetry Journal, Commonweal, Carolina Quarterly, Georgia Review, Kansas Quarterly, The Literary Review, Midwest Quarterly, Mississippi Review, Poetry Northwest, Prairie Schooner*, and *Virginia Quarterly Review*, and occasional reviews for the "Read This" column in *New York Review of Science Fiction*.

■ Work in Progress

The Lost and Found House, for Viking; *Ella and the Canary Prince*, for Cobblestone Press.

■ Sidelights

Michael Cadnum is a poet whose horror fiction has earned high praise from reviewers who point to his precise and lyrical use of language as one of his greatest strengths. While some critics are uncomfortable with Cadnum's dark and sometimes depressing portrayals of the lives of his adolescent characters, others admire the complexity of his fiction for young adults, which shuns simple resolutions and pat endings. "Cadnum is working in standard YA literature territory," Patrick Jones remarked in *Horn Book*, "but with his own edge. The edge is made sharper with the introduction of themes not often discussed in YA books: shame, guilt, and failure." Cadnum's adult novels of horror and mystery have earned him high praise as well. With the publication of Cadnum's second novel, *Locus* reviewer Edward Bryant proclaimed, "if he chooses to continue writing in

MICHAEL CADNUM

the field [of horror fiction, Cadnum] is on the fast-track to the top."

Of his original passion for verse, Cadnum told *SATA* that "poetry writing has been the major focus of my professional life." Ted Kooser wrote in *Georgia Review* that Cadnum's poems "startled me by their originality and delighted me by their precision." The critic made the following comment about one of his poems entitled "Dreams": "There have been thousands of poems written called 'Dreams,'... yet how quickly Cadnum knocks us off our platitudes and sends us sliding elsewhere."

Cadnum's passion for words and sounds is also clearly evident in his prose writing style. He broke into the world of fiction with the novel *Nightlight,* which features characters haunted by ghosts, insanity, and nightmares, and received high marks from Bryant, who called the work in a *Locus* review "literary horror at a high level." Mary Lee Tiernan compared *Nightlight* to a Stephen King novel, dubbing it "an adventure in horror" in her review in *Voice of Youth Advocates.* While Cadnum's second novel, *Sleepwalker,* suffered a little from overly high expectations created by the success of his first work, "we all should face such problems," Bryant ironically intoned in his laudatory review of the later book. A revival of the classic mummy tales of an earlier era, *Sleepwalker* concerns an archeolo-

gist haunted by the ghost of his dead wife, who travels to England to straighten out problems at an accident-plagued excavation site. Although *New York Times Book Review* critic Ed Weiner condemned the author's use of "classic bogeyman story elements and mummy movies in fashioning this slightly creepy, slightly musty and slightly slight novel," Bryant again highlighted Cadnum's precise prose style and effective characterization: "*Sleepwalker's* level of tale-telling and the author's attention to detail ... make this a stand-out novel."

The first of Cadnum's novels to be reviewed for the young adult audience was the author's third effort, *Saint Peter's Wolf.* In this work, Ben, a psychologist whose career and marriage have both failed, finds a set of teeth that give him the feeling of unlimited power and strength. While this helps his career at first, his life begins to whirl out of control until he is introduced to the other side of his new persona by another wolf-like character. "YAs are sure to identify with Ben's frustration and helplessness" remarked *School Library Journal* contributor Phillip Clark, who also praised Cadnum's compelling plot.

While other Cadnum novels are occasionally reviewed with young adults in mind, *Calling Home* and *Breaking the Fall* feature adolescent protagonists and were written specifically for this audience. In *Calling Home,* Peter turns to drowning his sorrows in alcohol after accidentally killing his best friend. However, drunkenness does not dull the feeling that he is gradually being inhabited by the spirit of his dead friend, whom he impersonates on the phone in reassuring calls to the boy's frantic parents. While a critic in *Kirkus Reviews* called this "a disturbing story" that will leave readers feeling "weighed down by the heavy atmosphere and events," Jones remarked that it "is not a pretty novel, nor is Peter particularly likable, but Cadnum locks his readers in ... and pulls them through as Peter daily wrestles with the horror of his action."

Like *Calling Home, Breaking the Fall* disturbed critics with its portrayal of a young man's antisocial behavior depicted against a background almost devoid of moral guidance. In this work, Stanley finds relief from the chaos and confusion of his home life by breaking into houses with a charismatic friend. "Tension hums beneath the surface of Cadnum's riveting novel," commented *Booklist* reviewer Stephanie Zvirin. Other critics singled out the author's signature evocative prose and careful characterization. "Mature teens may find it a more realistic reflection of a troubled world, in the manner of Robert Cormier, S. E. Hinton, and many adult writers," Susan L. Rogers wrote in *School Library Journal.*

Cadnum is also the author of *Ghostwright,* a "compelling, lyrically written thriller," according to a critic in *Publishers Weekly,* in which a successful playwright is haunted by a man from whom he stole the ideas for his early works. Goaded into killing his former friend by his attempts to blackmail him, playwright Speke continues to encounter the man, prompting Marylaine Block to comment in *Library Journal* that the "elliptical style keeps readers as uncertain as Speke about what is real, what only imagined."

The Horses of the Night retells the story of Faust, who sold his soul to the devil in exchange for earthly success. In Cadnum's version, Stratton Fields, an architect and member of a powerful San Francisco family, is cheated out of a job that will revive his career by an enemy of his family. When the man who wins the job and Fields' enemy both suddenly die, Cadnum's protagonist begins to wonder whether he hasn't inadvertently made a pact with the demon who continues to haunt him. A critic in *Kirkus Reviews* called *The Horses of the Night* "beautifully observed—typical of Cadnum—and effectively disturbing." A critic in *Publishers Weekly* complained that Cadnum's tale is "lightweight" and "melodramatic," but *Library Journal* reviewer A. M. B. Amantia wrote, "This well-written thriller takes its time, building evidence and events slowly so the reader can savor every scene."

Skyscape, Cadnum's next novel, again brought responses from critics that centered on the author's ability to keep his audience guessing about the true nature of his characters and on his tendency to slowly build tension to a shattering climax. In *Skyscape,* a successful painter suffering from a creative block is taken to the desert by a celebrity psychologist for a cure. By switching back and forth between these two protagonists' inner voices, Cadnum discusses issues of the media, fame, and art, while confounding readers' expectations about which of the men is insane. *Library Journal* critic Robert C. Moore concluded, "As a study of characters in the cultural spotlight, *Skyscape* is intriguing."

Critics often remark that Cadnum's background in writing poetry most clearly exhibits itself in his precise use of evocative language, a characteristic not commonly found in horror fiction. While some reviewers complained of the author's use of stock characters and situations of the horror genre such as mummies and ghosts, others emphasized that his narratives explore important social questions while presenting frightening and exciting stories. About the author's novels for young adults, Jones remarked: "Cadnum isn't offering simple tales of good and evil but complex stories written in simple yet tense prose about 'good kids' doing evil things." Often, even those critics who find Cadnum's novels for young adults too dark and unrelenting find much that is worthy in the author's prose style, plot construction, and depth of characterization.

■ Works Cited

Amantia, A. M. B., review of *The Horses of the Night, Library Journal,* July, 1993.

Block, Marylaine, review of *Ghostwright, Library Journal,* July, 1992.

Bryant, Edward, review of *Nightlight, Locus,* June, 1990, p. 23.

Bryant, Edward, review of *Sleepwalker, Locus,* December, 1990, pp. 23-24.

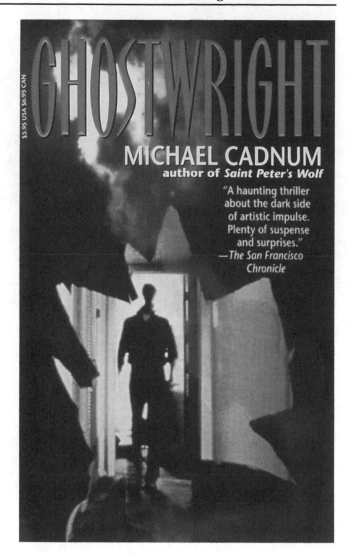

A famous playwright's life is suddenly threatened by an old friend he had believed to be dead in this psychological thriller.

Review of *Calling Home, Kirkus Reviews,* May 1, 1991.

Clark, Phillip, review of *Saint Peter's Wolf, School Library Journal,* February, 1992, p. 121.

Review of *Ghostwright, Publishers Weekly,* June 1, 1992.

Review of *The Horses of the Night, Kirkus Reviews,* June 1, 1993.

Review of *The Horses of the Night, Publishers Weekly,* June 21, 1993.

Jones, Patrick, "People Are Talking about ... Michael Cadnum," *Horn Book,* March/April, 1994, pp. 177-80.

Kooser, Ted, "A Few Attractive Strangers," *Georgia Review,* fall, 1990, pp. 503-5.

Moore, Robert C., review of *Skyscape, Library Journal,* September 1, 1994.

Rogers, Susan L., review of *Breaking the Fall, School Library Journal,* September, 1992.

Tiernan, Mary Lee, review of *Nightlight, Voice of Youth Advocates,* October, 1990, p. 225.

Weiner, Ed, review of *Sleepwalker, New York Times Book Review,* March 31, 1991, p. 16.

Zvirin, Stephanie, review of *Breaking the Fall, Booklist,*
November 15, 1992.

■ For More Information See

PERIODICALS

Booklist, July, 1991.
Horn Book, January/February, 1996, p. 77.
Kirkus Reviews, May 15, 1992.
Publishers Weekly, May 10, 1991; November 16, 1992;
August 22, 1994.
Voice of Youth Advocates, February, 1996, pp. 368-69.

—Sketch by Mary Gillis

* * *

CASELEY, Judith 1951-

■ Personal

Surname is pronounced *Case*-ley; born October 17,
1951, in Rahway, NJ; daughter of Lester (a writer) and
Dorothy Jean (a professor of mathematics) Goldberg;
married Roger Caseley, August 31, 1975 (divorced);
married Neil Brian Curtis (an educational evaluator),
August 3, 1985; children: (second marriage) Jenna
Lindsay, Michael Harrison. *Education:* Syracuse University, B.F.A. (cum laude), 1973.

■ Addresses

Home—32 Coolidge Ave., Glen Head, NY 11545.

■ Career

Sotheby Parke-Bernet, London, England, receptionist,
1975-80; artist. *Exhibitions:* With group and solo, in
New York, New Jersey, and London; paintings in
private collections in France, Spain, England, Russia,
Germany, and the United States. *Member:* Society for
Children's Book Writers and Illustrators, Authors
Guild, Authors League of America.

■ Awards, Honors

Author's Citation, New Jersey Writers Conference,
1986, for *Molly Pink* and *Molly Pink Goes Hiking.*

■ Writings

*FOR CHILDREN; SELF-ILLUSTRATED; PUBLISHED BY
GREENWILLOW*

Molly Pink, 1985.
Molly Pink Goes Hiking, 1985.
When Grandpa Came to Stay, 1986.
My Sister Celia, 1986.
Apple Pie and Onions, 1987.
Silly Baby, 1988.
Ada Potato, 1989.
Three Happy Birthdays, 1989.
Annie's Potty, 1990.
The Cousins, 1990.

JUDITH CASELEY

Grandpa's Garden Lunch, 1990.
Dear Annie, 1991.
Harry and Willy and Carrothead, 1991.
The Noisemakers, 1992.
Sophie and Sammy's Library Sleepover, 1993.
Mama, Coming and Going, 1994.
Mr. Green Peas, 1995.
Priscilla Twice, 1995.
Slumber Party!, 1996.

ILLUSTRATOR

Olga Norris, *The Garden of Eden,* Abelard, 1982.

FOR YOUNG READERS; NOVELS

Kisses, Knopf, 1990.
Hurricane Harry, Greenwillow, 1991.
Starring Dorothy Kane, Greenwillow, 1992.
My Father, the Nutcase, Knopf, 1992.
Chloe in the Know, Greenwillow, 1993.
Harry and Arney, Greenwillow, 1994.

■ Sidelights

Judith Caseley is the author and illustrator of a number
of picture books for young children inspired by moments from her own childhood. From stage fright,
moving, and dealing with physical or emotional handi-
caps to just plain being a kid, Caseley's young likeable
characters deal with the mixed feelings and emotions
with which young children can easily identify. Her

illustrations have been praised for their bright colors, framed format, and the artist's attention to the many small details that hold young children's interest. In addition, Caseley has written several novels for beginning and teen readers, which have been praised by critics for their realism and humor.

Caseley had an early interest in art and received her bachelor of fine arts degree from Syracuse University in 1973. After spending several years in London, England, painting, working in an auction gallery, and exhibiting her work both there and in the United States, she decided to change her artistic focus. "After trying to sustain myself by painting pictures for gallery viewing, I began to design and sell greeting cards and received several awards for tiny watercolors," Caseley once explained. "Eventually I found that writing and illustrating stories was more fulfilling work." Providing the illustrations for the biblical story *The Garden of Eden* was her first project for young children. The critics' positive reviews of her work in *The Garden of Eden* assured Caseley of a career as a successful children's illustrator. But she wanted to do more than just illustrate other people's stories. She wanted to write and illustrate her own.

"*Molly Pink* is based on a traumatic experience from my own childhood—horrible stage fright," she commented about her first book, published in 1985. In this story, Molly Pink is chosen by her music teacher, Mrs. Popper, to sing the solo at her school's recital. Molly practices every day: in the bathroom, on the way to school, to her teddy bear at bedtime, and to the muffin that awaits her every morning on the breakfast table. Everywhere, in fact, except in front of an audience. She can't even sing in front of her own family unless they cover their eyes. On the day of Molly's recital, her brother Joey pins a good-luck picture of a songbird on her coat and all goes well until Mrs. Popper raises her baton for Molly's solo. Suddenly, she can't make a sound, and it's not until she looks out into the audience and spies her mother, father, and Joey, all hiding their eyes, that Molly recovers and can sing. Through Caseley's pen and ink and soft, pink-toned watercolors, "Molly's paralyzing stage fright ... is communicated with sympathetic humor in [a] delightful first book," Charlotte W. Draper says in *Horn Book*.

Molly Pink appears again in *Molly Pink Goes Hiking,* as a pleasant walk through the woods with her family is disrupted by a scuffling noise in the woods that turns out to be another family, the Russells. Molly takes an instant dislike to young Robert Russell because he is fat. But when her curiosity causes her to disrupt the walk again by tumbling into a fast-moving stream, it is young Russell who comes to her rescue, and Molly takes another look at her attitudes about overweight people. "*Molly Pink Goes Hiking* recounts an adventure when I nearly drowned in a river and was saved—and embarrassed—by a boy who was *fat*," Caseley commented.

"*My Sister Celia* documents parts of my own wedding and the abandoned feelings of a young child," the author remarked. It is the story of a special bond

Caseley tells the story of a young girl whose favorite pen pal is her grandfather in this self-illustrated 1991 picture book, *Dear Annie.*

between sisters—and the insecurity that can sometimes result. Seven-year-old Emma and her grown-up sister Celia share a special time together each weekend drawing pictures and having "coffee." They also enjoy watching *The Wizard of Oz* with their mother. But when Celia and her boyfriend Ben become engaged, and he starts tagging along on the sisters' special day together, Emma feels left out. Wedding plans and the thought of being flower girl just make her sulk, and she pouts down in the basement to escape what's happening. But when Celia gives her little sister a pair of ruby-red, Wizard-of-Oz shoes to wear at the wedding and winks at her on her way down the aisle, Emma comes around. The following year she sits with Celia, Ben, and her baby nephew Evan, and they all watch *The Wizard of Oz* together as part of a new family tradition. Along similar lines, *Silly Baby* describes Lindsey's reaction to the news that a new baby is joining the family. When Callie is born, she seems pretty useless until Lindsey realizes that she acted pretty much the same way when she first joined the family.

Caseley's tales range from describing kids' relationships with siblings to their relationships with grandparents in books like *When Grandpa Came to Stay,* the story of a boy who learns to deal with grief and sadness after the death of his grandmother. And in *Grandpa's Garden Lunch,* Sarah works alongside her grandfather in his beloved garden, digging, planting vegetables, flowers, and herbs, watering, and pulling weeds. By summertime, the two gardeners are finally able to enjoy all that their hard work has made possible when Grandma prepares a "garden lunch" of mint tea, salad, basil and spaghetti, and zucchini cake for the hungry gardeners. In a review in *School Library Journal* Dorothy Houlihan describes *Grandpa's Garden Lunch* as "another story [by

Caseley] blooming with bright colors and bursting with familial love." In *Dear Annie,* a young girl develops a life-long correspondence with her loving grandfather. When she takes all eighty-eight of the letters he has written her to school for show and tell, her classmates are moved to seek pen pals of their own.

Show and tell time makes Norman feel like he's missing something in *Mr. Green Peas.* Other kids always tell about the pets they have at home, but Norman's dad is allergic to pet hair and his mom thinks gerbils are underfed rats. When his dad is asked to house-sit his boss's iguana for a month, Norman can't wait to tell about the amazing "Mr. Green Peas"; only none of his classmates believe him. Caseley's warm portrayal of a preschooler's desire for a pet is enhanced by illustrations that reviewers praised as sure to capture children's imaginations.

Caseley's colorfully illustrated *The Noisemakers* "gently underscores the idea that noisy imaginary games are wonderful fun, but sometimes quiet fun is best," writes Stephanie Zvirin in *Booklist.* The mothers of friends Sam and Laura wish their children would learn this lesson, but the two noisy youngsters *like* to be loud ... in department stores, in restaurants, and even in the local library, where they are scolded by the librarian.

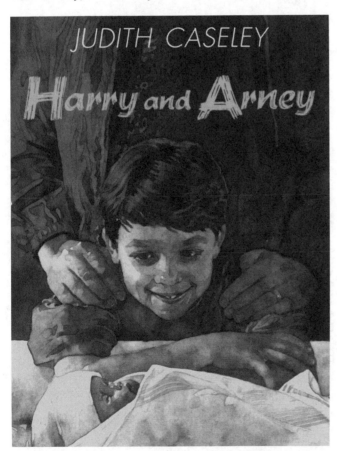

This fourth book in a series about the Kane family continues the adventures of a young boy whose bright ideas do not always turn out as planned. (Cover illustration by Ellen Thompson.)

Finally their mothers let them loose on a neighborhood playground, where Sam and Laura can be as noisy as they want, and learn that there is a time and place for everything, even lots of noise.

School-aged readers can also enjoy Caseley's stories in books like *Hurricane Harry, Starring Dorothy Kane, Harry and Arney,* and *Chloe in the Know.* Harry Kane lived up to his nickname when he was a three-year-old ball of energy; as a kindergartner, it follows him to a new school in *Hurricane Harry.* Caseley adds humorous touches to her portrayal of Harry's move to a new home, his first day at school—his sister accidentally puts him in a second-grade classroom—and the tragic death of his new pet turtle, "Personality," who meets an untimely end after seeking shelter in a pile of laundry destined for a spin in the washer and dryer. "Preschoolers will recognize much of themselves in this impetuous hero," *Booklist* critic Hazel Rochman writes. In *Starring Dorothy Kane,* we see the entire chain of events—from moving to their new home and going on a family camping trip to dealing with the bully in the new neighborhood and that terrifying first day of school—through the eyes of Harry's seven-year-old sister, Dorothy. And *Chloe in the Know* continues the story of the Kane family as older sister Chloe feels burdened in her "big sister" role, especially when she gets the news that her mother is pregnant again. Gradually, as she becomes involved in helping her mother through her pregnancy and gets added responsibilities, she begins to realize that being the oldest has its good points too.

Besides writing picture books and books for younger readers, Caseley has also written several books for teen readers. In *Kisses,* published in 1990, sixteen-year-old Hannah Gold tries to cope with the added problems that growing up brings: a secret admirer, a crush on good-looking Richard, dealing with disturbing advances from her violin teacher, problems at home between her parents, and being confidant to best friend Dierdre, who has become involved with a rough-talking older boy. Hannah gradually leaves behind her childhood illusions about finding the "perfect love" and learns to accept the realities of her own life—everything, at least, except her flat chest.

My Father, the Nutcase introduces fifteen-year-old Zoe Cohen, whose father has an emotional breakdown after a car accident and becomes clinically depressed. While she and her family cope with her father's problem—her two sisters deal with it by adopting some destructive behaviors, and Zoe's mom becomes stressed-out due to the added responsibilities—Zoe is confused by her anger at her dad for not being there for her, and she becomes further mixed up as she begins to date and wishes she had his advice. Gradually, her father begins to pull out of his depression, and Zoe starts to gain a stronger sense of her own self-worth as she deals with pushy dates, her situation at home, and her relationship with a fun guy in her school who also writes poetry.

Within the many picture books she has written and illustrated for young children, Caseley creates likeable young characters whose gentle, loving relationships with friends and family appeal to the bearers of young imaginations and their parents alike. And her novels for older readers are noted for their realistic portrayal of the attitudes, language, and situations common to teens and pre-teens. Caseley's skills as an illustrator have allowed her to open a perceptive window onto the many phases of childhood and provide a colorful, entertaining mirror of what it means to grow up.

■ Works Cited

Draper, Charlotte W., review of *Molly Pink, Horn Book,* July/August, 1985, pp. 435-36.
Houlihan, Dorothy, review of *Grandpa's Garden Lunch, School Library Journal,* October, 1990.
Rochman, Hazel, review of *Hurricane Harry, Booklist,* October 15, 1991.
Zvirin, Stephanie, review of *The Noisemakers, Booklist,* September 1, 1992.

■ For More Information See

PERIODICALS

Booklist, November 1, 1985, p. 402; February 15, 1988, p. 998; July, 1991, p. 2047; March 15, 1992, p. 1357; February 15, 1993, p. 1066; September 1, 1994, p. 39; February 15, 1995, p. 1092.
Bulletin of the Center for Children's Books, May, 1986, p. 162; March, 1988, p. 132; April, 1991, p. 186; June, 1993, p. 310; March, 1996, p. 221.
Horn Book, January/February, 1987, p. 42; January/February, 1991, p. 53; January/February, 1996, p. 61.
Junior Bookshelf, October, 1982, p. 182.
Publishers Weekly, February 15, 1985, p. 102; November 28, 1986, p. 74; November 2, 1992, p. 72.
School Library Journal, October, 1985, p. 149; February, 1986, p. 72; November, 1986, p. 73; April, 1988, p. 78; June, 1991, p. 74; November, 1992, p. 116; September, 1994, p. 182.
Times Educational Supplement, January 14, 1983, p. 34.
Voice of Youth Advocates, December, 1992, p. 319.

*   *   *

CHANEY, Jill 1932-

■ Personal

Born June 5, 1932, in Hertfordshire, England; daughter of Walter Sidney (a barrister) and Barbara (Webb) Chaney; married Walter Francis Leeming (a chartered civil engineer), August 26, 1960; children: Catherine Frances, Matthew John. *Education:* Attended private schools in England; attended Waterperry Horticultural School, 1949-51; Royal Horticultural Society diploma, 1950.

■ Addresses

Home—Glen Rosa, Colleyland, Chorleywood, Hertfordshire, England.

■ Career

Author. Worked as a gardener in London, England, 1951-61, mainly at a retirement home operated by the Jewish Board of Guardians. Director of Chorleywood Bookshop, 1971-88. *Member:* Royal Horticultural Society, Religious Society of Friends (Quakers), National Trust.

■ Writings

FICTION; FOR CHILDREN

On Primrose Hill, illustrated by Jane Paton, Methuen, 1962.
Half a Candle, illustrated by Carolyn Dinan, Dobson, 1968, Crown, 1969.
A Penny for the Guy, illustrated by John Dyke, Dobson, 1970.
Mottram Park (young adult), illustrated by Carolyn Dinan, Dobson, 1971.
Christopher's Dig, illustrated by John Dyke, Dobson, 1972.
Taking the Woffle to Pebblecombe-on-Sea, illustrated by Elizabeth Ogan, Dobson, 1974.
Return to Mottram Park (young adult), illustrated by Carolyn Dinan, Dobson, 1974.
Christopher's Find, illustrated by John Dyke, Dobson, 1975.
The Buttercup Field, illustrated by Elizabeth Ogan, Dobson, 1976.
Woffle, R.A., illustrated by daughter, Catherine Leeming, Dobson, 1976.
Canary Yellow (young adult), illustrated by Carolyn Dinan, Dobson, 1977.
Angel Face, illustrated by Carolyn Dinan, Dobson, 1979.
Vectis Diary, illustrated by Catherine Leeming, Dobson, 1979.
Leaving Mottram Park, (young adult), illustrated by Carolyn Dinan, Book Guild, 1989.
Three Weeks in August, Cross, 1995.

■ Sidelights

British author Jill Chaney "writes equally successfully for the eight-year-old level and the older adolescent reader," according to Ann G. Hay in *Twentieth-Century Children's Writers.* She has written several popular series of books for each audience. Chaney explained to Hay that her books "seem to be about people trying to get on well with each other, not wanting to quarrel. The books for older children are also about bridging the gap between childish expectations and adult reality."

Chaney shows a "real understanding of young love" in her popular "Mottram Park" series for young adults, according to Ann Thwaite in the *New Statesman.* The series follows the developing romance between Sheila and Gary. In *Mottram Park,* Sheila runs away from home, with the reluctant help of Gary, when she cannot get along with her domineering grandmother. When their decision to make love leads to a traumatic experience, however, the couple go their separate ways. In the

Joseph and Annabel continue their secret friendship with a friendly, invisible creature in this 1976 book illustrated by Chaney's daughter, Catherine Leeming.

anxiously awaited sequel *Return to Mottram Park,* Sheila's grandmother dies, which allows her family life to return to normal. She runs into Gary, whom she has not seen in a year, just after he finishes his examinations to enter university. They realize that they still love each other, though they both feel it is best for their relationship to proceed very slowly. Gary travels abroad for several weeks and returns to find that his parents have separated. In his shock, he asks Sheila to marry him. As a *Junior Bookshelf* reviewer noted, "I am sure that many young girls and some boys, perhaps secretly, will read this novel with real enjoyment and understanding." The story of Sheila and Gary continues in *Leaving Mottram Park,* published in 1989.

Chaney is also the author of three successful books for younger readers about Christopher, who wants nothing more than to dig up the bones of a dinosaur. After reading about Mary Anning, a girl from Dorset who dug up a plesiosaurus in the nineteenth century, Christopher decides to find a dinosaur himself. In *Christopher's Dig* he has a hard time finding a place to excavate in London, and he gets into trouble for digging in the city parks. His parents and friends are skeptical about his ambitions. While digging on the banks of the Thames,

however, Christopher finds a box of buried treasure that provides enough money to fund a real search for dinosaur bones on the Dorset coast. In the sequel, *Christopher's Find,* Christopher goes on holiday with his sister Margie and their friend Roy and again sets out to find his dinosaur skeleton, while Margie and Roy pursue their own interests. In a review for *Growing Point,* Margery Fisher remarked that Chaney "has an eye for youthful behaviour and a brisk, easy way of describing it."

Another of Chaney's popular series for younger readers features a big, hairy invisible creature known as the Woffle. In *Taking the Woffle to Pebblecombe-on-Sea,* Joseph and Annabel notice a pair of boots walking by themselves in the woods. They come to learn that the boots are actually being worn by the invisible Woffle, and they make friends with him. When the Woffle wants to go to Pebblecombe to visit his aunt, the children take him on the train with hilarious results. Unfortunately, the Woffle decides that he does not like his aunt and must return home. A *Junior Bookshelf* reviewer called it "a splendid imaginative book." The sequel, *Woffle, R.A.,* describes what happens when the children bring the Woffle home to live in their shed. In order to keep him out of trouble, Joseph and Annabel give the Woffle a set of paints. But his paintings turn out to be so popular that they appear in an exhibition, and the children are hard pressed by the people of the village to produce the artist. In a *Growing Point* review, Fisher considered the story to be "entertaining enough," but noted that "the humour cannot help but be interrupted by the intrusive improbabilities of the plot."

Chaney returned to writing for a young adult audience with the 1977 publication of *Canary Yellow.* In this novel, sixteen-year-old Julia has a fight with her parents and runs away from home. She meets an old man who shortly afterward has an accident, and while he is in the hospital she lives on his houseboat and takes care of his canary. Julia also baby-sits for a troubled neighbor family. When the kids are placed in foster care and the mother is institutionalized, however, Julia realizes that she has fallen for the father, Dave. Dave takes advantage of the situation, and their relationship turns out badly. In a review for *Times Literary Supplement,* David Rees praised Chaney for not glamorizing the life of a runaway, stating that she "is exceptionally good at conveying to the reader the feelings of boredom, loneliness and guilt which the young runaway usually experiences, also how the attraction and excitement of new experience can rapidly turn to fear and pain." Assessing Chaney's writing, Hay found that her stories tend to be "sensitively handled," so that "the teenager will not feel 'talked-down-to' as she reads them."

■ **Works Cited**

Fisher, Margery, "Making Their Mark," *Growing Point,* October, 1975, pp. 2721-23.
Fisher, Margery, "A Bonus of Laughter," *Growing Point,* April, 1976, pp. 2849-52.

Hay, Ann G., "Jill Chaney," in *Twentieth-Century Children's Writers,* St. James Press, 1995, pp. 196-97.

Rees, David, "She's Leaving Home," *Times Literary Supplement,* September 29, 1978, p. 1083.

Review of *Return to Mottram Park, Junior Bookshelf,* February, 1975, p. 57.

Review of *Taking the Woffle to Pebblecombe-on-Sea, Junior Bookshelf,* February, 1975, p. 33.

Thwaite, Ann, review of *Mottram Park, New Statesman,* November 12, 1971, p. 661.

■ For More Information See

PERIODICALS

Growing Point, January, 1977, pp. 3040-43; March, 1979, p. 3484.

Junior Bookshelf, August, 1976, pp. 195-96; April, 1977, p. 107; December, 1978, p. 326; April, 1979, p. 112; April, 1980, p. 92.

Kirkus Reviews, April 15, 1969, p. 450.

Times Literary Supplement, October 3, 1968, p. 1107; October 30, 1970, p. 1262; October 22, 1971, p. 1318; April 6, 1973, p. 383.

*   *   *

CHIPPERFIELD, Joseph E(ugene) 1912-1976
(John Eland Craig)

■ Personal

Born April 20, 1912, in St. Austell, Cornwall, England; died January 3, 1976; son of Edward and Lavinia (White) Chipperfield; married Mary Anne Tully, April 26, 1936. *Education:* Educated privately. *Politics:* Conservative. *Religion:* Catholic.

■ Career

Author's Literary Service, Cheapside, London, England, editor, 1930-34; editor and scriptwriter for documentary films, 1934-40; freelance writer, 1940-76. *Member:* Auto Club (Great Britain), German Shepherd Dog Club (Ireland).

■ Writings

FICTION FOR CHILDREN

Two Dartmoor Interludes, Boswell Press (London), 1935.

An Irish Mountain Tragedy, Boswell Press, 1936.

Three Stories (contains *Two Dartmoor Interludes, An Irish Mountain Tragedy,* and *The Ghosts from Baylough*), Boswell Press, 1936.

This Earth—My Home: A Tale of Irish Troubles, Padraic O'Follain (Dublin), 1937.

Storm of Dancerwood, illustrated by C. Gifford Ambler, Hutchinson, 1948, Longmans, Green, 1949, revised edition, Hutchinson, 1967.

JOSEPH E. CHIPPERFIELD

Greatheart, The Salvation Hunter: The Epic of a Shepherd Dog, illustrated by C. Gifford Ambler, Hutchinson, 1950, Roy, 1953.

Beyond the Timberland Trail, illustrated by Raymond Shepard, Hutchinson, 1951, Longmans, Green, 1953.

Windruff of Links Tor, illustrated by Helen Torrey, Longmans, Green, 1951.

Grey Chieftain, illustrated by C. Gifford Ambler, Hutchinson, 1952, Roy, 1954.

(Under pseudonym John Eland Craig) *The Dog of Castle Crag,* illustrated by Leslie Atkinson, Nelson, 1952.

Silver Star, Stallion of the Echoing Mountain, illustrated by C. Gifford Ambler, Hutchinson, 1953, Longmans, Green, 1955.

Greeka, Eagle of the Hebrides, illustrated by C. Gifford Ambler, Hutchinson, 1953, Longmans, Green, 1954, revised edition, Hutchinson, 1962.

Rooloo, Stag of the Dark Water, illustrated by C. Gifford Ambler, Hutchinson, 1955, Roy, 1962, revised edition, Hutchinson, 1962, Roy, 1963.

Dark Fury, Stallion of Lost River Valley, illustrated by C. Gifford Ambler, Hutchinson, 1956, Roy, 1957.

Wolf of Badenoch: Dog of the Grampian Hills, illustrated by C. Gifford Ambler, Hutchinson, 1958, Longmans, Green, 1959.

Ghost Horse: Stallion of the Oregon Trail, illustrated by C. Gifford Ambler, Hutchinson, 1959, Roy, 1962.

Grasson, Golden Eagle of the North, illustrated by C. Gifford Ambler, Hutchinson, 1960.

Petrus, Dog of the Hill Country, illustrated by Stuart Tresilian, Longmans, Green, 1960.

Seokoo of the Black Wind, illustrated by C. Gifford Ambler, Hutchinson, 1961, McKay, 1962.

The Grey Dog from Galtymore, illustrated by Stuart Tresilian, Heinemann, 1961, McKay, 1962.

Sabre of Storm Valley, illustrated by C. Gifford Ambler, Hutchinson, 1962, Roy, 1965.

A Dog against Darkness, illustrated by F. R. Exell, Heinemann, 1963, published as *A Dog to Trust: The Saga of a Seeing-Eye Dog,* McKay, 1964.

Checoba, Stallion of the Comanche, illustrated by C. Gifford Ambler, Hutchinson, 1964, Roy, 1966.

Boru, Dog of the O'Malley, illustrated by C. Gifford Ambler, Hutchinson, 1965, McKay, 1966.

The Two Fugitives, illustrated by John Lathey, Heinemann, 1966.

Lone Stands the Glen, illustrated by Barry Driscoll, Hutchinson, 1966.

The Watcher on the Hills, Heinemann, 1968.

Rex of Larkbarrow, illustrated by Robert Hales, Hutchinson, 1969.

Storm Island, illustrated by Gareth Floyd, Hutchinson, 1970.

Banner, The Pacing White Stallion, illustrated by Robert Hales, Hutchinson, 1972.

Lobo, Wolf of the Wind River Range, illustrated by Robert Hales, Hutchinson, 1974.

In his 1964 novel *Storm of Dancerwood,* Chipperfield tells the story of an Alsatian dog exploring the West Country of England. (Illustration by Helen Torrey.)

Hunter of Harter Fell, illustrated by Victor Ambrus, Hutchinson, 1976.

OTHER

The Story of a Great Ship: The Birth and Death of the Steamship Titanic, illustrated by Charles King, Hutchinson, 1957, Roy, 1959.

Also author of two short story collections and of filmscripts. Contributor of short stories, serials, and articles to periodicals.

■ Sidelights

Set in locales ranging from his native Cornwall to the American West, British author Joseph E. Chipperfield's stories dealt with a variety of animals, including wild horses, dogs, and even birds of prey. Some critics noted that his romantic tales of misunderstood creatures were reminiscent of the work of Jack London; according to Cecilia Gordon in *Twentieth-Century Children's Writers,* Chipperfield "had the same gift for interpreting animals' reactions without becoming too anthropomorphic." In addition to exploring the emotional bonds between man and beast, Chipperfield often included many facts about science and nature in his stories. Sharing information about the natural world was part of his intent in writing, as the author once explained to *SATA:* "Due to spending much time out of doors studying wild life in England, Scotland, Ireland and abroad, I found that most of the knowledge gained could be utilized in fictional form, based on facts."

Chipperfield continued: "Practically every title has been based on some personal experience, or some recorded fact.... *Storm of Dancerwood* came from a long camping holiday on Exmoor in the company of my then German Shepherd." In this novel, an Alsatian dog is drawn to the wilderness of his ancestors and develops a gentle relationship with a blind vixen. "The setting is an integral part of the story," a *New York Times Book Review* critic wrote, explaining that Chipperfield's portrayals of England's West country "are stirring and satisfying." "There is great beauty in the descriptions," Alice M. Jordan similarly observed in *Horn Book,* adding that "dog lovers will not be alone" in enjoying this "moving" story.

Chipperfield also wrote stories of wild animals and birds, and took care in creating believable backgrounds for them. "The wild horse books have been based on some American legend, and efforts taken to ensure their accuracy," the author once stated. "The Scottish and west of England books have all come out of personal experience and contact, and for the most part were planned or written in the actual locality." It was these dog stories based on his personal experiences in Britain that brought him the most critical praise. *Windruff of Links Tor,* for instance, is set on the moors of western England and contains the "thrilling action, lovely setting and the towering sentiment dog lovers demand," a *Kirkus Reviews* writer stated. The hills and shepherds of northern Scotland provide the background for *Wolf of*

Badenoch: Dog of the Grampian Hills. In this work, Chipperfield's writing "has the power to make the reader experience with all his senses the harshness and rugged beauty" of the setting, a *Horn Book* reviewer remarked. The "suspenseful" story, a *Booklist* critic concluded, will appeal to readers who enjoy "excellent writing with its fine characterization and evocative description."

■ Works Cited

Gordon, Cecilia, "Joseph E. Chipperfield," in *Twentieth Century Children's Writers,* 4th edition, St. James Press, 1995, pp. 200-201.

Jordan, Alice M., review of *Storm of Dancerwood, Horn Book,* September, 1949, pp. 421-22.

Review of *Storm of Dancerwood, New York Times Book Review,* November 13, 1949, pp. 28-29.

Review of *Windruff of Links Tor, Kirkus Reviews,* June 15, 1951, p. 296.

Review of *Wolf of Badenoch: Dog of the Grampian Hills, Booklist,* September 15, 1959, p. 56.

Review of *Wolf of Badenoch: Dog of the Grampian Hills, Horn Book,* August, 1959, p. 290.

■ For More Information See

PERIODICALS

Books and Bookmen, November, 1970.
Horn Book, October, 1953, p. 358.
New York Times Book Review, October 4, 1953, p. 28.
Young Readers' Review, December, 1966.*

* * *

CLAREMONT, Chris(topher Simon) 1950-

■ Personal

Born in 1950; married Beth Fleisher (a science fiction writer and editor).

■ Addresses

Office—Suite 270, 330 7th Ave., Brooklyn, NY 11215.

■ Career

Novelist. Marvel Comics, co-creator and writer of several top-selling comic book series, 1975-92; DC Comics, creator and owner of comic book series *Sovereign Seven,* 1995—.

■ Writings

COMIC COLLECTIONS

X-Men: God Loves, Man Kills, Marvel, 1982.
The Uncanny X-Men, Marvel, 1987.
Fantastic Four Versus the X-Men, Marvel, 1990.
(With Bill Sienkiewicz) *The New Mutants: The Demon Bear Saga,* Marvel, 1990.
X-Tinction Agenda, Marvel, 1992.
New Mutants: Bookshelf Edition, Marvel, 1994.

CHRIS CLAREMONT

X-Men: Greatest Battles, Marvel, 1994.

SCIENCE FICTION/FANTASY NOVELS

FirstFlight, Ace Books, 1988.
Grounded! (sequel to *FirstFlight*), Ace Books, 1991.
Cry, Vengeance ("Star Trek: The Next Generation" series), DC Comics, 1994.
(With wife, Beth Fleisher) *Dragon Moon,* illustrated by John Bolton, Bantam Books, 1994.
Sundowner (sequel to *Grounded!*), Berkley/Ace Books, 1994.
(With George Lucas) *Shadow Moon: The Saga of the Shadow War* (first book in trilogy entitled "Chronicles of the Shadow War"), Bantam Books, 1995.
Alien/Predator: The Deadliest of the Species, illustrated by Eduardo Baretto, Dark Horse Comics, 1995.

HISTORICAL FANTASY GRAPHIC NOVELS

Marada the She-Wolf, illustrated by John Bolton, Marvel/Epic Comics, 1982.
Marada: Wizard's Mask, illustrated by John Bolton, Marvel/Epic Comics, 1984.
The Black Dragon (a six-issue limited series), illustrated by John Bolton, Marvel/Epic Comics, 1985.

OTHER

Also author of *The Savage Land,* 1990; *X-Men: Asgardian Wars,* 1990; *X-Men: From the Ashes,* 1990; *Debt of Honor* ("Star Trek 25th Anniversary" graphic novel),

DC Comics; and (with Frank Miller) *Wolverine* (a monthly series, issues 1-10), Marvel, 1988-89.

■ Work in Progress

Two "Superman" projects for DC Comics, including a limited "Elseworlds" series entitled *Whom Gods Destroy;* "Chris Claremont's Huntsman" series for Image Comics; *Shadow Dawn,* second book in "Chronicles of the Shadow War" trilogy.

■ Sidelights

During his seventeen-year career as a writer and creator of comic book series for Marvel Comics, Chris Claremont helped establish a number of highly popular characters and sold over one hundred million comic books. His creations include *The Uncanny X-Men, Wolverine,* and *New Mutants.* Since leaving Marvel, Claremont has expanded upon his previous work, as well as gone on to launch new comic book characters and series.

In addition to his work in comics, Claremont has published several science fiction and fantasy novels and graphic novels for young adults. *FirstFlight* is the first book in a trilogy of futuristic novels centering around space pilot Nicole Shea. In *FirstFlight,* Nicole is nearly kicked out of the academy for her daredevil flying. Instead, she is sent on a routine mission to chart distant planets. The mission soon becomes dangerous, however, when the ship is attacked by pirates and Nicole must establish a relationship with powerful aliens in order to save the crew. A *Publishers Weekly* reviewer credited Claremont's background as a comic book writer for the book's "lean, tense storyline, the graphic visual sense, and the talent for action."

In *Grounded!,* the second book in the series, Nicole finds herself grounded due to the psychological stress of her previous mission. She is assigned to Edwards Air Force Base on earth, where she draws closer to her alien friends and receives death threats from the pirates she defeated. Meanwhile, the nations of Earth engage in a heated political debate about what approach the planet should take in dealing with the aliens. Mary K. Chelton, writing in *Voice of Youth Advocates,* called *Grounded!* "a wonderful military SF mystery with an engaging, competent, tough female protagonist, full of high tech descriptions and gadgetry." *Booklist* reviewer Roland Green also praised Claremont's characterization in the novel, calling Nicole "one of the more notable female warriors in recent science fiction." Nicole's adventures continue in *Sundowner,* published in 1994.

■ Works Cited

Chelton, Mary K., review of *Grounded!, Voice of Youth Advocates,* February, 1992, p. 379.
Review of *FirstFlight, Publishers Weekly,* November 27, 1987, p. 78.
Green, Roland, review of *Grounded!, Booklist,* August, 1991, p. 2108.

■ For More Information See

PERIODICALS

Booklist, July, 1994, p. 1927; November 1, 1994, p. 482.
Library Journal, November 15, 1994, p. 90.
Publishers Weekly, November 14, 1994, p. 64.
School Library Journal, September, 1992, p. 129.
Voice of Youth Advocates, February, 1994, p. 360.

*   *   *

CLARK, Ann Nolan 1896-1995 (Marie Dunne)

OBITUARY NOTICE—See index for *SATA* sketch: Born December 5, 1896, in Las Vegas, NM; died December 13, 1995, in Tucson, AZ. Educator, author. A prolific author of children's books, Clark is remembered for being one of the first Caucasian authors to write books for minority children using characters, situations, and values associated with the children's respective cultures. Specializing in books for Native American and Hispanic American children, Clark also wrote about Finnish immigrants to the American Midwest and Vietnamese children. She began her career as a school teacher near Las Vegas, New Mexico, in 1917. After stints in Tacoma, Washington, and at Highland University, she began some forty-two years with the Bureau of Indian Affairs in 1920. During her work at the Bureau, she realized that Native American children could learn more easily if primers were geared toward them to feature people and aspects of their culture. Her primers were often illustrated by Indian students, and she used poetic language that came to life when read aloud. Among these readers were *Who Wants to Be a Prairie Dog?, There Still Are Buffalo, About the Grass Mountain Mouse,* and *Singing Sioux Cowboy Reader.* She later expanded her scope to include books for Hispanic American children. In total, she authored more than forty books, including the Newbery Medal winner *Secret of the Andes.* The work dealt with the challenges faced by young protagonists as they try to live within the confines of two conflicting cultures. Clark, who penned articles for periodicals as Marie Dunne, also worked as an education consultant for the International Cooperation Administration's Latin American Bureau from 1945 to 1950. In 1962, she was awarded the Distinguished Service Award from the U.S. Department of the Interior. In 1984, she was named outstanding author in Arizona.

OBITUARIES AND OTHER SOURCES:

BOOKS

Twentieth-Century Children's Writers, St. James Press, 1995.

PERIODICALS

Washington Post, December 15, 1995, p. D5.

COOKE, Frank E. 1920-
(Eddie Franck)

■ Personal

Born June 26, 1920, in Sunbury, PA; son of Frank E.
and Josephine L. Cooke; married Ann H., August 21,
1947; children: Leslie, Jeffrey. *Education:* Bucknell
University, B.A.; graduate study at University of Iowa
and Springfield College. *Hobbies and other interests:*
Camping, backpacking, gardening, fishing, cycling, and
travel.

■ Addresses

Office—c/o Fiesta City Publishers, P.O. Box 5861,
Santa Barbara, CA 93150-5861.

■ Career

School headmaster in New York and California, 1957-
78; Fielding Institute, Santa Barbara, CA, director of
services, 1980-81; Children's Commission, Santa Barbara, commissioner, 1991-93. Fiesta City Publishers,
Santa Barbara, president, 1981—. Has also worked as a
composer/songwriter, music business consultant, and
academic placement consultant. *Military service:* U.S.
Army, 1941-46, received Mid East medal, American
Campaign medal, WWII Victory medal, American Defense medal, and Good Conduct medal. *Member:* American Society of Composers, Authors, and Publishers
(ASCAP), Santa Barbara Screenwriters' Association,
Santa Barbara Songwriters' Guild (founding president).

FRANK E. COOKE

■ Writings

Write That Song!, Fiesta City, 1981.
(With wife, Ann Cooke) *Cooking with Music,* Fiesta
City, 1982.
(Under pseudonym Eddie Franck) *Kids Can Write
Songs, Too!,* illustrated by Jeff Cooke, Fiesta City,
1988, revised edition, 1993.

*MUSICAL PLAYS FOR YOUNG ADULTS; PUBLISHED BY
FIESTA CITY*

Bent Twig, 1971, revised edition, 1993.
Carrie, 1972, revised edition, 1995.
El Canon Perdido (The Lost Cannon), 1973, revised
edition, 1994.
*The 9th Avenue Truck Trailor and Occasional Timepiece
Co.,* 1974, revised edition, in press.
The Late Jim Brown, 1975, revised edition, in press.
Break Point, 1995.

Also author of an untitled musical for junior high school
students.

■ Sidelights

Frank E. Cooke told *SATA,* "While serving as a teacher
and coach at a private school in Connecticut, I was
asked by several students to write a musical production
especially for them. This helped start me on a project
which continues to occupy my time and interests. I now
have four completed musicals with full piano music
scores for each. Some of these have been performed in
New York and in California. One of the most recent has
been purchased by the University of Washington.

"My approach to writing could be called sporadic.
When I do get started on a play or book, I put most of
my time on getting finished. At other times, the muse
eludes me, and I am off to the fishing spots, traveling,
gardening, and engaging in one of my primary interests:
cooking and inventing recipes. That endeavor produced
the book, *Cooking with Music,* written with my wife,
Ann, and with an introduction by Rod McKuen, famed
poet and songwriter.

"The musical plays I write are intended for young
teenagers. These include *Carrie,* the life and times of
Carry A. Nation, turn-of-the century prohibitionist;
Bent Twig, a play about the ultimate merging of a girls'
school and a boys' boarding school; *El Canon Perdido,*
the story of the lost cannon which figured in an 1847
misunderstanding between American soldiers and Cali-
fornios; *The Ninth Avenue Truck, Tailor, and Occasional
Timepiece Company,* about drug problems (the good
guys win in the end!); *Break Point,* three acts outlining
the wins and losses of a young and coming tennis player;
and *The (Almost) Late Jimmy Brown,* which emphasizes
sibling rivalry and parental preferences."*

CRAFT, Ruth 1935-

■ Personal

Born August 30, 1935, in Christchurch, New Zealand; daughter of a librarian; married Michael Craft; children: four sons. *Education:* Received B.Litt.

■ Career

Television writer, 1968—. Writer for *Playschool,* BBC-TV.

■ Awards, Honors

Children's Book Showcase Award, 1976, and Junior Literary Guild selection, both for *The Winter Bear;* The Owl Prize, 1980, for *Carrie Hepple's Garden.*

■ Writings

Play School, Play Ideas, illustrated by Quentin Blake, BBC Publications, 1971, revised edition, Hodder & Stoughton, 1983.
The Winter Bear, illustrated by Eric Blegvad, Collins, 1974, Atheneum, 1975.
Pieter Brueghel's "The Fair," Lippincott, 1975.
The King's Collection, illustrated by Elisa Trimby, Doubleday, 1978.
Carrie Hepple's Garden, illustrated by Irene Haas, Atheneum, 1979.
Wise Dog, illustrated by Nicola Smee, Collins, 1986.
Monster House, Collins, 1987.
Fancy Nancy, illustrated by Nicola Smee, Collins, 1987.
Fancy Nancy in Disguise, illustrated by Nicola Smee, Collins, 1989.
The Song That Sings the Bird, illustrated by John V. Lord, Collins, 1989.
The Day of the Rainbow, illustrated by Niki Daly, Puffin Books, 1991.

■ Sidelights

Ruth Craft once told *SATA* that she began her career in 1968 as a television writer. While watching a program for pre-schoolers on British TV, Craft decided to try submitting some of her own material. That led to her employment by the British Broadcasting Corp. (BBC) as writer, advisor, and consultant to the children's television show, *Playschool,* for which she relied on experiences from her own childhood, and on her children's ideas and games. Her work with the BBC resulted in the publication of *Play School, Play Ideas* in 1971, which contained suggestions of activities for under-fives, one for each day of the week.

Many of Craft's fictional books for children are written in rhymed verse, including her first picture book, *The Winter Bear,* which was a Junior Literary Guild selection. *The Winter Bear* was originally a script that was shown on *Playschool.* Adapting it for a picture book, Craft followed two rules she learned from writing for television: make sure the story has a strong visual

theme, and use interesting words which can be easily read aloud. A *Junior Literary Guild* reviewer quoted Craft as describing the story as "an attempt to recreate the delight of a winter's expedition on a rather unpromising day." The story concerns three children who go out for a walk on a winter's day. They see many sights and have numerous adventures, but the highlight of their day is finding a stuffed bear stuck high up in a tree.

Craft took a totally different tack in writing for children with her next book, *Pieter Brueghel's "The Fair."* In it she takes Brueghel the Younger's finely detailed painting, *The Village Fair,* divides it into sections, and creates rhymes to accompany the artwork. Elizabeth McCorkle, writing for the *School Library Journal,* called the book "a stimulating way to train children to view art."

Craft returned to pure fiction with her 1979 tale entitled *The King's Collection,* which a *Kirkus Reviews* contributor called "a book to excite the imagination." It is a story of a kindly ruler who collects all kinds of things— as long as they are all different from each other. He collects such fanciful items as laundry and hangers, buttons, toothbrushes, water faucets, and even mug shots, including one of a robber from Rio who "stole the milk from babies' bottles and wore a helmet made of battered tin trays."

In her 1979 book, *Carrie Hepple's Garden,* Craft told the story of three children who, trying to retrieve their lost ball, must climb over the fence into Carrie Hepple's yard. The old woman, rumored to be a witch, soon teaches the children that you can't believe everything you hear. A reviewer in *Publishers Weekly* wrote enthusiastically about *Carrie Hepple's Garden* and felt as

Three children in Ruth Craft's 1974 picture book discover a surprise souvenir from a crisp cold walk in the country. (Cover illustration by Erik Blegvad.)

In simple rhymed text, younger readers learn of Carrie Hepple's off-limits garden and the mysterious Carrie herself. (Cover illustration by Irene Haas.)

though the book taught a vital lesson "with no whiff of sentimentality or preaching."

It's the dog who teaches the lessons in Craft's 1986 *Wise Dog.* Vernon and his mother, both running late and irritated as they try to get out of the house in the morning, are watched by Rumble, the family dog. Rumble not only manages to smooth over the situation but also gets some extra breakfast treats for his trouble. And the lessons in *Fancy Nancy* (who reappears in Craft's 1989 *Fancy Nancy in Disguise*) come from an endearing five-year-old who has an unique way of looking at ordinary objects and events. Nancy can turn a dull party into a fun time when she finds a book about animals and starts envisioning guests as parrots, elephants, and other exotic creatures. She can even turn an earache into an adventure when she finds interesting objects down in the cracks between the sofa cushions. In a review for *Growing Point,* Margery Fisher praised the way Craft "leads us with demure humour some way into the mind of a small child."

In 1991, Craft paired with South African illustrator Niki Daly to create *The Day of the Rainbow,* which a *Kirkus Reviews* critic called "a celebration of urban life." This book, filled with the details of city life, interweaves the stories of three lost items. Nerinder, a little Indian girl, loses her library book as she straggles behind her mother and the baby; Leroy, a black roller-skater, loses a present he's bought for his girlfriend; and Dimitri Poppodopolous is angry because his wife has lost a favorite recipe. However, when the rain—and the rainbow that follows—finally comes, it cools down hot tempers as well as hot temperatures.

In a complete departure from her works of fiction, Craft's next book was *The Song That Sings the Bird,* an anthology of 118 poems by such diverse authors as Samuel Taylor Coleridge, Alexander Pope, Ogden Nash, and Sylvia Plath. Margery Fisher, again writing for *Growing Point,* called this a "superlative collection" and praised the book as a "notable addition to the growing library of anthologies for the young."

■ Works Cited

Review of *Carrie Hepple's Garden, Publishers Weekly,* January 1, 1979, p. 58.

Craft, Ruth, *The King's Collection,* Doubleday, 1978.

Review of *The Day of the Rainbow, Kirkus Reviews,* January 1, 1989, p. 47.

Fisher, Margery, review of *Fancy Nancy, Growing Point,* September, 1987, p. 4862.

Fisher, Margery, review of *The Song That Sings the Bird, Growing Point,* July, 1990, p. 5374.

Review of *The King's Collection, Kirkus Reviews,* April 15, 1979, pp. 447-48.

McCorkle, Elizabeth, review of *Pieter Brueghel's "The Fair," School Library Journal,* October, 1976, p. 96.

Review of *The Winter Bear, Junior Literary Guild,* September, 1975, p. 16.

■ For More Information See

PERIODICALS

Growing Point, March, 1983, p. 1050.
Junior Bookshelf, April, 1990, pp. 95-96.
Publishers Weekly, July 19, 1976, p. 132.
School Library Journal, September, 1979, p. 107.
Times Educational Supplement, August 7, 1987, p. 19; May 15, 1992, p. 7.*

*   *   *

CRAIG, John Eland
    See CHIPPERFIELD, Joseph E(ugene)

D

MARJORIE SHEILA DARKE

DARKE, Marjorie Sheila 1929-

■ Personal

Born January 25, 1929, in Birmingham, Warwickshire, England; daughter of Christopher and Sarah Ann (maiden name Palin) Darke; married 1952; children: two sons and one daughter. *Education:* Attended Leicester College of Art and Technology, 1946-50; Central School of Art, London, 1950. *Hobbies and other interests:* Reading, music, sewing, country walks, jogging.

■ Addresses

Home—Somerset, England. *Agent*—c/o Rogers, Coleridge & White, Ltd., Literary Agency, 20 Powis Mews, London W11 1JN, England.

■ Career

Writer. Textile designer, John Lewis Partnership, London, 1951-54. *Member:* Society of Authors, PEN.

■ Writings

NOVELS; FOR YOUNG ADULTS

Ride the Iron Horse, illustrated by Michael Jackson, Longman Young, 1973.
The Star Trap (sequel to *Ride the Iron Horse*), illustrated by Michael Jackson, Longman Young, 1974.
A Question of Courage, illustrated by Janet Archer, Crowell, 1975.
The First of Midnight, illustrated by Anthony Morris, Kestrel, 1977, Seabury Press, 1978.
A Long Way to Go (sequel to *The First of Midnight*), Kestrel, 1978.
Comeback, Kestrel, 1981.
Tom Post's Private Eye, Macmillan, 1983.
A Rose from Blighty (sequel to *A Question of Courage*), Collins, 1990.

FICTION; FOR CHILDREN

Mike's Bike, illustrated by Jim Russell, Kestrel, 1974.
What Can I Do?, illustrated by Barry Wilkinson, Kestrel, 1975.
The Big Brass Band, illustrated by Charles Front, Kestrel, 1976.
Kipper's Turn, illustrated by Mary Dinsdale, Blackie & Son, 1976.
My Uncle Charlie, illustrated by Jannat Houston, Kestrel, 1977.
Kipper Skips, illustrated by Thelma Lambert, Blackie & Son, 1979.
Carnival Day, illustrated by Nita Sowter, Kestrel, 1979.

Messages: A Collection of Shivery Tales, Viking Kestrel, 1984.
Imp, illustrated by Margaret Chamberlain, Heinemann, 1985.
The Rainbow Sandwich, illustrated by Joanna Worth, Methuen, 1989.
Night Windows, illustrated by Annabel Spenceley, Macmillan, 1990.
Emma's Monster, illustrated by Shelagh McNicholas, Walker, 1992.

OTHER

Also author of numerous short stories for younger and older readers.

■ **Sidelights**

"As far back as I can remember I have been a kind of dipsomaniac where words are concerned," Marjorie Sheila Darke told *SATA.* "A solitary child, reading was a major source of pleasure to me, becoming almost an obsession in my teens when I devoured a novel a day. At this point my father objected, book lover though he was, as my school work was suffering. He rationed me severely, I thought, allowing me no more than two books a week. Was this a blueprint for authorship? If it was, it did not bear fruit until long after I had left school, been to art college and to work, married, and had a family. By the time my children were going to school I felt a real need to swim out of the pleasurable but self-effacing seas of motherhood and do something totally different; something creative and personal. Writing seemed a natural answer and fitted easily into family life.

"A ten year apprenticeship followed when I tried my hand at innumerable forms of writing—thrillers, adult novels, short stories for young and old, television plays. Writing for children evolved out of these years of trial and error, and for the first time I found I was really happy; slotting without difficulty into this particular genre, perhaps because my own childhood and adolescence have remained very clear in my mind. The first novel I felt to be worthy of publication was born—*Ride the Iron Horse,* a story of the coming of an early railway to a remote part of England. It was a success and gave me the much needed encouragement to continue."

The lead characters of *Ride the Iron Horse,* and its sequel, *The Star Trap,* are John Gate, a farm boy who wishes to become an engineer despite his poverty and illiteracy, and Frances, the squire's daughter. In the first story, which a reviewer in *Times Literary Supplement* called a "mature first novel" and praised Darke's "mastery of the technical details of engineering," Frances clandestinely teaches John to read. When John and Frances save the squire's railroad from sabotage, John gets the chance to achieve his dreams. In the sequel, Frances defies her father (and social convention) and runs away to become an actress, eventually becoming engaged to John, now a full-fledged railroad engineer.

This was followed by two books for young readers. *Mike's Bike* is about a boy who longs for a bike but doesn't see that there's one sitting on the rubbish heap just waiting for rescue. *What Can I Do?* is the tale of a bored little girl who doesn't want to do the usual things. When she sees her next door neighbor repairing his car, she spends the rest of the day in oily happiness.

Darke soon returned to the historical novel and her interest in women's oppression in what has become her most popular work: *A Question of Courage.* On the surface, this is the story of Emily Palmer, a working girl who becomes more and more involved with England's Suffragette Movement. On a deeper level, it is the story of the movement itself. Emily loses her job and is eventually imprisoned for her involvement in the cause, where she is force fed when she attempts a hunger strike. Of this novel, Ann A. Flowers wrote in *Horn Book:* "The descriptions of mob and police brutality are shocking." *A Question of Courage* was to become the cornerstone for a series of books (written over the course of fifteen years and interspersed with many other works) concerning racist oppression combined with injustice to women. *The First of Midnight* is the story of two star-crossed lovers in England in the late 1700s. While imprisoned on a slave ship, Jess, a young white orphan, meets Midnight, an educated African who is the personal slave of the ship's captain. Jess is eventually sold to be a scullery maid to the Jarman sisters, and when Midnight escapes the ship he runs to Jess for safety. When Midnight gets a chance to make his life's dream come true and return to Africa, Jess realizes that she will not fit into his world, and remains behind without telling him she is pregnant.

Darke continues the saga in *A Long Way to Go,* a story about twins Bella and Luke, who are descendants of Midnight and Jess. It is World War I in London, and black-skinned Britons are rare. Despite suffering racial taunts, Luke decides to stand up for his beliefs and become a conscientious objector. Bella goes to work in a munitions plant, where she meets Emily Palmer (from *A Question of Courage*), and they both get fired for demanding pay equal to what the male workers receive. A reviewer for *Junior Bookshelf* described *A Long Way to Go* as "a good story which shows ordinary people, extraordinary only in their toughness and resistance to pressures, caught up in the tangle of grim events."

It wasn't until 1990, fifteen years after the original story appeared, that Darke picks up the story of Emily and Louise at the beginning of World War I, where she left them in *A Question of Courage.* Anne Everall, writing for *School Librarian,* described *A Rose from Blighty* as a novel that "examines the impact the war had on the suffragette movement." It's also the story of Emily's growing romance with Louise's brother Peter—in defiance of social class barriers—and Louise's consequent jealousy. This is vintage Darke, fast-paced, authentically detailed, and passionate.

Darke also wrote historical novels for younger readers, including *Night Windows,* a time-slip story in which a young artist named Ben, painting a mural of the Industrial Revolution, finds himself slipping into the world of the picture. In the two-book series of *Kipper's Turn* and *Kipper Skips,* a small boy in late Victorian England is forced into petty thievery to survive, while at the same time he is being harassed by the "Board Men" who want him to attend the newly compulsory elementary school. In a review for *Times Literary Supplement,* Aidan Warlow stated that his enjoyment of the books was due to "a well constructed and exciting plot."

"To date my novels for young adults all have historical settings," Darke once told *SATA,* "which may seem strange when one considers the fact that I found school history extremely dull. Acts of Parliament, foreign policies, battle strategy bored me into near sleep. My interest lay in ordinary people, their loves, trials, everyday lives. As a child I often begged my mother and grandmother: 'Tell me about when you were a little girl!' Their answers are with me still, so that I feel as strongly linked to the past as I do to the present and future. I love to sink myself into a chosen period, feel it in my bones, try to reproduce it so that the reader, too, may know what it was like to be a navvy building an early railway, a Victorian actress, a Suffragette, a slave . . . ."

"Ideas for my stories usually originate at unexpected moments—a chance remark in conversation; something I see in the street or on television; a phrase I read in a book, or a newspaper item. Any of these and many others may spark off a train of thought which I like to jot down straight away because they are rare treasures and easily lost. Once an idea takes hold I have a marvelous time letting my mind rove freely, even wildly, as the story begins to take shape, but before it evolves too far I begin research into the particular background. Much of this research is from books, but I find it equally important to visit places and talk to people connected with my current interest. In this way I can begin to experience the period within myself, and in doing so inadvertently have a lot of fun. There was the time I drove a steam traction engine at a rally, and another time when I crawled up and up alarmingly vertical ladders in an old water mill, peering down on the great cogs of wood and iron and the flat milling stones which once had pounded wheat into flour, worked by the mill race I could still hear thundering way beneath my feet.

"For the sake of *A Question of Courage* I spent a fascinating afternoon with a lady whose sheltered cousin defied her family, went to London, and smashed a window because she believed in the Suffragette cause. A deed which put her in prison. Holding the badges Mrs. Pankhurst had presented to her, was for me a very poignant moment. There are, of course, details which defy capture. I never did discover whether Bathbrick was in use as a pan scourer in the late eighteenth century, when researching for *The First of Midnight.* Neither did I find out whether charcoal irons were used by dressmakers in 1912, in the case of *A Question of Courage.* When this happens the only course left open to me is to ruthlessly discard any material where there is

the smallest element of doubt. It is only fair to the reader.

"Not all my books require this same intensive research. I like to alternate with stories for very young children which can be read aloud. It is a refreshing change playing with the words, building and developing the sounds as well as the storyline. These stories are closely bound to the pictures decorating the book, and I have always been most fortunate in the excellent and sympathetic artists chosen to illustrate them." Three of those picture books were *My Uncle Charlie,* a story of a sailor who returns from the sea with a trunk-load of gifts; *Carnival Day,* the tale of a sad little boy with the measles who must stay home and miss a trip to the carnival; and *Emma's Monster,* seven lively stories about a little girl and her strong-willed—though imaginary—monster.

"Ultimately there are the sheets of blank paper beside my typewriter," Darke told *SATA,* "a stack of notes and my head filled with broken jigsaw pieces. I know that the story is hovering there, already independent of me but hidden. Before other people can see it, there is an elusive wall of fog to be pushed away—and that is my job for the few weeks or months. It is not easy and sometimes it is exasperating, but the moment when my characters begin to direct their own lives and I am merely a recorder of events, then there is an exhilaration, a joy in the writing, which is impossible to define."

■ Works Cited

Everall, Anne, review of *A Rose from Blighty, School Librarian,* August, 1990, p. 116.
Flowers, Ann A., review of *A Question of Courage, Horn Book,* December, 1975, pp. 600-601.
Review of *A Long Way to Go, Junior Bookshelf,* February, 1979, pp. 48-49.
Review of *Ride the Iron Horse,* "Getting Steam Up," *Times Literary Supplement,* April 6, 1973, p. 388.
Warlow, Aidan, "Violent Outbursts," *Times Literary Supplement,* October 1, 1976, p. 1240.

■ For More Information See

PERIODICALS

Growing Point, November, 1990, p. 5435.
Junior Bookshelf, February, 1977, pp. 19-20; August, 1977, pp. 217-18; February, 1985, p. 22.
Kirkus Reviews, February 1, 1978.
School Librarian, August, 1992, p. 101.
School Library Journal, October, 1975, p. 105; May, 1978, p. 75.
Times Literary Supplement, March 29, 1974, p. 3265.

LIONEL DAVIDSON

DAVIDSON, Lionel 1922-
(David Line)

■ Personal

Born March 31, 1922, in Hull, Yorkshire, England; married Fay Jacobs, 1949 (died 1988); married Frances Ullman, 1989; children: (first marriage) two sons.

■ Addresses

Agent—Curtis Brown, 162-168 Regent St., London W1R 5TB, England.

■ Career

Writer and editor for several British magazines, 1954-59; novelist and screenwriter, 1959—. *Military service:* Royal Navy Submarine Service, 1941-46.

■ Awards, Honors

Silver Quill Award for most promising first novel, Authors' Club, 1960, for *The Night of Wenceslas;* Gold Dagger Award for best novel, Crime Writer's Association, 1960, for *The Night of Wenceslas,* 1967, for *The Menorah Men,* and 1978, for *The Chelsea Murders;* President's Prize for Literature (Israel), for *Smith's Gazelle.*

■ Writings

FOR CHILDREN; UNDER PSEUDONYM DAVID LINE, EXCEPT WHERE NOTED

Soldier and Me, Harper, 1965, published in England as *Run for Your Life,* J. Cape, 1966.
Mike and Me, J. Cape, 1974.
(Under name Lionel Davidson) *Under Plum Lake* (fantasy), Knopf, 1980.
Screaming High, Little, Brown, 1985.

NOVELS; FOR ADULTS

The Night of Wenceslas, Gollancz, 1960, Harper, 1961.
The Rose of Tibet, Harper, 1962.
The Menorah Men, Harper, 1966, published in England as *A Long Way to Shiloh,* Gollancz, 1966.
Making Good Again, Harper, 1968.
Smith's Gazelle, Knopf, 1971.
The Sun Chemist, Knopf, 1976.
Murder Games, Coward, 1978, published in England as *The Chelsea Murders,* J. Cape, 1978.
Kolymsky Heights, St. Martin's, 1994.

OTHER

Also author of screenplays. Contributor of short stories to *Alfred Hitchcock's Mystery Magazine* and *Suspense.* Contributor to anthologies, including *Winter's Crimes 13,* Macmillan, 1981, and *Winter's Crimes 16,* Macmillan, 1984.

■ Adaptations

Mike and Me was adapted into a British television series, c. 1974.

■ Sidelights

Using David Line as a pen name, popular British novelist Lionel Davidson is the author of several award-winning thrillers for young adult readers. In books like *Soldier and Me* and *Screaming High,* as in the webs of espionage he weaves in his novels for adults, Davidson is noted for his vividly drawn characters and colorful international settings, as well as the author's energetic style and engaging, suspense-filled plots. In addition to his novels of suspense, Davidson is also the author of the young adult fantasy novel *Under Plum Lake,* which he published under his own name in 1980.

Davidson's books for young adults "are deceptively simple both in narrative and language," notes Peter Hollindale in *Twentieth-Century Children's Writers.* Hollindale goes on to describe the novels as "taut, lean, strongly plotted thrillers, with fast-moving narratives filled with unrelenting excitement and suspense." But their success as a "good read" doesn't take away from the fact that they are also "highly literate and intelligent." According to the critic, "simplicity does not mean simplification, spareness and pace of language do not bring cliche, and familiar situations avoid hackneyed stereotypes by their freshness of particular setting and meticulous accuracy of technical detail."

Davidson was born on March 31, 1922, one of nine children of immigrant parents living in a poorer working-class neighborhood in Hull, Yorkshire, England. His father, who was of Polish descent, died when Lionel was only two years old; his Russian-born mother moved with the entire family to London four years later. Because of a lack of money, Davidson left school when he was fourteen and got a job in the office of a shipping company. Working there only a short while, he was soon hired in at the *Spectator,* which published his first story, written when he was only fifteen years old. From there, Davidson moved on to a wide variety of writing and editing assignments, taking time out from his writing career to join the Royal Navy and serve in the Submarine Service during World War II. After the war ended, he returned to England and married Fay Jacobs; by 1949 the couple was living in Europe where Davidson worked as a freelance journalist. The experiences he encountered over the next ten years through the course of investigating social and political events for the British press would provide the inspiration for his first novel, *The Night of Wenceslas,* published in 1960.

While *The Night of Wenceslas* had been written more for fun than as part of an attempt to become a novelist, Davidson's first work of fiction became an almost instant best seller in England and received a great deal of critical praise. The timing couldn't have been better for its author; Davidson was already at work on a second book, this time because he needed to supplement his income as a journalist due to his growing family. 1962's *The Rose of Tibet* also made its way up the best-seller charts and Davidson's career as a novelist was established. Several more adult novels would follow, many set in Israel, where Davidson and his family made their home during much of the 1970s, before returning to his native England. Davidson's wife would die in 1988; he remarried in 1989.

Davidson's output as a novelist has been relatively small, perhaps because of the time needed to fully research each book's location and its related historic framework, as well as the complex social and political elements that the author sets at play in each of his works of fiction. Besides researching such elements, Davidson spends a great deal of time plotting the actions of his characters to be sure that motivations ring true, and he also experiments with a variety of possible outcomes. For him, writing a novel is like piecing together a large and complex puzzle, from which many pieces are missing and must be hunted for.

His first children's novel, *Soldier and Me,* released in England under the title *Run for Your Life,* was published in 1965. It introduces fourteen-year-old Jim Woolcott, a quiet, unadventurous English student who accidentally stumbles upon some important political information through his friendship with Szolda, a young Hungarian refugee with a nose for trouble whom Jim nicknames "Soldier." When Soldier tells Jim that he overheard some Hungarians plotting a murder in the local library, Jim finds the story far-fetched. Finally Jim is persuaded, and he and Soldier trail the killers, only to witness the actual killing. When they go to the police to report the murder, they discover that both the corpse and the evidence have vanished and they are not believed. Given a deaf ear by the police, the boys find themselves caught up in a life-threatening situation as they try to prevent the Hungarians from getting away with their deadly deed. Forced to go into hiding after the killers realize the teens have witnessed their crime, the two young men are eventually captured by their devious foreign enemies, who are masters of disguise. Woolcott's ordeal forces him to adapt to unpleasant circumstances and brings out his inner resourcefulness and ability to make the best of things. "Not only is this an exciting story," writes a reviewer in the *Times Literary Supplement,* "but the boys remain recognizable and plausible boys, heroic against the grain."

Mike and Me is Davidson's sequel to *Soldier and Me,* although it was published almost a decade later in 1974. Even in the relative peacefulness of his hometown, Woolcott manages to stumble into more trouble after he uncovers a plot by dishonest land developers to get what they want through criminal means. This time it is bumbling cousin Mike who becomes his right-hand man, as Jim, young Soldier, friend Nixon, and Moggy, the boy's art teacher, attempt to stop the villainous land-grabbers.

Davidson published *Under Plum Lake* under his real name to differentiate it from his juvenile adventure novels. A utopian fantasy for young adults, *Under Plum Lake* is the story of the underwater society known as Egon, a parallel world where an intelligent race of humanoids has successfully battled such conditions as rapid aging, illness, and injury to enjoy living for ten times the normal human life span—thereby acquiring greater knowledge—in a peaceable realm where nothing unpleasant seems to happen. The story is told from the point of view of Barry Gordon, a creative and adventurous thirteen-year-old boy who stumbles upon—or rather swims through—the doorway to Egon while exploring caves along the rugged seaside coast during his family's vacation in Cornwall. Barry is taken to this world of the deep by Dido, a young man who, in appearance, seems to almost mirror Barry. Dido allows his earthbound twin a glimpse of the many facets of his almost-too-perfect underwater home and, together, the two boys go on a series of otherworldly adventures.

After the time comes for Barry to leave Egon's utopian paradise and return to his own world, an effort by the Egonians to erase all the boy's memories of his experiences there is unsuccessful and the magical world haunts him in the form of a recurring dream. Barry becomes confused and tormented by the contrasts between the possibilities for happiness embodied in his slight recollections of Egon and the realities of his own world, particularly his own growth towards adulthood, during which he must learn to accept and deal with greater responsibility and stresses and accept the inevitable aging and death common to his species.

"Egon thus joins the ranks of literature's ideal worlds such as Utopia, Shangri-la, and Islandia," states Anstiss Drake in the *Chicago Tribune Book World,* calling *Under Plum Lake* "a work of superb imagination." Such praise was hard earned by the book's writer, according to Rosemarie Mroz in the *Dictionary of Literary Biography.* Davidson found *Under Plum Lake* difficult to write "because it is told by a child as he ventures into the fantasy world of Egon and because it contains many philosophical thoughts." Davidson rewrote the novel more than ten times during the two years prior to its publication, according to Mroz.

As he did with the three novels that preceded it, the author of *Screaming High* adopted the pen name of David Line when publishing his 1985 novel. And, like all of its predecessors, it is a novel of riveting action and suspense, set mainly in England. Two young men show courage in the face of danger when they uncover a ring of drug-traffickers. Although shunned by his fellow students for his eccentric behavior, "Ratbag" Mountjoy is a talented teenaged trumpet-player whose musical talent is discovered by classmate Nick, who also befriends the young prodigy. When Ratbag joins the school band, they win a chance to perform at the

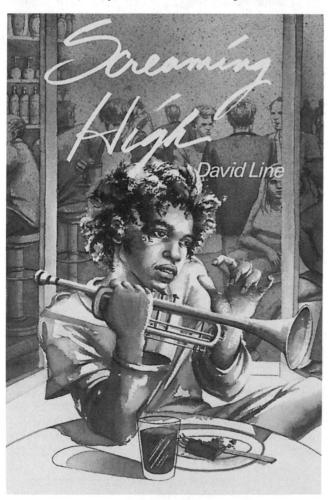

On their way to a music competition in Amsterdam, high schoolers Nick and trumpeter Ratbag inadvertently get mixed up with an international crime ring.

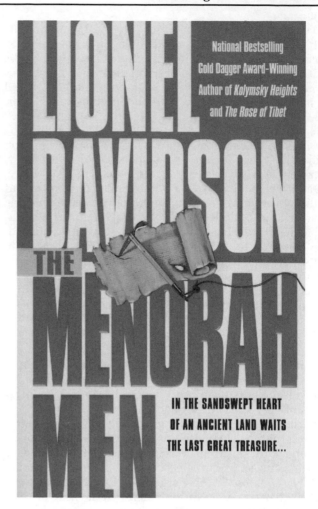

National Bestselling Gold Dagger Award-Winning Author of *Kolymsky Heights* and *The Rose of Tibet*

IN THE SANDSWEPT HEART OF AN ANCIENT LAND WAITS THE LAST GREAT TREASURE...

An archaeological mystery about a missing menorah pits a scholar against dangerous ancient and contemporary antagonists.

national band playoffs in Amsterdam. While there, the two boys witness drug trafficking and dutifully report it to the local Dutch authorities; when they are asked to return to Holland a second time—serving as unwitting bait for a police crackdown on the drug ring—plans to protect them backfire and Ratbag and Nick suddenly find themselves facing death. Finally, the criminals are captured. The boys return to England, and Ratbag goes back to pursuing his promising future as a jazz musician.

In addition to his novels for young adult readers, Davidson's works for adults include *The Night of Wenceslas,* the 1960 thriller that revolves around a phony inheritance and a smuggling operation in Prague; *The Rose of Tibet,* about the search for a missing Englishman in the mountains of Central Asia; *The Menorah Men* (published in England as *A Long Way to Shiloh*), the tale of a British archeologist's search for the original seven-branched lamp of Judaism while in tense competition with Arab rivals; and *The Chelsea Murders,* a mystery novel focusing on a series of seven murders, where the only clues to solving the crimes are hidden in numerous literary allusions that the murderer himself provides. Davidson has been awarded the Crime Writer's Association's prestigious Golden Dagger Award on three separate occasions: for his novels *The Night of Wenceslas, The Menorah Men,* and *The Chelsea Murders.* In each of these works Davidson has been praised by critics for, as Mroz contends, his "ability to blend fact and fiction smoothly, as well as his ability to capture the spirit of people and place."

■ Works Cited

Drake, Anstiss, review of *Under Plum Lake, Chicago Tribune Book World,* November 11, 1980, p. 7.

Hollindale, Peter, "David Line," in *Twentieth-Century Children's Writers,* 4th edition, edited by Laura Standley Berger, St. James Press, 1995, pp. 580-81.

Mroz, Rosemarie, "Lionel Davidson," in *Dictionary of Literary Biography,* Volume 14: *British Novelists since 1960, Part 1,* edited by Jay L. Halio, Gale Research, 1983, pp. 244-48.

Review of *Run for Your Life, Times Literary Supplement,* May 19, 1966, p. 442.

■ For More Information See

PERIODICALS

Bulletin of the Center for Children's Books, April, 1966, p. 133; October, 1985.

Library Journal, July-October, 1965, p. 3806.

Publishers Weekly, July 18, 1994, p. 234.

School Library Journal, December 1985, p. 103.*

* * *

DAVIS, Robin W(orks) 1962-

■ Personal

Born January 19, 1962, in Austin, TX; married Mark L. Switzer, 1984 (divorced, 1990); married James L. Davis (a postal employee), February 13, 1992; children: (second marriage) Caitlinn Nicole. *Education:* Baylor University, B.F.A., 1984; University of North Texas, M.L.S., 1992. *Hobbies and other interests:* Painting, collecting "Dia de los Muertos" crafts.

■ Addresses

Office—901 Precinct Line Rd., Hurst, TX 76053.

■ Career

Richardson Public Library, Richardson, TX, youth services librarian, 1987-91; Hurst Public Library, Hurst, TX, youth services librarian, 1991—. Consultant and workshop presenter, North Texas Library System, Texas Library Association, and Houston Area Library System. *Member:* American Library Association, Texas Library Association, Kappa Delta.

■ Awards, Honors

Recipient, National Reading Program grant, American Library Association; winner, Clever Creative Programs

ROBIN W. DAVIS

for Literacy, Cuyhahoga County, OH; Panhellenic scholar; Texas Library Association scholar; Patricia Johnston Memorial Art scholar; Student Foundation scholar.

■ Writings

Creature Features, Texas State Library, 1989.

Camp Wanna Read, Texas State Library, 1991.

Promoting Reading with Reading Programs, Neal Schuman, 1992.

An Alphabet of Books: Literature-Based Activities for Schools and Libraries, Alleyside (Fort Atkinson, WI), 1995.

An Alphabet of Authors, Alleyside, 1995.

Art Information through Children's Literature, Scarecrow, 1995.

Big Books for Little Readers, Scarecrow, 1996.

■ Sidelights

Robin W. Davis told *SATA:* "As an artist, I became very interested in the illustrations in children's picture books, particularly in the 1980s, when there was much change and revolution going on in the publishing of kids' books. These wonderful and new illustrations inspired creative ideas in me, which translated to some work I did for the Texas State Library's Reading Club Program Manuals in 1989 and 1991. My favorite children's author is Margaret Mahy, but I love all the illustrators and have no favorite."

PLEASANT DeSPAIN

DeSPAIN, Pleasant 1943-

■ Personal

Born September 30, 1943, in Denver, CO; son of Robert A. and Eleanor J. (Feazell) DeSpain. *Education:* Southern Illinois University, B.S., 1965, M.S., 1966. *Hobbies and other interests:* Travel worldwide.

■ Addresses

Home and office—3649 East 3rd St., #201, Tucson, AZ 85716.

■ Career

University of Massachusetts, Amherst, instructor in literature and speech, 1966-68; University of Washington, Seattle, instructor in literature and speech, 1970-72; KING-TV, Seattle, producer/writer and host of children's storytelling show, 1975-80. Professional storyteller/author (including school workshops), 1972—. Consultant/author for Rose Studios (computer software development for interactive children's story games), 1994—. *Member:* National Storytelling Association.

■ Awards, Honors

Officially named "Seattle's Resident Storyteller" by the mayor of Seattle, June, 1975.

■ Writings

Twenty-two Splendid Tales to Tell from around the World, Volumes 1-2, illustrated by Kirk Lyttle, August House (Little Rock, AR), 1993 (originally published as *Pleasant Journeys,* 1979).
Thirty-three Multicultural Tales to Tell, illustrated by Joe Shlichta, August House, 1993.
Eleven Turtle Tales: Adventure Tales from around the World, August House, 1994.
Strongheart Jack and the Beanstalk, August House, 1995.
The Mystery Artist, Willowisp Press (St. Petersburg, FL), 1995.
Eleven Nature Tales, August House, 1996.

Also author of a syndicated newspaper column.

■ Work in Progress

Eleven Latin American Tales, expected 1997.

■ Sidelights

Pleasant DeSpain has taught speech, literature, and drama at university and in public schools, has written, produced, and hosted an award-winning television program on KING-TV in Seattle, and was officially proclaimed "Seattle's Resident Storyteller" by the mayor. "I've been writing and telling stories since I was in the third grade," DeSpain told *SATA.* "I grew up, became educated, and started my career as a university instructor in literature and speech communication. In 1972, at the age of twenty-eight, I decided to make a living telling stories. There was no such thing as a professional storyteller in the U.S. in 1972, and thus I'm often referred to as one of the pioneers of America's storytelling renaissance. I began writing down many of the multicultural tales in the way that I tell them some twenty years ago. Soon after, my pure, simple retelling caught on with other storytellers, educators, and parents."

Critics have praised DeSpain's efforts. For example, *Booklist* reviewer Julie Corsaro described the traditional tales included in the first volume of DeSpain's *Twenty-two Splendid Tales to Tell from around the World* as "retold with simplicity and directness by an accomplished storyteller." The anthology includes tales from Europe, Asia, Africa, the East Indies, Japan, and North America. All the stories stress the triumph of common sense over brute strength, and good over evil. Volume two includes twenty-two more parables, myths, and fables of heroes and heroines, villains of all sorts, witches, giants, and leprechauns.

For *Thirty-three Multicultural Tales to Tell,* DeSpain collected stories from Native Americans, and from Brazil, China, Korea, Russia, Tibet, Africa, and other countries. These short (two- to three-page), nonsexist, action-oriented tales stress the similarities among peoples and the universality of their messages. A *Kirkus Reviews* critic noted that the stories would give readers a "stronger impression of human culture's unity than its diversity."

DeSpain narrowed his subject matter for his next collection, *Eleven Turtle Tales: Adventure Tales from around the World.* According to DeSpain, the turtle, who lives on land and in water and breathes air, joins these three elements of creation—land, water, and air—and becomes the primary symbol of Mother Earth. The turtle appears in many guises around the world and plays a variety of roles, from trickster to advisor. There are eleven different tales retold, including how the turtle got his protective shell, and how turtle sibling rivalry created the land that is now California and still causes the earthquakes that occur there.

"I've traveled to schools throughout the U.S. during the past twenty years, telling tales and teaching children the fundamentals of story making and writing," DeSpain told *SATA.* "Along the way, I began sharing some of the stories that I made up when I was in grade school. My motivation has always been the power of imagination and language and the joy of sharing. My basic belief is that we are all storytellers. Our lives are our stories. When we share our stories, we come alive."

■ Works Cited

Corsaro, Julie, review of *Twenty-two Splendid Tales to Tell from around the World, Booklist,* January 1, 1995, p. 828.
Review of *Thirty-three Multicultural Tales to Tell, Kirkus Reviews,* October 15, 1993, p. 1327.

■ For More Information See

PERIODICALS

Come-All-Ye, winter, 1993, p. 4; spring, 1995, p. 3.
Horn Book Guide, spring, 1994, p. 106.
School Library Journal, August, 1994, p. 16; November, 1994, p. 67.
Small Press Reviews, March, 1994, p. 6.

*   *   *

DORRITT, Susan
See SCHLEIN, Miriam

*   *   *

DOWNIE, John 1931-

■ Personal

Born December 12, 1931, in Glasgow, Scotland; naturalized Canadian citizen; married Mary Alice Dawe Hunter (an author), June 27, 1959; children: Christine, Jocelyn, Alexandra. *Education:* University of Glasgow, B.Sc., 1953; University of Toronto, M.A.Sc., 1956, Ph.D., 1959.

■ Addresses

Home—190 Union St., Kingston, Ontario, Canada K7L 2P6. *Office*—Department of Chemical Engineering, Queen's University, Kingston, Ontario, Canada K7L 3N6. *Electronic mail*—downiej@post.queensu.ca.

■ Career

Research engineer at Gulf Research & Development Co., 1959-62; Queen's University, Kingston, Ontario, professor, 1962-95, emeritus professor of chemical engineering, 1995—. Life visiting fellow, Clare Hall, Cambridge, 1989—. *Member:* Chemical Institute of Canada (fellow, 1978), Canadian Society of Chemical Engineering.

■ Awards, Honors

Second prize, children's section (with wife, Mary Alice Downie), 4th CBC Literary Competition, 1982, for "Bright Paddles."

■ Writings

(With wife, Mary Alice Downie) *Honor Bound,* illustrated by Joan Huffman, Oxford University Press, 1971, revised edition illustrated by Wesley Bates, Quarry Press, 1991.
(With Mary Alice Downie) *Alison's Ghosts,* illustrated by Paul McCusker, Thomas Nelson, 1984.

Also contributor, with Mary Alice Downie, to anthologies, including *Inside Outside,* Holt, 1978; *Measure Me Sky,* Ginn & Co., 1979; and *Thread the Needle,* Holt, 1987.

*   *   *

DOWNIE, Mary Alice (Dawe) 1934-
(Dawe Hunter)

■ Personal

Born February 12, 1934, in Alton, IL; brought to Canada, 1940; daughter of Robert Grant (a research scientist) and Doris Mary (Rogers) Hunter; married John Downie (a professor of chemical engineering), June 27, 1959; children: Christine, Jocelyn, Alexandra. *Education:* University of Toronto, B.A. (with honors), 1955. *Religion:* Anglican.

■ Addresses

Home—190 Union St., Kingston, Ontario, Canada, K7L 2P6. *Electronic mail*—downiej@post.queensu.ca.

■ Career

Writer, critic, and editor. Maclean-Hunter, Toronto, Ontario, stenographer, 1955; *Marketing Magazine,* Toronto, reporter, 1955-56; *Canadian Medical Association Journal,* Toronto, editorial assistant, 1956-57; Oxford

MARY ALICE DOWNIE

University Press, Toronto, librarian and publicity manager, 1958-59; Kingston *Whig-Standard*, Kingston, Ontario, book review editor, 1973-78. Founding editor, "Kids Canada" series, Kids Can Press, Toronto, and "Northern Lights" series, Peter Martin Associates, Toronto. Affiliated member, Senior Combination Room, Newnham College, Cambridge, 1988-89. Speaker at schools and workshops. *Member:* PEN, Writers Union of Canada (chairman, membership committee, 1987-88).

■ Awards, Honors

Ontario Arts Council Awards, 1970, 1975, 1978, 1981, 1987, 1989, 1990; Canada Council Arts Awards, 1972-73, 1981-82; Canada Council Short Term Award, 1979; (with John Downie) second prize, fourth CBC Literary Competition, Children's Section, 1982, for "The Bright Paddles"; Exploration Grant (with E. Greene and M. A. Thompson), 1984; Ontario Heritage Foundation grant, 1988; Multicultural Directorate grant, 1990.

■ Writings

FICTION FOR CHILDREN

(With husband, John Downie) *Honor Bound,* illustrated by Joan Huffman, Oxford University Press, 1971, revised edition illustrated by Wesley Bates, Quarry Press, 1991.

Scared Sarah, illustrated by Laszlo Gal, Thomas Nelson (Canada), 1974.

Dragon on Parade, illustrated by Mary Lynn Baker, PMA Books, 1974.

The King's Loon/Un Huart pour le Roi, illustrated by Ron Berg, Kids Can Press, 1979.

The Last Ship, illustrated by Lissa Calvert, PMA Books, 1980.

(With George Rawlyk) *A Proper Acadian,* illustrated by Ron Berg, Kids Can Press, 1981.

Jenny Greenteeth, illustrated by Anne Powell, Rhino Books, 1981, revised edition illustrated by Barbara Reid, Kids Can Press, 1984.

(With John Downie) *Alison's Ghosts,* illustrated by Paul McCusker, Thomas Nelson, 1984.

The Cat Park, illustrated by Kathryn Naylor, Quarry Press, 1993.

Snow Paws, illustrated by Kathryn Naylor, Stoddart, 1996.

FOLKTALES

The Magical Adventures of Pierre, illustrated by Yuksel Hassan, Thomas Nelson, 1974.

The Witch of the North: Folktales from French Canada, illustrated by Elizabeth Cleaver, Oberon Press, 1975.

The Wicked Fairy-Wife: A French-Canadian Folktale, illustrated by Kim Price, Kids Can Press, 1983.

How the Devil Got His Cat, illustrated by Jillian Gilliland, Quarry Press, 1988.

(With Mann Hwa Huang-Hsu) *The Buffalo Boy and the Weaver Girl,* illustrated by Jillian Gilliland, Quarry Press, 1989.

Cathal the Giant Killer and the Dun Shaggy Filly, illustrated by Jillian Gilliland, Quarry Press, 1991.

NONFICTION FOR CHILDREN

(With Jillian Gilliland) *Seeds and Weeds: A Book of Country Crafts,* Four Winds Press, 1981.

(With Jillian Gilliland) *Stones and Cones: Country Crafts for Kids,* Scholastic/TAB Publications, 1984.

EDITOR OR COMPILER

(With Barbara Robertson) *The Wind Has Wings: Poems from Canada,* illustrated by Elizabeth Cleaver, Oxford University Press, 1968, revised edition published as *The New Wind Has Wings: Poems from Canada,* 1984.

(With Mary Hamilton) *And Some Brought Flowers: Plants in a New World,* illustrated by John Revell, University of Toronto Press, 1980.

(With Elizabeth Greene and M. A. Thompson) *The Window of Dreams: New Canadian Writing for Children,* Methuen, 1986.

(With Barbara Robertson) *The Well-Filled Cupboard: Everyday Pleasures of Home and Garden,* Lester & Orpen Dennys, 1987.

(With Barbara Robertson) A. M. Klein, *Doctor Dwarf and Other Poems for Children,* illustrated by Gail Geltner, Quarry Press, 1990.

(With M. A. Thompson) *Written in Stone: A Kingston Reader,* Quarry Press, 1993.

OTHER

Contributor (sometimes with John Downie) to anthologies, including *Inside Outside*, Holt, 1978; *Measure Me Sky*, Ginn & Co., 1979; *Crossroads I*, Van Nostrand Reinhold, 1979; *Storytellers Rendezvous*, Canadian Library Association, 1980; *Out and About*, Academic Press, 1981; *All in Good Time*, McGraw-Hill, 1985; *Thread the Needle*, Holt, 1987; and *Winter Welcomes*, Thomas Nelson, 1987. Contributor of numerous stories, articles, and reviews to periodicals, including *Horn Book, Pittsburgh Press, Ottawa Citizen, Globe and Mail, OWL, Chickadee, Montreal Gazette, Canadian Gardening,* and *Century Home.*

■ **Sidelights**

Mary Alice Downie is one of the best-known children's authors and editors in Canada. Many of her ideas are drawn from the colonial period of Canada's past, which, as she once said, "is a short past when you consider the country but stretches out when the heritage of the immigrant is included." The result is fiction that "breathes life into distant periods of Canadian history," according to Joan McGrath in *Twentieth-Century Children's Writers.* "Her youthful Canadians of long ago are irresistible creations: believably of their period, yet as lively and full of fun as their distant descendants who people the playgrounds of today."

Downie's first book was a compilation of poems entitled *The Wind Has Wings: Poems from Canada* that reflects the great diversity of that country. Works by forty-eight poets include such subjects as ice and cold, animal life, and Indians, as well as translations from Yiddish, French, and Eskimo verses. Since then she has coedited several other anthologies that feature Canadian writing for children and adults, including an updated version of her first collection titled *The New Wind Has Wings,* which Zena Sutherland of the *Bulletin of the Center for Children's Books* called "a fine anthology" with "variety and vitality."

Downie's first, and most ambitious, historical novel, *Honor Bound,* was written in collaboration with her husband, John Downie. During the American Revolution in the thirteen colonies there were many people who remained loyal to England's King George III. After the war, many of these people decided to escape persecution from American colonists and move to the wilderness of Canada; they became known as United Empire Loyalists. *Honor Bound* tells the story of one such family who leaves their "civilized" Philadelphia home to start a new life in the Canadian backwoods. Not only must the family leave behind their home and possessions, they must also move without their daughter, Honor, who was visiting relatives when Yankee vigilantes struck, and they do not know her fate. Terence Scully, writing for *Canadian Children's Literature,* commented on the double meaning of the title—the family's search for dignity in their new home as well as their effort to reunite the family—and noted that "the narrative has a rousing beginning, a convincing progression from episode to episode ... and above all a satisfying distinct conclusion where 'Honor' has been reached."

An orphan is the central character in *The King's Loon,* a fictional story set against the real historical events of seventeenth-century Governor Frontenac's efforts to establish an agreement with an Iroquois tribe. Andre runs away from his well-meaning but nagging foster mother, Tante Louet, and stows away on the Governor's ship. After his discovery, he captures a rare loon, which will be his ticket to meeting the King of France. The loon languishes in its cage, however, and when Andre decides to set it free, he learns through the loon's ungrateful behavior how hurtful his own careless behavior has been to Tante Louet. The historical facts Downie relates supplement Andre's "appealing story," according to McGrath.

Details of seventeenth-century life are likewise vividly displayed in *The Last Ship,* seen through the eyes of ten-year-old Madeleine. Every year, when the last supply ship leaves Quebec to return to France, the inhabitants feel cut off and exiled from their old lives. In this story, which *In Review* contributor Mary Anne Buchowski-Monnin called "a pleasant introduction to Canadian history for young children," Madeleine fails in an attempt to sneak into the governor's ball, witnesses a fire, and realizes that it is Quebec, not France, that is now truly her home.

A Proper Acadian makes a complicated subject understandable for young readers. Twelve-year-old Timothy, living in Boston in the 1750s, is sent to live with his aunt when he is orphaned by his mother's death. His aunt and her family are Acadians, people of French descent living in Nova Scotia in an area that the French had ceded to England in the early 1700s. Timothy must make a choice between his native New England and his beloved adopted family when the deportation of Acadians is ordered, and his aunt's family must go into exile. McGrath called this story of conflicting family and national loyalties "vividly told."

Not all of Downie's works are historical novels. She has also written for much younger readers. Cynthia Kittleson, in a review for *School Library Journal,* said that *Jenny Greenteeth* was a "refreshing change," being a "silly story with a witch whose life goes beyond Halloween." In this story, everyone in the town of Denim is afraid of the once-popular water witch. The mayor orders her captured, and only young David is brave enough to confront her and offer a solution—a toothbrush and toothpaste. Praising the story's "light-hearted humor," *In Review* contributor Hope Bridgewater said that the idea that fears should be confronted logically makes for "a worthwhile message."

Downie is also well established as a reteller of folktales. Several of these are adaptations of French-Canadian tales, while others retell an old Chinese legend and a Scottish fable. *The Wicked Fairy-Wife* is a chilling tale, which, like many European-based folktales, contains a large measure of violence. A beautiful young farmgirl

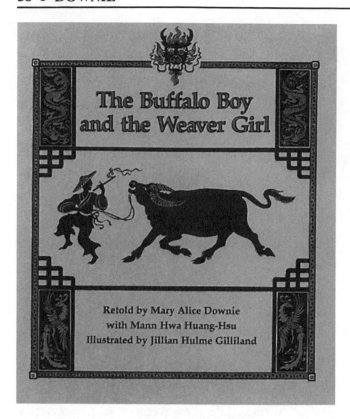

A Chinese legend about a young man, his magic buffalo, and his fairy princess bride introduces readers to Chinese art and literature in this 1989 book. (Cover illustration by Jillian Gilliland.)

named Josette is taken from her parents to marry the handsome prince of the realm. A few years later, an evil fairy comes along, usurps Josette's place as queen, and orders her killed. The executioners, however, take pity on her—merely plucking out her eyes and leaving her alone in the forest. There, Josette not only survives, she bears the king's son, who grows up to avenge his mother and reunite his parents. Reviewer Mary Ainslie Smith commented in *Books in Canada* that "in spite of the violence of many of the incidents, Downie tells the story with cheerful humour."

How the Devil Got His Cat is another French-Canadian tale about the clash between good and evil. At a convent in Quebec, an old wooden bridge collapses. No one can be found to build a new, stronger bridge until a stranger appears. He wants no money for the job—only the soul of the first creature to cross the bridge. Although the stranger (the devil, of course) tries to trick the Mother Superior into crossing first, she sends her beloved black cat instead, who remains with him forever. This traditional tale, combined with the striking silhouette illustrations of Jillian Gilliland, makes "a compelling and enjoyable story for young children," Eva Martin wrote in *Canadian Children's Literature.*

The Buffalo Boy and the Weaver Girl, written with Mann Hwa Huang-Hsu, is based on an ancient Chinese legend about a young man who is driven from his home by a jealous sister-in-law, who allows the man to leave

with the family's buffalo. Unbeknownst to her, the animal has magical powers which help the young man find a new home and a beautiful wife. The work features more silhouette art by Gilliland, which "perfectly complements" Downie's "well-crafted, compelling text," according to Bernie Goedhart in *Quill & Quire.* Downie explored her Scottish roots for the tale of *Cathal the Giant Killer and the Dun Shaggy Filly,* about a man's search for his wife, who has been stolen by a local giant. Downie creates a feeling of song with her words, which *Canadian Children's Literature* contributor Gillian Harding-Russell described as written "dialect, with the lovely flowing rhythms of that language emphasized by ... a periodic repetition." In *Cathal,* the critic added, "we feel the magic touch of an artist storyteller."

"As a writer I spend a great deal of my time on the wrong track; for every book that has been published there is another manuscript in the attic," Downie told *SATA.* "I get an idea (become obsessed by, is nearer the truth) or stumble across interesting material in the Queen's University stacks. With mounting enthusiasm I turn it into an un-publishable manuscript. After a certain amount of brooding about this, it occurs to me what I should really be doing and I set to work once more.

"*The Wind Has Wings* sprang from the ashes of an anthology for poetry for four-to-six-year olds (in that case the publisher saw what should be done); *Honor Bound* [came] from an eighteenth-century diary owned by a landlady. *The Witch of the North,* a collection of French-Canadian witch and devil legends, resulted from reading done for an ill-fated sequel to *Honor Bound.*

This retelling of a French-Canadian tale describes how a nun outwits the devil. (Cover illustration by Jillian Gilliland.)

"My husband, who acts as unpaid editor and occasionally as coauthor, describes me as a 'relentless follower of false trails.' There are undoubtedly more efficient ways of writing, but as the travel-articles say—the side roads are the most interesting. They still are."

■ Works Cited

Bridgewater, Hope, review of *Jenny Greenteeth, In Review,* April, 1982, p. 42.

Buchowski-Monnin, Mary Anne, review of *The Last Ship, In Review,* February, 1981, pp. 35-36.

Goedhart, Bernie, review of *The Buffalo Boy and the Weaver Girl, Quill & Quire,* September, 1989, p. 22.

Harding-Russell, Gillian, "Between the Lines, Stories Live," *Canadian Children's Literature,* Number 73, 1994, pp. 86-88.

Kittleson, Cynthia, review of *Jenny Greenteeth, School Library Journal,* May, 1985, p. 72.

Martin, Eva, "Fairy Tales Retold or Newly Created," *Canadian Children's Literature,* Number 57/58, 1990, pp. 116-17.

McGrath, Joan, "Mary Alice Downie," in *Twentieth-Century Children's Writers,* 4th edition, edited by Laura Standley Berger, St. James Press, 1995, pp. 301-303.

Scully, Terence, "Canadian Colonial Vignettes," *Canadian Children's Literature,* Number 23/24, 1981, pp. 97-98.

Smith, Mary Ainslie, review of *The Wicked Fairy-Wife: A French-Canadian Folktale, Books in Canada,* January, 1984, p. 26.

Sutherland, Zena, review of *The New Wind Has Wings: Poems from Canada, Bulletin of the Center for Children's Books,* April, 1985, p. 145.

■ For More Information See

PERIODICALS

Books for Young People, August, 1988, p. 4.
Books in Canada, October, 1986, p. 38.
Canadian Children's Literature, Number 29, 1983, pp. 77-80; Number 41, 1986, pp. 56-57.
Kirkus Reviews, January 1, 1972, p. 4.
Quill & Quire, June, 1982, p. 36; June, 1984, p. 35.
School Library Journal, May, 1981, p. 54; November, 1985, p. 83.
Times Literary Supplement, April 3, 1969, p. 353.

* * *

DUNLOP, Agnes M(ary) R(obertson) ?-1982
(Elisabeth Kyle, Jan Ralston)

■ Personal

Born in Ayr, Scotland; died February 23, 1982, in Ayr, Scotland; daughter of James (a lawyer) and Elizabeth (Riddell) Dunlop. *Education:* Educated privately. *Religion:* Presbyterian. *Hobbies and other interests:* European travel, history, music, collecting antiques, art.

■ Career

Writer.

■ Writings

FICTION FOR CHILDREN; UNDER PSEUDONYM ELISABETH KYLE

The Mirrors of Versailles, Constable, 1939.
Visitors from England, illustrated by A. Mason Trotter, Davies, 1941.
Vanishing Island, illustrated by A. Mason Trotter, Davies, 1942, published as *Disappearing Island,* Houghton, 1944.
Behind the Waterfall, illustrated by A. Mason Trotter, Davies, 1943.
The Seven Sapphires, illustrated by Nora Lavrin, Davies, 1944, Nelson, 1957.
Holly Hotel, illustrated by Nora Lavrin, Davies, 1945, Houghton, 1947.
Lost Karin, illustrated by Nora Lavrin, Davies, 1947, Houghton, 1948.
The Mirrors of Castle Doone, illustrated by Nora Lavrin, Davies, 1947, Houghton, 1949.
West Wind, illustrated by Francis Gower, Davies, 1948, Houghton, 1950.
The House on the Hill, illustrated by Francis Gower, Davies, 1949.
The Provost's Jewel, illustrated by Joy Colesworthy, Davies, 1950, Houghton, 1951.
The Lintowers, illustrated by Joy Colesworthy, Davies, 1951.
The Captain's House, illustrated by Joy Colesworthy, Davies, 1952, Houghton, 1953.
Forgotten as a Dream, Davies, 1953.
The Reiver's Road, illustrated by A. H. Watson, Nelson, 1953, published as *On Lennox Moor,* Nelson, 1954.
The House of the Pelican, illustrated by Peggy Fortnum, Nelson, 1954.
Caroline House, illustrated by Robert Hodgson, Nelson, 1955, published as *Carolina House,* Nelson, 1955.
A Stillness in the Air, Davies, 1956.
Run to Earth, illustrated by Mary Shillabeer, Nelson, 1957.
The Money Cat, illustrated by Cecil Leslie, Hamish Hamilton, 1958.
Oh Say, Can You See?, Davies, 1959.
Eagle's Nest, illustrated by Juliette Palmer, Nelson, 1961.
The Stilt Walkers, Heinemann, 1972.
Through the Wall, illustrated by Philip Moon, Heinemann, 1973.
The Yellow Coach, illustrated by Alexy Pendle, Heinemann, 1976.
The Key of the Castle, illustrated by Joanna Troughton, Heinemann, 1976.
The Burning Hill, Davies, 1977.

NONFICTION; UNDER PSEUDONYM ELISABETH KYLE

Queen of Scots: The Story of Mary Stuart, illustrated by Robert Hodgson, Nelson, 1957.
Maid of Orleans: The Story of Joan of Arc, illustrated by Robert Hodgson, Nelson, 1957.

Girl with a Lantern, illustrated by Douglas Relf, Evans, 1961, published as *The Story of Grizel,* Nelson, 1961.

Girl with an Easel, illustrated by Charles Mozley, Evans, 1962, published as *Portrait of Lisette,* Nelson, 1963.

Girl with a Pen: Charlotte Bronte, illustrated by Charles Mozley, Evans, 1963, Holt Rinehart, 1964.

Girl with a Song: The Story of Jenny Lind, illustrated by Charles Mozley, Evans, 1964, published as *The Swedish Nightingale: Jenny Lind,* Holt Rinehart, 1965.

Victoria: The Story of a Great Queen, illustrated by Annette Macarthur-Onslow, Nelson, 1964.

Girl with a Destiny: The Story of Mary of Orange, illustrated by Charles Mozley, Evans, 1965, published as *Princess of Orange,* Holt Rinehart, 1966.

The Boy Who Asked for More: The Early Life of Charles Dickens, Evans, 1966, published as *Great Ambitions,* Holt Rinehart, 1968.

Duet: The Story of Clara and Robert Schumann, Holt Rinehart, 1968.

Song of the Waterfall: The Story of Edvard and Nina Grieg, Holt Rinehart, 1970.

ADULT NOVELS; UNDER PSEUDONYM ELISABETH KYLE

The Begonia Bed, Bobbs Merrill, 1934.
Orangefield, Bobbs Merrill, 1938.
Broken Glass, Davies, 1940.
The White Lady, Davies, 1941.
But We Are Exiles, Davies, 1942.
The Pleasure Dome, Davies, 1943.
The Skaters' Waltz, Davies, 1944.
Carp Country, Davies, 1946.
Mally Lee, Doubleday, 1947.
A Man of Talent, Davies, 1948.
A Little Fire, Appleton, 1950 (published in England as *Douce,* Davies, 1950).
The Tontine Belle, Davies, 1951.
Conor Sands, Davies, 1952.
The Regent's Candlesticks, Davies, 1954.
The Other Miss Evans, Davies, 1958.
Return to the Alcazar, Davies, 1962.
Love Is for the Living, Davies, 1966, Holt Rinehart, 1967.
High Season, Davies, 1968.
Queen's Evidence, Davies, 1969.
Mirror Dance, Davies, 1970, Holt Rinehart, 1971.
The Scent of Danger, Davies, 1971, Holt Rinehart, 1972.
The Silver Pineapple, Davies, 1972.
The Heron Tree, Davies, 1973.
Free as Air, Davies, 1974.
Down the Water, Davies, 1975.
All the Nice Girls, Davies, 1976.
The Stark Inheritance, Davies, 1978.
A Summer Scandal, Davies, 1979.
The Deed Box, Hale, 1981.
Bridge of the Blind Man, Hale, 1983.

OTHER

(Under pseudonym Jan Ralston) *Mystery of the Good Adventure* (juvenile), illustrated by A. Mason Trotter, Dodd Mead, 1950.

(Under pseudonym Elisabeth Kyle; with Alec Robertson) *The Singing Wood* (play), produced in Glasgow, Scotland, 1957.

Dunlop's manuscripts are collected at the National Library of Scotland, Edinburgh.

■ Sidelights

Agnes M. R. Dunlop, using the pseudonym Elisabeth Kyle, wrote works ranging from children's fiction to biographies to adult romances and mysteries, often using her native Scotland as a backdrop. Although she produced no single masterpiece, according to Valerie Brinkley-Willsher in *Twentieth-Century Children's Writers,* she "provided interesting and exciting stories for young readers for 35 years." Her children's fiction ranged through several genres, including romances, mysteries, and historical novels, including *The Key to the Castle.* This novel, based on actual historical events, follows Willie Douglas, a young page whose theft of a key allowed Mary, Queen of Scots, to escape imprison-

Intriguing and well-researched, Dunlop's biography of Clara and Robert Schumann tells of their love, the obstacles they faced, and their world of music.

ment on Loch Leven. As Brinkley-Willsher noted, "Kyle's feeling for history enabled her to recreate the atmosphere" of the distant past.

Kyle was best known for her fictionalized biographies, which dramatized the lives of famous writers, musicians, and historical figures. In her biography of the author of *Wuthering Heights, Girl with a Pen: Charlotte Bronte,* Kyle "brings to life the ... yearning ambitions of the Bronte girls with a satisfying vividness," Millicent Taylor noted in the *Christian Science Monitor.* "One cannot recommend too highly the results of combined skill and research," Virginia Haviland asserted in her *Horn Book* review, adding praise for Kyle's ability to create realistic atmosphere, "brilliantly drawn characters," and "real suspense." The popular author of *A Christmas Carol* and *David Copperfield* is profiled in *Great Ambitions: A Story of the Early Years of Charles Dickens.* Calling it an "excellent introduction" to Dickens, a *Horn Book* reviewer observed that Kyle's book "provides insight into how an author thinks and creates." A critic for *Best Sellers* likewise found that Kyle "brings Dickens to life," and concluded that *Great Ambitions* "is an ideal way of presenting background" on Dickens's works to children.

The Swedish Nightingale: Jenny Lind
by Elisabeth Kyle

Agnes Dunlop recounts the inspiring story of the Swedish soprano who overcame incredible odds to become an international legend.

Similarly, *The Swedish Nightingale: Jenny Lind* "is another fine biographical novel," a *Saturday Review* critic remarked. In detailing the life of the Swedish singer who overcame the loss of her voice, Kyle "makes very real the humble but spirited Jenny ... and brings to life the people who played parts in her phenomenal career," Ruth Hill Viguers stated in *Horn Book. Duet: The Story of Clara and Robert Schumann* and *Song of the Waterfall: The Story of Edvard and Nina Grieg* provide information on two famed composers, the German musician who married a brilliant pianist and the Norwegian writer of *Peer Gynt.* A *Times Literary Supplement* critic called the former work "convincingly told," while in another *Horn Book* review Viguers stated of the latter: "With her usual vitality in presenting talented, appealing people, the author brings to life" Grieg and his wife, creating a work "so interesting" that musical novices "may find themselves eager to hear some of Grieg's" work.

"I always regarded myself a story-teller first and foremost," Dunlop once told *SATA.* "I enjoy the sort of book which, whatever its other excellencies, manages to keep alive the reader's interest in what will happen next."

■ Works Cited

Brinkley-Willsher, Valerie, "Elisabeth Kyle," in *Twentieth-Century Children's Writers,* 4th edition, St. James Press, 1995, pp. 545-47.

Review of *Duet: The Story of Clara and Robert Schumann, Times Literary Supplement,* March 14, 1968, p. 262.

Review of *Great Ambitions: A Story of the Early Years of Charles Dickens, Best Sellers,* March 1, 1968, p. 466.

Review of *Great Ambitions: A Story of the Early Years of Charles Dickens, Horn Book,* April, 1968, p. 190.

Haviland, Virginia, review of *Girl with a Pen: Charlotte Bronte, Horn Book,* April, 1964, p. 186.

Review of *The Swedish Nightingale: Jenny Lind, Saturday Review,* November 13, 1965, p. 62.

Taylor, Millicent, review of *Girl with a Pen: Charlotte Bronte, Christian Science Monitor,* May 7, 1964, p. 6B.

Viguers, Ruth Hill, review of *The Swedish Nightingale: Jenny Lind, Horn Book,* October, 1965, p. 508.

Viguers, Ruth Hill, review of *Song of the Waterfall: The Story of Edvard and Nina Grieg, Horn Book,* December, 1969, pp. 683-84.

■ For More Information See

PERIODICALS

Bulletin of the Center for Children's Books, September, 1966, p. 14.

Horn Book, October, 1968, p. 570.

New York Times Book Review, May 10, 1994, Part 2, p. 10; June 23, 1968, p. 22.

Times Literary Supplement, December 9, 1965, p. 1147.*

DUNNE, Marie
  See CLARK, Ann Nolan

E–F

ENGELMANN, Kim (V.) 1959-

■ Personal

Born July 30, 1959, in Boston, MA; daughter of James E. (a professor) and Arlene T. (Carr) Loder; married Timothy Charles Engelmann (a psychologist), June 20, 1981; children: Christopher Charles, Julie Kim. *Education:* Barnard College, Columbia University, B.A., 1981; Princeton Seminary, Master of Divinity, 1984; Boston University School of Theology, D.Min., 1993. *Religion:* Presbyterian. *Hobbies and other interests:* "I enjoy the outdoors and love to hike alone or with the family. Skiing, ice dancing, and canoeing are also favorite activities."

■ Addresses

Home—Pennsylvania.

■ Career

Minister and writer. First Presbyterian Church of Springfield, NJ, director of Christian education, 1984-85; Federated Church of Ashland, MA, minister of Christian education, 1985-89; Sudbury Presbyterian Church, Sudbury, MA, parish associate, 1989; Trinitarian Congregational Church, North Andover, MA, associate pastor, 1989-93; Lawrence General Hospital, Lawrence, MA, Protestant chaplain, 1991-92; Navigators Press, Colorado Springs, CO, author of young adult fiction, 1993—; First Presbyterian Church, Strasburg, PA, part-time minister of Christian education, 1995—. Lazarus House Ministries, coordinator of meals for the homeless, 1989-93; Greater Lawrence Council of Churches, "Moments with the Master" radio broadcast, regular speaker, 1989-93. Member of Donegal Presbytery (Missions Committee).

■ Writings

"JOONA TRILOGY"; YOUNG ADULT FANTASY

Journey to Joona, Navigators Press, 1995.
Defenders of Joona, Navigators Press, 1995.

The Crown of Joona, Navigators Press, 1995.

OTHER

Contributor of articles to periodicals, including *Baptist Leader, Monday Morning,* and *Guideposts.*

■ Work in Progress

Adventures in Thrusselylen, a novel for young adults featuring a winged horse named Annabelle.

■ Sidelights

Kim Engelmann is the author of the "Joona" trilogy, which follows the adventures of three children in a magical land populated by swans. In the first book, *Journey to Joona,* young Margaret and her friends meet a beautiful swan named Laurel who tells them about the swan world, Joona. The children accompany Laurel to Joona, only to find that an evil swan named Malcolm is threatening to take over the land and keep other swans out. They must assist the good swans in their battle against Malcolm and his selfish followers. The story continues in the sequel, *Defenders of Joona,* in which the swan kingdom is invaded and Margaret and her friends must help the swans regain their freedom. In *The Crown of Joona,* the third book in the trilogy, the action moves back to Earth as an evil swan named Sebastian begins practicing his dark magic there. Margaret and her friends face life-threatening danger in their efforts to thwart Sebastian's plot. In a review of *Journey to Joona* for *Library Journal,* Henry Carrigan Jr. referred to the book as a morality tale focusing on "the cosmic struggle between God's messengers and the messengers of Satan."

The religious undertones of Engelmann's fiction for young adults come from her extensive work in the Presbyterian Church. The subject of her doctoral thesis was pastoral care for hospitalized children, and her education also included many courses in counseling adults and adolescents. Since completing her education, Engelmann has directed Christian education and led worship in several churches. She explained her feelings

Laurel the talking swan seeks the help of three children to fight evil Sebastian, who blocks the way to Joona, the swans' paradise, in the first book of Kim V. Engelmann's trilogy.

about the role of the church in today's society to *SATA:* "Community is virtually extinct in American society. Loneliness is on the rise as long-term friendships are on the decline. The average length of stay for a family in any one location today is three to five years. Lack of roots and significant relationships with others have been for many replaced by an overload of activities in an effort to fill the voids created by our dehumanizing culture. Locked doors, indifference to the stranger, fear of being 'taken advantage of,' and unwillingness to risk in relationships for long-term gain are warning signs that our culture is suffering from deep fragmentation, loss of identity, and a pervasive anomie that resurfaces each time we realize that, despite all our activities and frenzied schedules, we are still searching for vision and purpose.

"It is essential that the church be on the cutting edge of these issues, continuing to define humanity's chief end, which is 'to glorify God and enjoy him forever.' This necessarily implies an openness to the stranger, a movement toward Christian community in the church of Christ, and a commitment to spiritual renewal as we recover our deep pietistic roots that call us into the most meaningful relationship of all—the relationship with Jesus Christ our risen Lord. He it is that gives vision and purpose to the human life and fills the voids of our transient existence with his eternal presence. From this reality springs the joy of community and the very awesome realization that we are called and empowered by the Holy Spirit to bring God's kingdom to earth in whatever way God moves us. This mission of the church is the hope for a world lost to the dehumanizing trends of our fallen nature."

■ Works Cited

Carrigan, Henry, Jr., *Library Journal,* February 1, 1995, p. 64.*

*   *   *

FIDLER, Kathleen (Annie) 1899-1980

■ Personal

Born August 10, 1899, in Coalville, Leicestershire, England; died August, 1980; daughter of Francis and Sarah H. B. (Ellison) Fidler; married James Hutchison Goldie (a banker), 1930 (deceased); children: Agnes, Francis. *Education:* St. Mary's College, Bangor, North Wales, teacher's certificate, 1920. *Politics:* Conservative. *Religion:* Presbyterian. *Hobbies and other interests:* Gardening and theatre.

■ Career

Writer. Scot Lane Evening Institute, Wigan, Lancashire, England, headmistress, 1924-30; St. Paul's Girls' School, Wigan, headmistress, 1925-30; Authors' Panel for Schools Broadcasting in Scotland, scriptwriter, 1938-62. Speaker on writing at libraries and schools. *Member:* Society of Authors, PEN (Scottish branch), Soroptimist Club.

■ Awards, Honors

Moscow Film Festival award, 1967, for *Flash the Sheep Dog* (screenplay); *Haki the Shetland Pony* was listed as one of Child Study Association's children's book of the year, 1970.

■ Writings

FOR CHILDREN

The Borrowed Garden, Lutterworth, 1944.
St. Jonathan's in the Country: A Sequel to "The Borrowed Garden," illustrated by Charles Koolman, Lutterworth, 1945, revised edition, 1952.
Fingal's Ghost (based on radio play), John Crowther (London), 1945.
The White Cockade Passes, Lutterworth, 1947.
The Mysterious Mr. Simister, Lutterworth, 1947.
Mr. Simister Appears Again, illustrated by Margaret Horder, Lutterworth, 1948.
Mr. Simister Is Unlucky, illustrated by Margaret Horder, Lutterworth, 1949.
Guest Castle, Lutterworth, 1949.

I Rode with the Covenanters, illustrated by E. Boyce Uden, Lutterworth, 1950.

(With Lennox Milne) *Stories from Scottish Heritage* (three volumes), Chambers, 1951.

The White-Starred Hare and Other Stories, illustrated by A. H. Watson, Lutterworth, 1951.

To the White North: The Story of Sir John Franklin, Lutterworth, 1952.

Fedora the Donkey, illustrated by Iris Gillespie, Lutterworth, 1952.

The Stallion from the Sea, Lutterworth, 1953.

Pete, Pam and Jim, the Investigators, illustrated by Lunt Roberts, Lutterworth, 1954.

The Bank House Twins, illustrated by Frank Bellamy, Lutterworth, 1955.

The Droving Lad, illustrated by Geoffrey Whittam, Lutterworth, 1955.

The Man Who Gave Away Millions: The Story of Andrew Carnegie, Lutterworth, 1955, Roy, 1956.

Mr. Punch's Cap, illustrated by Shirley Hughes, Lutterworth, 1956.

Lanterns over the Lune, illustrated by David Walsh, Lutterworth, 1958.

(With Jack Gillespie) *The McGills at Mystery Farm,* illustrated by Leo Davy, Lutterworth, 1958.

(With Jack Gillespie) *More Adventures of the McGills,* illustrated by Hodgson, Lutterworth, 1959.

Escape in Darkness, illustrated by Geoffrey Whittam, Lutterworth, 1961.

The Little Ship Dog, illustrated by Antony Maitland, Lutterworth, 1963.

The Desperate Journey, illustrated by Michael Charlton, Lutterworth, 1964.

New Lamps for Old (reader), Oliver & Boyd, 1965.

Flash the Sheep Dog, illustrated by Antony Maitland, Lutterworth, 1965.

Police Dog, illustrated by Sheila Rose, Lutterworth, 1966.

Adventure Underground (reader), Oliver & Boyd, 1966.

Forest Fire (reader), Oliver & Boyd, 1966.

The Boy with the Bronze Axe, illustrated by Edward Mortelmans, Chatto, Boyd & Oliver, 1968.

Haki the Shetland Pony, illustrated by Victor Ambrus, Lutterworth, 1968, Rand McNally, 1970.

Treasure of Ebba, illustrated by Trevor Ridley, Lutterworth, 1968.

Mountain Rescue Dog, illustrated by Mary Russon, Lutterworth, 1969.

School at Sea, illustrated by David Grice, Epworth (London), 1970.

The Gold of Fast Castle, illustrated by Trevor Ridley, Lutterworth, 1970.

Flodden Field, September 9, 1513, illustrated by F. R. Exell, Lutterworth, 1970.

The Thames in Story, Epworth, 1971.

Diggers of Lost Treasure, Epworth, 1972.

The '45 and Culloden, July 1745 to April 1746, illustrated by F. R. Exell, Lutterworth, 1973.

Stories of Old Inns, Epworth, 1973.

Pirate and Admiral: The Story of John Paul Jones, illustrated by Bernard Brett, Lutterworth, 1974.

Turk, the Border Collie, illustrated by Mary Dinsdale, Lutterworth, 1975.

(With Ian Morrison) *Wrecks, Wreckers and Rescuers,* Lutterworth, 1976.

The Railway Runaways, illustrated by Terry Gabbey, Blackie & Son, 1977.

The Lost Cave, Blackie & Son, 1978.

Seal Story, illustrated by Douglas Phillips, Lutterworth, 1979.

Pablos and the Bull, Blackie & Son, 1979.

The Ghosts of Sandeel Bay, illustrated by Annabel Large, Blackie & Son, 1981.

"BRYDON FAMILY" SERIES

The Brydons at Smuggler's Creek, illustrated by H. Tilden Reeves, Lutterworth, 1946.

More Adventures with the Brydons, illustrated by Victor Bertoglio, Lutterworth, 1947, new edition with new illustrations, 1952, revised edition, Knight Books, 1971.

The Brydons Go Camping, illustrated by A. H. Watson, Lutterworth, 1948.

The Brydons in Summer, illustrated by A. H. Watson, Lutterworth, 1949, revised edition, Knight Books, 1971.

The Brydons Do Battle, illustrated by A. H. Watson, Lutterworth, 1949.

The Brydons Look for Trouble, illustrated by T. R. Freeman, Lutterworth, 1950.

The Brydons in a Pickle, illustrated by T. R. Freeman, Lutterworth, 1950.

Surprises for the Brydons, illustrated by T. R. Freeman, Lutterworth, 1950.

The Brydons Get Things Going, illustrated by T. R. Freeman, Lutterworth, 1951, revised edition, Knight Books, 1971.

The Brydons Hunt for Treasure, illustrated by T. R. Freeman, Lutterworth, 1951.

The Brydons Catch Queer Fish, illustrated by T. R. Freeman, Lutterworth, 1952.

The Brydons Stick at Nothing, illustrated by T. R. Freeman, Lutterworth, 1952.

The Brydons Abroad, illustrated by T. R. Freeman, Lutterworth, 1953.

The Brydons on the Broads, illustrated by T. R. Freeman, Lutterworth, 1955, revised edition, Knight Books, 1971.

Challenge to the Brydons, illustrated by T. R. Freeman, Lutterworth, 1956.

The Brydons at Blackpool, illustrated by T. R. Freeman, Lutterworth, 1960.

The Brydons Go Canoeing, illustrated by T. R. Freeman, Lutterworth, 1963.

"HERITAGE OF BRITAIN" SERIES

Tales of the North Country, illustrated by Jack Matthew, Lutterworth, 1952.

Tales of London, illustrated by Douglas Relf, Lutterworth, 1953.

Tales of the Midlands, illustrated by Douglas Relf, Lutterworth, 1954.

Tales of Scotland, illustrated by Douglas Relf, Lutterworth, 1956.

Look to the West: Tales of Liverpool, illustrated by Henry Toothill, Lutterworth, 1957.

Tales of the Islands, illustrated by Douglas Relf, Lutterworth, 1959.

Tales of Pirates and Castaways, illustrated by Charles Keeping, Lutterworth, 1960.

Tales of the West Country, illustrated by Charles Keeping, Lutterworth, 1961.

True Tales of Treasure, illustrated by W. F. Phillipps, Lutterworth, 1962.

Tales of the South Country, illustrated by W. F. Phillipps, Lutterworth, 1962.

True Tales of Escapes, illustrated by W. F. Phillipps, Lutterworth, 1965.

True Tales of Mystery, illustrated by Bonar Dunlop, Lutterworth, 1967.

True Tales of Castles, illustrated by Imre Hofbauer, Lutterworth, 1969.

"DEAN FAMILY" SERIES; ILLUSTRATED BY REG FORSTER

The Deans Move In, Lutterworth, 1953.

The Deans Solve a Mystery, Lutterworth, 1954.

The Deans Follow a Clue, Lutterworth, 1954.

The Deans Defy Danger, Lutterworth, 1955.

The Deans Dive for Treasure, Lutterworth, 1956.

The Deans to the Rescue, Lutterworth, 1957.

The Deans' Lighthouse Adventure, Lutterworth, 1959.

The Deans and Mr. Popple, Lutterworth, 1960.

The Deans' Dutch Adventure, Lutterworth, 1962.

PLAYS

Flash the Sheep Dog (screenplay; based on book of same title), British Broadcasting Corp. (BBC), 1967.

Haki the Shetland Pony (teleplay; based on book of same title), BBC-TV, 1971.

Also author of numerous radio plays for the BBC-Radio program "Children's Hour" and for BBC-Radio schools' programs.

■ Sidelights

In a writing career that spanned four decades, Kathleen Fidler was the author of a host of stories that transformed the everyday into interesting books for young readers. Whether uncovering the past in tales of archeological discoveries and fictions based upon what such finds revealed about history, or recounting modern-day adventures featuring young people and animals exploring the world around them, Fidler's books were full of her enthusiasm for the people and places of her native England. Alan Edwin Day commented in an essay in *Twentieth-Century Children's Writers* that Fidler "portrays ordinary people caught up in slightly extraordinary circumstances, in exciting but not unduly perilous adventures.... The unlikely attains credibility by contrast with its mundane surroundings."

Animal stories have always been popular with children, and Fidler contributed to the list of good books about animals with titles that included *Police Dog, Mountain Rescue Dog, Turk, the Border Collie, Seal Story, Flash the Sheep Dog,* and *Haki the Shetland Pony.* In *Flash the Sheep Dog* the main canine—a hard-working sheep dog

Adam and his colt, Haki, join an English circus after winning first prize at the pony sale in Scotland in Kathleen Fidler's 1968 tale. (Illustration by Victor Ambrus from *Haki the Shetland Pony.*)

living on a farm—has, like each of Fidler's animal characters, a matter-of-fact approach to life and behaves in a convincingly dog-like fashion. The book was later made into an award-winning movie of the same name; Fidler would base the 1975 novel *Turk, the Border Collie* on the actual dog that performed the role of Flash in that film. In Fidler's story, Turk leaves the farm where he has been sent after the death of his master and encounters several adventures along the country roads and bustling riverways he travels on his way back to the place where he was born.

In another of Fidler's books that she later adapted for film—*Haki the Shetland Pony*—a fifteen-year-old boy named Adam and Haki, the pony he has trained to do tricks since it was a foal, are the main characters. When Adam and Haki win an award for their performance at a local fair, the talented pony attracts the attention of Mr. Wiggins, the owner of a circus on tour throughout Scotland. Mr. Wiggins offers to buy Haki and ends up hiring Adam too; the boy and his pony are able to stay together and explore the world while travelling with the circus troupe. Fidler's *Seal Story* introduces readers to the island of Lindisfarne, the home of nine-year-old

Dan. After he discovers a stranded seal cub near the island shore, Dan cares for the small animal through babyhood, feeding it condensed milk, playing it music on his mouth-organ, and teaching it to swim and fish. Finally, with the help of his grandfather, the seal becomes old enough to return to the sea. A *Junior Bookshelf* reviewer praises *Seal Story* as "a model of how things should be done," adding that "Fidler has a strong feeling for the landscape and its wild creatures."

Tales of animals are but one of the ways Fidler expressed her love for people and for the beautiful British countryside. She also wrote several books about British history in both fiction and nonfiction genres. In her "Heritage of Britain" series, which includes *Tales of London, Tales of Pirates and Castaways,* and *Tales of the West Country,* Fidler collected stories, legends, and anecdotes about different parts of historic England. Her story *The Desperate Journey* focuses on a nineteenth-century Scottish family that loses its home when their land is confiscated. The family moves to the dirty industrial city of Glasgow, but there only the children, Kirsty and Davie, can find work in the mills, forcing the family to live in poverty. Kirsty and Davie's parents finally decide to risk everything; they join the waves of emigrants who leave their homeland and sail across the sea to the Canadian wilderness in search of independence and a better life during the beginning of Britain's industrial era. *Flodden Field, September 9, 1513* is Fidler's description of the Battle of Flodden, in which the English army so roundly defeated an invading Scottish force under King James IV that the Scots would not attack England for another thirty years. A *Times Literary Supplement* reviewer calls *Flodden Field* "an unbiased account enlivened by [the author's] eye for the interesting anecdote." This book was followed by *The '45 and Culloden, July 1745 to April 1746,* Fidler's story of the famous battle led by Scotland's Bonny Prince Charlie in his move to win the crown of England. In the area of history, the author's enthusiasm for her subject is contagious. Alison Prince refers to Fidler's *The Thames in Story* as "a really un-put-downable history book" in a review in the *New Statesman.*

During her background study for *The Thames in Story,* Fidler and four of her grandchildren went for a cruise on the Thames River, which flows through the city of London. "One, aged eight, fell in, but bravely swam out herself," the author later recalled for *SATA.* "She had only learned to swim that year!" In the course of research for her other books, Fidler travelled throughout the United States, western and southern Europe, Scandinavia, and North Africa, trips that proved to be less eventful but equally as inspiring. In 1969 she observed an archaeological dig at Coldingham Priory in Scotland. "I visited Hadrian's Wall, the great Roman wall stretching across the north of England, to watch school children aged thirteen to fourteen making a week's supervised 'dig' at Vindolanda.... I was just *watching,* with a view to making it a background for a book.... Imagine our excitement when, in the first ten minutes's dig, three boys turned up a beautiful small bronze eagle, perhaps once part of the accoutrements of a Roman soldier, and shortly afterwards three girls turned up the handle and top of a large amphora that had come from southern Gaul and had once held olive oil, dated around 280 A.D."

Her lifelong fascination with uncovering the past served as a foundation for much of Fidler's writing. A visit to the Neolithic settlement of Skara Brae—a site on one of the Orkney islands off the northeast coast of Scotland that was uncovered by a storm in the 1850s—proved to be the inspiration for *The Boy with the Bronze Axe.* In this novel for younger readers, a boy named Tenko floats from his home to a treeless island where he makes friends with Berno and Kali, a brother and sister who live there in the Stone-Age village of Skara Brae. Arriving on this northern island—after leaving his own people and their more advanced culture—Tenko introduces Skara Brae's amazed residents to the technology of the Bronze Age with his sturdy bronze axe and his wealth of practical knowledge. The villagers begin changing their ways in light of this new technology until a storm comes and the village must be abandoned to the destruction of wind and sea. Fidler brings readers back to modern times in *The Lost Cave,* as four teenagers stumble upon Bronze-Age artifacts and drawings while exploring underground caverns in Yorkshire. But readers are drawn once again into the past as the ancient island-city of Crete becomes the setting for *Pablos and the Bull.* After a young boy and his pet bull are captured by pirates from their home on Knossos, they are brought to the city of Crete and sold as slaves. While leaving Crete in an effort to save the black bull from being put in the bullring to fight more powerful and aggressive beasts in an upcoming citywide contest, Pablos and his bull escape a violent earthquake that destroys much of the beautiful city. "Fidler's experienced hand in description has made the most of the natural disaster and its effect on the effete Cretan court," comments Margery Fisher in *Growing Point,* "and she has given her two central characters a sturdy courage and independence which helps them to fit plausibly into the ancient world where Pablos, with his knowledge of cattle-breeding, finds a logical future."

As Fidler's experience broadened so did the scope of her work: from entertaining adventure tales of animals and young people, she went on to explorations in the areas of archeology, history, and biography. In *Diggers of Lost Treasure* she combined her love of archeology, biography, and historical fiction to recount the life stories of two famous nineteenth-century archaeologists: British politician Sir Austen Henry Layard, who was active in excavations in Iraq's Tigris River valley, and Heinrich Schliemann, a German businessman who left his desk job and set out to find the remains of the lost city of Troy, the destruction of which was described in Homer's *Iliad.* A more modern form of archeological exploration is discussed in *Wrecks, Wreckers and Rescuers,* which Fidler co-wrote with Dr. Ian Morrison. This book introduces readers to eleven tragedies that occurred off the coasts of the British islands and recounts the investigations of marine archaeologists and salvage operations directors, as well as the development of sea-rescue efforts and advances in aquatic life-saving equipment over the years.

In addition to her realistic accounts of past and present events, Fidler also wrote several books of imaginative fiction for young readers. She created several series of books, including the "Brydon Family" series, which began as a radio program for the BBC before she adapted it as a set of novels for children. "The 'Brydon Family' series came out of my own happy family life," she once told *SATA*. Fidler introduces readers to another fun-loving family in her "Dean Family" series.

In *The Railway Runaways* rambunctious eight-year-old twins James and Jenny impulsively decide that they are going to see young Queen Victoria *and* take a ride on a train. They run away from their home in Edinburgh, Scotland, and, while they never reach Buckingham Palace to visit the Queen, they do get to ride on a train and meet many interesting people during their afternoon escapade. Another story for and about young people is *The Ghosts of Sandeel Bay*. It is a mystery story written in the classic vein, and Fidler posits a group of vacationing children in the middle of a secret smuggling operation. The seaswept Scottish coast provides the perfect dramatic backdrop for the story as the four children, who don't take to each other at first, eventually pull together and work as a team to outwit some local criminals. "The plot is sound and exciting, as one would expect from an author of Kathleen Fidler's standing," Margaret Banerjee notes in *British Book News*.

Throughout her long career, Fidler was praised for her admirable and likeable main characters, her well-researched, tightly constructed plots, and for the love for both everyday occurrences and mysteries of the past that she successfully wove throughout her books. Through her writing, especially in the area of British history, she opened up the eyes and imaginations of young readers to the riches hidden in the world around them.

■ Works Cited

Banerjee, Margaret, review of *The Ghosts of Sandeel Bay, British Book News,* autumn, 1981, p. 21.

Day, Alan Edwin, "Katheen Fidler," in *Twentieth-Century Children's Writers,* 4th edition, edited by Laura Standley Berger, St. James Press, 1995, pp. 339-41.

Fisher, Margery, "Past Tense," *Growing Point,* July, 1980, p. 3721.

Review of *Flodden Field, September 9, 1513, Times Literary Supplement,* October 22, 1971, p. 1344.

Prince, Alison, "Real Things," *New Statesman,* November 12, 1971, p. 667.

Review of *Seal Story, Junior Bookshelf,* December, 1979, p. 334.

■ For More Information See

PERIODICALS

Booklist, April 1, 1971, p. 663.

Growing Point, January, 1976, p. 2789; July, 1979, p. 3558; March, 1982, p. 4030.

Junior Bookshelf, February, 1976, p. 42; October, 1977, pp. 286-87; October, 1978, p. 265; December, 1980, p. 291; August, 1981, p. 158.

Publishers Weekly, September 28, 1970, p. 80.

School Library Journal, December 15, 1970, p. 4348.

Times Literary Supplement, December 9, 1965, p. 1134; June 6, 1968, p. 581; December 8, 1972, p. 1500.*

*   *   *

FILDERMAN, Diane E(lizabeth) 1959- (Diane Harris-Filderman)

■ Personal

Born August 22, 1959, in Washington, DC; daughter of Robert H. (a business owner) and Lucille V. (a homemaker; maiden name, Smith) Harris; married Franklyn T. Filderman (a business owner), December 9, 1982; children: Jordan, Marissa. *Education:* Kent State University, B.A.

■ Addresses

Home and office—10664 Quarterstaff Rd., Columbia, MD 21044.

■ Career

Children's book author.

DIANE E. FILDERMAN

■ Writings

Mickey Steals the Show, May Davenport Publishers, 1995.

■ Work in Progress

Two sequels to *Mickey Steals the Show* have been completed; seeking publisher for two other manuscripts for picture books; working on an adult novel.

■ Sidelights

Diane E. Filderman told *SATA:* "I have always had an inner need and desire to be creative. Writing has become a great outlet for that desire. It has been encouraging for me to see my children enjoy my stories. I hope that many other children will enjoy them as well. In a very real sense, my children motivated me to write my first book. I have always read with them and wanted to give them a story I thought they would enjoy. I have been compelled to write ever since I began that first book.

"I am grateful that I have had the time, energy, and desire to write. I feel blessed by the ideas and story lines that make their way into my mind. It would be wonderful to be able to continue expressing my creativity through writing and perhaps other artistic areas. To really have a career in this field would be something truly exciting."

*   *   *

FISK, Nicholas
See HIGGINBOTTOM, David

*   *   *

FRANCK, Eddie
See COOKE, Frank E.

*   *   *

FRANK, Anne(lies Marie) 1929-1945

■ Personal

Born June 12, 1929, in Frankfurt am Main, Germany; died of typhoid fever and malnutrition, March, 1945, in the Bergen-Belsen concentration camp, Germany; daughter of Otto (a banker and business owner) and Edith Frank.

■ Writings

Het Achterhuis (diary; title means "The House Behind"), foreword by Annie Romein-Verschoor, Contact (Amsterdam), 1947, translation from Dutch by B. M. Mooyaart-Doubleday published as *Diary of a Young Girl,* introduction by Eleanor Roosevelt, Doubleday, 1952; with preface by

George Stevens, Pocket Books, 1958; published as *Anne Frank: The Diary of a Young Girl,* Washington Square Press, 1963; published as *The Diary of Anne Frank,* foreword by Storm Jameson, illustrated by Elisabeth Trimby, Heron Books, 1973; published as *The Diary of Anne Frank: The Critical Edition,* edited by David Barnouw and Gerrold van der Stroom, translated by Arnold J. Pomerans and B. M. Mooyaart-Doubleday, introduction by Harry Paape, Gerrold van der Stroom, and David Barnouw, Doubleday, 1989; published as *The Diary of a Young Girl: The Definitive Edition,* edited by Otto H. Frank and Mirjam Pressler, translated by Susan Massotty, Doubleday, 1995.

The Works of Anne Frank, introduction by Ann Birstein and Alfred Kazin, Doubleday, 1959.

Tales from the House Behind: Fables, Personal Reminiscences and Short Stories, translation from original Dutch manuscript *Verhalen rondom het Achterhuis* by H. H. B. Mosberg and Michel Mok, illustrated by Peter Spier, World's Work, 1962.

Anne Frank's Tales from the Secret Annex (includes portions previously published in *The Works of Anne Frank* and *Tales from the House Behind* and translations from the original manuscript *Verhaaltjes en gebeurtenissen uit het Achterhuis*), by Ralph Manheim and Michel Mok, Doubleday, 1983.

The diary has been translated from the original Dutch into about sixty languages, including German, French, Italian, Spanish, Russian, Arabic, and Polish.

■ Adaptations

Anne Frank: Diary of a Young Girl was adapted by Frances Goodrich and Albert Hackett for a two-act stage play titled *Diary of Anne Frank,* first produced in New York in 1955 and published in 1956 as *The Diary of Anne Frank Dramatized by Frances Goodrich and Albert Hackett* by Random House with a foreword by Brooks Atkinson. The diary was also adapted for the film *The Diary of Anne Frank,* released by Twentieth-Century Fox in 1959 (starring Millie Perkins in the title role), and for a television movie of the same name (starring Melissa Gilbert) broadcast in 1980. Selections of the diary were read by Julie Harris for a recording by Spoken Arts, 1974, and by Claire Bloom for a recording by Caedmon, 1977.

■ Sidelights

Through her diary, Anne Frank's life has become a metaphor, a symbol for the six million Jews who were murdered in concentration camps during World War II, as well as for all people persecuted or discriminated against for their beliefs, their race, or any other reason given at that time or since. Today, the Franks' hiding place in Amsterdam is a site that about six hundred thousand people visit every year; her life story has been turned into a highly succesful Broadway play, a movie, and television fare. Not quite sixteen when she died, Anne Frank continues to live in the hearts and minds of millions of people worldwide. But beyond the name, beyond the symbolic stature is the fact that Anne Frank was a writer—a diarist and creator of short stories and fables. After all, if Frank had not turned her hand to writing in her diary, the world would never have heard of her. It was in a simple poetry album—often used by girls at the time—that she received for her thirteenth birthday that Frank began her musings: "Writing in a diary is a really strange experience for someone like me," she wrote on June 20, 1942. "Not only because I've never written anything before, but also because it seems to me that later on neither I nor anyone else will be interested in the musings of a thirteen-year-old schoolgirl." But she was wrong. Her subsequent musings have become "a classic," according to Karen D. Wood and Susan G. Avett in *Language Arts.*

In July of 1942, about a month after Frank received her diary, she and her family, along with four other Jews, went into hiding from the Nazis. Living in the cramped attic space above her father's business office in Amsterdam, Frank's coming of age is recorded in the pages of her diary. In Anne Frank's diary the reader comes face to face with the inner thoughts of the adolescent as she charts her own development—warts and all. The diary wonderfully describes "the conversion of a child into a person," as the poet John Berryman noted in *The Freedom of the Poet.* Meyer Levin, writing in the *New York Times Book Review,* similarly commented that Frank explores the "drama of puberty." For two years Frank kept the diary until she and her family were betrayed and arrested and sent to the concentration camps. But most of the diary was saved and later published in scores of editions and is best known to readers of English under the titles *The Diary of Anne Frank* or *Diary of a Young Girl.* Millions have wanted to read Frank's "unbosomings": over twenty-five million copies of the book have been sold worldwide in about sixty different languages; at one point it was the twelfth most borrowed book in United Kingdom libraries and remains a staple in schools decades after its initial publication in 1954. It is in the diary that the reader discovers the flesh and blood Anne Frank, not the metaphoric Frank, symbol of the Holocaust.

Anne Frank was born in Frankfurt am Main in 1929, the year of the economic crash in the United States and the onset of a global economic depression. Anne was the second daughter in the family; her sister Margot was three years her senior. The Franks, upper middle class and assimilated Jews, were well aware of the new direction Germany was taking. The father, Otto Frank, had served on the western front during World War I in an artillery regiment, attaining the rank of lieutenant. He had also spent time abroad, both in the United States and in the Netherlands. As a member of the Frank banking family, he had lived a rather privileged life, but was not an unrealistic man. Otto Frank saw the writing on the wall with the election of Hitler in 1933 to the office of chancellor. But he understood even before then that it was time for his family to move when the family bank was falsely denounced in a clearly anti-Semitic lawsuit against Otto Frank's brother—which was later proven unfounded. Although the allegations

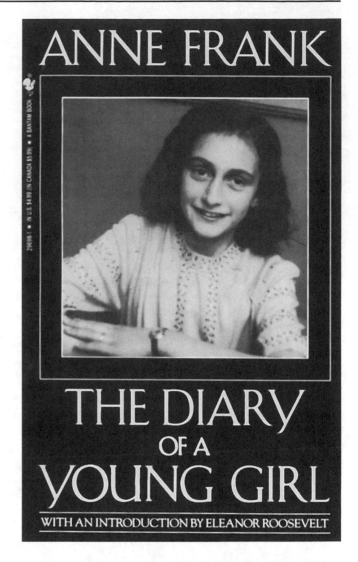

Editions of Anne Frank's diary, like this 1993 paperback, have remained in print since the late 1940s, keeping the personal and often insightful reflections of the spunky teenage girl alive for future generations.

were false, the bank suffered financially. Fortunately, Otto Frank managed to secure a Dutch branch of a pectin company and moved the family to Amsterdam.

Anne Frank was only four when the family moved from Germany to Holland, and she quickly picked up the new language and made new friends. She attended a Montessori school and was known as an average student, very sociable and fun-loving to the point of being prankish. Meanwhile, Otto Frank had expanded his pectin import business to include herbs, had a work force of eleven, and a combined office and warehouse on the Prinsengracht Canal. The coming of war in 1939 did not change things drastically in Amsterdam—that came only after the German occupation of the nation in 1940 and the "Aryanization" of businesses and social life. Otto Frank's business was signed over to a non-Jew—though he was still the boss and owner. Anne Frank and her sister Margot were forced to attend a Jewish lyceum, which they attended for the next two years. A close friend from Frank's school days, Lies Goslar Pick, later described Frank in *McCall's* as "a mischief-maker who annoyed the neighbors with her pranks and continually was in hot water at school for her conduct." She was nicknamed "Miss Chatterbox" and "Miss Quack-Quack," and was no stranger to teacher reprimands for talking in class.

This bubbly, joking, and playful exterior, however, belied a more introspective nature. Though she had numerous girlfriends and male admirers, Frank later confided to her diary, "[On] the surface I seem to have everything, except my one true friend. All I think about when I'm with friends is having a good time. I can't bring myself to talk about anything but ordinary everyday things. We don't seem to be able to get any closer, and that's the problem. Maybe it's my fault that we don't confide in each other. In any case, that's just how things are, and unfortunately they're not liable to change. This is why I've started the diary." She quickly hit upon a literary device: "To enhance the image of this long-awaited friend in my imagination, I don't want to jot down the facts in this diary the way most people would do, but I want the diary to be my friend, and I'm going to call this friend *Kitty*." Over the course of the

Photographed in Merwedeplein, Amsterdam, Anne and a girlfriend enjoy happier days before the Nazi occupation of 1942. (From *The Diary of Anne Frank: The Critical Edition*.)

next two years, Frank recorded her impressions, her ups and downs, fears and loves in letters she wrote to Kitty, the name of a fictional character in a popular Dutch novel for girls at the time (initially, she had written to several different characters in the novel, but she eventually settled on just one).

The pragmatic Otto Frank, wary of the situation by the summer of 1942, converted attic space in a rear annex to the company warehouse in case the family needed to go into hiding. Such an eventuality was soon thrust upon them: Margot was summoned for "working service" in Germany, which was just a hidden way of saying concentration camp, and the family quickly moved into the annex, the "house behind" that Frank later titled her diary. In addition to the four Franks, there was also Mr. and Mrs. Van Pels and their fifteen-year-old son Peter, and Fritz Pfeffer, a dentist. These eight people were supplied with food and news by Johannes Kleiman and Victor Kugler (who were officially the owners of Frank's business), Hermine (Miep) Gies-Santrouschitz, and Elly (Beb) Voskuijl. Another friend, Jan Gies, helped to secure their connection to the Dutch resistance. For two years these eight lived in the pressure cooker of the rooms in the secret annex. Their movements were greatly restricted both day and night: they could not open windows or leave the house, could talk only in whispers, and were loathe to use water or toilet facilities during those hours when strangers were in the warehouse. "We're as still as baby mice," Frank wrote in October 1, 1942. "Who would have guessed three months ago that quicksilver Anne would have to sit so quietly for hours on end, and what's more, that she could?" The diary was Frank's salvation, her quiet time activity, and along with the diary she also wrote part of a novel, short stories, and fables.

Daily life in the annex took up many diary entries. She faithfully recorded daily routines. She was also a quick study in character delineation, drawing portraits of the other inhabitants of the annex and of the strained relationships that inevitably develop in such close quarters. Into the diary also went Frank's own concerns and dreams, even her love for Peter Van Pels ("van Daan" in the diary) and their first clumsy kiss. She was honest, as well, about the difficult relations she and her mother had and was as critical of her own motives and actions as she was of others. And, too, there are events from the outside world that the group hears of: the invasion of Normandy and rising hopes; the continual fear of discovery. Never does the diary fall into the bald retelling of facts—the very thing she set out to avoid. As Levin pointed out, the "unfolding psychological drama of a girl's growth, mingled with the physical danger of the group ... frees Anne's book from the horizontal effect of most diaries." Frank's diary is rendered in dramatic form, constructed like a novel with rising action, tension, and denouement.

Anne Frank also grew into a young woman in the pages of her diary. It was an incredibly compressed journey, and along the way she discovered that she was an author, that what she wanted to do once the insanity of war was ended was to write books. She also realized that her diary would be her first book. Listening to the Dutch news from London in the spring of 1944, she heard it suggested—some interpreters of the diary believe she was listening to a speech by the Dutch Cabinet Minister of Education of the exiled government—that there should be a collection of letters and diaries after the war. "Just imagine how interesting it would be if I were to publish a novel about the Secret Annex," she wrote to Kitty. "The title alone would make people think it was a detective story. Seriously, though, ten years after the war people would find it very amusing to read how we lived, what we ate and what we talked about as Jews in hiding." About this time, Frank began rewriting the diary—from its beginning up to the entries from the spring of 1944—on loose-leaf paper for planned publication, thus accounting for the two versions of the diary that exist.

Perhaps the most often quoted entry of Anne Frank's diary was written on July 15, 1944: "It's difficult in times like these: ideals, dreams and cherished hopes rise within us, only to be crushed by grim reality. It's a wonder I haven't abandoned all my ideals, they seem so absurd and impractical, yet I cling to them because I still believe, in spite of everything, that people are truly good at heart. It's utterly impossible for me to build my life on a foundation of chaos, suffering and death. I see the world being slowly transformed into a wilderness, I hear the approaching thunder that, one day, will destroy us too, I feel the suffering of millions. And yet, when I look up at the sky, I somehow feel that everything will change for the better, that this cruelty too shall end, that peace and tranquility will return once more. In the meantime, I must hold on to my ideals. Perhaps the day will come when I'll be able to realize them!"

But it was not to be. In early August the secret annex was betrayed and all eight of its occupants were arrested, along with Kleiman and Kugler, who were sent to concentration camps in Holland. The diary, along with Frank's other writings, however, was left behind and kept by Miep Gies in her desk until after the war. All eight Jews were sent from Westerbork to Auschwitz, where Mrs. Frank died, along with countless other Jews, "from hunger and exhaustion," as the afterword in the diary notes; and Peter Van Pels was gassed to death. Anne Frank and her sister were later sent to Bergen-Belsen where, two months before the German surrender, first Margot and then Anne died of what some suspect was typhoid fever. That the two sisters caught such a fatal disease was no accident, since the Germans starved their prisoners, gave them no adequate shelter or medical care, and, some strongly suspect, deliberately contaminated the camp's meager water supply. The only survivor among the eight was Otto Frank. After Auschwitz was liberated in January, 1945, by the Soviets, he returned to Amsterdam, anxious to find news of his daughters. Although Anne and Margot were still alive when he was released, the trip to Amsterdam was long and arduous, and by the time Otto Frank tracked down Anne and Margot it was too late. The very day he learned of their deaths, Anne's diary and other writings were given to him by Miep Gies.

It was two years before the diary was published in an edited version by Otto Frank. At first he was shocked and amazed at what he read: he, like many others, including former teachers, had never suspected that his daughter possessed such a deep, insightful mind. Also, the content of some of the entries concerning Anne's relationship with her mother and descriptions of her budding sexuality were thought to be of too private a nature to share. Typed copies of this edited diary made the rounds of friends in Amsterdam, who finally convinced Otto Frank to publish the diary. In 1947 Anne Frank's journal appeared as *Het Achterhuis,* "The House Behind." In its Dutch publication, the book received unanimously favorable reviews. Reading the diary in manuscript in 1946, Jan Romein wrote in the newspaper *Het Parool* (and later collected in *A Tribute to Anne Frank*) that "the Government Institute for War Documentation is in possession of about two hundred similar dairies, but it would amaze me if there was one among them as pure, as intelligent, and yet as human as [Anne

Frank's father, Otto Frank, shown here in a 1939 photograph, at first felt his daughter's diary was too personal for publication, but he later relented and allowed an edited version to go to press in 1947. (From *The Diary of Anne Frank: The Critical Edition.*)

Frank's]." By 1950 there was a German edition of the book that suffered somewhat from a translation that changed some of the text so as not to be too offensive to people in that country. Where movie footage of the atrocities of Auschwitz and other death camps brought only derision from the Germans, the German edition of Anne Frank's diary brought real remorse. In 1952 the first American edition appeared with an introduction by former First Lady Eleanor Roosevelt, who called it a "remarkable book.... Anne's diary is an appropriate monument to her fine spirit and to the spirits of those who have worked and are working still for peace." The novelist and historian Frederic Morton commented in the *New York Times Book Review* that the diary may well be "the single most enduring thing to be born during the entire course of the Nazi nightmare." Upon translation and publication of the diary in the Soviet Union, the novelist and poet Ilya Ehrenburg declared in *Chekhov, Stendhal, and Other Essays* that "one voice out of six million has reached us. It is only a child's voice, but it has great power, the power of sincerity, of humanity, and also of talent."

With the production of a stage play in 1955—which enjoyed a long, successful run during the 1960s and again with a new production that ran in the 1980s and '90s—and of a film four years later, the insights of Anne Frank's diary were brought to an even wider audience across the globe. But the diary was not without its detractors. Nazi and neo-Nazi groups in Europe and the United States, the same who claim the Holocaust never happened, have argued that the diaries are too historically aware, too literate in style, and too overtly sexual in certain passages for a girl of fourteen or fifteen to have written. The diaries are, they argue, obvious forgeries. Such criticisms were laid to rest by the 1989 edition of the book, which included exhaustive forensic and handwriting analyses on the notebooks and concluded that the diaries were indeed the work of Anne Frank.

In 1959 some of the collected stories and fables of Anne Frank were published as *The Works of Anne Frank*. Not surprisingly, these did not approach the depth or power of the diary. One story does stand out, "The Wise Old Dwarf," as a fictional evocation of Frank's own situation. The dwarf keeps a couple of elves confined in order to teach them a lesson. Commenting on the collected works, Morton noted that they show "Anne followed instinctively the best of all platitudes: Write whereof you know.... [She] was at her best when ... she poured out her own personality." More of her stories were collected in the 1962 *Tales from the House Behind: Fables, Personal Reminiscences and Short Stories,* which included the fragment of a novel, "Cady's Life," about a young woman struggling to recover from being struck by a car. G. B. Stern, writing in the introduction to the book, felt that "Cady's Life" "corroborates all one has said about [Anne Frank's] potential powers." Stern found a sense of character and of plot development, as well as a feeling for religion in this unfinished novel.

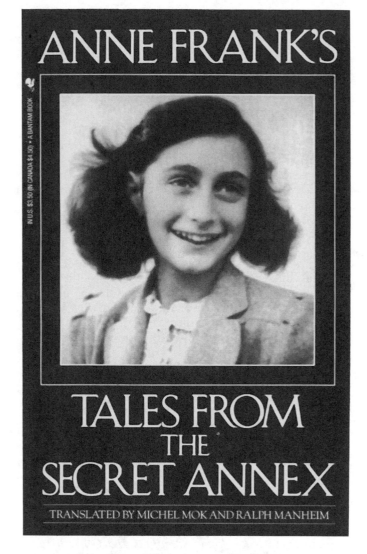

Here in the 1983 collection of Anne Frank's lesser-known writings are fables, short stories, an incomplete novel, and some previously unpublished parts of the world-famous diary.

With the death of Otto Frank in 1980, more of the Anne Frank archive was opened, for he had kept much of what he considered the less polished and perhaps objectionable material out of print. 1983's *Anne Frank's Tales from the Secret Annex* is a compilation of all of Anne Frank's known writings, including those she never intended for publication. Some of these pieces are girlish fantasies that, according to Jonathan Kirsch in the *Los Angeles Times Book Review,* "make [Frank] seem more human, and her passing even more tragic." Stefan Kanfer noted in *Time* that "most of the 30 pieces show a heartbreaking potential," and a critic in *Kirkus Reviews* commented that the best of the sketches "are the gently, sweetly optimistic fairy-tales and parables, occasionally heart-breaking in their earnest simplicity." Reviewing the book in *Horn Book,* Gregory Maguire wondered about the directions that Anne Frank's writing might have taken had she survived into adulthood. "It is not lost genius, however, that one mourns," he wrote, "but lost life of any sort."

Six years later, in 1989, *The Diary of Anne Frank: The Critical Edition,* provided readers for the first time with the complete texts of the diaries—both versions that Anne Frank herself wrote, and the edited version that her father initially put together from these two. As was noted, this edition also contained extensive forensic evidence with which to finally counter critics who claimed the diaries were not the work of Anne Frank. Ruth Wisse, writing in the *New York Times Book Review,* commented that "now there is a critical edition of the diary, with an apparatus that might put Shakespeare scholarship to shame." And in 1995, with *Diary of a Young Girl: The Definitive Edition,* the diary received a new English translation as well as being restored to its original form as Anne Frank herself had written it in the secret annex.

It is this sort of restoration that reminds the reader, after all, that the entire Anne Frank business—the films, books, houses, and foundations—rests on the musings of a young girl self-imprisoned above an oily Amsterdam canal living in fear of discovery at any moment, yet dealing with the daily grind with a quiet heroism. It is the diary that reveals the inner world of Anne Frank and that touches similar parts in all of us. When Anne Frank confided in *The Diary of a Young Girl* that "I want to be useful or bring enjoyment to all people, even those I've never met. I want to go on living even after my death!" she had no idea how prophetic those words would be.

■ Works Cited

Review of *Anne Frank's Tales from the Secret Annex, Kirkus Reviews,* December 15, 1983, p. 1287.
Berryman, John, *The Freedom of the Poet,* Farrar, Straus, 1976, pp. 91-106.
Ehrenburg, Ilya, *Chekhov, Stendhal, and Other Essays,* Knopf, 1963, pp. 258-64.
Frank, Anne, *Diary of a Young Girl,* Doubleday, 1952.
Frank, Anne, *The Works of Anne Frank,* Doubleday, 1959.
Frank Anne, *Tales from the House Behind: Fables, Personal Reminiscences, and Short Stories,* World's Work, 1962.
Frank, Anne, *The Diary of a Young Girl: The Definitive Edition,* Doubleday, 1995.
Kanfer, Stefan, "Child Sacrifice," *Time,* January 30, 1984, p. 77.
Kirsch, Jonathan, review of *Anne Frank's Tales from the Secret Annex, Los Angeles Times Book Review,* September 11, 1983, p. 14.
Levin, Meyer, "The Child behind the Secret Door," *New York Times Book Review,* June 15, 1952, pp. 1, 22.
Maguire, Gregory, "Outlook Tower," review of *Anne Frank's Tales from the Secret Annex, Horn Book,* June, 1984, p. 373.
Morton, Frederic, "Her Literary Legacy," *New York Times Book Review,* September 20, 1959, p. 22.
Pick, Lies Goslar, "I Knew Anne Frank," *McCall's,* July, 1958, pp. 30-31, 109-11, 114-15.
Romein, Jan, "A Child's Voice," in *A Tribute to Anne Frank,* Doubleday, 1971, p. 21.

Wisse, Ruth, "A Romance of the Secret Annex," *New York Times Book Review,* July 2, 1989, p. 2.
Wood, Karen D., and Susan G. Avett, review of *Anne Frank: Diary of a Young Girl, Language Arts,* January, 1993, pp. 64-65.

■ For More Information See

BOOKS

Bettelheim, Bruno, *Surviving and Other Essays,* Knopf, 1979.
Dunaway, Philip, and Melvin Evans, editors, *Treasury of the World's Great Diaries,* Doubleday, 1957.
Fradin, Dennis B., *Remarkable Children: Twenty Who Made History,* Little, Brown, 1987.
Gies, Miep, and Alison Leslie Gold, *Anne Frank Remembered: The Story of the Woman Who Helped to Hide the Franks,* Simon & Schuster, 1987.
Her Way: Biographies of Women for Young People, American Library Association, 1976.
Tridenti, Lina, *Anne Frank,* Silver Burdett, 1985.
Twentieth-Century Literary Criticism, Gale, Volume 17, 1985, pp. 98-122.
Twentieth-Century Young Adult Writers, St. James Press, 1994, pp. 221-22.

PERIODICALS

Booklist, February 1, 1991, p. 1122.
Christian Century, May 6, 1959.
Commonweal, October 31, 1968.
Holiday, September, 1969, pp. 16, 20-21.
Horn Book, May, 1993, p. 371.
Life, August 18, 1958.
Los Angeles Times Book Review, June 11, 1989, p. 6.
Ms., October, 1986, pp. 79-80.
Newsweek, June 25, 1979, pp. 14-15.
New York Times Book Review, February 26, 1967, p. 32.
New York Times Magazine, April 21, 1957; September 15, 1957, pp. 96, 98.
People, September 16, 1984.
Publishers Weekly, February 13, 1995, p. 70.
Saturday Review, July 19, 1952.
School Library Journal, January, 1984, p. 42; November, 1986, pp. 30-34; April, 1988, p. 43.
Seventeen, June, 1989, p. 112.
U.S. News & World Report, May 11, 1987, p. 77; August 1, 1989, p. 9.*

OTHER

Anne Frank Remembered (documentary film), Sony Pictures Classics, 1996.

—*Sketch by J. Sydney Jones*

*　　*　　*

FULLER, Roy (Broadbent) 1912-1991

■ Personal

Born February 11, 1912, in Failsworth, Lancashire, England; died September 27, 1991, in London, England; son of Leopold Charles (a factory manager) and Nellie

(Broadbent) Fuller; married Kathleen Smith, 1936; children: John. *Education:* Attended Blackpool High School, Lancashire; qualified as solicitor, 1934.

■ Career

Poet, novelist, and critic. Staff member of various legal firms, 1934-38; Woolwich Equitable Building Society, London, England, assistant solicitor, 1938-58, solicitor, 1958-69, director, 1969-88; Oxford University, Oxford, England, professor of poetry, 1968-73. Building Societies Association, London, chair of Legal Advisory Panel, 1958-69, vice-president, 1969-91. Member of Board of Governors, BBC, 1972-79. *Military service:* Royal Navy, 1941-46; Royal Naval Volunteer Reserve, lieutenant.

■ Awards, Honors

Fellow, Royal Society of Literature, 1958; Arts Council Poetry Award, 1959; Duff Cooper Memorial Prize for Poetry, 1968; Queen's Gold Medal for Poetry, 1970; Commander, Order of the British Empire, 1970; Cholmondeley award for poetry, 1980; D.Litt., University of Kent, Canterbury, 1986; M.A., Oxford University.

■ Writings

FOR CHILDREN

Savage Gold: A Story of Adventure, illustrated by Robert Medley, Lehmann, 1946, Penguin, 1957, illustrated by Douglas Hall, Hutchinson Educational, 1960.
With My Little Eye, illustrated by Alan Lindsay, Lehmann, 1948, Macmillan, 1957.
Catspaw, illustrated by David Gollins, Alan Ross, 1966.
Seen Grandpa Lately? (verse), illustrated by Joan Hickson, Deutsch, 1972.
Poor Roy (verse), illustrated by Nicolas Bentley, Deutsch, 1977.
The Other Planet and Three Other Fables, illustrated by Paul Peter Piech, Keepsake Press, 1979.
More about Tompkins and Other Light Verse, Tragara Press, 1981.
(With Barbara Giles and Adrian Rumble) *Upright, Downfall* (verse), Oxford University Press, 1983.
The World through the Window: Collected Poems for Children, illustrated by Nick Duffy, Blackie, 1989.

POETRY FOR ADULTS

Poems, Fortune Press, 1940.
The Middle of a War, Hogarth Press, 1942.
A Lost Season, Hogarth Press, 1944.
Epitaphs and Occasions, Lehmann, 1949.
Counterparts, Verschoyle, 1954.
Brutus's Orchard, Deutsch, 1957, Macmillan, 1958.
Collected Poems, 1936-1961, Deutsch, 1962, Dufour, 1962.
Buff, Deutsch, 1965, Dufour, 1965.
New Poems, Deutsch, 1968, Dufour, 1968.
(With R. S. Thomas) *Pergamon Poets 1,* edited by Evan Owen, Pergamon Press, 1968.
Off Course, Turret, 1969.
(With Alfred Alvarez and Anthony Thwaite) *Penguin Modern Poets 18,* Penguin, 1970.

ROY FULLER

To an Unknown Reader, Poem-of-the-Month Club, 1970.
Song Cycle from a Record Sleeve, Sycamore Press, 1972.
Tiny Tears, Deutsch, 1973.
An Old War, Tragara Press, 1974.
Waiting for the Barbarians: A Poem, Keepsake Press, 1974.
From the Joke Shop, Deutsch, 1975.
The Joke Shop Annexe, Tragara Press, 1975.
An Ill-Governed Coast, Ceolfrith Press, 1976.
Re-treads, Tragara Press, 1979.
The Reign of Sparrows, London Magazine Editions, 1980.
The Individual and His Times: A Selection of the Poetry of Roy Fuller, edited by V. J. Lee, Athlone Press, 1982.
House and Shop, Tragara Press, 1982.
As from the Thirties, Tragara Press, 1983.
Mianserin Sonnets, Tragara Press, 1984.
New and Collected Poems, 1934-1984, Secker & Warburg, 1985.
Subsequent to Summer, Salamander Press, 1985.
Outside the Canon, Tragara Press, 1986.
Consolations, Secker & Warburg, 1987.
Available for Dreams, Collins, 1989.

FICTION FOR ADULTS

The Second Curtain, Verschoyle, 1953, Macmillan, 1956.
Fantasy and Fugue, Verschoyle, 1954, Macmillan, 1956, published as *Murder in Mind,* Academy (Chicago), 1986.
Image of a Society, Deutsch, 1956, Macmillan, 1957.

The Ruined Boys, Deutsch, 1959, published as *That Distant Afternoon,* Macmillan, 1957.

The Father's Comedy, Deutsch, 1961.

The Perfect Fool, Deutsch, 1963.

My Child, My Sister, Deutsch, 1965.

The Carnal Island, Deutsch, 1970.

Omnibus (contains *With My Little Eye, The Second Curtain, Fantasy and Fugue*), Carcanet, 1988.

Stares, Sinclair-Stevenson, 1990.

NONFICTION FOR ADULTS

Owls and Artificers: Oxford Lectures on Poetry, Deutsch, 1971, Library Press, 1971.

Professors and Gods: Last Oxford Lectures on Poetry, Deutsch, 1973, St. Martin's Press, 1974.

Souvenirs (memoirs), London Magazine Editions, 1980.

Vamp till Ready: Further Memoirs, London Magazine Editions, 1982.

Home and Dry: Memoirs 3, London Magazine Editions, 1984.

Twelfth Night: A Personal View, Tragara Press, 1985.

The Strange and the Good: Collected Memoirs, Collins Harvill, 1989.

Spanner and Pen: Post-War Memoirs, Sinclair-Stevenson, 1991.

EDITOR

Byron for Today, Porcupine Press, 1948.

(With Clifford Dyment and Montagu Slater) *New Poems 1952,* Joseph, 1952.

The Building Societies Acts, 1874-1960: Great Britain and Northern Ireland, 3rd edition, Franey, 1957, 5th edition, Franey, 1961, 6th edition, Franey, 1962.

Supplement of New Poetry, Poetry Book Society, 1964.

Fellow Mortals: An Anthology of Animal Verse, illustrated by David Koster, Macdonald & Evans, 1981.

(With John Lehmann) *The Penguin New Writing, 1940-1950: An Anthology,* Penguin, 1985.

OTHER

Also legal correspondent for *Building Societies' Gazette,* as well as a contributor periodicals, including *Listener, New Statesman, Times Literary Supplement.* Fuller's papers are housed in manuscript collections at the Brotherton Collection, Leeds University, the State University of New York, Buffalo, and the British Library, London.

■ Sidelights

Roy Fuller was a poet of renown, a self-proclaimed chronicler of the everyday. According to Stephen Spender, as quoted by Michael Goldberg in the *Dictionary of Literary Biography,* Fuller was the norm against which "other poets of the past thirty years may be judged." Clear, lucid verses were Fuller's trademark, something that became unfashionable in the later twentieth century. Fuller was also a well respected novelist, turning his hand to stories about sensitive individuals fighting against the forces of an uncaring society or corporation. Among these novels are a trio of mysteries that fans of the genre still enjoy. Less well known are Fuller's works

for young readers. In the four fiction books and the five collections of poetry he wrote for a juvenile audience, Fuller explored many of the same themes and with much the same linguistic sophistication as his adult works. "There is no talking-down to a youthful audience here," Peter Reading commented in a *Times Literary Supplement* review of Fuller's *The World through the Window.*

Indeed, talking down was not Fuller's style. A poet's poet, his love of language shows in every stanza of every poem. A family man who understood the hurly-burly of corporate life, having served for thirty years as a solicitor for a British savings and loan association, Fuller once described his life as "part managerial, part poetic." But he managed to balance both aspects well enough to leave behind a body of work of which any full-time writer would be proud. In addition to his output of juvenile titles, there are thirty-one volumes of poetry, nine novels, eleven nonfiction works, and a score of edited works and reviews.

Born in 1912 into a lower-middle-class home in Failsworth, Lancashire, Fuller was one of two children whose father worked as manager of a rubber-proofing mill. But after his father's death when Fuller was only eight, his mother moved the family to Blackpool. At sixteen Fuller was articled—or apprenticed—to a solicitor; he studied the law, and by age twenty-one he passed his qualifying exams. This early life was not exactly the stuff that makes a great poet. As quoted by Goldberg, Fuller described his background as "provincial ... [and] unliterary," and his schooling as "uninspired ... [and] truncated." He worked for various law firms, married in 1936, and by the time of the outbreak of World War II had moved his family to the outskirts of London, where he took a post with the Woolwich Equitable Building Society. But for the war years during which he served in the Royal Navy, Fuller remained with this firm until his retirement in 1968, and he stayed in the London suburb of Blackheath until his death.

During the war, Fuller worked in the newly emerging field of radar and spent several years in Kenya as a radar technician. He had already begun to write poetry before the war, publishing his first volume in 1939. But it was during the war years that he gained some renown with *The Middle of a War* and *A Lost Season.* Influenced by W. H. Auden and Stephen Spender, these early poems are characterized by their liberal political slant—Fuller thought of himself as a Marxist at the time—and a concern for the individual in modern technological society. Many critics have mentioned these two volumes as among the best war poetry of the time.

Fuller's stay in Kenya provided other grist for the writer's mill. With the end of the war and his return to England, Fuller decided to try his hand at fiction. His son John, later to be a poet in his own right, stimulated Fuller to write books for younger readers. In a way he was apprenticing himself in the novelist's trade by starting out with juvenile novels. The first of these, *Savage Gold,* is set in East Africa. A couple of young boys are caught up in the rivalry of two mining companies in an action-adventure tale that Alan Edwin Day, writing in *Twentieth-Century Children's Writers*, characterized as "well told" and with "a fast and exciting pace." Next, Fuller tried out the mystery genre in *With My Little Eye*. Its youthful protagonist, Frederick French, the only son of a county judge, plays detective during a courtroom murder trial. Both literate and sophisticated, the book is, "in its small way a perfect example of a modern crime story," according to Julian Symons, writing in *Mortal Consequences*. But it is this very sophistication that bothered Day in *Twentieth-Century Children's Books*. For Day, this sophistication and plot complexity were too much for young readers: "We can only conclude that Fuller sadly misdirected his inventiveness," Day noted. In the same article, Fuller himself commented that "though writing for children has always given me a certain sense of freedom, I have never thought of my children's books as 'written down' to an audience. Indeed, I have erred the other way." Upon its publication in the United States, *With My Little Eye* was included on the adult lists.

As his son grew up, Fuller's inspirations changed and he returned to adult fiction and poetry for almost twenty years. It was during this time that his reputation was made with such poetry collections as *Epitaphs and Occasions, Counterparts,* and *Brutus's Orchard.* By the 1960s Fuller was considered one of the foremost British poets of his time. But he had not neglected fiction. In the 1950s he continued his experiments in the mystery genre with *The Second Curtain* and *Fantasy and Fugue*. His exploration of the theme of the individual against society was evidenced in books such as *Image of a Society, The Ruined Boys,* and *The Father's Comedy.* With these last three, Fuller used microcosms to stand for society as a whole; in *Image of a Society,* it is a building and loan association, something about which he had firsthand knowledge. With *The Ruined Boys,* society is represented by a second-rate public school. The book recounts the life of Gerald Bracher during three terms in which the protagonist tries to combat the corrosive effects and pressure of his society. *The Father's Comedy* takes place in Kenya, and here the forces of society are represented by a mysterious corporation called 'The Authority.' In this novel Fuller thrusts a comfortable middle-aged lawyer into combat when he is faced with the hard choice of compromising his own career and a potential knighthood by speaking up for his son, who is on trial in Kenya.

By the late 1960s, both Fuller's poetry and prose had reached a new and more personal level. Still a stickler for form, he now explored the themes of death, loss, aging, and the role of the artist. Much of the poetry is infused with a quiet and suburban enjoyment of nature, as well, influenced by back-garden musings at his home on Blackheath. His *Collected Poems* of 1962 and *The Individual and His Times* are considered touchstones of this middle to late period of Fuller's poetic development. The novels, too, took on this more private, personal theme, as in *My Child, My Sister,* which Fuller

Set in a Victorian mansion called Stares, a home for mental patients, this tragicomedy focuses on a recovering actor and his revealing rendition of Chekhov's *The Seagull*.

considered to be better than any of his poetry in structure.

With his retirement from Woolwich Equitable in 1968, Fuller's public life did not diminish. He became a professor of poetry at Oxford University for the next five years and served as governor on the board of the British Broadcasting Corporation (BBC) for the next decade. It was during this part of his career that Fuller returned to children's books. "The separation in time between the two groups of children's books," Fuller explained in *Twentieth-Century Children's Books*, "is to be accounted for by the fact that I was stimulated to write them first by my son's childhood, then my grandchildren's." Fuller's first return to juvenile fiction was *Catspaw,* a book in which little Victoria wanders into a land populated only by dogs who are continually worried about the machinations of the country called Pussia, populated only by cats. Published in 1966, *Catspaw* is in part an allegory of the Cold War, then at its height.

With the publication of *Seen Grandpa Lately?*, Fuller made his first verse contribution to children's literature.

In part comic and nonsensical, the volume also contains serious poems exploring many of Fuller's adult themes, such as death and loss. Throughout the 1970s, Fuller made further periodic sallies into juvenile fiction and verse. A second volume of children's verse, *Poor Roy,* appeared in 1977, followed by a book of stories, *The Other Planet and Three Other Fables* in 1979. Fuller's output for young readers in the 1980s was confined to verse: *More about Tompkins and Other Light Verse* in 1981, and *Upright, Downfall* in 1983. The latter was written with two other poets, which, according to a reviewer for *Book Report,* provides "a broad range of experience, discovery and delight."

Fuller won an Indian Summer of renown for his adult verse with *New and Collected Poems, 1934-1984,* which successfully reintroduced the poet to a new generation of readers. Other notable volumes of poetry followed, *Consolations* and *Available for Dreams* among them. He also wrote several volumes of memoirs as well as making a return to fiction with the 1990 *Stares,* which Lachlan Mackinnon, writing in the *Times Literary Supplement,* called a "frightening and memorable novel."

Fuller's verses for children was gathered together in the 1989 *The World through the Window: Collected Poems for Children.* Here is everything from childish doggerel—"There was a girl named Sheila Stables, / Who never really knew her tables"—to longer and more serious poems delving into the full range of Fuller's adult themes: the natural history of suburbia, daily tasks seen anew, growing old, facing death. Poetic forms vary from limericks and sonnets to more sophisticated styles. The tone is often humorous and sometimes at the expense of the author himself, as in the poem in which Fuller describes himself as a grandfather: "The truth is really that behind / The professional brow / There is a very simple mind / Thinking of crispy bacon rind . . . ." Reading noted that it "is at once enjoyable and informative," but that also because of its "wit, imagery, sophistication" it would probably not find the wide readership that other simpler texts do. A critic for *Observer Review* commented on Fuller's "light and genial touch" evident everywhere in the collected poems, while Judith Nichols, writing in *Books for Your Children,* concluded that *The World through the Window* would be "an ideal opportunity to catch up" on Fuller's work.

Catching up on the full range of Fuller's achievement is a job in itself. Into his seventies, the poet continued not only to produce but to grow, to strive for new artistic expression and creative development. For someone whose life was part poetic and part managerial, Fuller managed to blend the two amazingly well. A sophisticat-

ed choice for children then, but one not without rewards.

■ **Works Cited**

Day, Alan Edwin, "Fuller, Roy (Broadbent)," in *Twentieth-Century Children's Writers,* 4th ed., St. James Press, 1995, pp. 374-76.

Fuller, Roy, *The World through the Window: Collected Poems for Children,* Blackie, 1989.

Mackinnon, Lachlan, review of *Stares, Times Literary Supplement,* January 11, 1991, p. 17.

Nichols, Judith, review of *The World through the Window, Books for Your Children,* spring, 1990, p. 19.

Goldberg, Michael, "Roy Fuller," in *Dictionary of Literary Biography,* Volume 15: *British Novelists, 1930-1959,* Gale, 1983, pp. 98-106.

Reading, Peter, "A Natural Perversity," *Times Literary Supplement,* August 18, 1989, p. 905.

Symons, Julian, *Mortal Consequences: A History—From the Detective Story to the Crime Novel,* Harper, 1972, pp. 193-94.

Review of *Upright, Downfall, Book Report,* May-June, 1986, p. 36.

Review of *The World through the Window, Observer Review,* August 6, 1989, p. 40.

■ **For More Information See**

BOOKS

Austin, Alan E., *Roy Fuller,* Twayne, 1979.

Contemporary Authors Autobiography Series, Volume 10, Gale, 1991, pp. 111-28.

Contemporary Literary Criticism, Gale, Volume 4, 1975, pp. 177-79; Volume 28, 1984, pp. 147-59.

PERIODICALS

New York Times Book Review, April 13, 1986, p. 38.

Observer, September 5, 1965, p. 26; June 23, 1985, p. 23; February 8, 1987, p. 28; March 22, 1987, p. 27; April 23, 1989, p. 44; November 11, 1990, p. 67; March 10, 1991, p. 61.

Times Literary Supplement, November 1, 1985, p. 1223; April 25, 1986, p. 450; March 6, 1987, p. 244; June 23, 1989, p. 694; December 1, 1989, p. 1344; February 1, 1991, p. 21.

■ **Obituaries**

PERIODICALS

London Times, September 28, 1991, p. 14.
Los Angeles Times, September 30, 1991, p. A20.
Washington Post, September 29, 1991, p. B7.*

—Sketch by J. Sydney Jones

G

ADELE GERAS

GERAS, Adele (Daphne) 1944-

■ Personal

Surname begins with a hard "G" and rhymes with "terrace"; born March 15, 1944, in Jerusalem, Palestine (now Israel); daughter of Laurence David (a lawyer) and Leah (Hamburger) Weston; married Norman Geras (a lecturer and author), August 7, 1967; children: Sophie, Jenny. *Education:* St. Hilda's College, Oxford, B.A., 1966. *Religion:* Jewish. *Hobbies and other interests:* "I

enjoy the movies more than anything and read an enormous amount of everything, but my great love is thrillers and detective stories. I am very lazy, and like sleeping in the afternoons."

■ Addresses

Home—10 Danesmoor Rd., Manchester M20 3JS, England. *Agent*—Laura Cecil, 17 Alwyne Villas, London N1 2HG, England.

■ Career

Fairfield High School, Droylsden, Lancashire, England, French teacher, 1968-71; writer, 1976—. Actress in *Four Degrees Over* (play), London, 1966.

■ Awards, Honors

Taylor Award, 1991, for *My Grandmother's Stories: A Collection of Jewish Folktales;* National Jewish Book Council Award, 1994, for *Golden Windows and Other Stories of Jerusalem.*

■ Writings

FICTION FOR CHILDREN

Tea at Mrs. Manderby's, illustrated by Doreen Caldwell, Hamish Hamilton, 1976.
Apricots at Midnight and Other Stories from a Patchwork Quilt, illustrated by Doreen Caldwell, Hamish Hamilton, 1977, Atheneum, 1982.
Beyond the Cross-Stitch Mountains, illustrated by Mary Wilson, Hamish Hamilton, 1977.
The Painted Garden, illustrated by Doreen Caldwell, Hamish Hamilton, 1979.
A Thousand Yards of Sea, illustrated by Joanna Troughton, Hodder & Stoughton, 1980.
The Rug that Grew, illustrated by Priscilla Lamont, Hamish Hamilton, 1981.
The Christmas Cat, illustrated by Doreen Caldwell, Hamish Hamilton, 1983.
Little Elephant's Moon, Illustrated by Linda Birch, Hamish Hamilton, 1986.

Ritchie's Rabbit, illustrated by Vanessa Julian-Ottie, Hamish Hamilton, 1986, Random House, 1987.

Finding Annabel, illustrated by Alan Marks, Hamish Hamilton, 1987.

Fishpie for Flamingoes, illustrated by Linda Birch, Hamish Hamilton, 1987.

The Fantora Family Files, illustrated by Tony Ross, Hamish Hamilton, 1988.

The Strange Bird, illustrated by Linda Birch, Hamish Hamilton, 1988.

The Coronation Picnic, illustrated by Frances Wilson, Hamish Hamilton, 1989.

Bunk Bed Night, Dent, 1990.

My Grandmother's Stories: A Collection of Jewish Folktales, illustrated by Jael Jordan, Knopf, 1990, Heinemann, 1990.

Nina's Magic, Hamish Hamilton, 1990.

Pink Medicine, Dent, 1990.

A Magic Birthday, Simon & Schuster (London), 1992.

The Fantora Family Photographs, illustrated by Tony Ross, Hamish Hamilton, 1993.

Golden Windows and Other Stories of Jerusalem, HarperCollins, 1993, Heinemann, 1995.

Baby's Bedclothes, illustrated by Prue Greener, Longman, 1994.

The Dolls' House, illustrated by Prue Greener, Longman, 1994.

Keith's Croak, illustrated by Prue Greener, Longman, 1994.

Mary's Meadow, illustrated by Prue Greener, Longman, 1994.

Mimi; and, Apricot Max, illustrated by Teresa O'Brien, Longman, 1994.

Josephine, illustrated by Teresa O'Brien, Longman, 1994.

The Return of Archibald Gribbet, illustrated by Sumiko, Longman, 1994.

Toey, illustrated by Duncan Smith, Heinemann, 1994.

Gilly the Kid, illustrated by Sue Heap, Simon & Schuster, 1995.

Little Swan, illustrated by Johanna Westerman, Random House, 1995.

Stories for Bedtime (with cassette), illustrated by Amanda Benjamin, HarperCollins, 1995.

A Candle in the Dark (part of the "Flashbacks" historical fiction series), A. & C. Black, 1995.

Also contributor to periodicals, including *Cricket.*

FICTION FOR YOUNG ADULTS

The Girls in the Velvet Frame, Hamish Hamilton, 1978, Atheneum, 1979.

The Green behind the Glass, Hamish Hamilton, 1982, published as *Snapshots of Paradise: Love Stories,* Atheneum, 1984.

Other Echoes, Atheneum, 1983.

Voyage, Atheneum, 1983.

Letters of Fire and Other Unsettling Stories, Hamish Hamilton, 1984.

Happy Endings, Hamish Hamilton, 1986, Harcourt, 1991.

Daydreams on Video, Hodder & Stoughton, 1989.

The Tower Room, Hamish Hamilton, 1990, Harcourt, 1992.

Watching the Roses, Hamish Hamilton, 1991, Harcourt, 1992.

Pictures of the Night, Harcourt, 1993.

A Lane to the Land of the Dead, Hamish Hamilton, 1994.

OTHER

(With Pauline Stainer) *Up on the Roof* (adult poetry), Smith Doorstep (Huddersfield, England), 1987.

Yesterday (memoirs), Walker (London), 1992.

Voices from the Dolls' House (adult poetry), Rockingham Press (Ware, England), 1994.

Geras's work has been translated into several languages, including Dutch and German.

■ Sidelights

A childhood spent following her father on his wide-ranging assignments for the Colonial Service had a great influence on the work of novelist and short story writer Adele Geras. Using her experiences of historic Jerusalem, where she was born, exotic Africa, and Great Britain, where she attended boarding school and now lives, Geras weaves a strong sense of place and time into her fiction. Her portraits of vivid characters, also often drawn from recollections of the people she encountered during her childhood years, have been praised by reviewers and readers alike. Sea travel, Jewish culture, and a love of tradition also play strong roles in shaping her stories for children and teenage readers. "I write because I enjoy it," Geras once told *SATA.* "I write about places and things that have been important to me in one way or another."

"I used to write a lot as a child," Geras explained to Jean W. Ross in a 1987 interview for *Contemporary Authors,* "and then I found that what happened was, as you got more and more educated and had more and more academic work given to you, you had less and less time to do your own stuff. And of course the other thing is that, as you become an adolescent, you become very self-conscious, and you get the idea that if you can't be Tolstoy or Jane Austen, then you're not going to be anybody at all and you should stop. So I did stop when I was about fourteen, and I didn't start again until after my daughter was born. Then I rediscovered what fun it was—which is what every child knows."

Geras's first attempt at writing as an adult was spurred on by a competition in the London *Times.* "As soon as I saw the contest announced, . . . I wrote a story and sent it off," she recalled in an essay for *Something about the Author Autobiography Series* (*SAAS*), "and although it did not win, it did become the starting point for *Apricots at Midnight.* It's a ghost story called 'Rose' and the moment I'd finished it, I knew that this was what I wanted to do from now on."

"Rose" would be joined by several other short tales and published by Geras in 1977 as *Apricots at Midnight,* a collection of story "patches" narrated by Aunt Piney, a dressmaker, as she works on a quilt with her young niece. A *Publishers Weekly* reviewer found the collection an "unusual and entrancing book," while *Horn Book* contributor Kate M. Flanagan praised the tales as "rich in detail and delightfully recounted." Geras's enthusiasm for her newly found craft also found an outlet in writing picture books for young children. The first, *Tea at Mrs. Manderby's,* is a sensitive story about a young girl who resigns herself to taking afternoon tea with an elderly neighbor at her parent's urging. Several more books for young readers would follow, including *A Thousand Years of Sea,* about a fisherman who releases a mermaid from his net and is rewarded with beautiful sea-colored cloth that the ladies of his village make into swishing skirts; and *Toey,* about two children who hope for a new pet and end up with a pair of playful kittens. Geras has also published many short stories in magazines such as *Cricket;* several of her tales have been collected in 1995's *Stories for Bedtime.*

In addition to short stories and picture books for young children, Geras is the author of several collections of short fiction for older readers. In 1983 she wrote *The Green behind the Glass,* a set of eight tales about young love that was released in the United States as *Snapshots of Paradise: Love Stories.* Called "an intriguing departure from the sunny sentimentality of so many romance collections for young adults" by *Booklist* reviewer Stephanie Zvirin, *The Green behind the Glass* includes "Don't Sing Love Songs," narrated by a young woman who is on her own with a friend in Paris until their shared attraction towards handsome Jim threatens their friendship; the title story, which describes an emotion-laden situation where a young woman's older sister knows herself to be the real object of her sister's now-dead fiance's true affections; and "Tea in the Wendy House," a young, pregnant woman's lament for her soon-to-be-lost youth as she faces a shotgun wedding and a future as wife and mother in a tiny house. *Horn Book* writer Mary M. Burns hailed the variety of styles and settings of Geras's love stories, calling them "distinguished by perceptive insight into human nature, dexterity in plot construction, and a sense of style remarkable for its readability and its imagery and constraint."

In 1994's *A Lane to the Land of the Dead,* Geras uses suspense and elements of the supernatural to add spice and a touch of melancholy to the lives of her young protagonists; "Geras shows her usual lightness of touch," Elspeth S. Scott observed in *School Librarian,* predicting the collection would have wide appeal. In contrast, the five tales in *Golden Windows and Other Stories of Jerusalem* show readers what life was like in early twentieth-century Jerusalem. In "Beyond the Cross-Stitch Mountains," one story from this collection, eleven-year-old Daskeh conspires with friend Danny to escape the care of her aunt Phina and visit his own aunt, despite the danger in leaving the bomb shelter where they routinely spend the nights during Israel's 1948 War for Independence. And "Dreams of Fire" shows the after-effects of this experience on young Danny as memories of death and violence return to haunt him in

the form of a memorial built to honor the War. Reviewer Ellen Mandel praised *Golden Windows* in *Booklist* as "well-written, laced with subtleties of history, and rich in personal emotion."

In addition to being included in *Golden Windows,* Geras's "Beyond the Cross-Stitch Mountains" is the title of another book for younger readers that draws on the author's Jewish heritage. Similarly, the 1978 novel *The Girls in the Velvet Frame* takes as its setting the city of Jerusalem as it tells the story of five daughters of a widow whose only son, Isaac, has left for the United States, only to be unheard from for months. The year is 1913—just four years prior to the outbreak of World War I. While the close-knit family has little money, their wealthier Aunt Mimi provides a splash of magic in the lives of the sisters—Rifka, Chava, Naomi, Dvora, and Shoshie—with her dishes of candy, her comfortable home, and the photograph she arranges to have taken of them as a birthday gift for their mother. At the suggestion of their worldly aunt, the girls send a copy of the finished photograph to New York City, hoping that their brother will see it and contact them. "The appeal of this charming books comes ... from the accurate, penetrating and quite unsentimental portraits of the five children and of their elders," Marcus Crouch noted in

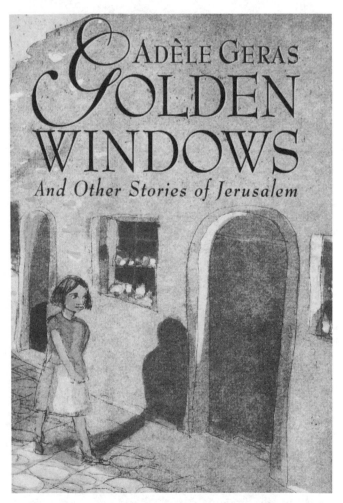

Five stories of related characters tell what growing up in historic Jerusalem was like in this 1993 book.

Inspired by a real photograph of the author's mother and four aunts, this story of five Bernstein girls and their mother is a vivid family tale of New York life before World War I. (Cover illustration by Douglas Hall.)

the *Times Literary Supplement.* Cyrisse Jaffee similarly acclaimed Geras's characters, adding in *School Library Journal* that "marvelous descriptions of time and place add contours."

The 1983 novel *Voyage* focuses on the history of the Jewish people, describing the passage of those who fled from the poverty of Eastern Europe by enduring the fifteen-day crossing of the Atlantic Ocean aboard a tightly packed ship. In Geras's novel, which takes place just after the turn of the century, readers are introduced to the hopes and fears of several vivid characters: spunky Mina, who must keep up the spirits of her worried mother and her brother; Golda, who is bringing her baby girl to join her husband in New York City; and Yankel, a bully who is making the trip with his mother. The sight of the Statue of Liberty in New York Harbor at journey's end marks the beginning of a new life for these people, as it has for the thousands of actual immigrants whose lives they symbolize. The book's vignettes "cleverly [reveal] not only the happenings on board but the thoughts, hopes, fears, and memories of the little community," Ethel L. Heins wrote in *Horn Book.*

Geras has also written several other novels for young adult readers. Among the most notable are three books that comprise her "Egerton Hall" series. Set in Egerton Hall boarding school in 1963, the stories revolve around three friends—Alice, Bella, and Megan—as the events of their lives take turns that resemble the fairy tales of old. In 1990's *The Tower Room,* Megan becomes a modern-day Rapunzel when she is freed from a lackluster tower room in the boarding school after falling in love with a handsome young laboratory assistant at Egerton Hall. Told in her own words as she looks back over the chain of events leading up to her life with her "Prince Charming" in a small, humble London apartment, Megan realizes that real life doesn't always end "happily ever after."

In 1991's *Watching the Roses,* Geras draws from the Sleeping Beauty legend in telling Alice's story. The reader eavesdrops upon the young woman, lying on her bed in her parent's large house, as she recounts to her diary the events surrounding her eighteenth birthday party. As preparations for the party—actually, a gala ball—are in their final stages, Alice recalls telling friends Megan and Bella stories about her estranged Aunt Violette, who had once dourly predicted that Alice

In a modern take-off on "Sleeping Beauty," eighteen-year-old Alice copes with rape and her budding sexuality, recording her thoughts in her diary.

would never live past eighteen. But her anticipation turned to tragedy, the reader soon learns, as the young woman reveals that she was attacked and raped by the uncouth son of her family's gardener on the very night of the ball. She now lies in her room recovering from the shock of the event and silently questioning her own culpability. As in the Sleeping Beauty legend, time seems to stop while Alice attempts to come to terms with the events of the past few days and deals with her sexuality and concerns over how the rape will affect her relationship with Jean-Luc, her own handsome prince. Florence H. Munat praised *Watching the Roses* in *Voice of Youth Advocates,* noting that Geras "has deftly added just the right modern twists and details to allure older readers back to the story that enchanted them as children."

Geras's fairy-tale trilogy is completed with a modern retelling of Snow White's story, casting eighteen-year-old Bella in the lead. Taking place in Paris during Bella's summer vacation from Egerton Hall, *Pictures of the Night* features an evil stepmother, Marjorie, who becomes so jealous of her stepdaughter's budding singing career that she actually tries to kill the beautiful young woman. However, Bella is saved from Marjorie's attempt to poison her—with apple-flavored liqueur—by the quick-thinking of Mark, a rich American medical student visiting France. In a *Kirkus Reviews* assessment of the novel, one critic called Geras "a writer distinguished for her imaginative power and fresh, vivid writing." "The fairy tale parallels become more apparent as the trilogy proceeds," notes Sheila Ray in *Twentieth-Century Young Adult Writers,* "gradually moving through the momentous year when the girls fall in love and face their emerging sexuality, creating a powerful tour de force, outstanding in young adult literature."

A prolific author whose work is consistently given high marks by reviewers, Geras has written several other novels, including *Other Echoes,* a work of historical fiction that takes place in Borneo, and a pair of books about the adventures of the humorous Fantora family, told from the point of view of their cat Ozymandias. As she once told *SATA:* "I write very quickly once I get started, but hate getting started—it's like diving from a high board into cold water—terrifying in prospect, but terrific when you've taken the plunge." Geras advised beginning writers: "Read all the time and learn to type. It used to take me almost as long to copy a novel out neatly for the typist as it did to write it."

■ Works Cited

Review of *Apricots at Midnight and Other Stories from a Patchwork Quilt, Publishers Weekly,* October 15, 1982, p. 66.

Burns, Mary M., review of *Snapshots of Paradise, Horn Book,* September/October, 1984, p. 596.

Crouch, Marcus, review of *The Girls in the Velvet Frame, Times Literary Supplement,* September 29, 1978, p. 1083.

Flanagan, Kate M., review of *Apricots at Midnight and Other Stories from a Patchwork Quilt, Horn Book,* February, 1983, pp. 43-44.

Geras, Adele, interview with Jean W. Ross in *Contemporary Authors New Revision Series,* Volume 19, Gale, 1987, pp. 200-203.

Geras, Adele, essay in *Something about the Author Autobiography Series,* Volume 21, Gale, 1996, pp. 185-204.

Heins, Ethel L., review of *Voyage, Horn Book,* August, 1983, p. 452.

Jaffee, Cyrisse, review of *The Girls in the Velvet Frame, School Library Journal,* September, 1979, p. 138.

Mandel, Ellen, review of *Golden Windows and Other Stories of Jerusalem, Booklist,* October 15, 1993.

Munat, Florence H., review of *Watching the Roses, Voice of Youth Advocates,* December, 1992, p. 278.

Review of *Pictures of the Night, Kirkus Reviews,* March 15, 1993.

Ray, Sheila, "Adele Geras," in *Twentieth-Century Young Adult Writers,* 4th edition, edited by Laura Standley Berger, St. James Press, 1994, pp. 242-44.

Scott, Elspeth S., review of *A Lane to the Land of the Dead, School Librarian,* May, 1995, p. 77.

Zvirin, Stephanie, review of *Snapshots of Paradise, Booklist,* August 1984, p. 1609.

■ For More Information See

PERIODICALS

Books for Your Children, autumn, 1992, p. 27.
Christian Science Monitor, May 13, 1983.
Horn Book, March/April, 1993, p. 211.
Junior Bookshelf, December, 1976, p. 326; June, 1994, p. 100; August, 1995, p. 134.
Kirkus Reviews, September 1, 1984, p. J8.
School Librarian, June, 1983, p. 162; November, 1992, p. 157; May, 1994, p. 60.
Times Literary Supplement, March 27, 1981, p. 340; January 27, 1984; November 30, 1984; June 6, 1986.

*   *   *

GILMORE, Kate 1931-

■ Personal

Born May 2, 1931, in Milwaukee, WI; daughter of Earl C. (an author, philosopher, and professor of secondary education) and Margaret (Webster) Kelley; married John W. Gilmore (a computer systems designer), October 28, 1960; children: Valerie, Geoffrey. *Education:* Antioch College, B.A., 1954. *Politics:* "Liberal as in 'old-fashioned' or 'bleeding-heart.'" *Religion:* "Long-lapsed Protestant." *Hobbies and other interests:* Gardening and photography.

■ Addresses

Home—30-53 36th St., Astoria, NY 11103.

■ Career

Novelist, 1983—. Temporary legal secretary, New York City, 1985—; Arboretal Artifacts, co-director and craftsman (making one-of-a-kind topiaries and wreaths from dried botanicals), 1989—. *Member:* New York Botanical Garden, Smithsonian Institution, New York Museum of Natural History.

■ Writings

Of Griffins and Graffiti, Penguin, 1986.
Remembrance of the Sun, Houghton Mifflin, 1986.
Enter Three Witches, Houghton Mifflin, 1991.
Jason and the Bard, Houghton Mifflin, 1993.

■ Work in Progress

The Exchange Student, a novel set in the near future and which centers around the role of animals in our lives, for Houghton Mifflin; reading about zoology.

■ Sidelights

Kate Gilmore has published several novels for young adults, each of which is quite different from the another. For example, *Of Griffins and Graffiti* tells the story of a group of teenagers who decide to paint a mural on the side of a jet plane that makes international flights, while *Enter Three Witches* follows the adventures of a teenage boy who tries to prevent his new girlfriend from discovering that he lives with a group of witches.

Remembrance of the Sun, published in 1986, is based upon Gilmore's own experience of living in a turbulent Iran in the late 1970s. It tells the story of Jill Alexander, a seventeen-year-old American whose family moves to Iran in 1978 due to her father's employment in the oil industry. During this time, many Iranians actively rebelled against the Shah and his tyrannical government, often with violent results. Jill falls in love with Shaheen, an Iranian classmate who shares her love of music and mountain climbing, just as he becomes involved in the revolutionary movement. Shaheen's father helps Jill's family to escape the country, and Jill is left to wonder what happened to her boyfriend. Carole Ann Barham stated in a *Voice of Youth Advocates* review that Gilmore's year in Iran helped her to create "a vividly detailed picture of its land, people, and culture at that violent time within the framework of an enjoyable story." Calling *Remembrance of the Sun* an "intelligent, many-layered novel," a critic for *Kirkus Reviews* noted that "the tension and beauty of this love story should keep any reader spellbound."

Gilmore's 1993 novel, *Jason and the Bard,* explores the world of professional theater through the eyes of Jason, a high school student whose love of acting earns him an apprenticeship with a summer Shakespeare festival. Along with several other young apprentices, Jason learns about every aspect of the theater, from lighting and props to selling tickets and rehearsing scenes. He also learns about the rivalries that divide the professional actors as well as the shared love of Shakespeare that brings them together. *Booklist* reviewer Carolyn Phelan called *Jason and the Bard* an "appealing novel" and a "good choice for lovers of Shakespeare" or theater.

Gilmore described the challenges of writing to *SATA:* "Each of my ... novels for young adults has been quite different from any of its predecessors, and each, with one exception, has been fun to write. Like everyone else I have had to edit and rewrite difficult passages, and especially I have had to cut to conform to my publisher's notion that no teenager will even pick up a book that is more than two hundred pages long. I had to cut my first book for Houghton Mifflin *in half,* not having been told before how times had changed since I was young and once cried when a good book came to an end. Yet even this traumatic experience seems trivial compared to my experiences with the book I am writing now and have been writing, it sometimes seems, for at least a century.

Living with three witches (including his mother and grandmother), Bren has a problem trying to keep his girlfriend, Erica, away from the house in Kate Gilmore's hilarious fantasy.

Jason and the Bard
Kate Gilmore

Although Jason came to the Avon Shakespeare Festival to act, he also learned to make props, develop swordplay skills, solve backstage mysteries, and balance work with fellowship and fun.

"I am trying to drape a vast, fascinating, and hugely important subject onto the back of a weak and underdeveloped plot. The subject keeps expanding; the plot keeps groaning and collapsing at the knees. I have already rewritten the first half twice, having never done any such thing in my life. I feel aggrieved, though it *is* better. And how will it all end? I haven't the faintest.

"The book is laid a hundred years in the future, something I have never done before and am resolved never to do again. It is called *The Exchange Student* because of a cute idea I had around five years ago about what fun it would be for a rowdy American family to have an exchange student from another planet. Somehow the other planet has become a place where, in the recent past, war, hunting, and above all technological folly have brought about the extinction of the higher animals. Only insects, scavenging rodents, and, of course, the perpetrators themselves remain in what was once a teeming wonderland. Earth itself has had a nearly catastrophic brush with environmental disaster and has suffered great losses while learning some hard lessons. Huge resources are now devoted to the preservation and propagation of endangered species.

"At the lower end of this effort is sixteen-year-old Daria Wells, who is a licensed breeder and has a small zoo in her own home—the home in which, whether by accident or design, the exchange student arrives. He and a few others have come to Earth with a passionate but ill-defined mission. They are to study our animals and they are to think about ways to repopulate their home planet. Being young, some of their ideas are simplistic to the point of comedy and doomed to fail. In the end, with the help of Daria's mentor, a great zoologist, a solution is found, and the vast project is underway.

"I have had to learn a lot about animals and ecology, and while it is hard to think of a more delightful research project (days and days wandering around zoos, piles and piles of wonderful books), the more I learn the harder it becomes to construct a viable novel—a 'good read,' suspenseful, amusing, and, yes, only two hundred pages long."

■ Works Cited

Barham, Carole Ann, review of *Remembrance of the Sun, Voice of Youth Advocates,* December, 1986, p. 216.
Phelan, Carolyn, review of *Jason and the Bard, Booklist,* March 15, 1993, p. 1313.
Review of *Remembrance of the Sun, Kirkus Reviews,* October 1, 1986, p. 1516.

■ For More Information See

PERIODICALS

Bulletin of the Center for Children's Books, December, 1986.
Kirkus Reviews, March 15, 1993, p. 371.
Publishers Weekly, April 12, 1993, pp. 64-65.*

*   *   *

GONZALEZ, Catherine Troxell 1917-

■ Personal

Born December 28, 1917, in Rhome, Texas; daughter of James Robert (a mail carrier) and Rena (a homemaker; maiden name, Morris) Troxell; married Jack Hastings, May 16, 1940 (divorced); married G. David Gonzalez, 1968 (divorced, 1973); children: (first marriage) James David. *Education:* Texas Technological University, B.A.; North Texas State University, M.A. *Politics:* Democrat. *Religion:* Methodist. *Hobbies and other interests:* Genealogy, writing, traveling, wild birds.

■ Addresses

Home—225 East First St., Rhome, TX 76078.
Office—P.O. Box 66, Rhome, TX 76078.

■ Career

Public school teacher, 1943-1978, for Bowie School District, Bowie, TX, Bridgeport School District, Bridge-

Sari Mednick overcomes prejudice and fear as a Catholic and a Czech in Catherine Gonzalez's vivid account of Texas Klan territory in the 1920s.

port, TX, Lubbock School District, Lubbock, TX, Northwest School District, Northwest, TX, Denton School District, Denton, TX, and Aldine School District, Aldine, TX; writer. Has also worked with the Wise Country Historical Commission and the Wise County Courthouse. *Member:* International Wildlife Federation, National Wild Federation, Daughters of the American Revolution, United Daughters of the Confederacy, Daughters of the Republic of Texas, Wise County Writers Ink, Denton Writers League.

■ Writings

Cynthia Ann Parker, Indian Captive illustrated by Virginia Scott Gholson, Eakin Press, 1980.
Lafitte, the Terror of the Gulf, Eakin Press, 1981.
Jane Long, the Mother of Texas, Eakin Press, 1982.
Tour Guide to North Texas, Eakin Press, 1982.
Quanah Parker, illustrated by Mark Mitchell, Eakin Press, 1987.
Cherub in the Stone, Texas Christian University Press, 1995.

Also author of *Rhome, A Pioneer History, Sam Houston,* and *Cynthia of the Comanches,* illustrated by Peggy Jenkins Logan, all Eakin Press.

■ Work in Progress

Chacho Sanchez, Citizen, for Eakin Press; historical stories about the hangings in Wise County (*Empty Bubbles*) and the Great Depression (*Gilly*); *Annie Cate, Trail Driver; The Sally Bowman Story.*

■ Sidelights

Catherine Troxell Gonzalez told *SATA:* "I wrote my first story in the fourth grade, using a spiral-back nickel notebook. (Wish I had kept that one! It was a thriller mystery story.) I started my serious writing in Lubbock, Texas, writing gardening articles for *Flower and Garden, Horticulture,* and *Workbasket,* to name a few. My next serious venture in writing was the history of my hometown. I wanted to set the record straight on a few stories about Rhome. Then my publisher, Edward Eakin, told me that he would publish anything I wrote for the elementary grades. That was all it took. I haven't stopped writing since that time."*

*   *   *

GREAVES, Margaret 1914-1995

■ Personal

Born June 13, 1914, in Birmingham, England; died June, 1995; daughter of Joseph William (a clergyman) and Jessie May (Greenup) Greaves. *Education:* Attended Alice Ottley School, 1927-33; St. Hugh's College, B.A. (with honors), 1936, B.Litt., 1938, M.A. *Religion:* Church of England.

■ Career

Lincoln High School for Girls, English teacher, 1938-40; Prior School, Shrewsbury, England, English teacher, 1940-41; Pate's Grammar School for Girls, Cheltenham, England, English teacher, 1943-46; St. Mary's College, Cheltenham, lecturer, 1946-60, principal lecturer and head of English department, 1960-70; writer. *Wartime service:* British Women's Land Army, 1941-43. *Member:* English Association, School Library Association.

■ Writings

"ENGLISH FOR JUNIORS" SERIES; FOR CHILDREN

Your Turn Next, illustrated by Jill McDonald, Methuen, 1966.
One World and Another, illustrated by Jill McDonald, Methuen, 1967.
Gallery (short stories), illustrated by Jill McDonald, Methuen, 1968.
Two at Number Twenty, illustrated by Jill McDonald, Methuen, 1970.
What Am I? illustrated by Jill McDonald, Methuen, 1972.

Gallery Wonders (includes *Your Turn Next, One World and Another, Gallery Two at Number Twenty,* and *What Am I?*), Bowmar, 1975.

"GALLIMAUFRY" SERIES: FOR CHILDREN

The Great Bell of Peking, illustrated by Jill McDonald, Methuen, 1971, Bowmar, 1975.

King Solomon and the Hoopoes, illustrated by Jill McDonald, Methuen, 1971, Bowmar, 1975.

The Rainbow Sun, illustrated by Jill McDonald, Methuen, 1971, Bowmar, 1975.

The Snowman of Biddle, illustrated by Jill McDonald, Methuen, 1971, Bowmar, 1975.

FICTION; FOR CHILDREN

The Dagger and the Bird: A Story of Suspense, illustrated by Jill McDonald, Methuen, 1971, illustrated by Laszlo Kubinyi, Harper, 1975.

The Grandmother Stone, Methuen, 1972, published as *Stone of Terror,* Harper, 1974, Target (London), 1974.

Little Jacko and the Wolf People, illustrated by Jill McDonald, Methuen, 1973.

The Gryphon Quest, Methuen, 1974.

Curfew, Methuen, 1975.

The Night of the Goat, illustrated by Trevor Ridley, Abelard Schuman (London), 1976.

Nothing Ever Happens on Sundays, illustrated by Gareth Floyd, BBC Publications, 1976.

A Net to Catch the Wind, illustrated by Stephen Gammell, Harper, 1979.

The Abbotsbury Ring, illustrated by Laszlo Acs, Methuen, 1979.

Charlie, Emma, and Alberic, illustrated by Eileen Browne, Methuen, 1979.

Cat's Magic, illustrated by Joanna Carey, Methuen, 1980, Harper, 1981.

The Snake Whistle, illustrated by Gareth Floyd, BBC Publications, 1980.

Charlie, Emma, and the Dragon Family, illustrated by Eileen Browne, Methuen, 1982.

Charlie, Emma, and the School Dragon, illustrated by Eileen Browne, Methuen, 1984.

The Monster of Roundwater, illustrated by Michael Bragg, Methuen, 1984.

(Reteller) *A Little Box of Witches* (four volumes; includes *The Witch Cat, Kate Crackernuts, The Witch's Servant,* and *Mother Cuspen*), illustrated by Francesca Crespi, Dial, 1985, Methuen, 1985.

(Reteller) *Fairy Tale* (four volumes; includes *The Princess and the Pea, Lucky Hans, The Musicians of Bremen,* and *Red Riding Hood*), illustrated by Annegart Fuchschuber, Michele Lemieux, Renate Mortl-Rangnick, and Eva Scherbarth, Methuen, 1985.

Once There Were No Pandas: A Chinese Legend, illustrated by Beverley Gooding, Dutton, 1985, Methuen, 1985.

(Reteller) *A Little Box of Ballet Stories* (three volumes), illustrated by Francesca Crespi, Dial, 1986, Methuen, 1986.

Little Bear and the Papagini Circus, illustrated by Francesca Crespi, Dial, 1986, Methuen, 1986.

Charlie, Emma, and Dragons to the Rescue, illustrated by Eileen Browne, Methuen, 1986.

(Reteller) *Goldilocks and the Three Bears,* illustrated by Maria Claret, Methuen, 1987.

Hetty Pegler, Half-Witch, illustrated by Derek Crowe, Methuen, 1987.

Charlie, Emma, and the Juggling Dragon, Methuen, 1989.

Mouse Mischief, illustrated by Jane Pinkney, M. Malin/ Deutsch (London), 1989.

The Magic Flute: The Story of Mozart's Opera, illustrated by Francesca Crespi, Greenwillow, 1989, Methuen, 1989.

Juniper's Journey, Methuen, 1990.

(Reteller) *Tattercoats,* illustrated by Margaret Chamberlain, Crown, 1990, F. Lincoln (London), 1990.

Magic from the Ground, Dent, 1990.

The Lucky Coin, illustrated by Liz Underhill, Stewart, Tabori & Chang, 1990.

Henry's Wild Morning, illustrated by Teresa O'Brien, Dent, 1990, Dial, 1991.

Amanda and the Star Child, illustrated by Diane Catchpole, Dent, 1991.

The Lost Ones (short stories), illustrated by Honey de Lacey, Dent, 1991.

Charlie, Emma, and the Runaway Dragon, Methuen, 1991.

Rosie's Lion, Dent, 1992.

The Naming, illustrated by Pauline Baynes, Dent, 1992, Harcourt, 1993.

The Star Horse, illustrated by Jan Nesbitt, Dent, 1992.

Littlemouse Alone, Scholastic, 1992.

Sarah's Lion, illustrated by Honey de Lacey, Barron's Educational (Hauppauge, NY), 1992.

The Ice Journey, illustrated by Alison Claire Darke, Dent, 1993.

Henry in the Dark, illustrated by Teresa O'Brien, Dent, 1993.

The Serpent Shell, illustrated by Jan Nesbitt, Barron's Educational, 1993.

Stories from the Ballet, illustrated by Lisa Kopper, Lincoln, 1993.

POETRY; FOR CHILDREN

Nicky's Knitting Granny and the Cat, illustrated by Alice Englander, Methuen, 1985.

The Mice of Nibbling Village, illustrated by Jane Pinkney, Dutton, 1986, M. Malin (London), 1986.

OTHER

The Blazon of Honor: A Study in Renaissance Magnanimity, Barnes & Noble, 1964, Methuen, 1964.

Regency Patron: Sir George Beaumont, Methuen, 1966.

(Editor) *Scrap-Box: Poems for Grown-ups to Share with Children,* illustrated by Jill McDonald, Methuen, 1969.

A Star for My Son (teleplay), produced by British Broadcast Corp., 1980.

Contributor of reviews to *Renaissance Quarterly.*

■ Sidelights

"Few children's writers have commanded the range, assurance, and depth of Margaret Greaves," notes Myles McDowell in an essay for *Twentieth-Century Children's Writers.* In her long career as both teacher and writer, Greaves has challenged young readers by presenting her young protagonists—and by extension, her audience—with real-life dilemmas that make them think long and hard about the choices they must make. From historical novels such as *Curfew,* where a young boy must question the meaning of justice in nineteenth-century Britain, to adaptations of stories as familiar as *Goldilocks and the Three Bears* and as sophisticated as *The Magic Flute: The Story of Mozart's Opera,* Greaves opens readers' eyes to the relationships between good and evil, fantasy and reality, and the roles that they play in the universal human drama.

Greaves was born in Birmingham, England, in 1914. After graduating from college, she dedicated herself to teaching English to young people. "I have made up stories ever since my childhood," Greaves once told *SATA,* "but never thought of publication until my own students needed an introduction to certain ideas about literature and art not easily available to them elsewhere." She decided that a series of English books for juniors containing original stories and anthologized poems would be of great help in the classroom, "because I believe that children can learn more from imaginative literature than from text-books." The "English for Juniors" series contains five volumes of poetry, collected short stories, and original fiction.

Greaves enjoyed writing the "English for Juniors" series so much that she decided to try her hand at a full-length novel for young readers. *The Dagger and the Bird: A Story of Suspense,* combines history and fantasy in a suspenseful tale that has been praised by reviewers. Bridget and Luke, the children of a country blacksmith and his wife, are subjected to the abusive ill temper of their younger brother, Simon, who also mistreats their parents, animals, and just about everything else. When they discover that Simon is afraid of the cold iron of the smithy shop and refuses to do his part in helping his ailing father, they become suspicious; Simon finally admits that he is not their brother at all but a changeling, a fairy imp left in place of the real Simon by the fairies who stole him. Bravely Bridget and Luke undertake a dangerous journey, with the help of the changeling himself, to the land of the fairies in order to rescue the real Simon. In addition to plotting a suspenseful yarn, Greaves illustrates the plight of both the human Simon and his changeling counterpart: raised in two separate worlds, they will never really feel at home in either.

"If Greaves has the courage to leave her heroes (and readers!) in uncertainty and nagging doubt," comments McDowell, "it is because, enriched in self-knowledge, they emerge from adventure equipped to face a more complex world." In *The Dagger and the Bird,* as well as her other fictional works, Greaves denies her readers a

In Margaret Greaves' *A Net to Catch the Wind* a king's obsession with capturing a beautiful wild colt leads him to disregard a wizard's warning and take advantage of his daughter's trust. (Illustration by Stephen Gammell.)

tidy ending; it is clear, instead, that the aftershocks of the children's adventures will continue to affect each of them; the reader has witnessed only a small part of their story. *The Grandmother Stone,* published in the United States as *Stone of Terror,* also combines history and fantasy with the personal growth of its young protagonists as Philip is sent by his dying mother to a small Channel Island to join his grandfather. Setting her tale in the seventeenth-century, Greaves posits her young hero amid witchcraft, violent storms, fear, and suspicion as he tries to convince Marie, the outcast niece of a fearful pagan priestess, to break away from her crazed and embittered aunt and her supposed bonds with the devil. *The Abbotsbury Ring* finds young Selina West suddenly equipped with the power to communicate with animals after she discovers a magic ring lying in a garden. Chatting with sea gulls and a stray dog running along the beach are fun, but when Selina and a friend are kidnapped by two ne'er-do-wells after witnessing a burglary, the power of the ring lets her call animal rescuers to their aid. In the end, Selina returns the ring to its original owner and learns that, with the love and caring she has for animals, she has no need for magic. And in Greaves's *A Net to Catch the Wind,* young Mirabelle is asked by her father, the king, to capture a beautiful silver-colored colt he has seen running wild in his royal forest. Despite the warning of the king's wizard to let the animal remain free, the king uses the trust that develops between his daughter and the colt she now calls Starlight to capture the wild beast; Starlight weakens in captivity until Mirabelle frees him and the two escape together. Now without his daughter, the king realizes his mistake in trying to possess something so beautiful and free-spirited; after he makes a gesture by freeing all the horses from the royal stable, Starlight, who has grown into a beautiful unicorn, and Mirabelle return.

Greaves enters the world of the fantastic even more fully in *Cat's Magic*. Travelling through time becomes a reality for Louise Higgs, a young girl who is sent to live on her Aunt Harriet's farm after the death of both her parents. Despite the friendship of a local boy named Charlie, she finds living in the country boring until she saves a young Abyssinian kitten from drowning. Louise wins the gratitude of Bast, the Egyptian cat goddess, who rewards the girl by sending her a hundred years into the past. Back in Victorian England, Louise finds herself working as a maid in a boarding house, where she actually meets one of her own ancestors. The owner of the boarding house is stealing from her guests and Louise resolves to help put the matter right with the help of several friends who are allowed to follow her through time.

The complexity of time travel is replaced by the confusion caused by having a dragon for a pet within the pages of *Charlie, Emma, and Alberic*. When Charlie finds a small lizard living in a hole in the road, he decides that it is the perfect pet, names it Alberic, and carries it home. However, as he and friend Emma watch the new pet, they realize that Alberic is growing larger and larger by the hour; he soon begins to talk and shows how he can become invisible at will. The children are quick to realize that this is no ordinary lizard—in fact, Alberic is a dragon, who, invisible to all in the house except Charlie and Emma, moves in as one of the family. When construction crews begin working on the road where Charlie found him—and beneath which Alberic's family still lives—the children quickly come to his aid and help the dragon and his family to safety. Alberic eventually marries and moves away, leaving Charlie and Emma with a new little dragon to take his place. Greaves continues the story of Charlie and his dragon friends in several sequels, including *Charlie, Emma, and the Dragon Family* and *Charlie, Emma, and Dragons to the Rescue,* where the children are joined by several of their magical friends in a holiday animal rescue mission, which finds several dragons joining the Animal Sanctuary parade through town—raising absolutely *no* eyebrows from the cheering townspeople.

While many of her books have been aimed at older readers, Greaves has also written many stories for younger children. *Little Bear and the Papagini Circus* is about a young bear unable to perform the stunts of the older, more experienced bear-family members, but his inadvertent antics end up stealing the show. Greaves's verses are combined with gentle watercolor drawings by illustrator Jane Pinkney to produce *The Mice of Nibbling Village,* fourteen poems about the small creatures that go about their daily chores under the floorboards of an old country house. In *Hetty Pegler, Half-Witch* the holiday guest of Toby, Jane, and Ben seems ordinary at first, but she turns out to be part witch and part human—and her spells tend to come out half-baked. Henry, the small tiger kitten, keeps things just as unpredictable in *Henry's Wild Morning* and *Henry in*

Greaves's entertaining story of a tiny striped kitten who wakes up one day feeling bold as a tiger is complemented by Teresa O'Brien's captivating illustrations. (Illustration by Teresa O'Brien from *Henry's Wild Morning.*)

the Dark as he decides to live up to his stripes. Nighttime excursions, the predicament of climbing too high in a tree, and other cat antics are shown through the eyes of a kitten to the enjoyment of young listeners. Also designed to be read aloud, *The Naming* is Greaves's account of how animals first got their names. To this Old Testament story is added a drop of magic as Greaves adds a single unicorn into the crowd of animals that appear in pairs before Adam to receive their names. "Wonderful moments are described in musical, precise language," according to reviewer Patricia Pearl Dole in *School Library Journal.*

The Naming is one of several adaptations of traditional stories that Greaves has done during her writing career. Her 1991 story collection *The Lost Ones* contains a dozen folktales that are perfect for reading aloud. "These are carefully turned pieces, lightly done so that the pathos of lost or enchanted children breathes through the settings of seashore or woodland, of riverside or ancient dwelling," notes Margery Fisher in *Growing Point. Once There Were No Pandas: A Chinese Legend* is Greaves's retelling of how panda bears came to have black spots, and *Tattercoats* is a classic folktale about a princess who is cast out of her home and befriended by a gooseherd and his flock. In *The Ice Journey,* Greaves explores the folk traditions of Iceland with a story that has everything from an evil stepmother to a nasty witch who puts the cauldron on to boil when little children come calling. And, in addition to folk and fairy tales from many cultures, Greaves transforms a personal love for the ballet into several books for young readers, including *A Little Box of Ballet Stories,* which contains the stories of "Firebird," "Petrushka," and

In this picture book based on Mozart's opera, the story of Prince Tamino's search for the beautiful Pamina is retold for young audiences. (Cover illustration by Francesca Crespi.)

"Coppelia," each in their own tiny volume. *Stories from the Ballet* expands the theme with outlines of seven of the most widely viewed ballets. And it's a quick step from the graceful world of the ballet to the colorful festivities that inhabit the stage during "The Magic Flute," an opera popular with children that Greaves outlines in *The Magic Flute: The Story of Mozart's Opera.*

Wide-ranging interests and an enthusiasm for sharing those interests with young readers have made Greaves's books lasting favorites. "My ideas spring from an interest in human relationships and a deep love of the countryside in which I have always lived," Greaves told *SATA,* "and from a heritage of folklore and history. My books often grow from a single image that comes to me quite unexpectedly—an ancient statue seen at a church gate in the Channel Islands, or a mental picture of the desolation of a changeling in a human household; and I recognize the image as the germ of a story that may become clear to me if I wait quietly and patiently. It is as if the story is there already and only waiting to be discovered."

■ Works Cited

Dole, Patricia Pearl, review of *The Naming, School Library Journal,* May, 1993, p. 84.

Fisher, Margery, "Words and Pictures," *Growing Point,* July, 1991, pp. 5538-41.

McDowell, Myles, "Margaret Greaves," in *Twentieth-Century Children's Writers,* 4th edition, edited by Laura Standley Berger, St. James Press, 1994, pp. 404-405.

■ For More Information See

PERIODICALS

Booklist, December 1, 1992, p. 675.

Horn Book, October, 1974; April, 1975.

Junior Bookshelf, June, 1982, p. 97; April, 1986, p. 67; October, 1990, p. 231; February, 1993, pp. 12-13; April, 1993, p. 60; December, 1993, p. 233; April, 1994, pp. 49-50.

New York Times Book Review, April 8, 1979, pp. 32-33; December 8, 1985, p. 74.

Publishers Weekly, October 14, 1974, p. 57; August 2, 1985, pp. 66-67.

School Library Journal, September, 1979, p. 110; April, 1981, p. 127; February, 1987, p. 68.

Times Literary Supplement, April 2, 1971; September 20, 1974; March 28, 1980, p. 361; March 30, 1984.

Wilson Library Bulletin, February, 1988, pp. 76-77.*

[Date of death provided by Marilyn Malin, copyright holder for Margaret Greaves' works.]

*   *   *

GREEN, Sheila Ellen 1934-
(Sheila Greenwald)

■ Personal

Born May 26, 1934, in New York, NY; daughter of Julius (a manufacturer) and Florence (Friedman) Greenwald; married George Green (a surgeon), February 18, 1960; children: Samuel, Benjamin. *Education:* Sarah Lawrence College, B.A., 1956. *Politics:* Democrat. *Religion:* Jewish.

■ Addresses

Home—175 Riverside Dr., New York, NY 10024.

■ Awards, Honors

Notable Children's Book, American Library Association, 1981, for *Give Us a Great Big Smile, Rosy Cole;* Junior Library Guild selection, 1983, for *Will the Real Gertrude Hollings Please Stand Up?* and 1989, for *Rosy's Romance;* and Parents Choice selection, 1985, for *Rosie Cole's Great American Guilt Club.*

■ Career

Writer and illustrator.

SHEILA ELLEN GREEN

■ Writings

SELF-ILLUSTRATED YOUNG ADULT FICTION; UNDER NAME SHEILA GREENWALD

A Metropolitan Love Story, Doubleday, 1962.
Willie Bryant and the Flying Otis, Grosset, 1971.
The Hot Day, Bobbs-Merrill, 1972.
Miss Amanda Snap, Bobbs-Merrill, 1972.
Mat Pit and the Tunnel Tenants, Lippincott, 1972.
The Secret Museum, Lippincott, 1974.
The Secret in Miranda's Closet, Houghton, 1977.
The Mariah Delany Lending Library Disaster, Houghton, 1977.
The Atrocious Two, Houghton, 1978.
All the Way to Wits' End, Little, Brown, 1979.
It All Began with Jane Eyre; or, The Secret Life of Franny Dillman, Little, Brown, 1980.
Give Us a Great Big Smile, Rosy Cole, Atlantic/Little, Brown, 1981.
Blissful Joy and the SATs: A Multiple-Choice Romance, Atlantic/Little, Brown, 1982.
Will the Real Gertrude Hollings Please Stand Up?, Atlantic/Little, Brown, 1983.
Valentine Rosy, Atlantic/Little, Brown, 1984.

Rosy Cole's Great American Guilt Club, Atlantic/Little, Brown, 1985.
Alvin Webster's Sure Fire Plan for Success and How It Failed, Little, Brown, 1987.
Write On, Rosy!: A Young Author in Crisis, Little, Brown, 1988.
Rosy's Romance, Little, Brown, 1989.
Mariah Delany's Author-of-the-Month Club, Little, Brown, 1990.
Here's Hermione: A Rosy Cole Production, Little, Brown, 1991.
Rosy Cole Discovers America!, Little, Brown, 1992.
My Fabulous New Life, Browndeer Press, 1993.
Rosy Cole: She Walks in Beauty, Little, Brown, 1994.
Emerald House, Browndeer Press, 1996.
The Rose Grows, Orchard, 1996.

ILLUSTRATOR; UNDER NAME SHEILA GREENWALD

Marie L. Allen, *Pocketful of Poems,* Harper, 1957.
Carol Ryrie Brink, *The Pink Motel,* Macmillan, 1959.
Florence Laughlin, *The Little Leftover Witch,* Macmillan, 1960.
Miriam Dreifus, *Brave Betsy,* Putnam, 1961.
Grace V. Curl, *Come A-Witching,* Bobbs-Merrill, 1964.
Laura H. Fisher, *Amy and the Sorrel Summer,* Holt, 1964.
Barbara Rinkoff, *The Remarkable Ramsey,* Morrow, 1965.
Hila Colman, *The Boy Who Couldn't Make Up His Mind,* Macmillan, 1965.
Anne Mallet, *Who'll Mind Henry?,* Doubleday, 1965.
Florence Laughlin, *The Seventh Cousin,* Macmillan, 1966.
Mary J. Roth, *The Pretender Princess,* Morrow, 1967.
James Playsted Wood, *When I Was Jersey,* Pantheon, 1967.
Emma V. Worstell, *Jump the Rope Jingles,* Macmillan, 1967.
Jean Bothwell, *The Mystery Cup,* Dial, 1968.
M. Jean Craig, *The New Boy on the Sidewalk,* Norton, 1968.
Nancy K. Robinson, *Veronica the Show Off,* Scholastic, 1982.
Henny Youngman, *Henny Youngman's Book of Jokes,* Carol Publishers, 1992.

OTHER

Contributor to periodicals, including *Cricket* and *New York Times;* contributor of illustrations to magazines, including *Harper's, Gourmet,* and *Reporter.*

■ Sidelights

Humorous and sensitive are the adjectives most often used to describe the work of Sheila Ellen Green, who writes under her maiden name, Shiela Greenwald. She is an author-artist best known for her "Rosy Cole" stories that trace the misadventures of the eponymous pre-teen heroine through trials of romance, violin playing, and self-beautification schemes. Greenwald's books for middle readers and young adults, while not of the hard-hitting realistic school, *do* deal with contemporary problems, including divorce, mental illness, anorexia, and unwanted pregnancy. However, Greenwald's gift is that she is always able to find humor in the bleakest of predicaments; her characters are thus able, as Maryclare O'Donnell Himmel wrote in *Twentieth-Century Young Adult Writers*, "to laugh at themselves and their seemingly hopeless situations."

Greenwald has turned an ironic and rather whimsical vision of the world into a genre. Her scratchy pen-and-ink drawings complement her written portraits of characters who are slightly offbeat, full of bravado, and just mischievous enough to feel like old friends to the reader. Though she does not necessarily write autobiographically, Greenwald confesses to exploring and expanding the situations that touch her life through her fiction. "My challenge," Greenwald once told *SATA*, "is to invent characters, plots, and scenes which will develop and define my feelings and opinions. In fact, my books often begin with strong opinions which I then have to soften and obscure so they aren't boring and polemical."

Polemics were the last thing Greenwald was thinking of, however, when beginning her career. "I started drawing too far back to remember," she told *SATA*, "and I did it all the time, as a habit, as a way to amuse myself." Reading comic books was another form of addiction for the young Greenwald, one that greatly influenced her drawing style. Growing up in New York City, she studied at the High School of Music and Art and then attended Sarah Lawrence, majoring in literature. At this point she stopped her formal study of painting, but continued to draw—in doodles on the margins of her papers. An interested professor suggested she put these drawings together and show them to publishers, which Greenwald did, and this ultimately led to a fourteen-year career as an illustrator not only for children's books, but for magazines, humor collections, and cookbooks. "After illustrating other people's books for a number of years, I decided to try writing my own and found this doubly rewarding," Greenwald recalled for *SATA*. Part of the inspiration for beginning to write books was having her own children demand ever more complex and humorous tales. Employing literary models from Jane Austen to Evelyn Waugh and Nancy Mitford, Greenwald concocted a strange brew of wit and humor with which to confront life's hardships and hurdles.

"I write down ideas that appeal to me—some work out, some don't," she explained to *SATA*. "*The Hot Day* was based on an incident from my father's childhood." One of her earliest books, *The Hot Day* tells the story of a family sweltering in summer heat, before the days of air conditioning, and of their roomer who remains cool—he's got the only fan in the place. One night the kids of the family blow talcum powder over themselves in the breeze from the fan and scare away the roomer—who thinks they are apparitions. "A mischievous idea," noted a *Kirkus Reviews* critic, and it sets the tone for much of Greenwald's juvenile fiction. With *Miss Amanda Snap,* she tells the story of a writer of children's books whose main character—Kirby the mouse—comes to life and slowly changes into a man whom the author promptly marries. No happy ending, however, for her

Enterprising Mariah Delany bites off more than she can chew when she creates the Author-of-the-Month Club and invites real authors to come and sign books. (Cover illustration by Robert Sauber.)

next Kirby-the-mouse book is a flop. "A witty and imaginative plot and pictures," commented one *Publishers Weekly* contributor.

Dolls are prominently featured in both *The Secret Museum* and *The Secret in Miranda's Closet*. In the former, elements of fantasy and fairy tale are blended when Jennifer Fairfax moves to the country with her potter mother (humorously named Beatrice) and weaver father. But at first business goes badly for the former teachers-turned-craftspeople, and Jennifer is left to her own devices. Soon she discovers a playhouse in the woods that contains a priceless collection of dolls who talk to Jennifer about how lonely and neglected they feel. With the help of a friend, Jennifer opens a museum and puts on puppet plays, giving her parents a lesson in enterprise at the same time. They subsequently adopt more businesslike practices, making their own luck. A *Publishers Weekly* reviewer described *The Secret Museum* as "a lovely low-keyed offering." With *The Secret in Miranda's Closet,* Greenwald once again uses a doll and a secret to power the plot, but in a more realistic vein. Miranda is a pudgy and stolid sort of girl whose feminist mother made a name for herself writing about how she has raised her daughter without the usual stifling role definers, such as dolls. But Miranda's secret is that she has a doll, given to her by a friend and tucked away in her closet. When the secret comes out, the mother realizes that she has been trying to force Miranda into a mold she has created for her, every bit as strict as society's. This is a story that has "vigor and warmth and humor," noted a *Bulletin of the Center for Children's Books* contributor, and a writer for *Kirkus Reviews* commented that "the assertiveness that the whole experience brings to the lumpy little girl is heartening."

Mischievous, plucky young girls play a prominent part in Greenwald's literary landscape. Mariah Delany figures in two such books, *The Mariah Delany Lending Library Disaster* and *Mariah Delany's Author-of-the-Month Club*. In the first, cutbacks in the New York City Public Library inspire Mariah to concoct a money-making scheme: she'll open her own library using her parents' huge collection of books and then collect a fortune on the overdue fines. It all works wonderfully until she discovers the universal truth of libraries: it is much easier to loan than to retrieve. "Mariah is an entertaining schemer," concluded Christine McDonnell in *School Library Journal*. Entrepreneurial dreams also inspire *Mariah Delany's Author-of-the-Month Club*, with much the same disastrous results as the earlier book. Bombing after three attempts to enlist authors, Mariah reluctantly gives up her plan to run her own author-of-the-month club and deals instead with the mountain of accumulated homework waiting for her. Joy Fleishhacker, writing in *School Library Journal*, noted that Greenwald's "humorous pen-and-ink sketches capture the energy and determination of this enjoyable character."

Another example of the slightly precocious, vaguely mischievous protagonists that Greenwald so effortlessly portrays is thirteen-year-old Franny Dillman in *It All Began with Jane Eyre; or, the Secret Life of Franny Dillman*. Franny inhales books whole and is mesmerized by Jane Eyre's situation. Her mother, alarmed at Franny's identification with this mature fictional heroine, attempts to bring Franny into touch with problems more her own age by introducing her to contemporary realistic juvenile fiction. Instead of lessening Franny's imaginative identification, these books only heighten it. Suddenly she is discovering divorce, teenage pregnancy, abortion and disease among her own family. Her detective work in trying to uncover such problems only lands her in hot water when her family in turn suspects her of being pregnant. "The results are hilarious and unpredictable," wrote McDonnell in *Horn Book*, describing the work as "a fast-paced, light-hearted spoof." It is also a book that pokes fun at contemporary teenage problem novels. *Bulletin of the Center for Children's Books* writer Zena Sutherland found that "the strength of the book is in the characterization and dialogue, both of which ring true."

In many ways, it is as if Greenwald's teenage and preteen protagonists up to 1980 were all a preparation for the series of books for which she is best known, the Rosy Cole novels, the first of which, *Give Us a Great Big*

Smile, Rosy Cole, appeared in 1981. Ten-year-old Rosy has the spotlight turned on her by her photographer uncle, who wants to create a book of photographs about her as he has done for her older sisters—one a ballet student and the other an equestrian. Hers is to be about her violin playing, and for a time even Rosy falls for fame, being brought up short, however, after hearing a recording of her own terrible playing. The heat is then on to stop publication of her uncle's book before the whole world discovers what a non-prodigy Rosy is. "The author never loses touch with her heroine," noted Kate M. Flanagan in *Horn Book*, "a refreshingly ordinary child whose basic good sense saves her from the foibles of adults." Marilyn Kaye, writing in *School Library Journal*, found this first Rosy Cole adventure "a cheerful, zesty story with a potential for wide appeal." *Give Us a Great Big Smile, Rosy Cole* went on to win an ALA Notable Children's Book award.

Valentine Rosy continues the adventures when Rosy Cole finds herself hosting a Valentine's Day party that will be competing with one being thrown by a crowd of boy-crazy classmates. Rosy is doubly surprised when she learns she will actually have to invite boys. "Rosy is an exceedingly likable heroine, and her realization that

With two teenage sisters at home, Rosy embarks on an ambitious research project to find out all about romance. (Cover illustration by Cly Wallace.)

Determined to out-beautify her child-model friend, Christi, Rosy tries to emulate paintings at the art museum in this funny tale.

everyone grows up at his or her own pace strikes a reassuring note," commented a *Booklist* critic, while a *Bulletin of the Center for Children's Books* reviewer found that Greenwald's creation was "shrewdly perceptive on pre-teens." Karen Jameyson concluded in *Horn Book* that the author "has created another wholly successful book about her refreshingly down-to-earth heroine." With *Rosy Cole's Great American Guilt Club,* Greenwald dealt with the theme of greedy materialism and peer pressure, and in *Write On, Rosy!: A Young Author in Crisis* she continued Rosy's search for individual talent, one that leads to investigative reporting and trouble for Rosy when she spies on the school principal. *Bulletin of the Center for Children's Books* contributor Roger Sutton noted of the latter book that "Rosy's unself-conscious charm is in great evidence." In *Rosy's Romance* Rosy and her buddy Hermione become obsessed with romance novels and try to turn Rosy's arty sisters into the kind of teens they've been reading about. Rosy is so busy trying to get her sisters regular dates that she almost misses romance staring her in the face. Partly a spoof on juvenile series books and their lack of depth, *Rosy's Romance* might prove the antidote to such books, according to Sylvia S. Margantz in *School Library Journal:* "If anyone can woo girls from series

books to a bit more substantial plotting and character depiction, it will be Rosy."

Further Rosy Cole adventures feature her best friend in *Here's Hermione: A Rosy Cole Production,* examine family history and heritage in *Rosy Cole Discovers America!,* and question what true beauty is in *Rosy Cole: She Walks in Beauty.* Commenting on the last mentioned title, Lauren Peterson noted in *Booklist* that "while there's plenty of light fun, Greenwald also shows that even preteens feel tremendous pressure to be thin and beautiful." It is this blending of light humor with what are essentially weighty themes that makes the Rosy Cole books so effective.

Apart from Rosy Cole, Greenwald is perhaps best known for her young adult novel, *Blissful Joy and the SATs: A Multiple-Choice Romance.* A multi-layered and complex novel, it tells the story of sixteen-year-old Blissful Joy Bowman who takes herself to be the only practical member of a family consisting of her and her two divorced actor parents. Low scores on Blissful's first SAT attempt shake her self-image, and her schoolfriend Colin helps her to see that maybe she is more romantic and fanciful than she has allowed herself to be. Befriending a mutt that follows her home helps in the process of self-discovery, as do the cast of quirky individuals the dog brings into her well organized life. First love in the form of MPRWOS (Meaningful Peer Relationships With the Opposite Sex) rocks Bliss and introduces her to a world far larger than she had allowed herself to see. A *Publishers Weekly* critic felt Greenwald outdid herself with this book: "Greenwald's piquant wit and velvety prose transform stories into delights, although she does not underestimate the dilemmas that teens face." And Himmel concluded that "Greenwald's expert use of irony and satire is one of the qualities that lifts this novel above other, more mundane 'problem novels.'"

"I write and draw because I enjoy writing and drawing," Greenwald once told *SATA.* "My books are intended for whoever enjoys my pleasure in these things." It is a large category, and Greenwald's legion of readers have come to rely on her quirky takes, her sardonic glimpses. As many reviewers have noted, her books have helped countless readers move on to chapter books, especially with the Rosy Cole series. Additionally, Greenwald's insistence on maintaining a sense of humor might help young readers deal effectively with life in the real world.

■ Works Cited

Review of *Blissful Joy and the SATs: A Multiple-Choice Romance, Publishers Weekly,* March 19, 1982, p. 71.

Flanagan, Kate M., review of *Give Us a Great Big Smile, Rosy Cole, Horn Book,* August, 1981, pp. 421-22.

Fleishhacker, Joy, review of *Mariah Delany's Author-of-the-Month Club, School Library Journal,* December, 1991, p. 114.

Himmel, Maryclare O'Donnell, "Sheila Greenwald," in *Twentieth-Century Young Adult Writers,* 1st edition, edited by Laura Standley Berger, St. James Press, 1994, pp. 259-60.

Review of *The Hot Day, Kirkus Reviews,* March 15, 1972, p. 320.

Jameyson, Karen, review of *Valentine Rosy, Horn Book,* January-February, 1985, p. 50.

Kaye, Marilyn, review of *Give Us a Great Big Smile, Rosy Cole, School Library Journal,* September, 1981, p. 125.

Margantz, Sylvia S., review of *Rosy's Romance, School Library Journal,* August, 1989, pp. 139-40.

McDonnell, Christine, review of *The Mariah Delany Lending Library Disaster, School Library Journal,* November, 1977, p. 56.

McDonnell, Christine, review of *It All Began with Jane Eyre; or, The Secret Life of Franny Dillman, Horn Book,* August, 1980, p. 407.

Review of *Miss Amanda Snap, Publishers Weekly,* August 7, 1972, p. 50.

Peterson, Lauren, review of *Rosy Cole: She Walks in Beauty, Booklist,* December 15, 1994, p. 753.

Review of *The Secret in Miranda's Closet, Kirkus Reviews,* March 1, 1977, p. 223.

Review of *The Secret in Miranda's Closet, Bulletin of the Center for Children's Books,* September, 1977, p. 15.

Review of *The Secret Museum, Publishers Weekly,* March 25, 1974, p. 56.

Sutherland, Zena, review of *It All Began with Jane Eyre; or, the Secret Life of Franny Dillman, Bulletin of the Center for Children's Books,* September, 1980, p. 10.

Sutton, Roger, review of *Write On, Rosy!: A Young Author in Crisis, Bulletin of the Center for Children's Books,* January, 1989, p. 121.

Review of *Valentine Rosy, Bulletin of the Center for Children's Books,* January, 1985, p. 84.

Review of *Valentine Rosy, Booklist,* March 1, 1985, p. 982.

■ **For More Information See**

PERIODICALS

Bulletin of the Center for Children's Books, December, 1972, p. 56; July, 1974, p. 177; February, 1978, p. 93; July, 1981, p. 193; December, 1983, p. 67; January, 1986, p. 86; July, 1989, p. 276; September, 1991, p. 11; January, 1993, p. 146; January, 1995, p. 165.

Horn Book, February, 1978, p. 45; February, 1980, p. 55; August, 1982, p. 412; August, 1983, p. 443; January, 1986, p. 58; March, 1988, p. 201; March, 1989, p. 233; September, 1989, p. 647; November, 1991, p. 735.

School Library Journal, May, 1977, p. 61; March, 1981, p. 108; August, 1983, p. 65; December, 1984, p. 80; January, 1986, p. 67; January, 1988, p. 74; January, 1989, p. 77; November, 1991, p. 96; January, 1993, p. 98; October, 1993, p. 124; January, 1995, p. 106.

Voice of Youth Advocates, January, 1982, p. 33; October, 1983, p. 202; June, 1994, p. 82.*

—*Sketch by J. Sydney Jones*

GREENWALD, Sheila
See GREEN, Sheila Ellen

*   *   *

GRIFFITH, Helen V(irginia) 1934-

■ **Personal**

Born October 31, 1934, in Wilmington, DE; daughter of John (a railroad machinist) and Helen (a wholesale building materials company president; maiden name, Williams) Griffith; divorced. *Education:* Attended high school in Woodcrest, DE. *Politics:* Republican. *Religion:* Christian. *Hobbies and other interests:* Birdwatching.

■ **Addresses**

Home—410 Country Club Dr., Wilmington, DE 19803. *Office*—S. G. Williams & Bros. Co., 301 Tatnall St., Wilmington, DE 19801.

■ **Career**

Secretary and clerk at various companies, 1953-76; S. G. Williams & Bros. Co., Wilmington, DE, secretary-treasurer, 1976—; writer of books for children. *Member:* Authors League of America, Authors Guild, Delmarva Ornithological Society.

HELEN V. GRIFFITH

■ Awards, Honors

Children's Choice Award, International Reading Association/Children's Book Council, 1981, for *"Mine Will," Said John;* Best Books citation, *School Library Journal,* 1982, for *Alex and the Cat;* Boston Globe-Horn Book Honor Book selection, 1987, and Notable Book citation, American Library Association (ALA), both for *Georgia Music; Junior Library Guild* selections for *Alex and the Cat, Alex Remembers,* and *More Alex and the Cat;* ALA Notable Book citations for *Grandaddy's Place* and *Grandaddy and Janetta.*

■ Writings

"Mine Will," Said John, illustrated by Muriel Batherman, Greenwillow, 1980, published with illustrations by Joseph A. Smith, 1992.

Alex and the Cat, illustrated by Joseph Low, Greenwillow, 1982.

Alex Remembers, illustrated by Donald Carrick, Greenwillow, 1983.

More Alex and the Cat, illustrated by Donald Carrick, Greenwillow, 1983.

Foxy, Greenwillow, 1984.

Nata, illustrated by Nancy Tafuri, Greenwillow, 1985.

Georgia Music, illustrated by James Stevenson, Greenwillow, 1986.

Journal of a Teenage Genius, Greenwillow, 1987.

Grandaddy's Place, illustrated by James Stevenson, Greenwillow, 1987.

Emily and the Enchanted Frog, illustrated by Susan Condie Lamb, Greenwillow, 1989.

Caitlin's Holiday, illustrated by Susan Condie Lamb, Greenwillow, 1990.

Plunk's Dreams, illustrated by Susan Condie Lamb, Greenwillow, 1990.

Doll Trouble, illustrated by Susan Condie Lamb, Greenwillow, 1993.

Grandaddy and Janetta, illustrated by James Stevenson, Greenwillow, 1993.

Dream Meadow, illustrated by Nancy Barnet, Greenwillow, 1994.

Grandaddy's Stars, illustrated by James Stevenson, Greenwillow, 1995.

Also author of stories and articles published in various magazines.

■ Sidelights

Helen V. Griffith won critical notice with her first published book for children, 1980's *"Mine Will," Said John.* She "emerged on the children's books scene in a way reminiscent of her prose: quiet, poetic, and subtly powerful," Cathryn M. Mercier wrote in *Twentieth-Century Children's Writers.* Since then, Griffith has continued "to attain success in a variety of forms," including picture books, chapter books, and novels for intermediate readers. While the tone or technique of her work may vary, "a gentle humor and ardent respect for human integrity and frailty permeate all her works," Mercier stated. Of all of Griffith's books, those featuring

After three trips to the pet store, John finally finds the ideal pet that both pleases his parents and lets him sleep. (Illustration by Jos. A. Smith from *"Mine Will," Said John.*)

the dog Alex and his cat friend and another series begun with *Georgia Music,* which portrays the relationship between a young girl and her grandfather, have elicited the most praise from critics.

Griffith once told *SATA* how her career as a writer developed: "I have been writing and drawing since I could handle a pencil, but I never took it seriously. When I was very young I wrote poetry, usually about animals. Later I began several novels which I illustrated profusely, but never finished. In high school I wrote funny sketches which still make me laugh—interviews with my dog, Wooly, about current events and little skits about school life that were very unflattering (and unfair) to our teachers.

"My tenth grade English teacher liked my writing (she never saw the skits) and encouraged me to send a poem to a magazine for teenagers. They published it and paid me, and if I'd had any sense, that would have been the beginning of my writing career. Instead, I never submitted another thing anywhere until I was forty years old. I started out writing nonfiction articles for magazines. Then I had an idea for a story about some boys and a tape recorder. I wrote it and found that I preferred writing fiction and that's what I've done ever since."

Griffith explained to *SATA* that since she loves nature and has "always liked animals," many of her books feature dogs. "I don't begin by thinking, 'I'm going to write a book about a dog,' but that's what happens."

"Mine Will," Said John, Griffith's first book, is all about a young boy's desire for a dog. When his parents suggest that a gerbil would be a nice pet, John insists that the best pet for him is a puppy; he predicts that the gerbil will cry at night. After John complains that the gerbil does cry all night, his parents replace the gerbil with a chameleon. But the chameleon does not make a good pet either—it bothers John by glowing purple and orange and pink at night. A frog would not be a good pet for John, either; according to him, it will chew the furniture. Finally, John's parents give in and buy him the perfect pet—a puppy. According to *School Library Journal* contributor Mary Rinato Berman, *"Mine Will," Said John* is "an amusing story for reading aloud, and it's easy enough for beginning readers." Children who enjoy *"Mine Will," Said John* will also appreciate *Plunk's Dreams,* in which a boy named John wonders about his dog's dreams as the pet twitches and yelps in his sleep. In *Booklist,* Ellen Mandel praised the author's "pertly phrased text" as "reminiscent of her spunky *Mine Will, Said John.*"

Griffith has delighted cat and dog lovers with her stories about Alex, a small, naive dog, and his wise feline friend. *Alex and the Cat* contains three stories involving the pair. In the first, Alex laments his dog's life of baths and tricks and tries out the cat's lifestyle. Failing at that, he decides to become a wild animal. Instead of bravely hunting a meal when it gets dark, however, Alex finds an excuse to return to the safety of his home. In the final story, Alex mistakes a baby chick for a baby robin and tries to put it in a robin's nest. Reviewers of *Alex and the Cat* appreciated the humorous dialogue shared by the dog and the cat. *School Library Journal* contributor Nancy Palmer found the book to be "warm, funny and involving—a rare gem in the genre"; and Zena Sutherland of *Bulletin of the Center for Children's Books* concluded that *Alex and the Cat* is a "joy to read aloud or alone."

Alex Remembers begins when the restless dog and cat are let out for a nighttime walk. When they see a large orange moon in the sky, Alex begins to howl without knowing why, and the cat assures him that he is remembering things from the long-ago past. Finally, Robbie, the animals' young owner, joins them as they watch the moon, and Alex wonders if Robbie is remembering as well. "The idea of animals responding to ancestral instincts is conveyed with feeling and dignity," concluded a critic for *Kirkus Reviews. More Alex and the Cat* provides three more stories for Alex's fans: Alex obsessively searches for a buried bone, uncontrollably chews family possessions, complains about the cold weather and then enjoys the first snow of winter. Of course, Alex's antics are accompanied by the wry comments of the cat. According to *Horn Book* critic Kate M. Flanagan, the "comic misunderstandings" of the dog and cat's conversations in one of these stories "calls to mind an Abbott and Costello routine."

Griffith's first story about "Grandaddy" and his grand-daughter appeared with the publication of *Georgia Music.* In this book, a girl visits her grandfather for the

summer in Georgia, and she enjoys sharing his quiet, peaceful life. Grandaddy finds her a hat and a hoe, and she helps him in the garden tending melons and black-eyed peas. The pair takes naps in the afternoon, and Grandaddy plays the mouth organ in the evening. Although the girl plans to visit her grandfather the next summer, he falls ill and comes to live in Baltimore with the girl and her family. Grandaddy longs for his cabin and Georgia afternoons; he sadly languishes until the girl plays "Georgia music" on the mouth organ for him and makes him laugh. Many critics appreciated *Georgia Music* and the watercolor illustrations of James Stevenson. In the opinion of *Horn Book* contributor Ann A. Flowers, *Georgia Music* presents "a blissful idyll of a nearly vanished style of life and a picture of quiet affection between the generations." Kathleen Brachmann similarly described *Georgia Music* in *School Library Journal* as a "very special love story" that "unwinds slowly and with an appealing gentleness."

Grandaddy's Place describes Janetta's initial relation-ship with her grandfather. The very first time she arrives at her grandfather's farm, she is disheartened: the farm is old, the yard looks barren, she sees a huge mule, and she thinks Grandaddy's cat looks mean. Grandaddy does not push Janetta into enjoying his home. Instead, he tells her an incredible tale about a falling star and how his old, big mule named Star, sent it back up again; and Janetta gradually begins to have fun and appreciate her grandfather and the farm. "This is an eye-catching,

Janetta doesn't think much about Grandaddy's ramshackle house or woods at first, but special events cause her to gradually change her mind. (Illustration by James Stevenson from *Grandaddy's Place.*)

heart-grabbing jewel that children won't want to miss," concluded Mary Lou Budd in *School Library Journal.*

In the first of the six chapters of *Grandaddy and Janetta,* Janetta travels alone to Georgia to visit her grandfather. Although she is a bit concerned because she hasn't visited Grandaddy in over a year, she soon falls into Grandaddy's happy routine. He tells her yet another funny tale, and the cat, who is absent for the first part of Janetta's visit, surprises her with a litter of kittens. When Janetta prepares to return home, Grandaddy allows her to take one of the kittens, which has a star on its head, back home to her mother. According to a *Kirkus Reviews* critic, this book possesses the "unusual charm and unassuming lyricism" of the other books about Grandaddy and Janetta. "Kudos to Griffith and Stevenson for another poignant collaboration," wrote a reviewer for *Publishers Weekly.* In 1995, Griffith and Stevenson worked together once again to describe Grandaddy's visit to Baltimore in *Grandaddy's Stars.*

Griffith has penned other books in a variety of styles for diverse audiences. Kindergartners may appreciate *Nata,* a book about the mischief created by a normally well-behaved fairy that *New York Times Book Review* contributor Alice Hoffman thought could "spark an interest in magical creatures and imaginative fantasy." *Caitlin's Holiday* and *Doll Trouble* provide amusing stories for primary school readers about Holiday, a doll who comes to life and causes problems for her owner. Another comical book for younger readers is *Emily and the Enchanted Frog,* three modern twists involving fairy tale characters that are "fast-moving stories with satisfying endings," Elizabeth Huntoon commented in *School Library Journal.* Griffith's novels for preteens include *Foxy,* a thoughtful drama about an abandoned dog set in the Florida Keys, and *Journal of a Teenage Genius,* a humorous fantasy. The picture book *Dream Meadow* quietly describes the peaceful dreams of an elderly woman and her loyal dog; as a *Kirkus Reviews* critic noted, *Dream Meadow* will provide children "upset by an approaching death" with "tender reassurance."

When she is not writing, Griffith works as a secretary and treasurer for her family's business, S. G. Williams & Brothers Co., watches birds, and reads. As she told *SATA,* "I don't count reading as a hobby—it's more of a vice. I wish I would spend less time reading and more time writing."

■ Works Cited

Review of *Alex Remembers, Kirkus Reviews,* April 15, 1983, p. 457.

Berman, Mary Rinato, review of *"Mine Will," Said John, School Library Journal,* October, 1992, p. 87.

Brachmann, Kathleen, review of *Georgia Music, School Library Journal,* October, 1986, pp. 160-61.

Budd, Mary Lou, review of *Grandaddy's Place, School Library Journal,* October, 1987, p. 112.

Review of *Dream Meadow, Kirkus Reviews,* April 15, 1994, p. 556.

Flanagan, Kate M., review of *More Alex and the Cat, Horn Book,* October, 1983, p. 568.

Flowers, Ann A., review of *Georgia Music, Horn Book,* November/December, 1986, p. 733.

Review of *Grandaddy and Janetta, Publishers Weekly,* May 3, 1993, p. 83.

Review of *Grandaddy and Janetta, Kirkus Reviews,* June 1, 1993, p. 722.

Hoffman, Alice, review of *Nata, New York Times Book Review,* November 24, 1985, p. 20.

Huntoon, Elizabeth, review of *Emily and the Enchanted Frog, School Library Journal,* September, 1989, pp. 226-27.

Mandel, Ellen, review of *Plunk's Dreams, Booklist,* March 15, 1990, p. 1462.

Mercier, Cathryn M., "Helen V. Griffith," in *Twentieth-Century Children's Writers,* 4th edition, edited by Laura Standley Berger, St. James Press, 1995, pp. 415-16.

Palmer, Nancy, review of *Alex and the Cat, School Library Journal,* May, 1982, p. 77.

Sutherland, Zena, review of *Alex and the Cat, Bulletin of the Center for Children's Books,* May, 1982, p. 170.

■ For More Information See

PERIODICALS

Booklist, April 1, 1993, p. 1431; May 1, 1994, p. 1608.

Bulletin of the Center for Children's Books, October, 1989, p. 33; October, 1990, p. 29; January, 1994, p. 155.

Publishers Weekly, March 28, 1994, p. 80.

School Library Journal, October, 1983, p. 149; April, 1990, p. 90; October, 1990, pp. 92-93; May, 1993, p. 85.

Voice of Youth Advocates, June, 1984, p. 95.

H

HALL, Katy
See McMULLAN, Kate (Hall)

* * *

HARLEY, Bill 1954-

■ Personal

Born July 1, 1954, in Greenville, OH; son of Max (a law editor) and Ruth (an editor and writer; maiden name, Wolf) Harley; married Debbie Block (an artist manager), June 7, 1980; children: Noah, Dylan. *Education:* Hamilton College, B.A., 1977. *Religion:* Quaker. *Hobbies and other interests:* Sailing, gardening.

■ Addresses

Home and office—301 Jacob St., Seekonk, MA 02771. *Agent*—Marian Reiner, 20 Cedar St., New Rochelle, NY 10801.

■ Career

American Friends Service Committee, Syracuse, NY, social worker, 1977-80; storyteller, author, songwriter, and musical performer with band, the Troublemakers, 1980—. Founder, Providence Learning Connection; cofounder, Stone Soup Coffeehouse, Providence, RI; vice-president and board member, Pokanoket Watershed Alliance. Speaker at numerous conferences and workshops; regular commentator, *All Things Considered*, National Public Radio, 1991—. *Member:* National Storytelling Association, Authors Guild, Authors League of America, Children's Music Network.

■ Awards, Honors

National Association of Independent Record Distributors and Manufacturers' (NAIRD) honorable mention, 1984, for *Monsters in the Bathroom;* Gold Choice Awards, *Parents' Magazine,* 1987, for *50 Ways to Fool Your Mother,* 1989, for *You're in Trouble* and for (with Peter Alsop) *Peter Alsop and Bill Harley: In the Hospital,*

BILL HARLEY

1990, for *I'm Gonna Let It Shine: A Gathering of Voices for Freedom,* and 1992, for *Who Made This Mess?;* Choice Silver Award, *Parents Magazine,* 1987, for *Cool in School: Tales from 6th Grade,* 1990, for *Come On Out and Play;* NAIRD Indie Award, 1987, for *Dinosaurs Never Say Please,* 1990, for *Come On Out and Play* and *Grownups Are Strange;* American Library Association Notable Recording, 1990, for *I'm Gonna Let It Shine;* National Association of Performing Arts Award, 1992, for *Who Made This Mess?*, 1993, for *Big Big World;* Choice Award, *Parents Magazine,* 1995, for *Wacka Wacka Woo and Other Stuff.*

■ Writings

FOR CHILDREN

(Contributor) *Ready-to-Tell Tales,* edited by David Holt and Bill Mooney, August House Press, 1994.

Carna and the Boots of Seven Strides, Riverbank Press (Berkeley, CA), 1994.

Nothing Happened, illustrated by Ann Miya, Tricycle Press (Berkeley, CA), 1995.

Sarah's Story, Tricycle Press, in press.

Sitting Down to Eat, August House, in press.

RECORDINGS

Monsters in the Bathroom, Round River Records (Seekonk, MA), 1984.

50 Ways to Fool Your Mother, Round River Records, 1986.

Coyote, Round River Records, 1987.

(With Peter Alsop) *Peter Alsop and Bill Harley: In the Hospital,* Round River Records, 1989.

Cool in School: Tales from 6th Grade, Round River Records, 1990.

Grownups Are Strange, Round River Records, 1990.

Come On Out and Play, Round River Records, 1990.

I'm Gonna Let It Shine: A Gathering of Voices for Freedom, Round River Records, 1990.

Who Made This Mess?, A & M Records, 1992.

You're in Trouble, A & M, 1992.

Dinosaurs Never Say Please, A & M, 1992.

Big Big World, A & M, 1993.

Already Someplace Warm, Round River Records, 1994.

From the Back of the Bus: Completely True Stories by Bill Harley, Round River Records, 1995.

Wacka Wacka Woo and Other Stuff, Round River Records, 1995.

Sitting on My Hands: A Collection of Commentaries as Aired on National Public Radio's "All Things Considered," Round River Records, 1995.

Also featured in video *Bill Harley: Who Made This Mess?* 1992.

■ Work in Progress

You're in Trouble, for August House, 1997; *The Night of the Spade-Footed Toads* (tentative title), a young adult novel about a biology teacher and the student who makes him reevaluate his work; currently researching arctic terns (in Scotland) for another novel, as well as developing a new touring show for the theater.

■ Sidelights

"If Calvin, of *Calvin and Hobbes* fame, were to grow up, he'd be Bill Harley," Catherine Cella stated in *Billboard,* describing the popular children's author, storyteller, and musician. A full-time performer since 1980, the anything but cartoonish Harley has made the rounds—everywhere from elementary school gymnasiums to outdoor festivals and concert stages—entertaining audiences of adults and children alike with his delightfully humorous and universally recognizable vignettes about growing up. He has captured on paper the spirit of his most popular routines in *Carna and the Boots of Seven Strides* and *Nothing Happened.* Continuing to cement the historic bond between story and song for his young audiences, Harley has produced several award-winning recordings for elementary school children.

"My mother writes for children," Harley explained to *SATA,* "[and] some of the stories I made up as a kid ended up in basal readers. I suppose my development as an author is only coming full circle. In between, though, I developed an interest in oral traditions and have done most of my work live, as a storyteller and singer and on tape. I am fascinated by the spoken word and the connection between story and song."

Many of Harley's snicker-inducing sagas draw on the rich legacies of folk music and storytelling traditions, while others lapse into lunacy while touching on more modern absurdities, as in "Dad Threw the TV out the

Harley has entertained young audiences across the country with his songs, some of which, including "Pizza Shake," "Who Made This Mess?," and the Cajun-sounding "I Don't Wanna Wait," are recorded on this cassette. (Cover illustration by Frank Bolle.)

Window." But such surface silliness does not mask Harley's message: "I've got a lot of concerns that this world we're leaving our kids is not in real good shape," he told Michael J. Vieira in *Providence Journal.* One of the insights he tries to leave behind with kids and their parents is where their own—and each other's—feelings are coming from, so that they can relate to each other more fairly and understand their own actions better. "There is a child in each of us," Harley told Alexis Magner Miller in *Providence Sunday Journal,* "and we'd all be a little healthier if we could honor that part of ourselves."

Transforming the energy and physical humor from his stage performances into equally entertaining books provided Harley with a fresh challenge when he began *Carna and the Boots of Seven Strides.* "As a storyteller or songwriter, there is constant feedback from the audience about what is working," Harley told *SATA.* "It's in performance that I discover what the story is about—if I'm listening, the audience will tell me things about the story I don't know." In his writing Harley has relied instead on an audience composed of friends and family that he counts on for an honest opinion—as well as the advice of his editor. "Writing for children or adults, I'm still writing for myself," he confided to *SATA.* "I try to keep this thought in front of me when I'm working . . . . I remember hearing Fred Rogers [of public television's long-running *Mr. Rogers' Neighborhood*] say that he views himself as an 'emotional archeologist,' and I'm very much interested in having the same vocation— digging down to the feelings that we all have. Of course," he added, "I'd like to have some fun while I'm doing it. I enjoy bringing adults up short—calling attention to their behavior, as well as honoring the kid's perspective." David Yonke praised Harley's success in achieving that goal in the *Toledo Blade:* "It's his openness and honesty that enable him to reach different generations at the same time. After all, every parent was once a child. The pressures, fears, joys, silliness, and insights of childhood are stored, in varying degrees, somewhere in every adult's memory bank."

Harley has reinforced the close relationship between children and adults through his work on National Public Radio's popular *All Things Considered,* where he entertains listeners with regular commentaries on everything from the problems of Nintendo addiction to militant feminist commandeering of men's rooms. "Almost invariably, the ones that get the strongest response are the ones that have to do with memories or issues of childhood," he explained to *SATA.* "And that's from a bunch of grownups." While his work for radio allows him to make a focussed point, Harley usually likes to let his audience arrive at their own conclusions. "Giving someone a story because they need it, and not because you love it, is a rock my ship tries to avoid," added Harley of his ongoing work with children. "After having spent so much time listening to kids' interests and concerns, and spent so much time wandering around in my own memories and past, I think it's possible to speak seriously (and humorously!) about issues that matter to children."

Even with a touring schedule that sometimes keeps him away from his own family for weeks at a time, Harley considers himself pretty fortunate. "While the hardest thing for me to do is to sit down and write with no one making me do it, it is also very satisfying. I am fascinated by the stuff that comes out. And when I'm not doing that, I get to take a guitar and a handful of songs and stories and hang out with people who want to hear me . . . . Stories help us understand and make sense of the world. When you have a lot of stories inside, you can make your own. That's what I do."

■ **Works Cited**

Cella, Catherine, "Talent 4 Children," *Billboard,* February 22, 1992.
Miller, Alexis Magner, "A Class Clown with a Message Youngsters Can Understand," *Providence Sunday Journal,* April 14, 1991, pp. HZ1-2.
Vieira, Michael J., "Silliness Is Serious Business for Singer of Children's Songs," *Providence Journal,* December 27, 1990.
Yonke, David, "Tales That Touch the Entire Family," *Toledo Blade,* February 26, 1993.

■ **For More Information See**

PERIODICALS

Los Angeles Times, January 3, 1991.
Providence Phoenix, April 8, 1994.

* * *

**HARRIS-FILDERMAN, Diane
See FILDERMAN, Diane E.**

* * *

HENBA, Bobbie 1926-

■ **Personal**

Born March 31, 1926, in Lantana, FL; daughter of John H. (a superintendent of construction) and Isabella (a homemaker; maiden name, Gillon) Flagg; married Alexander Henba (an artist and musician), July 23, 1955; children: Jordon. *Education:* Attended New England School of Art and Fashion, 1944-46. *Politics:* Independent. *Religion:* Christian. *Hobbies and other interests:* Reading, gardening, painting.

■ **Addresses**

Home and office—348 Calef Hill Rd., Tilton, NH 03276.

■ **Career**

Cohn, Hall, Marx, New York City, textile designer, 1950-55; freelance greeting card and advertising illustrator, 1956-62; Maurice F. Bloun, Inc. (advertising agency), Rollinsford, NH, illustrator and designer, 1962-77;

BOBBIE HENBA

painter. Volunteer librarian and lecturer. Participant in the Writers and Publishers Project (Concord, NH). *Exhibitions:* One-woman shows include Folk Art Gallery, Marblehead, MA, and Red Gate Gallery, Center Sandwich, NH.

■ Illustrator

Joy Dveland, *A Voice from Paris,* Cobblestone, 1982. Mary Lyn Ray, *Pianna,* Harcourt, 1994.

■ Work in Progress

Writing and illustrating a picture book about her father for Harcourt, a self-discovery picture book, and other picture books.

■ Sidelights

Bobbie Henba told *SATA:* "I have little memory of myself without pencil and colors in my hands. At the many social gatherings my parents hosted, I was the one curled up in a corner watching and listening—storing away in my mental closet images of people being people. I have spent my career committing that imagery to paper and canvas. Drawing the human scene has been as natural and necessary as breathing. When I discovered Norman Rockwell I had found my first idol!

"In 1977 when my financial responsibilities to my son were over I 'flew the coop' from commercial art and began painting family scenes of rural New England as I remembered it and 'heard tell of' from my elders. As a typical child of that era, I felt kinship with a family much larger than that contained within the walls of our farmhouse—I belonged to the whole town! The community spirit fostered in me back then now begs to speak to the needs of today's youngsters. If I can open doors to needed quiet places in which children can hear their own selfhood unfold, then I will feel that I'm tying up my life's work with rainbow ribbons."

■ For More Information See

PERIODICALS

Publishers Weekly, July 4, 1994, p. 38.

* * *

HERZIG, Alison Cragin 1935-

■ Personal

Born August 20, 1935; daughter of Stuart Wilson (a banker) and Mary (a homemaker; maiden name, Washburn) Cragin; divorced; children: Amy, Jill. *Education:* Bryn Mawr College, B.A., 1957.

■ Addresses

Home and office—15 West 81st St., New York, NY 10024.

■ Career

Writer and founding partner of Editors Ink; worked for a number of years as an art dealer and briefly as a fiction editor and writer for a national magazine. *Member:* Society of Children's Book Writers and Illustrators, Authors Guild, Authors League of America, California Writer's Club, Northern California Science Writers.

■ Awards, Honors

American Book Award for nonfiction hardcover, Association of American Publishers, 1981, for *Oh, Boy! Babies!;* two Notable Books in Social Studies; two Children's Editor's Choice books, American Library Association; two American Bookseller "Pick of the Lists"; Edgar Allan Poe Award nomination. Four books have been Junior Library Guild selections.

■ Writings

(With Jane Lawrence Mali) *A Word to the Wise,* illustrated by Martha Perske, Little, Brown, 1978.
(With Jane Lawrence Mali) *Oh, Boy! Babies!,* illustrated by Katrina Thomas, Little, Brown, 1980.
(With Jane Lawrence Mali) *A Season of Secrets,* Little, Brown, 1982.
(With Jane Lawrence Mali) *Thaddeus,* illustrated by Stephen Gammell, Little, Brown, 1984.

ALISON CRAGIN HERZIG

Shadows on the Pond, Little, Brown, 1985.

(With Jane Lawrence Mali) *The Ten-Speed Babysitter,* Dutton, 1987.

(With Jane Lawrence Mali) *Sam and the Moon Queen,* Clarion, 1992.

The Big Deal, illustrated by Scott Gladden, Viking, 1992.

The Boonsville Bombers, illustrated by Dan Andreasen, Viking, 1993.

(With Jane Lawrence Mali) *Mystery on October Road,* Viking, 1993.

(With Jane Lawrence Mali) *The Wimp of the World,* Viking, 1994.

Herzig's works have been translated into German, Swedish, French, Norwegian, Danish, and Japanese.

■ Adaptations

Oh, Boy! Babies! was made into an ABC primetime television special.

■ Work in Progress

The Boat in the Bottle, for Scholastic; *The Bronco Busters,* for Putnam.

■ Sidelights

Alison Cragin Herzig told *SATA:* "On my thirteenth birthday I asked my parents to paint my bedroom dark green and build bookcases on every available wall. My mother was horrified. It seemed like living in a cave to her. But it felt like a library to me and I loved books. Louisa May Alcott, Felix Salten, E. B. White, Marjorie Rawlings, Frances Hodgson Burnett, Dumas, Kipling, Stevenson, Harper Lee, Mary O'Hara, Eric Knight. The list goes on and on. I read at meals and under the covers at night and dreamed of growing up to be a story teller.

"I also loved baseball and sailing and animals of all sorts. One of my earliest memories is of wading the wild stream that ran past our house with a friend and springing all the traps a muskrat hunter had set along the banks. I used that experience as part of the plot in *Shadows on the Pond.* Of course you use everything when you write; old and new emotions and interests, your children, other people's children, everybody's pets, places where you once lived or live now, the bolt of lightning that came right through your roof into your living room during a thunderstorm, a father you know who defrosts frozen chicken wings by sitting on them, even brief encounters. *The Boat in the Bottle* was inspired by an old man I passed on a New York street pushing a large sailboat in a baby carriage. There was a story there, but it took a couple of years before I figured out what it was. And then my old boating days came back to help me.

"That brief encounter was a fortuitous one. Others have been less fortunate and even more haunting. Many homeless people live in the doorways and parks near my apartment. Their plight made me feel sad and helpless and fearful, feelings that were shared by my children and the teenagers I met volunteering at shelters and soup kitchens. They didn't know how to make it better and neither did I, so I wrote about it in *Sam and the Moon Queen.*" The relationship that forms between thirteen-year-old Sam and a homeless girl named December is the centerpiece of *Sam and the Moon Queen.* Barbara Chatton, writing for *School Library Journal,* said that this is "a readable and engaging portrait of several courageous people who carve out a kind of life on city streets."

"And then there were the animals I loved as a child," Herzig continued for *SATA.* "There are animals in many of my books. *The Big Deal* is dedicated to my dog, Football. Football is tiny, but what if he weren't? What if I were a ten year old boy, very small for my age, who was finally given the puppy he'd longed for for Christmas. And what if the deal was that I could keep him as long as I fed him and brushed him and walked him. And what if that puppy grew into a humongous dog, as big as a bear, and as strong as one too, and I wasn't big or strong enough to walk him anymore. What would I do?

"And what about baseball? Baseball the way it used to be played, in the sunlight on real grass. I was captain of the softball team in high school and college, but I always wanted to play hardball with the boys. And I always knew that someday I would write a baseball book. And finally I did. I'd been thinking about it for so long that *The Boonsville Bombers* turned out to be a gift book. That is to say, it seemed to write itself." Julie Corsaro, a critic for *Booklist,* found the chapter book to be "warm and funny" and commended Herzig for proving that "America's greatest pastime is not just for boys."

Herzig's first book (coauthored with Jane Lawrence Mali), *A Word to the Wise,* is a reflection of her love of words and phrases. It's the story of eight fifth-graders who are in a special reading group. They resent their teacher, Mrs. Dillworth, who only lets them read baby books. When they overhear her talking about a "treasure" of a book they are not allowed to read, they steal it and take turns taking it home. The book turns out to be a thesaurus, and a problem-solver for each of the children. A review in the *Bulletin of the Center for Children's Books* stated that there was a "nice display of comradeship and enterprise in the story."

Another collaboration with Mali resulted in a photodocumentary of a 1981 elective course in infant care given to fifth- and sixth-grade boys—*Oh, Boy! Babies!.* The authors' text is accompanied by comments and questions from the boys themselves. Cathi Edgerton, writing for *Voice of Youth Advocates,* called it an "inspiring" book, showing not only the "natural" fathering abilities boys have, "but celebrating learning and sharing and communication among people."

Herzig and Mali returned to fiction with *A Season of Secrets,* the story of fourteen-year-old Brooke and her six-year-old brother, Benji. Benji suffers from fainting spells, and their parents won't tell Brooke the cause. Another secret is that Benji is keeping and taming a bat hidden in his room. Eventually, Brooke learns what her parents have been trying to hide—Benji has epilepsy. Writing for *Voice of Youth Advocates,* Mary Lynn Copan praised the book for illustrating "the myths, fear and prejudices that lack of knowledge often brings."

In *Thaddeus,* yet another story about special relationships, young Tad and his Great-Great-Uncle (and namesake) Thaddeus work together to resolve a problem. Since Tad was born on Christmas day, Uncle Thaddeus has always tried to find clever ways to celebrate. For his seventh birthday, Uncle Thaddeus has written a book entitled "Tad's Birthday Book; or How Against All Odds We Solved the Unsolvable Problem and Got from There to This Very Day." Uncle Thaddeus' solution is to give Tad his October birthday, since he hardly uses it anymore. Zena Sutherland commented in the *Bulletin of the Center for Children's Books* that *Thaddeus* is a "loving" and "ingenious" story.

Problem-solving and skilled planning are also the theme of *The Ten-Speed Babysitter.* In this story, fourteen-year-old Tony comes to Connecticut to begin his summer live-in baby-sitting job. No sooner does he arrive than his employer goes off to the Bahamas for the weekend, leaving Tony and three-year-old Duncan to fend for themselves. Catastrophes abound, including a hurricane, a pair of thieves, and a duck egg about to hatch. It is through Tony's growing resourcefulness, and the help of a new-found friend, that he and Duncan get through the weekend. *Bulletin of the Center for Children's Books* reviewer Betsy Hearne considered the book to be "exuberant and entertaining" as well as "a prime example of a book whose crafting lives up to its popular appeal."

Herzig and Mali strike a light note with *The Wimp of the World.* Ten-year-old Bridget has three older brothers who are teaching her how not to be a wimp. She must do push-ups and she can't wear dresses. Then Great-Aunt Dawsie announces she is getting married and she wants Bridget to be maid of honor—for which she'll have to wear a dress, of course. This is an action-packed story; *Booklist* critic Stephanie Zvirin admired how the authors "manage to capture the hubbub of a big, close, hardworking family ... and there's not a slow moment in their sweet, warm story."

After her many collaborations with Jane Mali, Herzig went solo to write *Shadows on the Pond.* The story concerns fourteen-year-old Jill, whose parents are going through a separation. Jill and her mother go off for the

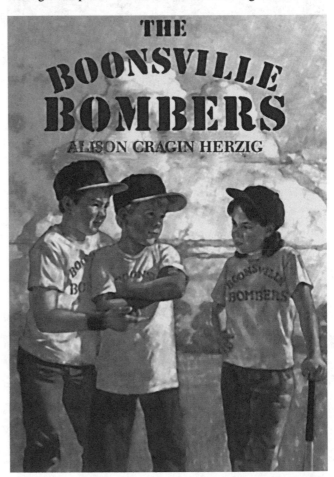

How can Emma get to play on her older brother's baseball team when they don't want a girl—and a younger one at that? (Cover illustration by Daniel Andreasen.)

summer to the family's cabin in Vermont. There, Jill and her long-time friend Migan head for the beaver pond, their special sanctuary. But someone is setting traps, and the girls become dangerously involved in efforts to stop the trapper. A *Publishers Weekly* reviewer called this an "unusual thriller" and a "timely treatment of major environmental issues."

Herzig also soloed on two books for younger readers: *The Big Deal* and *The Boonsville Bombers*. Reflecting Herzig's own interest in baseball, *The Boonsville Bombers* is the story of Emma Lee Benson's determination to earn a place on her brother's baseball team. In *The Big Deal*, young Sam, the shortest fourth-grader in school, chooses the runt of the litter for his new pet. But soon Wally grows into a humongous, though beloved, pet who tears up lawns and garden parties. *Booklist* contributor Hazel Rochman called this a "warm, funny story" and advised: "Just read aloud the first chapter and you'll have kids hooked."

Herzig told *SATA:* "I've written all over the map; from picture books to middle grade readers to young adult novels. One of my books was even reviewed as an adult title by the *New York Times*. If there is any constant about my work, it is in the area of sexual stereotyping. Most of the heroes I read about as a child were boys. I have wanted to balance the boat. So there are girl heroes as well as boy heroes in all my books. And there are fathers who cook and mothers who are occupied with careers and boys taking care of babies and girls going out in the night to do battle for what they love armed only with a flashlight and a shovel. And there's a bit of me in all of them."

■ Works Cited

Chatton, Barbara, review of *Sam and the Moon Queen, School Library Journal,* September, 1990.
Copan, Mary Lynn, review of *A Season of Secrets, Voice of Youth Advocates,* April, 1983, p. 37.
Corsaro, Julie, review of *The Boonsville Bombers, Booklist,* October 1, 1987, p. 327.
Edgerton, Cathi, review of *Oh, Boy! Babies!, Voice of Youth Advocates,* June, 1981, p. 43.
Hearne, Betsy, review of *The Ten-Speed Babysitter, Bulletin of the Center for Children's Books,* October, 1987, p. 30.
Rochman, Hazel, review of *The Big Deal, Booklist,* July, 1992.
Review of *Shadows on the Pond, Publishers Weekly,* November 29, 1985, p. 46.
Sutherland, Zena, review of *Thaddeus, Bulletin of the Center for Children's Books,* January, 1985, p. 86.
Review of *A Word to the Wise, Bulletin of the Center for Children's Books,* March, 1979, p. 118.
Zvirin, Stephanie, review of *The Wimp of the World, Booklist,* April 1, 1994.

■ For More Information See

PERIODICALS

Booklist, July, 1991, p. 2045.

Bulletin of the Center for Children's Books, February, 1986, p. 110.
Kirkus Reviews, January 1, 1979, p. 5.
Publishers Weekly, December 14, 1984, p. 54.
School Library Journal, November, 1982, p. 85; March, 1986, p. 176.*

*   *   *

HIGGINBOTTOM, David 1923-
(Nicholas Fisk)

■ Personal

Born October 14, 1923, in London England; married Dorothy Antoinette, 1949; children: Moyra and Nicola (twins), Steven, Christopher. *Education:* Ardingly College, Sussex, England.

■ Addresses

Home—59 Elstree Rd., Bushey Heath, Hertfordshire, WD2 3QX, England. *Agent*—Laura Cecil, 17 Alwyne Villas, Canonbury, London, N1 2HG, England.

■ Career

Writer and illustrator. Head of creative groups, Lund Humphries Ltd. (printers/publishers), London, England. Former advertising creative director, head of creative groups, and consultant. Has worked as an actor, publisher, editor, journalist, musician, and speaker to children

DAVID HIGGINBOTTOM

and adults. *Military service:* Royal Air Force; served during World War II. *Member:* Saville Club.

■ Writings

SCIENCE FICTION FOR YOUNG ADULTS; UNDER PSEUDONYM NICHOLAS FISK

Space Hostages, Hamish Hamilton, 1967, Macmillan, 1969.
Trillions, Hamish Hamilton, 1971, Pantheon, 1973.
Grinny, Heinemann, 1973, Nelson, 1974.
High Way Home, Hamish Hamilton, 1973.
Little Green Spaceman, illustrated by Trevor Stubley, Heinemann, 1974.
Time Trap, Gollancz, 1976.
Wheelie in the Stars, Gollancz, 1976.
Antigrav, Viking Kestrel, 1978.
Escape from Splatterbang, Pelham, 1978, Macmillan, 1979, published as *Flamers,* Knight, 1979.
Monster Maker, Pelham, 1979, Macmillan, 1980.
A Rag, a Bone, and a Hank of Hair, Viking Kestrel, 1980, Crown, 1982.
Robot Revolt, Pelham, 1981.
Sweets from a Stranger and Other Science Fiction Stories, Viking Kestrel, 1982.
On the Flip Side, Viking Kestrel, 1983.
You Remember Me!, Viking Kestrel, 1984, G. K. Hall, 1987.
Bonkers Clocks, illustrated by Colin West, Viking Kestrel, 1985.
Dark Sun, Bright Sun, illustrated by Brigid Marlin, Blackie, 1986.
Living Fire (short stories), Corgi, 1987.
Mindbenders, Viking Kestrel, 1987.
Backlash, Walker (London), 1988.
The Talking Car, illustrated by Ann John, Macmillan, 1988.
The Telly Is Watching You, Macdonald, 1989.
The Model Village, illustrated by Alan Cracknell, Walker, 1990.
A Hole in the Head, Walker, 1991.
Extraterrestrial Tales, Puffin, 1991.
Broops! Down the Chimney, illustrated by Russell Ayto, Walker, 1991.
(Editor) *The Penguin Book of Science Fiction: Stories Chosen by Nicholas Fisk,* Viking, 1993, published as *The Puffin Book of Science Fiction: Stories Chosen by Nicholas Fisk,* Puffin, 1994.

Also contributor to *Twisted Circuits,* edited by Mick Gowar, Beaver Books, 1987; and *Electric Heroes,* edited by Mick Gowar, Bodley Head, 1988.

"STARSTORMER SAGA"; SCIENCE FICTION FOR YOUNG ADULTS; UNDER PSEUDONYM NICHOLAS FISK

Starstormers, Knight, 1980.
Sunburst, Knight, 1980.
Catfang, Knight, 1981.
Evil Eye, Knight, 1982.
Volcano, Knight, 1985.

FICTION; UNDER PSEUDONYM NICHOLAS FISK

(And illustrator) *The Bouncers,* Hamish Hamilton, 1964.

The Fast Green Car, illustrated by Bernard Wragg, Hamish Hamilton, 1965.
There's Something on the Roof, illustrated by Dugald Macdougall, Hamish Hamilton, 1966.
Emma Borrows a Cup of Sugar (for children), illustrated by Carol Baker, Heinemann, 1973.
Der Ballon, Junior Press (Germany), 1974.
The Witches of Wimmering, illustrated by Trevor Stubley, Pelham, 1976.
Leadfoot, Pelham, 1980, revised edition, Piper, 1992.
Snatched, Hodder & Stoughton, 1983.
The Worm Charmers, Walker, 1989.
The Back-Yard War, illustrated by Valeria Petrone, Macmillan, 1990.
Fantastico, illustrated by Mick Reid, Longman, 1994.

Also contributor to *Young Winter's Tales,* edited by D. J. Denney, Macmillan, 1978; *An Oxford Book of Christmas Stories,* edited by Dennis Pepper, Oxford University Press, 1986; and *I Like This Story,* Puffin, 1986.

NONFICTION; UNDER PSEUDONYM NICHOLAS FISK

(And illustrator) *Look at Cars* (for children), Hamish Hamilton, 1959, revised edition, Panther, 1969.
Look at Newspapers (for children), illustrated by Eric Thomas, Hamish Hamilton, 1962.
Cars, Parrish, 1963.
The Young Man's Guide to Advertising, Hamish Hamilton, 1963.
Making Music, illustrated by Donald Green, Joseph, 1966, Crescendo, 1969.
Lindbergh the Lone Flier (for children), illustrated by Raymond Briggs, Hamish Hamilton/Coward McCann, 1968.
Richthofen the Red Baron, Raymond Briggs, Hamish Hamilton/Coward McCann, 1968.
(Editor and contributor of photographs) Eric Fenby, *Menuhin's House of Music,* Icon Books, 1970.
Pig Ignorant (a teenage memoir), Walker, 1991.

Contributor to *The Thorny Paradise* (anthology for children), edited by Edward Blishen, Viking Kestrel, 1975.

ILLUSTRATOR; UNDER PSEUDONYM NICHOLAS FISK

Beryl Cooke, *A Fishy Tale* (fiction), Angus & Robertson, 1957.
Sir Philip Joubert de la Ferte, *Look at Aircraft* (nonfiction), Hamish Hamilton, 1960.
Lettice Cooper, *The Bear Who Was Too Big* (fiction), Parrish, 1963.
Geoffrey Morgan, *Tea with Mr. Timothy* (fiction), Parrish, 1964, Little, Brown, 1966, Chapman, 1991.
William Mayne, *Skiffy* (fiction), Hamish Hamilton, 1973.

OTHER

Also writer for television; author of scripts for cassettes. General editor of "Hamish Hamilton Monographs," Hamish Hamilton, 1964. Contributor, "Take Part" series, Ward Lock, 1977; contributor to *Pears Junior Encyclopaedia.* Contributor of articles and science fiction stories to magazines.

■ Adaptations

Grinny was adapted for "CBS Storybreak," 1985.

■ Sidelights

David Higginbottom, who is better known to his readers by his pseudonym Nicholas Fisk, is an English author popular for his young adult science fiction stories. "[While] my main interest lies in writing books for children," Higginbottom once commented, "I am also an illustrator and photographer and often an impresario of adult printed works." Higginbottom can further add to this list his work as a journalist, sometime musician, public speaker, and creative consultant. Although he writes both fiction and nonfiction, Higginbottom's name is primarily associated with his science fiction works. "I write science fiction because it is liberating," the author once told *SATA*. "I greatly regret the label 'SF,' incidentally. SF were better named IF—stories centered on an If, a possibility, a leap." Often employing the traditional sci-fi plot device of the outside threat of an advanced technology, Higginbottom always returns to character development to carry the story. According to Gillian Cross, writing in *Times Literary Supplement*, Higginbottom "has a gift for combining the fantastic with the down-to-earth. In books like *Grinny* and *Trillions*, the interest comes not merely from the central events, but also from the effect of those events on recognizable characters."

Higginbottom, who served in the Royal Air Force during World War II, began writing and illustrating for children with nonfiction titles such as *Look at Cars, Look at Aircraft, Look at Newspapers,* and *The Young Man's Guide to Advertising,* combining his knowledge of things mechanical with the world of the publicist. With *Lindbergh the Lone Flier* and *Richthofen the Red Baron,* Higginbottom continued writing about his interests: the world of flight and of individual achievement. In 1967 he published the first of his science fiction novels, *Space Hostages,* and since that time has, with a few departures into children's picture books and mainstream juvenile novels, written almost solely in the science fiction field. Higginbottom once noted for *SATA* that he began writing science fiction because "the writer is free to invent his own games, rules, and players." That invention can be seen in the best of his science fiction novels, *Trillions, Grinny, Antigrav, You Remember Me!,* and *A Rag, a Bone, and a Hank of Hair,* and his sequence of five novels that make up the "Starstormer Saga."

Trillions deals with an invasion from outer space in a completely novel form: trillions of glittering multi-faceted baubles rain down on earth, charming the children and alarming the militarists who declare martial law and prepare to nuke the mysterious jewel-like objects. Young Scott manages to communicate with the sentient trillions and warn them away in time to prevent their mass destruction. In one of his earliest sci-fi attempts, then, Higginbottom had already set one of his thematic agendas: uncorrupted youths who are able to understand and see more clearly than their befuddled elders.

"Higginbottom has created an exciting story that should be enjoyed by all," noted Jean Mercier in a *Publishers Weekly* review of *Trillions.*

One of Higginbottom's best-known science fiction novels—which was also adapted for television—*Grinny,* tells another story of a disguised planetary visitor to earth, but with a new twist. In this case the visitor comes in the form of a sweet old lady who claims to be a long-lost great-aunt to a family who has never met her, and whose words, "You remember me!," seem to have the power to make adults forgetful enough to accept her as kin. Not so, however, for young Tim and Beth, who soon realize Great-Aunt Emma is not the sweetheart she pretends to be but a sinister extraterrestrial, and they therefore manage to foil her mission. "The nicely crafted story has suspense, action, and a frisson here and there," noted a reviewer for the *Bulletin of the Center for Children's Books.* A *Kirkus Reviews* critic commented that "the children have substantial, well-differentiated personalities not usually encountered in genre sci fi."

Higginbottom continued his science fiction explorations with the Cold War allegory *Antigrav,* in which a group of children vacationing with their parents on a tiny island off the coast of Scotland discover a red stone with the power to defy gravity. They set up clever experiments to prove the stone's power, but soon become the object of a chase by scientists trying to steal the antigravity rock. Finally the children throw the stone into the sea to keep its power out of the wrong hands.

Writing in *The Thorny Paradise,* an anthology on the art of children's fiction, Higginbottom noted his own development as a writer from his initial "childish little books for little children," to the point where his own children were demanding something quite different from him. "My child readers might, occasionally, be persuaded to share my nostalgias and fancies—even my childhood—but this was not to be relied upon. Better to devise stories that belonged either to a period the reader would recognize—the period of *now;* or to go so far back, or so far forward, that the reader must simply take my word for it."

This insight perfectly fits science fiction, and Higginbottom was even able to return to his own youth in England with one of his most well-received books. Venturing into the realms of DNA engineering, he created an altered world of the twenty-third century with *A Rag, a Bone, and a Hank of Hair.* As a result of a nuclear accident, very few humans can give birth, and so to avoid extinction the human race is now repopulated from the gene patterns found in fragments (the bits and pieces of the title) of those who died before the accident. These humans are known as Reborns, and young, brilliant Brin is given the job of observing three who have been resurrected from the twentieth century in an experiment to see how well such Reborns might adapt to the brave new world of Brin's time. These three, a boy, a girl, and a cleaning lady, inhabit a shabby kitchen in the London of the Blitz—something out of Higginbottom's own memories. Initially contemptuous of these primitive forms, Brin soon comes to sympathize with their plucky free will, so at odds with the controlled, sterile society he lives in. Finally Brin allies himself with these Reborns against the Seniors who have engineered them, creating a "heart-stopping crisis in Higginbottom's unforgettable novel," according to one *Publishers Weekly* reviewer. Norman Culpan, writing in *School Librarian,* found the book to be "absorbing and thought-provoking," and *Horn Book* contributor Paul Heins called it an "unconventional science fiction novel that develops a moral theme." This play of individual self-determination pitted against regulated human society helps to make *A Rag, a Bone, and a Hank of Hair* Higginbottom's "science fiction masterpiece," according to Dennis Hamley in *Twentieth-Century Young Adult Writers.*

Higginbottom returned to his earlier protagonists Tim and Beth from *Grinny* with *You Remember Me!,* enlisting them once again in the fight against a disguised alien. This time the invasion comes in the form of beautiful television personality Lisa Treadgood who is able to charm an entire nation—even the clever writer N. Fisk who has a cameo appearance in his own book—but not cub reporter Tim or his sister Beth. Treadgood attracts a huge following to her proto-fascist political party that marches under a banner of Decency, Discipline, and Dedication. Beth and Tim once again are able to defeat the evil machinations of this extraterrestrial. A *Junior Bookshelf* critic noted that the book had "enough tension and buoyancy to keep young readers eager to find out what happens next," while *Times Literary Supplement* contributor Stephanie Nettell thought it was "a lively sequel" to *Grinny.*

Higginbottom's obvious love for adventure stories gets full play in the "Starstormer Saga," a five-novel sequence in which four young protagonists—Vawn, Ispex, Tsu, and Makenzi—blast off from twenty-first-century Earth in a homemade rocket ship, partly in search of their space colonist parents, partly in search of adventure. They get plenty of the latter, including a fight against the power-drunk maniac, the Emperor of Tyrannopolis, who wants to rule the universe, and a test of survival on a hostile planet populated by talking lizards. "Mr. Fisk manipulates the cut and thrust of disturbing forces and sinister conflict with assured professionalism," commented a reviewer for *Junior Bookshelf* on the second installment in the series, *Sunburst.* Summing up the appeal of the series as a whole, another *Junior Bookshelf* critic concluded in a review of *Volcano* that it is the "futuristic thrills and spills and the enterprise of the children who face and solve what so often appear to be overwhelming challenges" that make the stories a success.

Higginbottom has also tried his hand at thrillers and adventure novels for young readers, without the science fiction angle. Books such as *Leadfoot,* about a young boy's dream of being a racing car driver and the real-life accident that forces him into that role, and *Snatched,* about the kidnapping of an ambassador's two children, set the realistic tone for such stories. "Higginbottom's characters inhabit a world in which millions starve and

individuals struggle, hit, love and hate," noted Mike Hayhoe in a review of *Snatched* for *School Librarian.* Higginbottom's realism was also noted by Margery Fisher in a *Growing Point* review of *Leadfoot:* "Terse and low-keyed even in moments of crisis, the book goes beyond the pace and excitement of action."

Writing in *The Thorny Paradise,* Higginbottom summarized why he writes for children and teenagers, whether it is science fiction or any other genre. "It is arguable," Higginbottom wrote, "that the highest expression of humankind takes the form of a child. It is very easy indeed to argue that the human mind is at its most agile, adventurous, generous and receptive stage during childhood. So the children's writer is mixing with and working for the Right People."

■ Works Cited

Cross, Gillian, review of *Antigrav, Times Literary Supplement,* July 7, 1978, p. 764.

Culpan, Norman, review of *A Rag, a Bone, and a Hank of Hair, School Librarian,* June, 1981, pp. 150-51.

Fisher, Margery, review of *Leadfoot, Growing Point,* November, 1980, p. 3782.

Fisk, Nicholas, "One Thumping Lie Only," *The Thorny Paradise,* edited by Edward Blishen, Viking Kestrel, 1975.

Review of *Grinny, Kirkus Reviews,* August 1, 1974, p. 804.

Review of *Grinny, Bulletin of the Center for Children's Books,* March, 1975, p. 112.

Hamley, Dennis, "Fisk, Nicholas," *Twentieth-Century Young Adult Writers,* 1st edition, edited by Laura Standley Berger, St. James Press, 1994, pp. 213-14.

Hayhoe, Mike, review of *Snatched, School Librarian,* December, 1983, p. 376.

Heins, Paul, review of *A Rag, a Bone, and a Hank of Hair, Horn Book,* June, 1982, pp. 286-87.

Mercier, Jean, review of *Trillions, Publishers Weekly,* March 26, 1973.

Nettell, Stephanie, review of *You Remember Me!, Times Literary Supplement,* March 23, 1986, p. 574.

Review of *A Rag, a Bone, and a Hank of Hair, Publishers Weekly,* June 4, 1982, p. 67.

Review of *Sunburst, Junior Bookshelf,* June, 1985, p. 139.

Review of *Volcano, Junior Bookshelf,* December, 1986, p. 224.

Review of *You Remember Me!, Junior Bookshelf,* February, 1985, p. 38.

■ For More Information See

PERIODICALS

Growing Point, May, 1976, p. 2887; December, 1976, p. 3011; November, 1979, p. 3614; January, 1981, p. 3816; September, 1982, p. 3953; May, 1983, p. 4077; November, 1985, p. 4538; July, 1988, p. 5004; May, 1989, p. 5155.

Junior Bookshelf, August, 1976, p. 198; February, 1977, p. 32; August, 1977, p. 234; October, 1978, p. 266; October, 1979, p. 277; August, 1980, p. 188; August, 1982, p. 151; June, 1983, p. 122; April, 1985, p. 89; February, 1987, p. 27; August, 1987, p. 178; June, 1988, p. 137; April, 1990, p. 84; April, 1992, p. 61; June, 1993, p. 104.

School Library Journal, March, 1979, p. 138; March, 1980, p. 139; April, 1982, p. 81.

Times Educational Supplement, November 23, 1984, p. 38; March 1, 1985, p. 29; April 5, 1985, p. 22; February 14, 1986, p. 28; June 17, 1988, p. B3; May 26, 1989, p. B15; July 10, 1992, p. 28; March 5, 1993, p. 12.

Times Literary Supplement, June 17, 1965, p. 500; May 19, 1966, p. 447; November 30, 1967, p. 1160; June 6, 1968, p. 582; April 6, 1973, p. 380; March 29, 1974, p. 331; December 10, 1976, p. 1553; July 18, 1980, p. 812; November 20, 1981, p. 1361; July 23, 1982, p. 791.*

—Sketch by J. Sydney Jones

*   *   *

HOWARD, Jane R(uble) 1924-

■ Personal

Born July 24, 1924, in Bloomington, IN; daughter of Vern Wright (a lawyer) and Lenore (a homemaker; maiden name, Vance) Ruble; married Ray A. Howard (a lawyer and certified public accountant), September 6, 1947 (divorced, June 6, 1986); children: Nancy Lenore Howard Dewar. *Education:* Indiana University, A.B., 1946. *Politics:* Republican. *Religion:* "Raised Presbyterian." *Hobbies and other interests:* Theater, reading, travel, "spending time with my grandsons, and a bit of bird-watching."

■ Addresses

Home and office—370 Satinwood Ct., North, Buffalo Grove, IL 60089.

■ Career

Children's book writer, playwright, and "occasional poet"; also teacher, editor, and theatrical director. Cole Marionettes, Chicago, IL, puppeteer, 1946-47; Hingham High School, Hingham, MA, English teacher and drama coach, 1948-51; Scott Foresman & Co. (textbook publisher), editorial assistant, 1951-52, part-time editor, 1967-69; Apple Tree Theatre, Highland Park, IL, public relations worker, manager of children's theatre, and assistant director of various productions, 1986-90; The Standard Club, Chicago, editor of newsletter, 1990-95. Speaker and lecturer at various schools and writers' workshops; writer in residence, Acts Institute, Lake Ozark, MO, 1984, 1985; guest lecturer, University of Illinois-Chicago, 1990. Former president of Off Campus Writers Workshop and The Writers, and member of other writing workshops. *Member:* Society of Children's Book Writers and Illustrators, Dramatists Guild, Authors Guild, Authors League of America, Children's

JANE R. HOWARD

Reading Round Table of Chicago, Society of Midland Authors (drama award committee chairman, 1985-87).

■ Awards, Honors

New York Poetry Forum Award for a Narrative Poem, 1974; Fiction Skills Award, Indiana University Writers Conference, 1974; Rainbow Company Children's Theatre National Playwriting Competition finalist, 1981, for *Maria's Loom;* Cummings/Taylor Playwriting Award, 1982, for *Marquee;* Midwest Theatre Network competition finalist, 1995, in children's theatre category for *Maria's Loom,* and in musical theatre category for *Dreamzzz.*

■ Writings

FOR CHILDREN

When I'm Sleepy, illustrated by Lynne Cherry, Dutton, 1985.

When I'm Hungry, illustrated by Teri Sloat, Dutton, 1992.

PLAYS

The Porch Swing (one-act), Baker's Plays, 1974.

Maria's Loom (play with music), produced in Winnetka, IL, 1976.

Frank + Marianne, rehearsed staged reading by Alley Theatre, Houston, TX, 1982.

Marquee (musical comedy), produced by the Sierra Repertory Theatre, Sonora, CA, 1983.

Also collaborative author of "Nelly's Fishy Fate" (one-act), published in *Plays, the Drama Magazine for Children,* 1972.

OTHER

Contributor to *Ocean Almanac,* Doubleday, 1984; contributor of short stories to *Highlights for Children, North American Review, Woman's World, Story World, Today's Family, Progressive Woman, Green's Magazine,* and *Ball State University Forum.*

■ Adaptations

Howard's short story "Season's Greetings" was adapted by Writers Theatre Chicago for production as *In the Heart of Winter,* 1995.

■ Work in Progress

Dreamzzz, a musical comedy; several picture book texts; several adult short stories; and a few poems.

■ Sidelights

Jane R. Howard told *SATA:* "When I was a child, my father built a stage in our basement for my sister and me where we put on little plays we created. We'd dress up in our mother's high heels and cast-off dresses, choose which movie star to pretend we looked like and act out a life for our characters, improvising the dialogue as we went along. In late grade school, I was a member of Miss Alice Brumblay's Shakespeare Club, where I played a very youthful Helena in *A Midsummer Night's Dream.* My mother rehearsed my lines with me, and the night of the show I wore a Juliet cap covered with gold sequins and a costume with an overlay of blue net sprinkled with rhinestones, all so glamorous I never ever forgot it. I was sure I wanted to be an actress when I grew up.

"In high school, I was in many of the plays—and also on the staff of the school newspaper—writing. As a senior, I was one of four girls invited to be in an Indiana University outdoor production of *A Midsummer Night's Dream.* I was Moth, one of the fairies in Titania's court. I can still sing all the words and dance all the steps we did to Mendelssohn's wonderful music. Later, in college, I was either onstage or backstage for most of the productions. In my senior year, I played Corliss Archer in the comedy *Kiss and Tell,* for which I was nominated—though I didn't win—as Best Actress of the Year.

"Out of college and still following my theatrical star, I became half of a puppeteering team for the Cole Marionettes, performing *The Tinder Box* and a clown circus act in Chicago schools. I manipulated the strings and spoke for six of the characters, including the dog, while my partner operated the other six. He and I travelled around in his station wagon, setting up our specially-designed stage wherever we went. Sometimes, on weekends, we performed for parties . . . .

"In 1966, as a girl scout leader, I wrote a stage adaptation of a children's book entitled *A Pint of Judgment,* by Elizabeth Morrow. Performing in this play, several troop members—including my own daughter Nancy—earned their Troop Dramatics badge. A few years later, under my guidance, eight cadette girl scouts earned their Player/Producer badge by writing and producing a wild and crazy melodrama called 'Nelly's Fishy Fate,' that was later published in *Plays, the Drama Magazine for Children.* Writing, I decided, was a talent I'd like to pursue seriously.

"So when Nancy entered high school, I started attending Off Campus Writers Workshop and The Writers, two workshops that became an invaluable source of inspiration and help to me. I've belonged for twenty-five years. The members and I have seen one another through many rejections as well as some solid successes, and I hold as special treasures the lifelong friendships I've made in these talented groups.

"Many of those friends were in the audience when *Maria's Loom,* for which I wrote book, music, and lyrics, was performed by the Winnetka Children's Theatre. The play was based on a children's story of mine entitled 'The Three Wishes' that had appeared in *Highlights for Children.*"

"In 1985," Howard continued, "my first picture book was published by E. P. Dutton. *When I'm Sleepy,* illustrated by Lynne Cherry, was greeted with enthusiastic reviews and has continued to thrive to this very day. *When I'm Hungry,* illustrated by Teri Sloat, came out in 1992, making a perfect companion for *Sleepy.* The simple texts tell of how animals sleep and eat and show a child trying to adapt to the animal ways and winding up preferring the human way. I love the way children laugh and are amused when I read the books to them. I'm frequently invited to speak at local kindergartens, grade schools and libraries, and the children often bring along their own copies of these books for me to autograph. A source of particular satisfaction to me was dedicating *Sleepy* to my daughter, Nancy, and *Hungry* to my sister, Harriet Ruble Pritchard, and her family.

"For four recent years of my life (1986-1990), I had the pleasure of working at Apple Tree, a professional theatre located in Highland Park, IL. There I did a wide variety of work, much of which involved writing, and was lucky enough to serve as assistant director for five of their productions. What better way to hone one's playwriting skills!

"Looking back, two special thrills stand out in my career as a writer. One was having my first picture book, *When I'm Sleepy,* published in England, Denmark, Germany, Holland, Sweden, and Japan. The second was having my award-winning musical comedy, *Marquee,* produced in 1983 and flying to California for the opening night . . . .

"Today I look upon the plays and stories and lyrics and songs and poems I have written as being both the

A bedtime book invites children to imagine falling asleep like a kitten, a bird, or some other sleepy animal. (Illustration by Lynne Cherry from *When I'm Sleepy.*)

challenge and the offspring of my creative life. What I've learned is that I must first make my work the best I can—with re-writing, polishing, finding just the right word, the right detail—and then I must be patient, optimistic and very tenacious about keeping my literary 'children' in the mail until they connect with an editor who likes and appreciates them. For me, being a writer is a deeply satisfying, highly demanding, sometimes very frustrating profession. I'm glad it's what I became when I grew up."

Howard's picture books for children feature small children using their imaginations to explore different ways of doing ordinary things. *When I'm Sleepy* is a "quiet, gentle story," according to *School Library Jour-*

nal contributor Nancy Kewish, in which a little girl snuggles down into her bed, and dreams about going to sleep the way animals do. From a bird in a nest, to a bear in a cave, to bats hanging from a tree, the little girl tries out each situation in her mind before happily settling in her own bed, surrounded by a group of toy animals. "Beyond a doubt, the author and the artist possess intimate knowledge of small children," remarked a reviewer for *Publishers Weekly.*

Using a similar format, *When I'm Hungry* pictures a little boy eating a breakfast of cereal and daydreaming about what animals eat. From imagining himself dining with creatures he sees outside his window, including a squirrel, a puppy, and birds, the boy ventures to more exotic locales, eating bananas with monkeys in the jungle, and dining in the mud with a group of hippopotamuses. "Howard rings some clever changes on her droll concept," noted *Booklist* reviewer Hazel Rochman, and Nancy Seiner of *School Library Journal* found something to appeal to both preschoolers and elementary-school children in *When I'm Hungry,* concluding: "It's bound to be popular with them all."

■ Works Cited

Kewish, Nancy, review of *When I'm Sleepy, School Library Journal,* December, 1985, p. 74.
Rochman, Hazel, review of *When I'm Hungry, Booklist,* December 1, 1992, p. 675.
Seiner, Nancy, review of *When I'm Hungry, School Library Journal,* January, 1993, p. 78.
Review of *When I'm Sleepy, Publishers Weekly,* September 20, 1985, p. 109.

■ For More Information See

PERIODICALS

Bulletin of the Center for Children's Books, February, 1986, p. 110.
Kirkus Reviews, August 15, 1992, p. 1061.
Newsweek, December 9, 1985, p. 86.

*   *   *

HUNTER, Dawe
See DOWNIE, Mary Alice

I–J

ISAACSON, Philip M(arshal) 1924-

■ Personal

Born June 16, 1924, in Lewiston, ME; son of Harris M. (a lawyer) and Goldie (Resnick) Isaacson; married Deborah Naomi Rosen, October 19, 1952; children: Elizabeth, Thomas, John. *Education:* Bates College, B.A., 1947; Harvard University, LL.B., 1950. *Hobbies and other interests:* Writing, architectural photography.

■ Addresses

Home—2 Benson St., Lewiston, ME 04240. *Office*—75 Park Street, Lewiston, ME 04240.

■ Career

Lawyer in Lewiston, ME, 1950—. Chairman of Maine Arts Commission, 1975-78; member of Federal-State Advisory Panel of National Endowment for the Arts. *Military Service:* U.S. Naval Reserve, 1942-46; became lieutenant junior grade. *Member:* Maine Bar Association.

■ Awards, Honors

D.F.A. from Bowdoin College, 1984; Nonfiction Honor, Boston Globe/Horn Book, 1989, for *Round Buildings, Square Buildings, and Buildings That Wiggle Like a Fish.*

■ Writings

The American Eagle, Little, Brown, 1975.
(And photographer) *Round Buildings, Square Buildings, and Buildings That Wiggle Like a Fish*, Knopf, 1988.
(And photographer) *A Short Walk Around the Pyramids and Through the World of Art*, Knopf, 1993.

Also art critic for *Maine Sunday Telegram*, 1966—.

■ Sidelights

Philip M. Isaacson's contributions to children's literature allow young people to access and appreciate the wonders of art and architecture. Critics have praised his simple and straightforward style, noting his talent for encouraging his readers to think about the way buildings look and feel in a manner that avoids both pedantic language and condescension. According to Paul Goldberger of the *New York Times Book Review*, Isaacson is "the best introductory writer on architecture we have." Goldberger adds: "Mr. Isaacson sees buildings in exactly the right way: as beautiful objects and as pieces of social and cultural history."

Isaacson has explained his approach to writing about architecture for children: "My special interest relates to the sensual aspects of architecture. It is easy to describe the spiritual qualities of a building and fix its place in history. It is more difficult to analyze our emotional response to a building—how it makes one feel—and then explain it to young readers. *Round Buildings* is my attempt to do so. It deals with the relationship between materials, proportion, physical components, site, and light, among other things, to create a harmonious whole."

While Isaacson worked as a lawyer after his graduation from Harvard in 1950, his appreciation of art and architecture led him into a writing career. He began to write as an art critic for a Maine newspaper in 1966, and his first book, *The American Eagle*, was published in 1975. *The American Eagle* provides a history of the national symbol and traces its official and unofficial uses on seals, plates, metal, clothing, and furniture, and as an architectural detail on buildings.

Isaacson's books on architecture feature his own photographs along with his instructive narratives. *Round Buildings, Square Buildings, and Buildings that Wiggle Like a Fish* allows readers an opportunity to contrast the walls, structures, and beginnings and endings of famous buildings. A critic for *Kirkus Reviews* appreciated the cross references that inspire comparisons, the wide page format, and Isaacson's "creative and poetic" ideas.

A Short Walk Around the Pyramids and Through The World of Art, in the words of a *Publisher's Weekly* critic, demonstrates the "power of art to communicate across both centuries and cultures." From paintings, sculptures, and photographs to industrial designs and plans for cities, Isaacson discusses universal uses of color, shape, and composition. Along with the "fascinating juxtapositions" in this book, Shirley Wilton of *School Library Journal* appreciated the book's introduction to "the pleasures to be gained in everyday life and work and travel when one has a knowledge of art and its principles."

■ Works Cited

Goldberger, Paul, review of *Round Buildings, Square Buildings, & Buildings that Wiggle Like a Fish, New York Times Book Review,* November 13, 1988.
Review of *Round Buildings, Square Buildings, and Buildings that Wiggle Like a Fish, Kirkus Reviews,* September 1, 1988, p. 1324.
Review of *A Short Walk Around the Pyramids and Through the World of Art, Publishers Weekly,* September 13, 1993, p. 137.
Wilton, Shirley, review of *A Short Walk Around the Pyramids and Through the World of Art, School Library Journal,* August, 1993, p. 175.

■ For More Information See

PERIODICALS

Booklist, March 15, 1994, p. 1355.
Horn Book Guide, spring, 1994, p. 140.
Library Journal, December 15, 1975, p. 2317.
New York Times Book Review, November 14, 1993, p. 53.*

*   *   *

JACKSON, Garnet Nelson 1944-

■ Personal

Born May 27, 1944, in New Orleans, LA; daughter of Israel Nelson and Carrie Brent Nelson Sherman (a businesswoman); married Anthony Jackson, January 2, 1970 (divorced, 1978); children: Damon. *Education:* Dillard University, B.A., 1968; graduate studies at Eastern Michigan University, 1970-73. *Politics:* Democrat. *Religion:* Baptist.

■ Career

Flint Public School System, Flint, MI, full-time elementary school teacher, 1968—. Columnist, *Flint Journal. Member:* International Reading Association, National Association for the Advancement of Colored Persons (NAACP), Michigan Reading Association, Urban League, Greater Flint Optimist Club.

GARNET NELSON JACKSON

■ Awards, Honors

Harambe Medal, and Dorothy Duke Evans Educator of the Year Award, both NAACP, both 1991; Christa McAuliffe Special Tribute Award, Michigan House of Representatives, 1992; governor's letter of commendation, State of Michigan, 1992; congressional record for the reading of one of her stories, 1992; Mayor's Award, Flint, MI, 1992; Womanhood Hall of Fame award, Zeta Phi Beta, 1993.

■ Writings

I Am an African American Child, African like Me, Inc. (Flint, MI), 1990.
The Little African King, King Tut, African like Me, Inc., 1990.
Phillis Wheatley, Poet, African like Me, Inc., 1990, illustrated by Cheryl Hanna, Modern Curriculum Press, 1992.
Benjamin Banneker, Scientist, African like Me, Inc., 1990, illustrated by Rodney Pate, Modern Curriculum Press, 1992.
Frederick Douglass, Freedom Fighter, African like Me, Inc., 1990, illustrated by Keaf Holliday, Modern Curriculum Press, 1992.
Garrett Morgan, Inventor, illustrated by Thomas Hudson, Modern Curriculum Press, 1992.
Rosa Parks: Hero of Our Time, illustrated by Tony Wade, Modern Curriculum Press, 1992.
Elijah McCoy, Inventor, illustrated by Gary Thomas, Modern Curriculum Press, 1992.
Charles Drew, Doctor, illustrated by Gary Thomas, Modern Curriculum Press, 1994.

Jackson's *Mae Jemison: Astronaut* tells how a five-year-old girl's dream to reach the stars became a reality.

Mae Jemison, Astronaut, Modern Curriculum Press, 1994.

Maggie Walker, Business Leader, Modern Curriculum Press, 1994.

Selma Burke, Artist, Modern Curriculum Press, 1994.

Shirley Chisholm, Congresswoman, illustrated by Thomas Hudson, Modern Curriculum Press, 1994.

Thurgood Marshall, Supreme Court Justice, illustrated by Higgins Bond, Modern Curriculum Press, 1994.

Toni Morrison, Author, Modern Curriculum Press, 1995.

Also contributor of poem "A Composite of Experiences" to *The Griot Speaks,* 1986.

■ Work in Progress

Nine manuscripts being reviewed; an adult novel in progress.

■ Sidelights

Garnet Nelson Jackson is an author, teacher, and pioneer in the development of ethnic biographies for young children. Jackson told *SATA:* "Before my books, first written in 1989, there was nothing of this type written for young children. My publishing company expanded on the idea and have published Beginning Biographies of other minority groups—Hispanics, Native American, Women, Asian Americans." In easy-to-read prose and stories, she has introduced students to the rich legacy of the contributions made by Blacks in areas as diverse as science, poetry, and space travel.

Born May 27, 1944, in New Orleans, Louisiana, Jackson was the second of three daughters. "I was raised in an atmosphere of warmth and love," she told *SATA*, "being surrounded by many relatives. My parents' family home and grandparents' home were side by side. I had many cousins and we spent the sunny days of our childhood laughing and playing."

Jackson's mother, Carrie Sherman, was a businesswoman who, as a young woman living in New Orleans, opened one of the first grocery stores in that city to be owned and operated by an African American. With her knack for business, Sherman soon became the owner of an ice-cream parlor and a barber shop. "With the family being an intricate part of the business community, we enjoyed a middle-class upbringing," recalled Jackson.

Jackson attended both public and private catholic schools before enrolling in New Orleans' Dillard University in 1963. "I began writing when I was a teenager," she explained. "I wrote several short stories and poems that I sent to various publishers. I even wrote a novella, but it was never published. So I put my writing career on hold and dedicated my early adulthood to teaching." After receiving her degree in education from Dillard in 1968, she visited a friend living in Flint, Michigan, liked the area, and stayed. She married and became an elementary teacher in the Flint public school system, where she has worked with young people ever since. "Although I began teaching, I never totally gave up my dream of becoming a writer," Jackson stated. "In 1980 I began writing poetry again. I joined Rejoti Writer's club of New Jersey. I had several poems published and received honorable mention for my poem 'A Composite of Experiences,' published in *The Griot Speaks* in 1986."

"As a teacher I strive always to instill cultural pride in my students, which ultimately led to my career as a published author," Jackson explained. Frustrated by not being able to find books for her class of primarily black first-grade students, she decided to publish her own. She wrote five books, which she published under the series name "African like Me." "I started writing them during Black History Month because there was nothing in the library on the early reader's level about outstanding African American people," she explained to Jeff Smith in the *Flint Journal.* When the books proved a success in her own classrooms, she spread the word and soon had orders for the series from as far away as Texas. In 1992, Modern Curriculum Press included several of these biographies in its series of a dozen books entitled "Beginning Biographies: African Americans," of which Jackson is the author. "They promote self-esteem and cultural awareness for the young child," she explains of the biography series. Covering the contributions of Black Americans in all areas of life, the series includes *Mae Jemison, Astronaut,* about the first African American woman in space, and *Garrett Morgan, Inventor,* a

discussion of the man who invented both the gas mask and the stoplight.

In addition to teaching and writing books for young readers, Jackson's dedication to children has another outlet: she writes a column on issues concerning young children for her local newspaper. "I owe my success to God," Jackson declares, "to my mother, who was such a beautiful role model; to my son, who inspires me; and to the children whose smiles delight and inspire me every day."

■ Works Cited

Smith, Jeff, "Reading, Writing, Authorship," *Flint Journal,* April 16, 1994, pp. B1-2.

■ For More Information See

PERIODICALS

Classroom Today, Modern Curriculum Press, 1993, p. 1.
Ebony, October, 1991.
Essence, February, 1995, p. 118.

*   *   *

JENKINS, Debra Reid
See REID JENKINS, Debra

*   *   *

JOHNSON, Sherrie 1948-

■ Personal

Born February 5, 1948, in Salt Lake City, UT; daughter of Ivo Dell (a salesman) and Geraldine (a secretary; maiden name, Young) Mills; married Carl M. Johnson (a business manager), August 26, 1967; children: Laresa J. Campbell, Talena J. Kerr, Breana J. Tilley, Anissa, Mariah, Kirsha, Meleah, Patrea, Joshua. *Education:* Weber State University, B.A., 1995. *Religion:* The Church of Jesus Christ of Latter-day Saints (Mormon). *Hobbies and other interests:* Swimming, reading, classical music, racquetball.

■ Addresses

Home—1021 North 700 West, West Bountiful, UT 84087.

■ Career

Writer, mother. Adjunct instructor, Weber State University. *Member:* Society of Children's Book Writers and Illustrators.

SHERRIE JOHNSON

■ Writings

FOR CHILDREN; PICTURE BOOKS, PUBLISHED BY DESERET BOOK

The Broken Bow, illustrated by Tyler Lybbert, 1994.
The Gadianton Robbers, illustrated by Lybbert, 1994.
Nephi and Lehi in Prison, illustrated by Lybbert, 1994.
Abinadi, illustrated by Lybbert, 1994.
Ammon and the King, illustrated by Lybbert, 1994.
Captain Moroni's Title of Liberty, illustrated by Lybbert, 1994.
Alma at the Waters of Mormon, illustrated by Lybbert, 1994.
Jesus Is Born, illustrated by Lybbert, 1994.
Enos Prays, illustrated by Lybbert, 1995.
Jesus Visits the Nephites, illustrated by Lybbert, 1995.
Jared and His Brother, illustrated by Mark McCune, 1995.
Abish, illustrated by McCune, 1995.

HISTORICAL FICTION

A House with Wings, Aspen Books, 1995.

FOR ADULTS

Spiritually Centered Motherhood, Bookcraft, 1983.
Man, Woman and Deity, Bookcraft, 1991.

OTHER

Has also published more than one hundred articles and short stories.

■ Work in Progress

Two contemporary children's novels, *Yaddow* and *Nabby II.*

■ Sidelights

Sherrie Johnson told *SATA:* "'How could you have known at five years of age?' I've often been asked. I have no answer. All I know is that before I could read, I watched my father knowing that whatever was inside his book was so captivating he was unaware of my presence. When he put the book down and left the room, I hurried to open it and examined the black marks on the white paper. I recognized it at once as magic. I remember the way the air jumped from the pages to caress my face as I flipped them and the stale odor that scented the air. But most of all I remember the feeling in my stomach. It was an intense longing as compelling as any hunger, as urgent as any thirst I have ever known. I wanted to read! I needed to read! I had to read because somehow I knew that only then could I write my own books.

"By incessantly asking Mother, 'What sound does this make?' I learned to read before I began school. It was my first taste of power. On my own accord I had stepped into my future and grasped what I wanted. Anxious to be on to the real goal, I wrote, illustrated, collated, and stapled books, then boldly marched door to door selling them. And that's how it all began.

"In my latest book, *A House with Wings,* I was able to combine my love of writing with my love of history. The story takes place 146 years ago on the very property where my home now stands. The 'old-timers' around here had shown me arrow heads they'd found in their fields and told me about the Indians living in teepees just north of my house. Then, while doing some historical research, I happened on a journal of a man who told of the hardships the trek west had been on his child named Millennium. As I read the name, I suddenly knew the girl and so I built her a cabin next to the Indians and began writing to see what would happen. That's how *A House with Wings* began to fly."

*   *   *

JONES, Geraldine
   See McCAUGHREAN, Geraldine

K

SALLY M. KEEHN

KEEHN, Sally M. 1947-

■ Personal

Born August 11, 1947, in London, England; daughter of Shirley (a naval officer) and Mary (a homemaker; maiden name, Giffen) Miller; married David C. Keehn (an attorney), December 30, 1972; children: Alison, Molly. *Education:* Hood College, B.A., 1969; Drexel University, M.L.S., 1972. *Religion:* United Church of Christ.

■ Addresses

Home—Allentown, PA.

■ Career

Anne Arundel County Public Library, Annapolis, MD, young adult librarian, 1972-75, part-time reference librarian, 1975-1979; freelance writer, 1981—. Part-time and volunteer reference librarian, Parkland Community Library, 1980-91; part-time tour guide, Lehigh County Historical Society, 1985-86. Also worked for the American Red Cross in Korea. *Member:* Society of Children's Book Writers and Illustrators, Authors Guild, Inkweavers.

■ Awards, Honors

New York Public Library "Reading and Sharing" citation, and Notable Trade Book in the Field of Social Studies citation, both 1991, Carolyn W. Field Award, and Jefferson Cup Honor Book, both 1992, International Reading Association Young Adults' Choice citation, 1993, and Favorite Paperback citation, 1994, Hodge Podger Society Award, 1994, and Texas Lone Star Reading List citation, 1994-95, all for *I Am Regina;* New York Public Library "Reading and Sharing" citation, 1995, for *Moon of Two Dark Horses.*

■ Writings

(With husband David C. Keehn) *Hexcursions: Daytripping in and around Pennsylvania's Dutch Country,* Hastings House, 1982.
I Am Regina (young adult novel), Philomel, 1991.
Moon of Two Dark Horses (young adult novel), Philomel, 1995.

I Am Regina has been published in Denmark, Germany, and Italy.

■ Sidelights

Sally M. Keehn told *SATA:* "The Native Americans say that a story stalks a writer and, if it finds you worthy, comes to live in your heart. The story of Regina Leininger, on which my first historical novel *I Am Regina* is based, stalked me for nine years. Her story did come to live in my heart. It still does.

"I came upon the incident that gave rise to the story while researching a travel book on Pennsylvania's Dutch Country. I attended the Kutztown Folk Festival where I read in the program about a reenactment of the French and Indian Wars. I never saw the reenactment, but what I read started me on a journey that led from a few words in a program to a 237-page novel. Why? I was curious. To be an author you have to be.

"I wanted to know why she was kidnapped. By whom. What was going on at the time? The French and Indian Wars? What were they? I wanted to know what life was like back then: for the Pennsylvania Germans with whom Regina lived for ten years; for the Native Americans with whom she lived nine. I didn't know that the Eastern Woodland Indians lived in bark-covered huts. That, at times, they ate the inner bark of trees, wild garlic, and mice to stay alive. That the men plucked hair from their faces. That they often adopted white captives and made them part of the family.

"I sifted through many secondary sources to find out about these things, but what truly inspired me to keep on going were the primary sources that detailed Regina's life. This story happened and I was fortunate to discover first-hand accounts that told about it. I call these accounts my 'voices from the past.' During the three years I worked on the novel, these voices stalked me. They told me, don't give up. This story's worth telling.

"My second historical novel, *Moon of Two Dark Horses,* stalked me for thirteen years. Four of these years I spent researching, writing, and revising the book. It, too, was sparked by a single incident—a massacre that happened during the American Revolution in northeastern Pennsylvania at a place now known as the 'Bloody Rock.' I wanted to know why the bloodshed happened. Through extensive research and a lot of thought, I discovered the reason and that tragic incident became two lines in a 218-page novel about friendship.

"For my third novel, I'm exploring an event that occurred when I was a teenager. Why did *it* happen? What was going on? Was our planet really on 'the eve of destruction'? As an author, I find that I'm much like the kids for whom I write—full of questions."

■ For More Information See

PERIODICALS

Bulletin of the Center for Children's Books, April, 1991, p. 198.
Kirkus Reviews, June 1, 1991, p. 730.
School Library Journal, June, 1991, p. 108.

Voice of Youth Advocates, August, 1991, p. 172.

* * *

KELLY, Joanne (W.) 1934-

■ Personal

Born August 22, 1934, in Chicago, IL; daughter of William J. Walters (an engineer) and Bernice Fawcett Leech (a teacher); married Charles Kelly (an engineer), June 11, 1954; children: Charles Jr., Douglas. *Education:* University of Illinois, B.S., 1968, M.S., 1970, C.A.S., 1980. *Religion:* Presbyterian.

■ Addresses

Home—2110 Galen Dr., Champaign, IL 61821.

■ Career

Thomas Paine Elementary School, Urbana, IL, librarian, 1967; Urbana School District, Urbana, elementary librarian, 1968-92, coordinator of libraries, 1984-92.

■ Awards, Honors

"Teacher Plus" citation, *Instructor Magazine,* 1978; "Those Who Excel" citation, Illinois State Board of Education, 1983.

■ Writings

The Battle of Books, illustrated by Pat Martin, Libraries Unlimited, 1990.
(With Martin and Kay V. Grabow) *Rebuses for Readers,* illustrated by Martin, Libraries Unlimited, 1991.
On Location: Settings from Famous Children's Books, illustrated by Martin, photographs by Charles Kelly, Libraries Unlimited, 1992.
Newbery Authors of the Eastern Seaboard: Integrating Social Studies and Literature, Grades 5-8, illustrated by Martin, photographs by Kelly, Libraries Unlimited, 1994.

■ Work in Progress

Beverly Cleary Handbook; Battle of Books 2.

■ Sidelights

Joanne Kelly told *SATA:* "I have had an active and avid interest in children's literature since I haunted my school and public libraries as a youngster. Books were my passion and my best friends. Happily I was blessed with a wonderful school librarian who fed my interests by providing me with the very best in juvenile literature, and—the greatest kindness of all—presented opportunities for discussion and other kinds of responses to the stories. I found deeper meaning and value in the books I loved because she offered activities to extend them.

Joanne Kelly's *On Location* combines geography, literature, and history by introducing students to the settings of beloved children's books, such as this reconstruction of Laura Ingalls Wilder's home from *Little House in the Big Woods*.

"When I became a school librarian many years later, I tried to promote the same love of good books in my students by showing them that the fun and learning of a favorite book can continue to be savored when the last page has been turned."

■ For More Information See

PERIODICALS

Library Talk, May/June 1991, p. 39; March/April 1993, p. 49.

*   *   *

KENDALL, Martha E.

■ Personal

Education: University of Michigan, B.A.; San Jose State University, M.A.; Stanford University, M.A. *Hobbies and other interests:* "I sing, and I play cello, fiddle, mandolin, guitar, and bass. I play classical music, and also perform regularly in bluegrass and swing ensembles."

■ Addresses

Home—25525 Mt. Bache Rd., Los Gatos, CA 95030.

■ Career

San Jose City College, professor of English and women's studies. *Member:* Phi Beta Kappa.

■ Awards, Honors

Charlie Parkhurst Award for Research, 1987, Santa Cruz Women's Commission; Honored at the National Women's Hall of Fame, 1987, Seneca Falls, NY; President's Award for Excellence in Teaching, 1988, 1990, San Jose City College; Re-Entry Students' Best Teacher Award, 1991, San Jose City College.

■ Writings

Scenes of American Life (video and book), Highland, 1986.
Elizabeth Cady Stanton: Founder of the Women's Rights Movement in America, Highland, 1988.
Nellie Bly: Reporter for the World, Millbrook, 1992.
John James Audubon: Artist of the Wild, Millbrook, 1993.

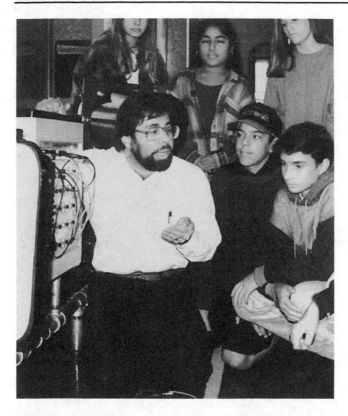

In *Steve Wozniak: Inventor of the Apple Computer,*
**Martha E. Kendall tells the story of how Wozniak
(pictured here at the Children's Discovery Museum in
San Jose) forever changed office technology.**

Pinata Party, Willowisp, 1993.
The Real Thing (video and book), Highland, 1993.
Benjamin Franklin, Willowisp, 1994.
Steve Wozniak: The Man Who Grew the Apple, Walker,
   1994.
Steve Wozniak: Inventor of the Apple Computer, Walker,
   1995.
One of the Family: Jane Goodall and the Chimps,
   Willowisp, 1995.

Also executive editor for *College Teaching,* 1989—.

■ For More Information See

PERIODICALS

Horn Book Guide, spring, 1993, p. 138; fall, 1994, p.
   376.*

* * *

KENNEDY, Pamela 1946-

■ Personal

Born October 22, 1946, in Renton, WA; daughter of
Douglas Haig (an insurance agent) and Mattie (a secre-
tary and homemaker; maiden name, Clark) Gwinnett;
married Kraig Michael Kennedy (a captain in the U.S.
Navy), June 16, 1969; children: Joshua, Douglas, Anne.
Education: University of Washington, B.A. (cum laude),

1968. *Politics:* Independent. *Religion:* Protestant. *Hobbies and other interests:* Reading, sewing, teaching Bible
classes to children and women.

■ Addresses

Home—1 Hale Alii, Honolulu, HI 96818.

■ Career

Teacher of reading and English, Olympic Junior High
School, Auburn, WA, 1969-71; supplemental teacher,
Pine Tree Elementary School, Kent, WA, 1972-73;
teacher of English and speech, San Diego College for
Electrical Engineers, San Diego, CA, 1973-75; freelance
writer, 1975—. Bible Study Fellowship, teaching leader,
1988-94. *Member:* Friends of Family Services Center
(vice-president, 1994-95).

■ Writings

COTTONTALE PICTURE BOOK SERIES

A, B, C Bunny, Focus on the Family, 1990.
1, 2, 3 Bunny, Focus on the Family, 1990.
Red, Yellow, Blue Bunny, Focus on the Family, 1990.
Oh, Oh, Bunny, Focus on the Family, 1990.
Night, Night, Bunny, Focus on the Family, 1990.
All Mine, Bunny, Focus on the Family, 1990.
No, No, Bunny, Focus on the Family, 1992.
So Mad, Bunny, Focus on the Family, 1992.

PAMELA J. KENNEDY

A CHRISTMAS CELEBRATION

TRADITIONS AND CUSTOMS FROM AROUND THE WORLD

WRITTEN BY PAMELA KENNEDY

Kennedy explains to children the origin and meaning of Christmas traditions using reproductions of fine art, line engravings, and old photographs in this 1992 book.

Big Brother Bunny, Focus on the Family, 1992.

"GOD MADE ME" SERIES

Now I'm 1!, Chariot Family, 1994.
Now I'm 2!, Chariot Family, 1994.
Now I'm 3!, Chariot Family, 1994.

OTHER

Dickens' Christmas Carol, Ideals, 1985.
The Story of the Swan Lake Ballet, Ideals, 1986.
A Child's Book of Prayers, Ideals, 1988.
A Little Treasury of Prayers, Ideals, 1989.
Prayers at Eastertime, Ideals, 1989.
The Other Wiseman, Ideals, 1989.
Prayers at Christmastime, Ideals, 1990.
Hymns of Faith and Inspiration, Ideals, 1990.
(Compiler) *Nursery Songs and Lap Games,* Ideals, 1990.
An Easter Celebration: Traditions and Customs from Around the World, Ideals, 1991.
A Christmas Celebration: Traditions and Customs from Around the World, Ideals, 1992.

Psalms for Moms, Concordia, 1997.

Contributing editor of *Ideals Magazine,* 1990—.

■ Work in Progress

Essays for *Ideals Magazine.*

■ Sidelights

Although Pamela Kennedy has written many books for toddlers, she is perhaps best known for her studies of Christian religious traditions, including her two volumes *An Easter Celebration: Traditions and Customs from Around the World* and *A Christmas Celebration: Traditions and Customs from Around the World.*

Reviewing *An Easter Celebration* in *Booklist,* Ilene Cooper wrote that "Kennedy does an excellent job of gathering various Easter traditions and customs and presenting them in a useful manner for children."

Cooper suggested that *An Easter Celebration* is "a handy volume for the holiday shelves."

School Library Journal reviewer Patricia Pearl observed that Kennedy's *An Easter Celebration* is "a pleasantly instructive look at the Christian meaning of Easter that suits various ages and faiths." However, Pearl pointed out that the work is narrower in scope than other books on this topic.

Lisa Napoli, reviewing Kennedy's *A Christmas Celebration* in *Booklist,* found it to be "accessible while supplying a wealth of information," and concluded that this book is "a practical and engaging overview of 'the most festive Christian holiday.'"

Kennedy told *SATA:* "Writing has been a love of mine since I was in elementary school. I enjoyed embellishing school writing assignments with characters (real and fictional) and settings that were more exciting than the everyday. By high school I had decided to pursue a career as an English teacher and, after graduation, attended the University of Washington, where I worked toward a degree in English. Because of a late registration one quarter, I was unable to get into a short story writing course I wanted to attend. The only other available writing course that fit into my schedule was one in expository writing. With little enthusiasm, I signed up. It was the best thing that could have happened! I had an excellent teacher who really focused on the basics of clear, concise writing, and helped me 'quit beating around the literary bush.'

"After college graduation, I married a young Naval officer and began teaching English in junior and senior high. For several years I wrote only in my journals and letters until my husband suggested I might make a contribution to our family income if I quit talking about writing and finally submitted something for publication. I countered his suggestion with a remark about not knowing how to get published, and he—not easily deterred—offered to take me to the library so I could find out."

Within a year Kennedy's first article on planning a party, complete with recipes, was printed in a magazine. Over the years more articles followed until one of her family's moves landed them in Milwaukee. There Kennedy wrote her first children's book, a retelling of Dickens' *A Christmas Carol.*

While Kennedy is no longer employed as a high school English teacher, she often visits schools as a guest lecturer speaking about her freelance work and her writing habits. She told *SATA:* "I often speak to writing classes at my own children's schools and encourage young writers to see that all stories and books begin with an idea in the writer's mind. If they have an idea, they have the first step of a story. I enjoy 'de-mystifying' the writing process and share anecdotes about how I have written manuscripts in airports, while riding in cars, even while holding a cranky baby on my lap," she explained. "I believe our schools are filled with writers who just need to be encouraged to learn the skills that will enable them to put their thoughts on paper with confidence and clarity. Just think of all the stories waiting to be told!

"After twenty-five years of marriage and seventeen moves, I have found great satisfaction and fulfillment in my very portable career," Kennedy concluded. "It is a creative outlet that allows me to share ideas and encourage others through the artistry of the written word."

■ Works Cited

Cooper, Ilene, review of *An Easter Celebration: Traditions and Customs from Around the World, Booklist,* March 15, 1991.

Napoli, Lisa, review of *A Christmas Celebration: Traditions and Customs from Around the World, Booklist,* November 1, 1992.

Pearl, Patricia, review of *An Easter Celebration: Traditions and Customs from Around the World, School Library Journal,* June 1991.

*   *   *

KHEMIR, Sabiha

■ Personal

Born in Tunisia. *Education:* Ecole Normale Superieure, Tunis, B.A.; London University, M.A., 1986, Ph.D., 1990.

■ Addresses

Office—69 Lady Margaret Road, London NW5 2NN, England.

■ Career

Art historian, writer, and illustrator. Worked as site supervisor on archaeological excavations in Egypt and as a research assistant at the University of Pennsylvania. Consultant on Islamic art for Metropolitan Museum of Art, New York City. Lecturer on Islamic art throughout the world.

■ Writings

Waiting in the Future for the Past to Come (novel), Quartet (London), 1993.

(And Presenter) *Rear Window: The Khalili Collection* (television program), Channel Four Television, 1993.

ILLUSTRATOR

Nacer Khemir, *L'Ogresse,* Maspero (Paris), 1975.

Nazim Hikmet, *Le Nuage Amoureux,* Maspero, 1979.

Denys Johnson-Davies, *The Island of Animals,* Quartet, 1994.

SABIHA KHEMIR

Also illustrator of twelve children's books for Institute of Ismaili Studies, London, 1983, and several book covers. Contributor of illustrations to magazines.

■ Sidelights

Sabiha Khemir draws on her strong background in Islamic art in both her work as an art historian and as an illustrator. Trained in both her native Tunisia and London as an expert in Islamic art and archaeology, Khemir has divided her time between creating exotic pen-and-ink illustrations for several books and magazines and a successful career as an art consultant in both England and the United States.

Khemir's first illustrations appeared in two books for children that were published in Paris in the mid-1970s. In 1983, after moving to England to attend London University, she participated in a Nursery Project sponsored by the Institute of Ismaili Studies in London, and illustrated a dozen books for young readers. Other projects filled the next decade, including work towards her Ph.D. in Islamic Art and archeology, which Khemir received in 1990. 1993 found her not only involved in writing and presenting a series of documentary films on Islamic Art for British television's Channel 4, but receiving praise for her first novel. Khemir's *Waiting in the Future for the Past to Come* is set in Tunisia and traces cultural shifts over three generations; it was praised by reviewers for being as creative and intricate

as her drawings. The following year, Denys Johnson-Davies' *Island of the Animals* was published, full of intricate illustrations of animals done by Khemir.

Born in Tunisia, Khemir now makes her home in England, where she is becoming increasingly more active in her field, speaking on Islamic Art and sharing her expertise on the subject with museums around the world, including the Metropolitan Museum of Art in New York City. She has also been involved in archaeological research, both on a major "dig" in Egypt and through work as a research assistant at the University of Pennsylvania. Khemir is fluent in four languages: Arabic, French, English, and Spanish.

■ For More Information See

PERIODICALS

Irish Times, September 25, 1993.
London Times, June 15, 1993.
Panurge, Spring, 1994.

BOOKS

(Exhibition catalogue) *Forces of Change: Artists of the Arab World,* The National Museum of Women in the Arts, Washington, D.C., 1994.

*   *   *

KOONS, James
See PERNU, Dennis

*   *   *

KRAUS, Joanna Halpert 1937-

■ Personal

Born December 7, 1937, in Portland, ME; daughter of Harold (a merchant) and Florence Halpert; married Ted M. Kraus (an editor and publisher), 1966; children: Timothy Yang Kun. *Education:* Attended Westfield College, London, 1957-58; Sarah Lawrence College, A.B., 1959; University of California, Los Angeles, M.A., 1963; Columbia University, Ed.D., 1972.

■ Addresses

Home—1209 Skycrest Dr., #2, Walnut Creek, CA 94595. *Agent*—Susan Schulman, 454 West 44th St., New York, NY 10036.

■ Career

Children's Theatre Association, Baltimore, MD, associate director and creative drama teacher, 1960-61; Strathmere School of the Arts, North Gower, Ontario, drama director, summers, 1961-63; New Rochelle Academy, New Rochelle, NY, director of drama program, 1962-63; Clark Center for the Performing Arts, New York City, assistant director and supervisor of performance program, 1963-65; Young Men's and Young Women's Hebrew Association (YM-YWHA), New York

JOANNA HALPERT KRAUS

City, creative drama teacher, 1965-70; New York City Community College, New York City, instructor in public speaking and oral interpretation, 1966-69; Columbia University, Teacher's College, New York City, supervisor of student teachers in speech and theatre, 1970-71; State University of New York College at Purchase, instructor in theatre and drama, 1970-72; State University of New York College at New Paltz, lecturer, 1972-73, assistant professor of theatre and education, 1973-79; State University of New York College at Brockport, associate professor, 1979-85, professor of theatre, 1986-95, coordinator of interdisciplinary arts for children, 1981-90, graduate coordinator, Interdisciplinary Arts for Children, 1990-95.

Chairperson of Children's Theatre Showcase, 1963-65. Guest storyteller on WEVD-Radio show *Let's Tell Tales,* 1973-75. Guest lecturer at Western Washington University Institute for Drama and the Child, summer, 1978. Director of plays, including *The Indian Captive,* 1973, *A Christmas Carol,* 1979, *Tom Sawyer,* 1980, *A Wrinkle in Time,* 1984, *Step on a Crack,* 1993, and *Ms. Courageous,* 1995. Coordinator of Arts for Children program, 1980, and children's theatre mini-tours, 1980, 1981, 1984, 1985. *Member:* International Association of Theatre for Young People, American Alliance for Theatre and Education, Dramatists Guild, United University Professions, Children's Theatre Association of America (recording secretary, 1982-84).

■ Awards, Honors

Charlotte B. Chorpenning Cup, American Theatre Association, 1971, for achievement in playwriting; Creative Artists Public Service fellowship in playwriting, 1976-77; first prize, Indiana University-Purdue University at Indianapolis (IUPUI) National Playwriting Competition, for *Remember My Name: A Story of Survival in Wartime France;* winner, American Voices New Play Reading Series, Rochester, NY, 1995, for *For the Glory;* Special Achievement Award, New York State Theatre Education Association, 1995.

■ Writings

PLAYS

The Ice Wolf (two-act; produced in New York City, 1964), New Plays, 1967.
Mean to Be Free (two-act; produced in New York City, 1968; produced Off-Off Broadway, 1992), New Plays, 1968.
Vasalisa (two-act; produced in Davidson, NC, 1972), New Plays, 1973.
The Dragon Hammer (one-act; produced in Rowayton, CT, 1977), New Plays, 1978.
Two Plays from the Far East (includes *The Dragon Hammer* and *The Tale of Oniroku*), New Plays, 1977.
Circus Home (two-act; produced in Seattle, WA, 1977), New Plays, 1979.
The Last Baron of Arizona (two-act; produced in Tempe, AZ, 1984), New Plays, 1986.
"Kimchi Kid" (two-act; produced in New Brunswick, NJ, 1986), New Plays, 1988.
The Shaggy Dog Murder Trial (one-act; produced in Brockport, NY), Anchorage Press, 1988.
Remember My Name: A Story of Survival in Wartime France (produced at Indiana University-Purdue University at Indianapolis), Samuel French, 1989.
Plays Plus, Collins Educational, 1990.
Angel in the Night (two-act; first produced in Evanston, IL, 1991), Dramatic Publishing, 1995.
(With Greer Woodward) *Tenure Track (Snapshots of Women in Academe),* (first produced at Megan Terry's Magic Theatre), Players Press, 1993.
For the Glory, produced in Rochester, NY, 1995.

Also author of play *Ms. Courageous,* first produced in 1995.

OTHER

Seven Sound and Motion Stories (fiction), New Plays, 1971, revised edition as *Sound and Motion Stories,* 1980.
The Great American Train Ride: Using Creative Dramatics for a Multi-Disciplinary Classroom Project (nonfiction), New Plays, 1975.
(Editor with Vicki Lewin) *In My Mind/In Your Mind: Rochester Kids Write,* State University of New York College at Brockport, 1982.
Tall Boy's Journey (children's fiction), illustrated by Karen Ritz, Carolrhoda Books, 1992.

Contributor to *New Women's Theatre,* edited by Honor Moore, Vintage Book, 1977, and *Children and Drama,* 2nd edition, edited by Nellie McCaslin, Longman, 1980. Contributor of reviews and articles to periodicals, including *Times Herald Record, Children and Drama, Children's Theatre Review,* and *Critical Digest.*

■ Work in Progress

A play about North Carolina history commissioned by the Raleigh Little Theatre and North Carolina Museum of History.

■ Sidelights

Joanna Halpert Kraus is an accomplished playwright and director of children's theater whose works, according to *Twentieth-Century Children's Writers* essayist Rachel Fordyce, "unlike many contemporary plays for children, [have] value, in Horatian terms, to educate and entertain both children and adults." Her plays include *The Ice Wolf,* which tells the story of an Eskimo village dominated by superstition, *Mean to Be Free,* an adaptation of the story of Harriet Tubman and the Underground Railroad, and *Vasalisa,* in which the supreme Russian witch of legend, Baba Yaga, is thwarted by the virtue of the title character. Through works such as these Kraus has become known for her extensive

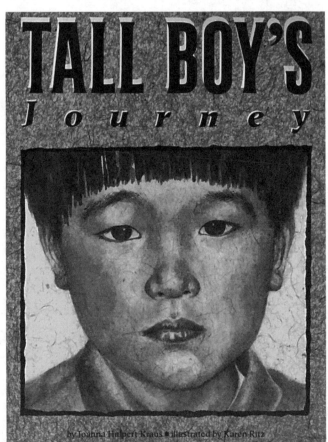

Dedicated to the author's adopted Korean son, this is the combined true story of several adopted international children. (Cover illustration by Karen Ritz.)

period research, lyrical use of language, and effective use of action, music, and visual effects, according to Fordyce. Kraus draws on legends and tales from societies ranging from Alaska to Africa to make what Fordyce termed "well-honed, undogmatic plea[s] for sanity, humanity, mercy, justice, and compassion."

Kraus is also the author of a children's book, *Tall Boy's Journey,* which tells the story of a Korean orphan, Kim Moo Yong, who travels to the United States to the home of adoptive parents in New York state. The boy finds life with his new parents strange, from the way they look to the lack of spirit posts in the community, but with the help of a Korean friend of his new father, he begins to make friends and settle down to his new life. While she found *Tall Boy's Journey* awkwardly written and somewhat predictable, *School Library Journal* reviewer Diane S. Marton remarked that the book nonetheless "details some of the cultural differences and fears that a young person coming from Asia to adoptive parents in the United States might experience." A *Kirkus Reviews* critic noted that Kraus "brings a poignant authenticity to the boy's arrival" and praised the "unusually perceptive and detailed portrayal" of an international adoption.

Kraus once commented: "When I was thirteen, my life was changed by a marvelous director of children's theatre, Margaret Dutton. We toured towns in Maine where no live theatre for young audiences had ever appeared. The children were spellbound, but no more so than we, the players. I vowed then to pass on that touch of magic. Accuracy and artistry were our goals, and now, as a writer, they are still the same for me. Children should have stories to grow on and should never have anything less than the best. Young people are a wonderful audience, for they listen with their hearts as well as their minds."

■ Works Cited

Fordyce, Rachel, "Joanna Halpert Kraus," *Twentieth-Century Children's Writers,* 4th edition, St. James Press, 1995, pp. 537-38.

Marton, Diane S., review of *Tall Boy's Journey, School Library Journal,* February, 1993, pp. 73-74.

Review of *Tall Boy's Journey, Kirkus Reviews,* November 15, 1992, p. 1445.

■ For More Information See

PERIODICALS

Publishers Weekly, November 30, 1992, p. 55.
School Library Journal, January, 1980, p. 72.
Times Educational Supplement, February 28, 1992, p. 34.

*   *   *

KYLE, Elisabeth
   See DUNLOP, Agnes M(ary) R(obertson)

L

LAMPMAN, Evelyn Sibley 1907-1980 (Lynn Bronson)

■ Personal

Born April 18, 1907, in Dallas, OR; died June 13, 1980; daughter of Joseph E. and Harrier (Bronson) Sibley; married Herbert Sheldon Lampman in 1934 (died, 1943); children: Linda Sibley Lampman McIsaac, Anne Hathaway Lampman Knutson. *Education:* Oregon State University, B.S., 1929. *Religion:* Episcopalian.

■ Career

Radio Station KEX, Portland, OR, continuity writer, 1929-34, continuity chief, 1937-45; Radio Station KGW, Portland, educational director, 1945-52; full-time writer of children's books, 1952-80.

■ Awards, Honors

Western Writers of America Spur award, 1968, 1971.

■ Writings

FICTION

Crazy Creek, illustrated by Grace Paull, Doubleday, 1948.

Treasure Mountain, illustrated by Richard Bennett, Doubleday, 1949.

The Bounces of Cynthiann', illustrated by Paull, Doubleday, 1950, World's Work, 1960.

Elder Brother, illustrated by Bennett, Doubleday, 1951.

Captain Apple's Ghost, illustrated by Ninon MacKnight, Doubleday, 1952, Hodder & Stoughton, 1953.

Tree Wagon, illustrated by Robert Frankenberg, Doubleday, 1953.

Witch Doctor's Son, illustrated by Bennett, Doubleday, 1954.

The Shy Stegosaurus of Cricket Creek, illustrated by Hubert Buel, Doubleday, 1955.

Navaho Sister, illustrated by Paul Lantz, Doubleday, 1956.

Rusty's Space Ship, illustrated by Bernard Krigstein, Doubleday, 1957.

Rock Hounds, illustrated by Arnold Spilka, Doubleday, 1958.

Special Year, illustrated by Genia, Doubleday, 1959.

The City under the Back Steps, illustrated by Honore Valintcourt, Doubleday, 1960, Faber, 1962.

Princess of Fort Vancouver, illustrated by Douglas Gorsline, Doubleday, 1962.

The Shy Stegosaurus at Indian Springs, illustrated by Paul Galdone, Doubleday, 1962.

Mrs. Updaisy, illustrated by Cyndy Szekeres, Doubleday, 1963.

Temple of the Sun, illustrated by Lili Rethi, Doubleday, 1964.

Wheels West: The Story of Tabitha Brown, illustrated by Gil Walker, Doubleday, 1965.

The Tilted Sombrero, illustrated by Ray Cruz, Doubleday, 1966.

Half-Breed, illustrated by Ann Grifalconi, Doubleday, 1967.

The Bandit of Mok Hill, illustrated by Marvin Friedman, Doubleday, 1969.

Cayuse Courage, Harcourt, 1970.

Once upon Little Big Horn, illustrated by John Gretzer, Crowell, 1971.

The Year of the Small Shadow, Harcourt, 1971.

Go up the Road, illustrated by Charles Robinson, Atheneum, 1972.

Rattlesnake Cave, illustrated by Pamela Johnson, Atheneum, 1974.

White Captives, Atheneum, 1975.

The Potlatch Family, Atheneum, 1976.

Bargain Bride, Atheneum, 1977.

Squaw Man's Son, Atheneum, 1978.

Three Knocks on the Wall, Atheneum, 1980.

FICTION; UNDER PSEUDONYM LYNN BRONSON

Timberland Adventure, Lippincott, 1950.
Coyote Kid, Lippincott, 1951.
Rogue's Valley, Lippincott, 1952.
The Runaway, Lippincott, 1953.

Evelyn Sibley Lampman's *The Bounces of Cynthiann'* recounts the story of how the four Bounce orphans from Rhode Island are placed in separate homes in Oregon in the 1800s but eventually manage to be reunited. (Illustration by Grace Paull.)

Darcy's Harvest, illustrated by Paul Galdone, Double-day, 1956.
Popular Girl, Doubleday, 1957.

OTHER

Also author of adult book, *Of Mikes and Men,* a 1951 fictionalized account of Lampman's early experiences as a writer for Portland radio stations. A collection of Lampman's manuscript is located at University of Oregon Library, Eugene.

■ Sidelights

Evelyn Sibley Lampman, writing at times under the pen name of Lynn Bronson, was a prolific and versatile author of biographies, historical fiction, and contemporary fiction. She was most praised and best known, however, for fiction involving members of minority groups, particularly Native Americans.

Lampman's maternal grandparents were pioneers who arrived in Oregon by covered wagons. Many of her stories were based on tales of the journey her grandmother told her. She once told *SATA:* "My father, who came to Oregon from Illinois in 1889 as a young lawyer

... always defended Indians in court, and so far as I know never sent a bill. He learned to speak Chinook jargon so he could talk with the older Indians who refused to speak English. Sometimes they brought their children, who always played with me in our front yard.... I grew up like them, too, which is probably why so many of my books have been about that race."

Lampman began by writing children's stories, both serious and light-hearted. Two of the more light-hearted, which don't focus on any ethnic groups, are *Captain Apple's Ghost* and *The Bounces of Cynthiann'.* In the first book, a ghost returns to his former home and helps to preserve a children's museum. In the second, a small town comes vividly to life when it takes in the motherless Bounce children.

Lampman first wrote about an ethnic minority in *Elder Brother,* which concerns the cultural conflicts of a Chinese-American family who adopt a son from China. The story takes place at the turn of the century, and even then the daughters of the household rebel against the boys' traditional views of feminine roles. Two of the books that introduced Indian characters also introduced a popular Lampman creation—the shy stegosaurus. *The Shy Stegosaurus of Cricket Creek* was followed by *The Shy Stegosaurus of Indian Springs,* in which a modern day (1962) Indian boy and his great-grandfather, struggling to reconcile old and new ways on the reservation, are aided with their problem by the giant dinosaur.

These books were followed by two very different historical fictions. One, *Temple of the Sun,* is the story of the conquest of the Aztecs in the sixteenth century, and of a young boy named Chimal who is chosen to fraternize with the Spaniards, learn their language, and become a spy for the Aztecs. A review in *Horn Book* commented that "without romanticizing the historical facts, the author has given a balanced picture of the conquerors and the conquered." *Wheels West* is a biography, based on several historical sources, of Tabitha Brown, who eventually became the first house-mother at what is now Pacific University. At the age of sixty-six, Brown crossed the country from Missouri to Oregon in covered wagons.

Lampman returned to the subject of ethnic persecution and conflict with *The Tilted Sombrero.* It is set at the beginning of the Mexican War of Independence and describes the first Indian revolt against Spanish rule. A thirteen-year-old Mexican Creole (a Mexican of Spanish descent) finds out that he has Indian blood and it changes his view of his country's political situation. A reviewer in the *Bulletin of the Center for Children's Books* stated that the story "gives a vivid picture of the stratified society that united to fight the oppressive rule of Spain."

Lampman moves from Mexico back up to her native Oregon in *Half-Breed,* the story of the son of a white man and a Crow mother. When his mother remarries (despite Crow taboos), Pale-Eyes rejects his Indian name and heritage, takes the name Hardy, and sets out for the Oregon Territory to find his father. His father, however, is a wanderer and never stays around long enough to form a relationship, which Hardy eventually finds with his Aunt Rhody. "The portrayal of the difficult adjustment of the half-breed in an essentially white society is skillfully handled," noted Elva Harmon in her *Library Journal* review.

Many of Lampman's books reflect the complicated relationships between cultures. In *Cayuse Courage,* Lampman tells the story of the 1847 Whitman massacre, in which several missionaries were killed by Cayuse Indians. In this fictionalized version, Lampman tells the story through the eyes of an Indian boy, Samuel Little Pony. Samuel's dreams of being a great warrior are shattered when his arm is caught in a white man's buffalo trap. He can't understand Dr. Whitman's decision to amputate when gangrene sets in, and he becomes bitter and ungrateful. However, when he is rejected by his own people because of his handicap, he develops a friendship with the Whitmans. When smallpox breaks out amongst the tribespeople, many Indians feel that the white people are purposely trying to wipe them out, and vow to take revenge. Samuel is caught between the two sides. In her review for *Horn Book,* Ruth Hill Vigners praised Lampman's balanced viewpoint, stating the "the author presents a consistently Indian point of view and an understand of the white people who had given up much to follow the dictates of their consciences." Robin McKown, writing for the *New York Times Book Review,* commented that "the whole tragedy of Indian relations lies in Mrs. Lampman's brief story, told effectively and with passion."

In quest of his white father, Pale Eyes leaves his mother and Crow Indian home to go to Oregon City and discovers an unfamiliar world, deep disappointment, and a new maturity. (Illustration by Ann Grifalconi from *Half-Breed.*)

An even more famous Indian massacre is the subject of *Once upon the Little Big Horn.* Wilson Sullivan's review for the *New York Times Book Review* gave the book high praise, stating that Lampman's "prose is as luminous as a perch in a pond and as cogent as a Sioux arrow" and that "both Sitting Bull and 'Long Hair' Custer emerge with a three-dimensional reality."

Lampman moved into the more modern problems of Native Americans with her 1976 work *The Potlatch Family.* Plum Longor feels rejected by her high school classmates, and she's sure it's because she's an Indian and her father is often drunk. When her brother, Simon, returns home from a veteran's hospital, he suggests that Plum and the other Indian families begin a weekly potlatch to share customs and traditions with tourists and interested townsfolk. To Plum's surprise, the venture is highly successful, and continues even after Simon's death. Marily Richards, writing for *School Library Journal* commented that the "carefully developed plot" and "well-sustained mood" make this an "engrossing story which successfully integrates historical information and the present-day situation of two tribal groups of the Oregon coast."

The book that perhaps more than any other displays Lampman's objectivity in seeing both the white and Native American point of view is *White Captives,* based on Olive Oatman's account of her five-year captivity after being kidnapped from her Mormon wagon train. Lampman shows just how far apart the two cultures were—Olive could not adjust to the "heathen" ways of the Indians, and the Indians could not understand her farming methods nor her hymn singing. Olive is horrified when a Mohave girl has Olive tattooed so that her soul will find peace, and the Mohave are shocked when Olive's sister dies of tuberculosis and Olive wants to bury her underground. Roberta Rogow, in her review for *School Library Journal,* commented that "all the characters are well rounded, and the conflict of white versus Indian ideas is made particularly real."

■ Works Cited

Harmon, Elva, review of *Half-Breed, Library Journal,* October 15, 1967.

McKown, Robin, review of *Cayuse Courage, New York Times Book Review,* April 12, 1970, p. 26.

Richards, Marily, review of *The Potlatch Family, School Library Journal,* May, 1976, p. 70.

Rogow, Roberta, review of *White Captives, School Library Journal,* May, 1975, p. 65.

Sullivan, Wilson, review of *Once upon the Little Big Horn, New York Times Book Review,* July 11, 1971, p. 8.

Review of *Temple of the Sun, Horn Book,* December, 1964.

Review of *The Tilted Sombrero, Bulletin of the Center for Children's Books,* October, 1966, p. 28.

Vigners, Ruth Hill, review of *Cayuse Courage, Horn Book,* June, 1970, p. 302.

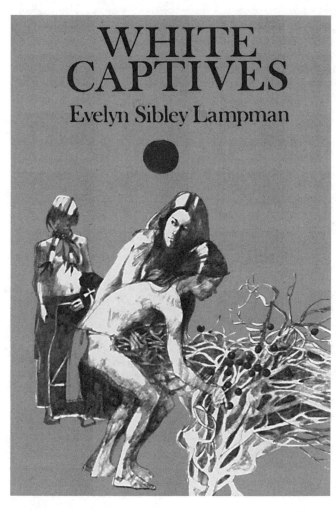

WHITE CAPTIVES

Evelyn Sibley Lampman

In this 1975 novel, two Mormon girls are kidnapped by Indians in 1851, and are kept captive for five long years. (Cover art by Robert Baxter.)

■ For More Information See

PERIODICALS

Booklist, January 1, 1968, p. 546.
Bulletin of the Center for Children's Books, October, 1965, p. 34; December, 1971, p. 59; June, 1978, p. 162.
Horn Book, December, 1971, pp. 611-12.
Kirkus Reviews, May 15, 1966, p. 513; August 15, 1967, p. 959; March 15, 1975, p. 307.
Library Journal, September 15, 1969, pp. 3220-21; September 15, 1974, p. 2273.
Publishers Weekly, August 2, 1971, p. 64; February 15, 1980, p. 110.*

*   *   *

LINE, David
See DAVIDSON, Lionel

LOCKE, Elsie (Violet) 1912-

■ Personal

Born August 17, 1912, in Hamilton, New Zealand; daughter of William John (a builder) and Ellen (Bryan) Farrelly; married John Gibson Locke (a meat worker); children: Donald Bryan, Keith James, Maire Frances, Alison Gwyneth. *Education:* University of Auckland, B.A., 1933. *Politics:* "No political affiliation." *Religion:* "Agnostic-humanist."

■ Addresses

Home—392 Oxford Ter., Christchurch 1, New Zealand.

■ Career

Writer. Has worked in libraries in New Zealand and in a number of other occupations.

■ Awards, Honors

Katherine Mansfield Award, 1959, for essay "Looking for Answers," published in *Landfall;* D.Litt., University of Canterbury, Christchurch, 1987.

■ Writings

FOR CHILDREN

A Land without a Master, Wellington Department of Education, 1962.
Viet-nam, Wellington Department of Education, 1963.
Six Colonies in One Country, illustrated by Stephen Furlonger, Wellington Department of Education, 1964.
Provincial Jigsaw Puzzle, illustrated by Stephen Furlonger, Wellington Department of Education, 1965.
The Runaway Settlers (fiction), illustrated by Antony Maitland, Blackwood, 1965, new edition illustrated by Gary Hebley, Hazard Press, 1993.
The Long Uphill Climb: New Zealand 1876-1891, illustrated by David A. Cowe, Wellington Department of Education, 1966.
High Ground for a New Nation, illustrated by David A. Cowe, Wellington Department of Education, 1967.
The End of the Harbour (fiction), illustrated by Katrina Mataira, Blackwood, 1968.
The Hopeful Peace and the Hopeful War, illustrated by David A. Cowe, Wellington Department of Education, 1968.
Growing Points and Prickles: Life in New Zealand 1920-1960, illustrated by Cath Brown and R. E. Brockie, Whitcombe & Tombs, 1971.
It's the Same Old Earth, illustrated by Victor Ambrus, Wellington Department of Education, 1973.
Maori King and British Queen (textbook), illustrated by Murray Grimsdale, Hulton, 1974.
Look under the Leaves (ecology), edited by David Young and David Ault, illustrated by David Waddington, Pumpkin Press, 1975.

ELSIE LOCKE

Moko's Hideout (fiction), illustrated by Elisabeth Plumridge and Beatrice Foster-Barham, Whitcoulls, 1976.

(With Ken Dawson) *The Boy with the Snowgrass Hair* (fiction), illustrated by Jean Oates, Whitcoulls, 1976, Price Milburn, 1983.

Snow to Low Levels: Interaction in a Disaster, Whitcoulls, 1976.

Crayfishermen and the Sea: Interaction of Man and Environment, Whitcoulls, 1976.

Explorer Zach (fiction), illustrated by David Waddington, Pumpkin Press, 1978.

A Land without Taxes: New Zealand from 1800 to 1840, Wellington Department of Education, 1979, revised edition published as *The Kauri and the Willow: How We Lived and Grew from 1801-1942*, Wellington Government Printer, 1984.

Journey under Warning (fiction), Oxford University Press, 1983.

A Canoe in the Mist (fiction), illustrated by John Shelley, Cape, 1984.

The Kauri and the Willow, Wellington Government Printer, 1984.

Two Peoples, One Land: A History of Aotearoa/New Zealand, illustrated by Elisabeth Plumridge, Wellington Government Printer, 1988.

Joe's Ruby, illustrated by Gary Hebley, Cape, 1995.

FOR ADULTS

(Editor) *Gordon Watson, New Zealander 1912-1945: His Life and Writings*, New Zealand Communist Party, 1949.

The Shepherd and the Scullery-Maid, New Zealand Communist Party, 1950.

The Time of the Child: A Sequence of Poems, privately printed, 1954.

The Human Conveyor Belt, Caxton Press, 1968.

The Roots of the Clover: The Story of the Collett Sisters and Their Families, privately printed, 1971.

Discovering the Morrisons (and the Smiths and the Wallaces): A Pioneer Family History, privately printed, 1976.

The Gaoler (biography), Dunmore Press, 1978.

Student at the Gates (memoir), Whitcoulls, 1981.

Co-operation and Conflict: Pakeha and Maori in Historical Perspective, New Zealand Foundation for Peace Studies, 1988.

(Editor with Janet Paul) *Mrs. Hobson's Album*, Auckland University Press, 1990.

Peace People: A History of Peace Activities in New Zealand, Hazard Press, 1992.

Contributor to *Landfall*, December, 1958.

■ Sidelights

Elsie Locke told *Twentieth-Century Children's Writers:* "Although as a child I walked to school with serial stories writing themselves in my head, I did not settle down to being a writer until my own children were growing into their teens. By that time I was thoroughly hooked on children's books, and my own ideas were budding, and still keep budding from year to year. To me, writing a story for children is a way of sharing. Naturally I share those themes that stir my interest, imagination, sympathy, sense of fun, delight, and concern. History, nature, and peace get into my books because I am keen about these matters. My grandparents and great-grandparents were pioneers in the early days of New Zealand. Around the family fireside I listened to many adventurous tales and I think today's children might like to do the same. Whether my readers live in New Zealand and enjoy the familiar settings, or somewhere else and find the settings exotic, I am giving them a small piece of a big world whose glory is the great variety of places and peoples and languages and customs—not to mention all the other living things, the sky and land and the sea."

Locke's historical novels for young adults incorporate adventure and lessons about the Maori, the native people of New Zealand, and their culture. Her interest in ecology and preserving the natural environment is often demonstrated in her nonfiction works, and a strong sense of place permeates her novels. In addition, Locke has garnered praise for the excitement of her plots and the detailed complexity of her historical settings.

In her first, and best known, novel, *The Runaway Settlers,* Locke presents a fictionalized version of the story of some of New Zealand's nineteenth-century pioneers. Mary Small, married to a drunken and abusive man, leaves her home in Australia in 1859 with her six children in tow, and ends up in New Zealand. Always fearful that her husband will appear to reclaim them all, Small changes the family name to Phipps and doggedly carves out a living from the land. Critics noted the similarities between the experiences of these pioneers and those who came to America in the same era. Many praised the exciting adventures depicted in *The Runaway Settlers,* and the author's artful incorporation of Maori language through descriptions of New Zealand flora and fauna. While critics disagreed about the effectiveness of Locke's characterization, most praised what *Kirkus Reviews* called "excellent land, people and history detail."

Other Locke novels for young adults similarly draw on New Zealand history for their basic story, augmented by themes of respect for the Maori culture and people, and for the land. The struggle between European settlers and native Maoris over ownership of the land take center stage in *The End of the Harbour.* In this work, a friendship that develops between two boys becomes "a binding symbol of hope" for peace between the two peoples, according to Diane Hebley in *Twentieth-Century Children's Writers.* Land rights are again the source of narrative tension in Locke's novel *Journey under Warning.* It depicts the Wairau Affray of 1843, as seen through the eyes of fifteen-year-old Gibby Banks and the adult Will Morrison, who works for the land company whose claim is under dispute. *Journey under Warning* is a sympathetic portrayal of the "passions, prejudices, and different points of view" on both sides of the bloody conflict, according to Hebley.

A natural disaster is at the center of *A Canoe in the Mist,* in which the 1886 eruption of Mount Tarawera in New Zealand, its destruction of a Maori village, and the legendary omens that preceded the disaster are told through the viewpoint of a preadolescent survivor. "This highly dramatic novel" is solidly set within the beauty of the New Zealand countryside, according to Hebley, and offers the young adult reader much information on Maori culture. Although Jeanette Larson, writing for *School Library Journal,* found fault with Locke's pacing and dialogue, she also deemed that, for American youth, "the exotic locale and the mystique of a natural disaster ... [make] this a worthwhile addition to most collections."

The Runaway Settlers, **Locke's first and best-known novel, tells of nineteenth-century Australian pioneers in New Zealand, whose lives were similar to American pioneers of that time.** (Illustration by Antony Maitland.)

Locke's concern for the environment is at the forefront of such nonfiction works as *It's the Same Old Earth* and *Look under the Leaves,* and in the short stories in *Moko's Hideout.* Two other novels, *Explorer Zach* and *The Boy with the Snowgrass Hair,* the latter coauthored by Ken Dawson, are adventure tales featuring young protagonists confronting the wilds of frontier New Zealand. "Above all," wrote Hebley about *The Boy with the Snowgrass Hair,* "the reader is made aware of the power and beauty of this New Zealand mountain country."

■ Works Cited

Hebley, Diane, "Elsie Locke," *Twentieth-Century Children's Writers,* St. James Press, 1995, pp. 597-99.
Larson, Jeanette, review of *A Canoe in the Mist, School Library Journal,* December, 1985, p. 91.

Review of *The Runaway Settlers, Kirkus Reviews,* March 15, 1966, p. 305.

■ For More Information See

PERIODICALS

Booklist, September 1, 1966, p. 217.
Horn Book, August, 1966.
Library Journal, May 15, 1966, p. 2710.
National Observer, July 4, 1966, p. 17.
Observer (London), September 7, 1971, p. 23; July 3, 1977, p. 22.

*　　*　　*

LOURIE, Helen
See STORR, Catherine (Cole)

M

PETER MANDEL

MANDEL, Peter (Bevan) 1957-

■ Personal

Born June 7, 1957, in New York, NY; son of Paul (an author and associate editor of *Life* magazine) and Sheila (a writer and staff member of *Life* magazine; maiden name, Emslie) Mandel; married Kathryn Byrd (a tax accountant), June 13, 1981. *Education:* Middlebury College, B.A., 1979; Brown University, M.A., 1981. *Hobbies and other interests:* Animals, birds, trees, ocean liners, travel, playing and watching baseball.

■ Addresses

Home—239 Transit St., Providence, RI 02906. *Agent*—Emilie Jacobson, Curtis Brown Ltd., 10 Astor Pl., New York, NY 10003.

■ Career

Part-time publications editor, Institute for Family Enterprise at Bryant College, Smithfield, RI; previously assistant to the president, Bryant College. *Member:* Volunteer Services for Animals (member of board of directors), Cat Writers Association.

■ Awards, Honors

Cat Medallion, Cat Writers Association, 1994, for Best Humor Piece; *Red Cat, White Cat* was named an *American Bookseller* "Pick of the Lists."

■ Writings

PICTURE BOOKS

Red Cat, White Cat, illustrated by Clare Mackie, Holt, 1994.

NOVELS; FOR YOUNG PEOPLE

Haunted House Mystery, Antioch, 1986.
Revenge of the Ghosts, Antioch, 1986.
Cry of the Wolf, Antioch, 1987.
Whisper's Secret Dream, Antioch, 1987.

HUMOR; FOR ADULTS

The Official Cat I.Q. Test, HarperCollins, 1991.
The Cat Dictionary, Penguin Books (Australia, South Africa and New Zealand), 1994.
The Official Dog I.Q. Test, Bonus Books, 1995.

Works have been published in China, Japan, Germany, Italy, Holland, Sweden, and Denmark.

OTHER

If One Lived on the Equator (poetry), Nightshade Press, 1993.

Contributor to *Reader's Digest, Cosmopolitan, Cats Magazine, Harper's,* and *Yankee Magazine.* Former sports and book review editor, *Brown Alumni Monthly* magazine, Brown University.

■ Sidelights

Peter Mandel told *SATA* that much of his success as a writer could be traced directly to his progressive New York City grade school, the City and Country School or "C and C." "At 'C and C' we did a lot of art, writing, and research projects," Mandel explained to *SATA.* "When I was eight years old my class spent a week at the Otis Farm in Massachusetts, milking cows and spending time with the animals. That sort of stuff stays with you—at least it did with me. And, a lot of my classmates at the City and Country School have become artists and writers," he said. Mandel confessed to *SATA* that the high school he attended, the Fieldston School, "was too competitive for me. I hated it."

When asked about his favorite books as a child, Mandel told *SATA:* "Growing up in New York City I was fascinated with information about Manhattan. One of my favorite books was *This Is New York.* It had lots of information that I found fascinating. It was jam-packed with facts and statistics—why New York has skyscrapers; heights of the tallest buildings; facts about all kinds of Manhattan things—the subways, the bridges, industries, the ports. And, since I was fascinated by ships— every kind of ship from ocean liners to tug boats—I loved *Tuffy, the Tug Boat,*" he continued. "Another favorite of mine was a series of books about Max, a guinea pig who wore a sombrero that he would also sleep in. The Max books had great illustrations."

Mandel is best known to adult readers as a regular contributor to national magazines (including *Reader's Digest, Cosmopolitan,* and *Cats Magazine*), a poet published in *Harper's* and *Yankee Magazine,* and the author of humorous spoofs, *The Official Cat I.Q. Test* and *The Official Dog I.Q. Test.* But children do not have to be accomplished readers to appreciate Mandel's talent. His wit was introduced to the pre-reading set in 1994 with the publication of *Red Cat, White Cat.* This book was inspired by Mandel's own red-and-white tomcat, Chuck, who tries as much as possible to keep Mandel from writing. "Since I hand-write all my manuscripts before I enter them on computer, Chuck (who's an indoor cat) likes to plunk his fat body right down in front of me, directly on whatever I'm trying to write," lamented Mandel to *SATA.* "Chuck doesn't try to *help* with my writing. He'd much rather *hinder* me by dragging his tail across my face or swishing it across the paper as I try to write."

But Chuck's disruptive tactics did not deter Mandel from writing *Red Cat, White Cat* in his honor. Mandel and British illustrator Clare Mackie collaborated to create paired pictures of cats with sets of rhymed, double-word captions representing antonyms ("Up Cat, Down Cat") and contrasts ("Farm Cat, Town Cat") on each page. Cavorting and leaping across the pages are grinning felines with long whiskers. Readers discover cats in a humorous set of circumstances and activities: Farm Cat dozes on the back of a cud-chewing cow, angling as she naps with a fishing cork tied to her tail. On another page a fish-bone Valentine, tagged with tiny hearts and Shy Cat's signature paw print, is what the timid tom uses to woo his sweetheart. According to a review in *Bulletin of the Center for Children's Books,* the work is "deft and appealing, with a controlled vocabulary that is accessible to the earliest beginning readers."

Grade-school readers may be familiar with Mandel's early books which feature characters from the television program, *The Real Ghostbusters: Haunted House Mystery* and *Revenge of the Ghosts,* as well as two other books which star "Whisper, the Winged Unicorn," *Cry of the Wolf* and *Whisper's Secret Dream.* Mandel told *SATA* that writing these books was just like an assignment at school: "The publishing house gave me the cast of characters. I had to write the story following various guidelines, just like an English class assignment, only with more rules. It was an interesting bridge between being in school and becoming a writer."

The idea of opposites is introduced through easy rhyming verse, droll illustrations of cats, and amusing wordplay. (Cover illustration by Clare Mackie.)

If you want to know how your dog ranks among hundreds of others, try completing *The Official Dog I.Q. Test,* designed to distinguish canine geniuses from dimwits. (Illustration by Lesa Nash.)

■ Works Cited

Mandel, Peter, telephone interview with Mel Wathen for *Something about the Author,* 1995.
Review of *Red Cat, White Cat, Bulletin of the Center for Children's Books,* November, 1994.

■ For More Information See

PERIODICALS

Kirkus Reviews, October 15, 1994, p. 1412.
Publishers Weekly, November 14, 1994.
School Library Journal, December, 1994.

*   *   *

McCAUGHREAN, Geraldine 1951-
(Geraldine Jones)

■ Personal

Surname is pronounced "Mc-*cork*-ran"; born June 6, 1951, in Enfield, London, England; daughter of Leslie Arthur (a fireman) and Ethel (a teacher; maiden name, Thomas) Jones; married John McCaughrean. *Education:* Attended Southgate Technical College, Middlesex, 1969-70; Christ Church College, Oxford, B.A. (honors),

1977. *Religion:* "Almost Catholic." *Hobbies and other interests:* Playing the concertina; "I have a dilapidated cabin cruiser on the local canal."

■ Addresses

Home—3 Melton Dr., Didcot, Oxfordshire OX11 7JP, England. *Agent*—Giles Gordon, Anthony Sheil Associates Ltd., 43 Doughty St., London WC1N 2LF, England.

■ Career

Thames Television, London, England, secretary, 1970-73; Marshall Cavendish Ltd., London, assistant editor, 1977-80, subeditor, 1978-79, staff writer, 1982, 1983-88; Carreras-Rothman Ltd., Aylesbury, England, editorial assistant, 1980-81; writer, 1981—. *Member:* National Union of Journalists, Journalists Against Nuclear Extermination.

■ Awards, Honors

Winner in short story category, All-London Literary Competition, Wandsworth Borough Council, 1979, for "The Pike"; Whitbread Award, 1987, for *A Little Lower Than the Angels;* Carnegie Medal, British Library Association, and *Guardian* Award, both 1989, for *A Pack of Lies.*

■ Writings

YOUNG ADULT FICTION

A Little Lower Than the Angels, Oxford University Press, 1987.
A Pack of Lies, Oxford University Press, 1988.
Gold Dust, Oxford University Press, 1993.

RETELLINGS

One Thousand and One Arabian Nights, illustrated by Stephen Lavis, Oxford University Press, 1982.
The Canterbury Tales, illustrated by Victor Ambrus, Oxford University Press, 1984, Rand McNally, 1985.
The Story of Noah and the Ark, illustrated by Helen Ward, Templar, 1987.
The Story of Christmas, illustrated by Ward, Templar, 1988.
Saint George and the Dragon, illustrated by Nicki Palin, Doubleday, 1989.
El Cid, Oxford University Press, 1989.
The Orchard Book of Greek Myths, Orchard, 1992.
Greek Myths, illustrated by Emma Chichester Clark, Margaret K. McElderry Books, 1993.
The Odyssey, illustrated by Ambrus, Oxford University Press, 1993.
Stories from Shakespeare, illustrated by Antony Maitland, Orion Children's, 1994.
The Orchard Book of Stories from the Ballet, illustrated by Angela Barrett, Orchard, 1994, published as *The Random House Book of Stories from the Ballet,* Random House, 1995.

GERALDINE McCAUGHREAN

The Golden Hoard: Myths and Legends of the World,
    illustrated by Bee Willey, Simon & Schuster/Marga-
    ret K. McElderry, 1996.

FOR CHILDREN

Seaside Adventure, illustrated by Chrissie Wells, Ham-
    lyn, 1986.
(With Wells) *Tell the Time,* illustrated by Wells, Ham-
    lyn, 1986.
(Translator) Michel Tilde, *Who's That Knocking on My
    Door?,* Oxford University Press, 1986.
My First Space Pop-Up Book, illustrated by Mike
    Peterkin, Little Simon, 1989.
My First Earth Pop-up Book, illustrated by Peterkin,
    Little Simon, 1990.
(Translator) *The Snow Country Prince,* Knopf, 1991.
(Translator) Daisaku Ikeda, *The Princess and the Moon,*
    Oxford University Press, 1991, Knopf, 1991.
(Translator) Ikeda, *The Cherry Tree,* illustrated by Brian
    Wildsmith, Knopf, 1992.
(Translator) Ikeda, *Over the Deep Blue Sea,* illustrated
    by Wildsmith, Knopf, 1993.
Blue Moon Mountain, illustrated by Palin, Golden,
    1994.
Blue Moo, illustrated by Colin Smithson, Longman,
    1994.
How the Reindeer Got Their Antlers, illustrated by Debi
    Gliori, Orchard, 1995.
On the Day the World Began, illustrated by Norman
    Bancroft-Hunt, Longman, 1995.
The Quest of Isis, illustrated by David Sim, Longman,
    1995.
Wizziwig and the Crazy Cooker, Orchard, 1995.

Wizziwig and the Singing Chair, Orchard, 1995.
Wizziwig and the Sweet Machine, Orchard, 1995.
Wizziwig and the Wacky Weather Machine, Orchard,
    1995.

OTHER

(Under name Geraldine Jones) *Adventure in New York*
    (textbook), illustrated by Cynthia Back, Oxford
    University Press, 1979.
(Under name Geraldine Jones) *Raise the Titanic* (text-
    book) Oxford University Press, 1980.
(Under name Geraldine Jones) *Modesty Blaise* (text-
    book), Oxford University Press, 1981.
The Maypole (adult novel), 1989.
Fires' Astonishment, Minerva, 1991.
Vainglory (adult novel), Cape, 1991.

Also author of *Heart's Blood* (adult novel), 1994. Editor,
Banbury Focus, 1981-82; subeditor and writer of stories
for *Storyteller* and *Great Composers.*

■ Sidelights

It is almost impossible to categorize Geraldine Mc-
Caughrean as a writer. She has written novels for young
adults and stories for young children; she has translated
and adapted tales, myths, and legends from various
cultures; and she has written adult fiction and text-
books. Whatever her subject, however, the author brings
a flair for intricate prose and exciting storytelling to her
writing. "Reading McCaughrean," Eileen Dunlop asserted in *Twentieth-Century Children's Writers,* "rein-
forces the belief that a good book is for everyone capable
of reading it, regardless of its intended primary audience."

A former editor and writer for various British publishers, McCaughrean started writing for young people by
retelling the stories of *One Thousand and One Arabian
Nights,* the series of tales told by the legendary Shahrazad to her royal husband as a way to postpone her
execution. McCaughrean was immediately praised for
her inspired storytelling, and her ability to make the
familiar stories of Sinbad, Aladdin, and Ali Baba seem
exciting and original. M. Crouch commented in *Junior
Bookshelf* that with *One Thousand and One Arabian
Nights* McCaughrean had achieved a "brilliant tour de
force in what is not so much a translation as a thorough
reworking of the tales" and that she had "used the
original as the starting point of a piece of individual
creative enterprise." Several reviewers also praised the
way McCaughrean interpreted Shahrazad's own story;
Anne Wilson, for instance, noted in *Signal* that "the
personal story of Shahrazad, which links her tales much
as the sources do, can never have been told with so
much warmth, suspense and appreciation of the ridicu-
lousness of her situation." The result, added the critic, is
"spellbinding. The language in which the stories are told
is a constant excitement throughout the book. . . .
Feelings and scenes are powerfully evoked, and Geraldine McCaughrean's arts show limitless versatility in
the undertaking of a variety of narrative."

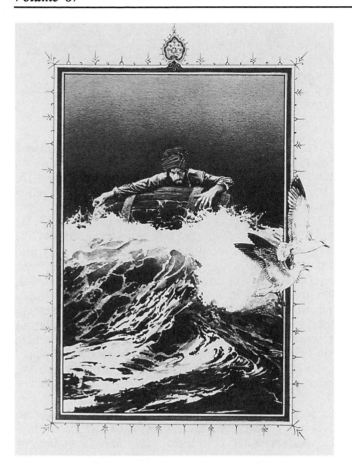

McCaughrean's retelling of *One Thousand One Arabian Nights* was lauded by critics for its lively interpretation that brings the original characters to life. (Illustration by Stephen Lavis.)

In *The Canterbury Tales,* McCaughrean takes Geoffrey Chaucer's classic series of stories from the fourteenth century and focuses on the pilgrimage to Canterbury itself. The author tones down the content of some of the more ribald tales, and then, "in colorful style and language, ... creatively reconstructs and adds conversation, event and detail, in keeping with the medieval times, to stitch the tales together," as Ruth M. McConnell described it in *School Library Journal.* While he felt that some of the tales lose something in the retelling, *Times Educational Supplement* contributor Terry Jones noted that "McCaughrean's real achievement is the way she has succeeded in turning the whole pilgrimage itself into a story, and has brought that far-off medieval expedition to life in a quite remarkable way." Calling *The Canterbury Tales* "one of the best buys of 1984" in another *Junior Bookshelf* review, Crouch concluded that McCaughrean "captures most beautifully the mood of the pilgrimage, the high spirits, the smell of the countryside and the muddy road."

McCaughrean' first novel, *A Little Lower Than the Angels,* was published to great acclaim, winning the Whitbread Children's Novel Award in 1987. It is a complex, multi-level drama of medieval England during the time when travelling players performed their Mystery and Morality in towns and villages across the countryside. The story centers around Gabriel, a stonemason's apprentice who runs away from his cruel master to join a troupe of players. The boy's flowing blond curls make him a natural to play the part of the angel Gabriel. Then the superficially benevolent playmaster Garvey, seizing a chance to increase the troupe's wealth and popularity, convinces Gabriel to play an off-stage role as a "miracle healer." Gabriel himself almost believes in his own power until he is confronted by townspeople, dying of the plague and desperate for a miracle, who think that Gabriel may be their answer. McCaughrean "has triumphed in her first novel in presenting the lives of ordinary people of the past, in direct, present-day language, with just a few archaisms to set the scene, and relevant historical information," Jessica Yates wrote in *British Book News Children's Books.* As Crouch similarly concluded in *Junior Bookshelf:* "This is a very good novel, rich in uncluttered historical detail, written with sensitive fluency, and with a gallery of memorable characters."

McCaughrean' versatility was highlighted by her next book, *A Pack of Lies.* This 1988 winner of the *Guardian* Children's Fiction Award and the Carnegie Medal demonstrates several different approaches to storytell-

Unlike Geoffrey Chaucer's fourteenth-century *Canterbury Tales,* McCaughrean has reworked each story to focus on its content rather than the narrator. (Illustration by Victor G. Ambrus.)

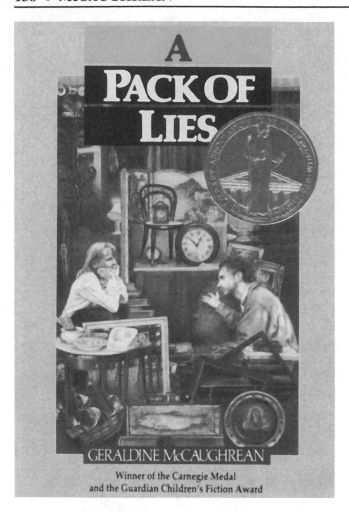

This 1988 *Guardian* Children's Fiction Award and Carnegie Medal winner is a unique collection of diverse tales from varied genres with a surprising twist at the end. (Cover illustration by Robina Green.)

ing. Ailsa Povery and her mother eke out a living selling antiques out of their dilapidated shop. One day, Ailsa meets a mysterious young man named MCC Berkshire, who offers to help in the shop in exchange for room and board. He is spectacularly successful, as he weaves elaborate stories about each item in the shop, enthralling customers into making purchases. Every tale displays his (and McCaughrean's) brilliance as a storyteller, as each one is written in a different literary style. "Each is an utterly convincing example of its kind, enthralling the reader in a web of make-believe," Valerie Caless observed in *School Librarian*. A reviewer in *Publishers Weekly* similarly hailed the author's "leaps from genre to genre, in the writing equivalent of sleight of hand," and added that she "pulls off each meta-fictional complexity with finesse and humor."

A Pack of Lies is more than just a collection of stories, however, as the ending reveals. MCC does not stay around the shop for long. After his departure, the disconsolate Ailsa picks up a book and finds herself a character in a story about MCC, their meeting, and his time in the shop. Caless asked, "Who, then, is the fiction and who the liar telling it? Is Ailsa a figment of MCC's

imagination or he of hers?" As Stephanie Nettell concluded in introducing this award-winner in *Books for Keeps:* "More than anything, *A Pack of Lies* is an exuberant celebration of fiction's spell, a smiling surrender to the grip of the unruly imagination, a playful introduction to the riches of style that lie waiting in books."

At the same time McCaughrean was writing fiction, she continued her retelling and translating activities, in 1989 producing her version of *Saint George and the Dragon,* the story of England's patron saint. Traveling across the countryside, George of Lydda comes across Sabra, the king's daughter, who has been tied to the stake as a sacrifice to the dragon—a slimy, lizard-like creature called Wickedness, whose father is Evil and whose mother is Darkness. In *El Cid,* McCaughrean retells the story of one of Spain's most famous heroes, Rodrigo Diaz, who was exiled from Castile only to become a brilliant warrior who recaptured territory from the invading Moors. "McCaughrean shows herself a grand storyteller," a *Kirkus Reviews* critic remarked; "she presents this prototypical chivalric knight in a lively narrative sparked with humor, drama, and her hero's daring trickery."

In both *The Odyssey* and *Greek Myths,* McCaughrean uses humor to create interest and excitement for younger readers. Janet Tayler, reviewing for *School Librarian,* noted that the adventures of Odysseus had been retold in a "lively, rather tongue-in-cheek manner," while Hazel Rochman, writing for *Booklist,* called the stories in *Greek Myths* "direct, robust, and gleeful." While Pauline Long noted that *Greek Myths* would not serve as a reference tool, she added in *School Librarian* that "its real purpose is to delight and entertain—and this it does in flamboyant style." As Rochman commented, the stories have the "dramatic immediacy" of familiar legends: "'Long ago, when fortune-tellers told the truth, there lived a very frightened man.' How can you not read on?"

McCaughrean has been widely praised for her translations as well as her adaptations. She has translated several books by Japanese author Daisaku Ikeda, including *The Cherry Tree* and *Over the Deep Blue Sea.* The first is the story of a sister and brother in a village that has been devastated by war. The children's father is now dead, and their mother goes off to work every day. They find hope and the possibility of rebirth when they work to help an old man protect a badly damaged cherry tree against the winter months, and watch as it blooms again in the spring. A *Kirkus Reviews* critic commented that McCaughrean's translation had "poetic vigor and grace." *Over the Deep Blue Sea* is a story of hatred dissipated through friendship. When a Japanese family goes to live on a South Sea island, the children make friends with a native boy named Pablo. But Pablo cuts off the friendship when he learns that the Japanese had bombed the island during the war. In the end, the children reunite and are told that they may have all come from the "same place" in "tiny boats" from around the world. Although some reviewers found the ending trite, a *Kirkus Reviews* writer praised the "vividly phrased text."

McCaughrean again showed the depth of her imagination with her third novel, 1993's *Gold Dust,* which is set in a poor mining town in Brazil. The effects of uncontrolled greed caused by the discovery of gold are seen through the eyes of Inez de Souza and her brother Maro, who watch as their town is slowly destroyed and its inhabitants corrupted by a gold rush. "Sharp observations on a kaleidoscope of topics enliven every page, often underlined by ironic humour, whether understated ... or sharper," Brian Slough wrote in *Times Educational Supplement.* "All we can be confident about each book [by McCaughrean] is that it will be admirable—but in which way?" Crouch asked in his *Junior Bookshelf* review. With its "sparkling" language and "wonderfully inventive, consistent and hideously convincing" plot, the critic concluded, *Gold Dust* is "an engrossing, funny, tragic blockbuster of a story."

Geraldine McCaughrean once told *SATA:* "Having struggled with several unsuccessful and unpublished novels, I have now found that my true talent lies in writing for children. In doing so, I have cleaned up a previously elaborate and overwritten style into one that is both more valid and of more use to publishers. This pure luck of being in the right place at the right time has led to the remarkable good fortune of making a living from the thing I like doing best."

■ Works Cited

Caless, Valerie, review of *A Pack of Lies, School Librarian,* February, 1989, p. 31.

Review of *The Cherry Tree, Kirkus Reviews,* April 1, 1992, p. 466.

Crouch, M., review of *One Thousand and One Arabian Nights, Junior Bookshelf,* February, 1983, p. 44.

Crouch, M., review of *The Canterbury Tales, Junior Bookshelf,* February, 1985, pp. 41-42.

Crouch, M., review of *A Little Lower Than the Angels, Junior Bookshelf,* June, 1987, p. 135.

Crouch, M., review of *Gold Dust, Junior Bookshelf,* February, 1994, pp. 34-35.

Dunlop, Eileen, "Geraldine McCaughrean," *Twentieth-Century Children's Writers,* 4th edition, St. James Press, 1995, pp. 434-36.

Review of *El Cid, Kirkus Reviews,* October 15, 1989, p. 1532.

Jones, Terry, "Pilgrims' Way," *Times Educational Supplement,* February 1, 1985, p. 27.

Long, Pauline, review of *The Orchard Book of Greek Myths, School Librarian,* February, 1993, p. 22.

McConnell, Ruth M., review of *The Canterbury Tales, School Library Journal,* February, 1986, p. 82.

Nettell, Stephanie, review of *A Pack of Lies, Books for Keeps,* May, 1989, p. 25.

Review of *Over the Deep Blue Sea, Kirkus Reviews,* May 15, 1993.

Review of *A Pack of Lies, Publishers Weekly,* April 28, 1989, p. 82.

Rochman, Hazel, review of *Greek Myths, Booklist,* February 1, 1993, p. 982.

Slough, Brian, "Gold Fever," *Times Educational Supplement,* November 12, 1993, p. III.

Tayler, Janet, review of *The Odyssey, School Librarian,* May, 1994, p. 62.

Wilson, Anne, "A New Arabian Nights," *Signal,* January, 1983, pp. 26-29.

Yates, Jessica, review of *A Little Lower Than the Angels, British Book News Children's Books,* June, 1987, p. 30.

■ For More Information See

BOOKS

Children's Literature Review, Volume 38, Gale, 1996.

PERIODICALS

Booklist, March 15, 1986, p. 1079; October 15, 1989, p. 461; December 15, 1989, p. 834.

Bulletin of the Center for Children's Books, April, 1988, pp. 161-62.

Growing Point, July, 1987, pp. 4824-26.

Horn Book, June, 1983, pp. 342-43.

Junior Bookshelf, August, 1989, pp. 159-60; February, 1990, p. 47; February, 1995, pp. 38-39; February, 1996, p. 26.

Kirkus Reviews, November 1, 1987, p. 1577; September 15, 1989, p. 1406.

School Librarian, December, 1982, pp. 339-40; September, 1985, p. 239; May, 1994, pp. 72, 74; February, 1996, p. 21.

School Library Journal, April, 1988, p. 102; March, 1990, p. 209; April, 1993, pp. 136-37; March, 1996, pp. 211-12.

Times Educational Supplemental, January 14, 1983, p. 33; March 10, 1989, p. B13; June 9, 1989, p. B12; November 10, 1989, p. 58; October 30, 1992, sec. 2, p. 7.

Times Literary Supplement, November 25-December 1, 1988, p. 1322.*

*   *   *

McMULLAN, Jim 1934-

■ Personal

Full name, James Burroughs McMullan; born in 1934; married Kate Hall (a writer and teacher), June 9, 1979; children: Leigh Fenwick.

■ Addresses

Home—88 Lexington Ave., Apt. 12E, New York, NY 10016.

■ Career

Illustrator and writer.

■ Awards, Honors

Best Illustrated Book, *New York Times,* 1965, for *Kangaroo & Kangaroo;* Pick of the List, *American Bookseller,* and one of the Ten Best Picture Books of 1993, *New York Times,* both for *Nutcracker Noel;* Ten Best Picture Books of 1995 selection, *New York Times,* 1995 Picture Book Award, Parents' Choice, Reading Magic Award, *Parenting,* 1995, all for *Hey, Pipsqueak!*

■ Writings

SELF-ILLUSTRATED CHILDREN'S BOOKS

(With wife, Kate McMullan) *The Noisy Giants' Tea Party,* HarperCollins, 1992.
(With Kate McMullan) *Nutcracker Noel,* HarperCollins, 1993.
(With Kate McMullan) *Hey, Pipsqueak!,* HarperCollins, 1995.

FOR ADULTS

Revealing Illustrations, Watson Guptil, 1980.
High Focus Drawing, Overlook, 1995.

OTHER

(Illustrator) Kathy Braun, *Kangaroo & Kangaroo,* Doubleday, 1965.

■ Sidelights

For joint sidelights covering illustrator Jim McMullan and his wife, author Kate McMullan, please see the *SATA* entry on Kate McMullan in this volume.

■ For More Information See

PERIODICALS

Booklist, December 15, 1992, p. 738; October 15, 1993, p. 454.
Kirkus Reviews, November 1, 1992, p. 1381; December 15, 1993, p. 1594.
New York Times, December 2, 1993, p. C18.
New York Times Book Review, November 28, 1993, p. 22.
Publishers Weekly, November 9, 1992.
School Library Journal, February, 1993, p. 76; March, 1994, p. 204.

*   *   *

McMULLAN, Kate (Hall) 1947-
   (Katy Hall)

■ Personal

Born January 16, 1947, in St. Louis, MO; daughter of Lee Aker (a physician) and Kathryn (a teacher and flight attendant; maiden name, Huey) Hall; married James Burroughs McMullan (an illustrator), June 9, 1979; children: Leigh Fenwick. *Education:* University of Tulsa, B.S., 1969; Ohio State University, M.A., 1972. *Hobbies and other interests:* Gardening, birding, reading.

KATE and JIM McMULLAN

■ Addresses

Home and office—88 Lexington Ave., Apt. 12E, New York, NY 10016. *Agent*—Rosemary Sandberg Ltd., 6 Bayley St., London WC1B 3HB, England.

■ Career

Writer and teacher. Magnolia School District, Los Angeles, CA, teacher, 1969; Long Beach School District, Los Angeles, teacher, 1969-71; U.S. Department of Defense, Washington, DC, teacher in Hahn, West Germany, 1972-75; Harcourt, Brace, Jovanovich, Inc., New York City, editor, 1976-78; freelance writer, 1978—; New York University School of Continuing Education, lecturer in "Writing for Children," 1989—. *Member:* Authors Guild, PEN, Society of Children's Book Writers and Illustrators.

■ Awards, Honors

Mark Twain List of Excellent Books, Missouri, 1989, and Bluebonnet List of Excellent Books, Texas, 1989-90, both for *The Great Ideas of Lila Fenwick;* Children's Book Award List, West Virginia, 1989-90, for *Great Advice from Lila Fenwick;* Intellectual Freedom Award honorable mention, New York Library Association, 1993; Pick of the List, *American Bookseller,* and one of the Ten Best Picture Books of 1993, *New York Times,* both for *Nutcracker Noel;* CRABbery honor, 1993, for *The Great Eggspectations of Lila Fenwick;* Ten Best Picture Books of 1995 selection, *New York Times,* 1995 Picture Book Award, Parents' Choice, Reading Magic Award, *Parenting,* 1995, all for *Hey, Pipsqueak!*

■ Writings

UNDER NAME KATE McMULLAN

The Mystery of the Missing Mummy, Scholastic, 1984.

(Adapter) Robert Louis Stevenson, *Dr. Jekyll and Mr. Hyde,* illustrated by Paul Van Munching, Random House, 1984.

The Great Ideas of Lila Fenwick, illustrated by Diane de Groat, Dial, 1986.

Great Advice from Lila Fenwick, Dial, 1988.

Dinosaur Hunters, illustrated by John R. Jones, Random House, 1989.

(Adapter) Gaston Leroux, *Phantom of the Opera,* Random House, 1989.

The Story of Harriet Tubman, Dell, 1990.

The Great Eggspectations of Lila Fenwick, illustrated by de Groat, Farrar, Straus, 1991.

(With husband, Jim McMullan) *The Noisy Giants' Tea Party,* illustrated by J. McMullan, HarperCollins, 1992.

Under the Mummy's Spell, Farrar, Straus, 1992.

The Biggest Mouth in Baseball, illustrated by Anna DiVito, Grosset & Dunlap, 1993.

(With J. McMullan) *Nutcracker Noel,* illustrated by J. McMullan, HarperCollins, 1993.

The Story of Bill Clinton and Al Gore: Our Nation's Leaders, Dell, 1993.

Good Night, Stella, illustrated by Emma Chichester Clark, Candlewick, 1994.

(With J. McMullan) *Hey, Pipsqueak!,* illustrated by J. McMullan, HarperCollins, 1995.

If You Were My Bunny, illustrated by David McPhail, Scholastic, 1996.

UNDER NAME KATY HALL

Nothing but Soup, Follett, 1976.

(With Lisa Eisenberg) *Chicken Jokes and Puzzles,* Scholastic, 1977.

(With Eisenberg) *A Gallery of Monsters,* Random House, 1980.

(With Jane O'Connor) *Magic in the Movies: The Story of Special Effects,* Doubleday, 1980.

(With Eisenberg) *Fishy Riddles,* illustrated by Simms Taback, Dial, 1983.

(With Eisenberg) *Pig Jokes and Puzzles,* Scholastic, 1983.

Garfield: Jokes, Riddles, and Other Silly Stuff, illustrated by Mike Fentz, Random House, 1984.

Garfield: The Big Fat Book of Jokes and Riddles, illustrated by Fentz, Random House, 1984.

(With Eisenberg) *101 Bug Jokes,* Scholastic, 1984.

(With Eisenberg) *Buggy Riddles,* illustrated by Taback, Dial, 1986.

(With Eisenberg) *101 School Jokes,* Scholastic, 1987.

(With Eisenberg) *Grizzly Riddles,* Dial, 1989.

(With Eisenberg) *Snakey Riddles,* Dial, 1990.

Skeletons! Skeletons! All about Bones!, Grosset & Dunlap, 1991.

(With Eisenberg) *Batty Riddles,* Dial, 1992.

(With Eisenberg) *Spacy Riddles,* Dial, 1992.

The Paxton Cheerleader Series, Pocket Books, 1994.

(With Eisenberg) *The Summer Camp Survival Handbook,* HarperCollins, 1995.

■ Adaptations

Fishy Riddles was released on audio cassette, Live Oak Media, 1985.

■ Work in Progress

Noel the First, a sequel to *Nutcracker Noel;* a first chapter book series called "The Dragon Diaries"; *Oh, No, Jo!,* a book for babies about a naughty kitten.

■ Sidelights

Kate McMullan has written a variety of books for young people, ranging from collections of jokes and riddles to picture books and middle-grade fiction. In 1992, she began collaborating with her husband, illustrator Jim McMullan, on picture books inspired by the experiences of their young daughter. "One of the joys of the past few years has been collaborating on picture books with my husband," McMullan told *SATA.* "Our first book emerged because we live in a noisy part of New York City, where garbage trucks crunch trash beneath our window at 3:00 a.m. and fire engine sirens wail all night long. When our daughter was young, these noises frightened her. My husband and I tried to soothe her fears with a story that became *The Noisy Giants' Tea Party.*"

The Noisy Giants' Tea Party describes the imaginative dreams a young boy named Andrew has due to the sounds in his house and outside his window. While Andrew sleeps fitfully in his room, his gerbils run around in their cage, a vacuum cleaner is turned on, a fire truck rushes by blaring its siren, and three drunken men walk by singing loudly. Andrew incorporates all of these sounds into a vivid dream about a group of raucous giants who have a tea party. Each page features two sets of illustrations: watercolor paintings at the top show the goings-on in Andrew's dream, while monochromatic line drawings at the bottom show the corresponding events taking place in the real world. In a review in *Booklist,* Janice Del Negro praised Jim McMullan's artwork, calling the illustrations "admirable and cleverly laid out." Similarly, a contributor in *Kirkus Reviews* noted that his "expertly rendered art . . . creates some amusing links between the racket and its lively imaginary counterpart." Mary Rinato Berman in *School Library Journal* stated that the book is "sure to appeal to children familiar with crunching, banging noises beneath their windows at night."

The McMullans' next collaboration, *Nutcracker Noel,* was published in 1993. As Kate McMullan explained to *SATA,* "*Nutcracker Noel* came from our years of attending Nutcracker Ballets to watch our daughter dance. Like Noel in the book, our daughter's first role really was that of a tree. And what a fine tree she was!" In the story, young Noel is ecstatic when she learns that the ballet school she attends is planning a production of "The Nutcracker." But Noel is soon disappointed when she is picked to portray a tree, while her rival Mia is chosen to play a gingerbread cookie doll. Noel tries in

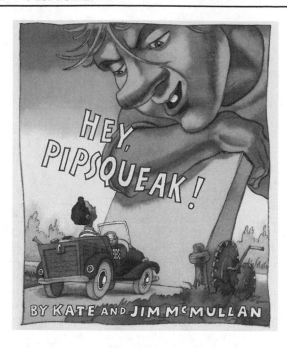

A giant troll has taken over the bridge Jack must cross in this 1995 picture book illustrated by the McMullans. (Cover illustration by Jim McMullan.)

vain to win a different part, but gradually she comes to terms with her role and decides to be the best tree she can be. On the day of the performance, Noel is delighted to find that her costume is beautiful and flowing with sparkles of snow, while Mia's is brown and baggy with a large, awkward head. In a review in *Booklist,* Ilene Cooper called Jim McMullan's watercolor illustrations "delightfully distinctive, lively, and full of wit," and a *Kirkus Reviews* critic wrote that he "portrays the denizens of the dance class with amused affection, satirizing postures and posturing with equal skill." Delia Peters, writing in the *New York Times Book Review,* commented that "Kate McMullan's text, especially the dialogue, is snappy and earthy," adding that the lesson in *Nutcracker Noel* "is one that every child and many adults must learn and relearn. It's wonderful to dream, but the true path to self-fulfillment is to be the best you can at what you are given."

The McMullans collaborated again in 1995, as Kate McMullan told *SATA:* "*Hey, Pipsqueak!,* our third book, came from somewhere deep in my husband's psyche. He had a strong image in his mind of a big troll guarding a bridge and a little boy trying to drive across the bridge in his car. He couldn't seem to make a story out of the image, so he asked me to have a try. Sometimes I felt as if I were doing a rubbing—that the story was there but hidden, and my job was to keep trying to bring it to the light. Finally, with considerable encouragement from our wonderful editors, Michael di Capua and Holly McGhee, it did emerge."

In addition to her picture-book collaborations with her husband, Kate McMullan has written many other popular books for children and young adults. She has published three popular novels for middle-grade readers

chronicling the adventures of Lila Fenwick. After becoming well-known for her "great ideas" and "great advice" in the first two books of the series, Lila suddenly finds everything going wrong in *The Great Eggspectations of Lila Fenwick.* First, Lila decides to try to become president of her sixth-grade class, but instead her best friend Gayle is nominated. Then she becomes Gayle's campaign manager, but this scheme does not work out either. Responding to a class project where each student must care for an egg as if it were a newborn baby, Lila sets up a day-care center to help her classmates. Unfortunately, one of the eggs is kidnapped. But everything works out in the end, as Lila learns from her mistakes and becomes editor of the school newspaper. A critic in *Kirkus Reviews* noted that "though light, [the book] touches on serious issues of responsibility; McMullan deserves praise for creating its well-rounded, individualized characters." Writing in *School Library Journal,* Susannah Price added that "the dialogue and feelings ring true for eleven-year-olds just learning to act responsibly and think clearly."

Good Night, Stella, published in 1994, is another story about an imaginative child's trouble sleeping. Stella

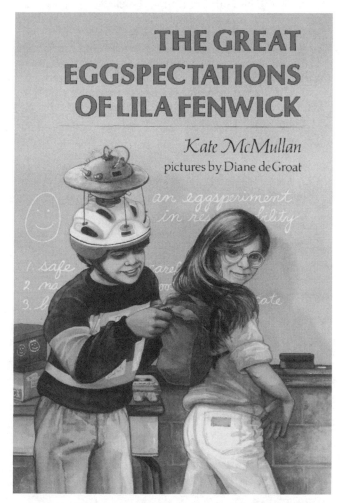

Known for her trademark "Great Ideas" and "Great Advice," sixth grader Lila Fenwick suddenly finds everything going awry in this 1991 story for middle graders. (Cover illustration by Diane de Groat.)

A host of disturbing questions keep Stella's mind racing, much to her father's chagrin, in this familiar bedtime story. (Cover illustration by Emma Chichester Clark.)

concocts all sorts of scary scenarios that prevent her from falling asleep. When her father grows weary of reassuring her, he instead uses reverse psychology, suggesting that Stella stay up to wait for her mother to return from the movies while he goes to bed. Stella is elated and passes the time by dressing up in high heels, dancing with her dolls, and telling scary stories to her stuffed animals. Finally, she exhausts herself and falls asleep. Writing in *School Library Journal*, Karen K. Radtke noted that "Stella is a creative, amusing little girl whom youngsters will enjoy meeting," and called *Good Night, Stella* "an appealing bedtime choice." *Booklist* reviewer Hazel Rochman added that "kids and their parents will laugh at Stella's attention-seeking tricks, even while they sympathize with those wild fears that creep up on you when you're left alone in the dark."

■ **Works Cited**

Berman, Mary Rinato, review of *The Noisy Giants' Tea Party, School Library Journal*, February, 1993, p. 76.

Cooper, Ilene, review of *Nutcracker Noel, Booklist*, October 15, 1993, p. 454.

Del Negro, Janice, review of *The Noisy Giants' Tea Party, Booklist*, December 15, 1992, p. 738.

Review of *The Great Eggspectations of Lila Fenwick, Kirkus Reviews*, June 15, 1991.

Review of *The Noisy Giants' Tea Party, Kirkus Reviews*, November 1, 1992, p. 1381.

Review of *Nutcracker Noel, Kirkus Reviews*, December 15, 1993, p. 1594.

Peters, Delia, review of *Nutcracker Noel, New York Times Book Review*, November 28, 1993, p. 22.

Price, Susannah, review of *The Great Eggspectations of Lila Fenwick, School Library Journal*, August, 1991.

Radtke, Karen K., review of *Good Night, Stella, School Library Journal*, March, 1995.

Rochman, Hazel, review of *Good Night, Stella, Booklist*, November 15, 1994, p. 612.

■ **For More Information See**

PERIODICALS

Booklist, June 15, 1991; July, 1992; July, 1993.
Horn Book, November, 1994, p. 722.
Kirkus Reviews, June 15, 1992; December 15, 1994.
New York Times, December 2, 1993, p. C18.
Publishers Weekly, June 9, 1989, p. 66; June 8, 1992; November 9, 1992; November 28, 1994, p. 60.
School Library Journal, September, 1989, p. 241; July, 1992; March, 1994, p. 204.

*   *   *

McNEILL, Janet 1907-1994

■ **Personal**

Born September 14, 1907, in Dublin, Ireland; died October 9, 1994; daughter of William (a minister) and Jeannie P. (Hogg) McNeill; married Robert P. Alexander (a civil engineer), June 24, 1933 (deceased); chil-

JANET McNEILL

dren: Robert McNeill, David Bradbury, James Connor, Frances Margaret. *Education:* University of St. Andrews, M.A., 1929.

■ Addresses

Agent—A. P. Watt & Son, 26/28 Bedford Row, London WC1R 4HL, England.

■ Career

Freelance writer. *Belfast Telegraph,* Belfast, Northern Ireland, staff member, 1929-33; member of Northern Ireland British Broadcasting Corp. Advisory Council, 1959-63; has appeared on British Broadcasting Corp. Television and on Ulster Television. *Member:* Royal Ulster Academy of Art (patron), Irish PEN Club (chairman, Belfast branch, 1956-57).

■ Writings

FICTION FOR CHILDREN

My Friend Specs McCann, illustrated by Rowel Friers, Faber, 1955.
A Pinch of Salt, illustrated by Friers, Faber, 1956.
A Light Dozen: Eleven More Stories, illustrated by Friers, Faber, 1957.
Specs Fortissimo, illustrated by Friers, Faber, 1959.
This Happy Morning, illustrated by Friers, Faber, 1959.
Special Occasions: Eleven More Stories, illustrated by Friers, Faber, 1960.
Various Specs, illustrated by Friers, Faber, 1961, Nelson, 1971.
Try These for Size, illustrated by Friers, Faber, 1963.
The Giant's Birthday, illustrated by Walter Erhard, Walck, 1964.
Tom's Tower, illustrated by Mary Russon, Faber, 1965, Little, Brown, 1967.
The Mouse and the Mirage, illustrated by Erhard, Walck, 1966.
The Battle of St. George Without, illustrated by Russon, Faber, 1966, Puffin Books, 1978.
I Didn't Invite You to My Party, illustrated by Jane Paton, Hamish Hamilton, 1967.
The Run-Around Robins, illustrated by Monica Brasier-Creagh, Hamish Hamilton, 1967.
It's Snowing Outside (reader), illustrated by Carol Barker, Macmillan, 1968.
The Day They Lost Grandad (reader), illustrated by Julius, Macmillan, 1968.
Goodbye, Dove Square, illustrated by Russon, Faber, 1969, Little, Brown, 1969.
Dragons, Come Home! And Other Stories, illustrated by John Lawrence, Hamish Hamilton, 1969.
Umbrella Thursday, illustrated by Carolyn Dinan, Hamish Hamilton, 1969.
Best Specs: His Most Remarkable Adventures, illustrated by Friers, Faber, 1970.
The Other People, Little, Brown, 1970, Chatto & Windus, 1973.
The Youngest Kite, illustrated by Elizabeth Haines, Hamish Hamilton, 1970.

The Prisoner in the Park, Faber, 1971, Little, Brown, 1971.
Much Too Much Magic, illustrated by Carolyn Harrison, Hamish Hamilton, 1971.
A Helping Hand, illustrated by Paton, Hamish Hamilton, 1971.
Wait for It and Other Stories, Faber, 1972.
A Monster Too Many, illustrated by Ingrid Fetz, Little, Brown, 1972.
The Nest Spotters (reader), illustrated by Geraldine Spence, Macmillan, 1972.
The Family Upstairs (reader), illustrated by Trevor Stubley, Macmillan, 1973.
A Snow-Clean Pony, illustrated by Krystyna Turksa, Hamish Hamilton, 1973.
A Fairy Called Andy Perks, illustrated by Lawrence, Hamish Hamilton, 1973.
We Three Kings, Faber, 1974, Little, Brown, 1974.
Ever After, Chatto & Windus, 1975, Little, Brown, 1975.
The Magic Lollipop, illustrated by Linda Birch, Brockhampton Press, 1975, Children's Press, 1976.
The Three Crowns of Kind Hullabaloo, illustrated by Mike Cole, Brockhampton Press, 1975, Children's Press, 1976.
My Auntie (reader), illustrated by George Him, Macmillan, 1975.
Go on, Then (reader), illustrated by Terrie Reid, Macmillan, 1975.
Growlings (reader), illustrated by Richard Rose, Macmillan, 1975.
The Day Mum Came Home (reader), illustrated by Prudence Seward, Macmillan, 1976.
Look Who's Here (reader), illustrated by Gerald Rose, Macmillan, 1976.
The Hermit's Purple Shirts (reader), Macmillan, 1976.
Billy Brewer Goes on Tour (reader), Macmillan, 1976.
Just Turn the Key and Other Stories, illustrated by Douglas Hall, Hamish Hamilton, 1976, published as *Free Parking and Other Stories,* Beaver, 1978.

PLAYS FOR CHILDREN

Finn and the Black Hag, music by Raymond Warren, Novello, 1962.
Switch On-Switch Off and Other Plays, Faber, 1968.
Graduation Ode, music by Warren, produced in Belfast, 1968.

NOVELS FOR ADULTS

A Child in the House, Hodder & Stoughton, 1955.
Tea at Four O'Clock, Hodder & Stoughton, 1956.
The Other Side of the Wall, Hodder & Stoughton, 1956.
A Furnished Room, Hodder & Stoughton, 1958.
Search Party, Hodder & Stoughton, 1959.
As Strangers Here, Hodder & Stoughton, 1960.
The Early Harvest, Bles, 1962.
The Maiden Dinosaur, Bles, 1964, published as *The Belfast Friends,* Houghton, 1966.
Talk to Me, Bles, 1965.
The Small Widow, Bles, 1967, Atheneum, 1968.

PLAYS FOR ADULTS

Gospel Truth, Carter, 1951.

Also author of more than twenty other radio plays.

■ Sidelights

Janet McNeill was a prolific author of books for readers of all ages. In addition to her adult fiction and plays, she has written books about mice and giants for the very young, and about teenage angst and confused adolescents.

Even her books for the youngest readers contain the quirky humor that is a McNeill trademark. In her 1966 *The Mouse and the Mirage,* McNeill invented an extremely clever rodent who hitches a ride across the desert on the nose of a camel. When the two meet a lion, the mouse convinces the lion into believing himself a wonderful mirage, who therefore cannot eat the travelers. Later, when they meet the lion again, the mouse convinces the lion that he and the camel are a mirage. Writing for *Horn Book,* Ruth Hill Viguers called this "an attractive, very amusing picture book."

Another book for young readers is *A Monster Too Many,* which is the story of two young boys who start out as enemies until they come upon the "monster" in the park—a walrus with "eyes like gooseberries that have been forgotten and have ripened on the bush" unites the boys in their efforts to return the animal to the sea. In McNeill's 1976 *The Magic Lollipop,* young Dan is on his way to spend the night at Gran's when he passes the house of the neighborhood witch. Catching her off guard, he dips his lollipop into her pot of magic spells. However, he's not really sure how to use the magic he's stolen, and the joke turns out to be on him when the spell turns out to make "rude boys behave politely."

McNeill also wrote a collection of short stories for grades three to seven, entitled *Wait for It and Other Stories.* The stories all feature the same cast of characters, but each can stand on its own. Writing for *School Library Journal,* Mary B. Nickerson praised the book's style as being "lively, graceful, and precise" and added that "every phrase is bright with meaning and rhythm." In *Tom's Tower,* a fantasy written for eight to eleven-year-olds, McNeill's central character is a young boy named Tom, who, sitting in his schoolroom one day, finds himself suddenly transported to a magic land where he is appointed a Guardian of the Treasure in the Castle. This is "an original, wittily and amusingly written" tale, according to Virginia Haviland in *Horn Book,* which ends when Tom finds himself in the classroom again, having mysteriously completed his assigned composition with the words, "Impossible things don't happen, not very often."

Another imaginative young boy who turns up in several of McNeill's books for young readers is Specs McCann. He and his friend Curly, along with several other schoolmates, share in-jokes and peculiar speech patterns, as well as the viewpoint that the world is controlled by (to them) unpredictable and prejudiced adults. Eccentric, though believable adults, are also central to McNeill's 1966 *The Battle of St. George*

Without and its sequel, *Goodbye, Dove Square.* In the first book we meet Matt ("DoorMatt") Mudge, who "discovers" an abandoned church within the rapidly decaying neighborhood of Dove Square. A review in the *Times Literary Supplement* complimented McNeill's "elegance of phrase and simile" that could "create a magical atmosphere."

Unfortunately, the children's efforts to save the church from demolition are unsuccessful. In fact, as we find out in *Goodbye, Dove Square,* the entire neighborhood has been cleared for renewal. Two years have gone by, and Matt, now living in a high-rise flat, is facing adjustments in every facet of his life. He is growing up quickly, and is having trouble understanding all he sees—including himself and his own feelings. Matt does reunite the old gang to solve a mystery and save an old man living in a deserted basement in the old neighborhood. A reviewer in the *Bulletin of the Center for Children's Books* called the novel a "deftly written and realistic picture of urban life" with characters that "have both individuality and universality."

Matt McGinley and his friends must battle a gang of toughs to protect the dilapidated, abandoned church that they have discovered and made their own. (Illustration by Mary Russon from *The Battle of St. George Without.*)

Two young boys are enemies until they discover a real sea monster in the park and become determined to work together to protect the creature from imprisonment in the zoo. (Illustration by Ingrid Fetz from *A Monster Too Many.*)

The heroine of McNeill's much-praised *The Other People* is also struggling with upsetting changes in her life. Thirteen-year-old Kate's mother has remarried and gone off on her honeymoon, leaving Kate at her Aunt Poppy's guest house. Although Kate had envisioned a grand establishment, the guest house is dreary, run-down, and overcrowded. Like Matt, Kate finds a way of piecing together the complicated jigsaws of adult life as she becomes embroiled in the lives of her aunt and the sometimes comic, sometimes sadly pathetic guests, such as the would-be poet Miss Dilys Darlington, who "wafted in, festooned in scarves, with dozens of loose ends, like the little cherubs ... on painted ceilings." Ethel L. Heins, writing for *Horn Book,* stated that "the art of the book is not [in] plot invention but the devastatingly subtle characterizations."

One of the reasons that McNeill's books are so appealing is her uncanny ability to capture the ways children think and behave. This ability is particularly noticeable in *The Prisoner in the Park,* in which Ned and his friends are bullied by a strange boy they meet in the wooded end of a public park. The boy blackmails the group into bringing him food. A *Kirkus Reviews* critic praised

McNeill's observations of the children's thoughts and feelings, "which are never expected but always exactly how such a child would react in the situation."

This realistic portrayal of characters shines through again in *We Three Kings,* which *Publishers Weekly* called "wonderfully down to earth and, at the same time, inspirational." This is the story of Dan Agnew, who is dealing with his father's depression over a bike accident he feels responsible for, as well as his relationship with his bullying cousin Roger. The story culminates when the two boys must work together to salvage the school's nativity play. A reviewer in the *Bulletin of the Center for Children's Books* cited the closing scene of the book as "honest sentiment rather than sentimentality" which "strikes just the right note after the abrasion and tension of the rest of the book."

Janet McNeill once commented: "I began writing fantasy for children because an active imagination is a great help to a child confronted by the facts of a largely materialistic world. I then found it possible, and interesting, to write of the children in this world and their reaction to it. I am always glad if I can make a child laugh and remember laughing."

■ Works Cited

Review of *The Battle of St. George Without, Times Literary Supplement,* November 24, 1966.
Review of *Goodbye, Dove Square, Bulletin of the Center for Children's Books,* September, 1969, p. 13.
Haviland, Virginia, review of *Tom's Tower, Horn Book,* August, 1967, p. 464.
Heins, Ethel L., review of *The Other People, Horn Book,* October, 1970, p. 482-83.
Nickerson, Mary B., review of *Wait for It and Other Stories, School Library Journal,* December, 1979, pp. 87-88.
Review of *The Prisoner in the Park, Kirkus Reviews,* September 1, 1972, p. 1028.
Viguers, Ruth Hill, review of *The Mouse and the Mirage, Horn Book,* December, 1966, p. 704.
Review of *We Three Kings, Bulletin of the Center for Children's Books,* November, 1974, p. 48.
Review of *We Three Kings, Publishers Weekly,* October 28, 1974, p. 49.

■ For More Information See

PERIODICALS

Booklist, June 15, 1978, p. 1470.
Bulletin of the Center for Children's Books, March, 1971, p. 109; November, 1972, p. 45.
Horn Book, October, 1969, pp. 536-537; February, 1976, pp. 56-57.
Kirkus Reviews, October 1, 1966, p. 1045; March 1, 1968, p. 272; October 1, 1975, p. 1138.
New York Times Book Review, September 25, 1966, p. 34.
School Library Journal, September, 1976, p. 97.

[Sketch reviewed by son, David Alexander]

VIRGINIA MEACHUM

MEACHUM, Virginia 1918-

■ Personal

Born May 10, 1918, in Chicago, IL; daughter of Fred (an elevator operator) and Marie (a homemaker; maiden name, DeBender) Harvin; married Clyde Meachum (an attorney), December 30, 1942; children: Bruce, Carol, Walter, Connie. *Education:* Illinois State University, B.Ed., 1943. *Politics:* Independent. *Religion:* Protestant. *Hobbies and other interests:* Travel in Europe, Eastern Asia, and the United States, collecting cat books and cats in art, gatherings with children and grandchildren.

■ Addresses

Office—110 North Vermilion, Danville, IL 61832.

■ Career

Elementary school teacher, New London, CT, 1943-45; University of Illinois, Champaign, administrative secretary, 1946-48; freelance feature writer, Danville, IL, 1948—. Lakeview Hospital, gift shop volunteer, 1958-90; PEO Sisterhood, Chapter KE, president, 1987-89. *Member:* Society of Children's Book Writers and Illustrators.

■ Writings

Janet Reno: United States Attorney General, Enslow Publishers, 1995.

Steven Spielberg: Hollywood Filmmaker, Enslow Publishers, 1996.

Contributor of articles to *Chicago Tribune* and *Glamour Magazine.* Contributor to *Moments to Treasure,* Ideals Publishing, 1975.

■ Work in Progress

Jane Goodall: Naturalist, a biography for young adults.

■ Writings

Virginia Meachum told *SATA:* "Although my formal education was in business and elementary education, I've always had an irrepressible need to express my thoughts on paper. Hence, I turned to writing humorous articles for women, for which there happened to be a market. Meanwhile, I experimented with books for children, short fiction, and even novels (all under cover!), and attended an occasional writers conference for guidance from professionals and to gain confidence.

"Recently, I found my niche in writing biographies for young adults. Researching the background of an outstanding person, and presenting a portrait of his or her life to young readers, is endlessly fascinating.

"At my advanced age, immersed in what I really like to do, I feel like the Grandma Moses of writing."

■ For More Information See

PERIODICALS

School Library Journal, August, 1995.

*　*　*

MILLER, Ellanita 1957-

■ Personal

Born December 12, 1957, in St. Louis, MO; daughter of Tyree Riley and Hazel Robinson; married Ernest S. Miller (an electrician and safety representative); children: James Lee Wright, Jr., Tiffany L. Miller, Ernest S. Miller, Jr. *Education:* Attended Florissant Valley Community College, McDonnell Douglas VIP School, and University of Missouri—St. Louis. *Religion:* Catholic.

■ Addresses

Office—3936 Affirmed, St. Louis, MO 63034.

■ Career

St. Louis Association of Retarded Children, St. Louis, MO, respite care provider, beginning 1984; E & E Rentals, St. Louis, owner, beginning 1984; Washington University School of Medicine, St. Louis, affiliated with minority student affairs, beginning 1994. St. Louis County election board, judge, 1992. *Member:* Impact

ELLANITA MILLER

Association, Ltd. (treasurer, 1994; vice president, 1995), Power Learning Systems.

■ Awards, Honors

Employee Suggestion Awards, McDonnell Douglas Corp., 1980, 1982, 1983 (twice), 1984, 1985; certificate, Saturday Scholars Program, 1995, for coordination of program.

■ Writings

Never, Never Talk to Strangers, Dorrance, 1995.

■ Work in Progress

Never Do Anything to Cause Others to Be Punished; I Am Human; Witch Haiti; Beau Font (the Cat) No Where to Go.

■ Sidelights

Ellanita Miller told *SATA:* "When several children were kidnapped and killed in St. Louis, Missouri, I was prompted to write my first published book, *Never, Never Talk to Strangers,* in an effort to help protect children. The book was written to make children aware of how easily gifts can lure them into the hands of strangers. Sometimes persuading a child to listen is very hard and

we must reach them at their level to get our point across. Most children enjoy bedtime stories or any story if given personal time. As a writer, there is nothing more fulfilling than being able to write meaningful stories that are beneficial to others.

"I was influenced by John Grisham, a prominent author, after listening to an interview. He stumbled across many tribulations before marketing his books. The result has brought him success. Many first time writers will receive very harsh criticism from agents, friends, and publishers, but do not let this discourage you. I have always believed that sometimes criticism is good, because it will either 'make you' or 'break you.' You must decide which phrase fits you."

*   *   *

MORRISON, Gordon 1944-

■ Personal

Born June 30, 1944, in Allston, MA; son of Hugh L. (a lithographic plate worker) and Margaret (an electronics assembler; maiden name, Vincent) Morrison; married Nancy Clapp (in library and technical services), October 7, 1967; children: Aimee, Suzanne, J. Seth. *Education:* Attended School of the Museum of Fine Art, Boston, MA, 1963-64; Butera School of Art, Boston, MA, graduated 1967. *Politics:* Independent. *Religion:* None. *Hobbies and other interests:* Camping, hiking, bird watching.

■ Addresses

Home and office—52 Bulfinch St., North Attleborough, MA 02760.

■ Career

Freelance illustrator, 1967—. B & B Studio, Boston, MA, illustrator, 1967-69; Butera School of Art, Boston, MA, substitute drawing teacher, 1968-69; North Attleborough High School Adult Education, North Attleborough, MA, painting teacher, 1978-80; Rhode Island School of Design, Providence, RI, continuing education instructor of biological illustration, 1985-87, independent studies mentor, final portfolio reviewer, curriculum consultant, 1985—. Appalachian Mountain Club guest lecturer, "Art and Nature Seminar," 1977-80. *Exhibitions:* Exhibitor at group shows at galleries including Cross Roads of Sport, New York City; Left Bank Gallery, Wellfleet, MA; "Fur, Feathers & Scales," Sanibel Island, FL; The Orvis Co., Manchester Center, VT. Exhibitor in one-man shows at museums and galleries including Marine and Science Museum, Virginia Beach, VA; New England Wildflower Society, Framingham, MA; Thoreau Lyceum, Concord, MA; Tremellen Gallery, PA; Madeleine Clark Wallace Library, Wheaton College, Norton, MA; Attleborough Museum of Art, Attleborough, MA; Dennison/Pequotsepos Nature Center, Mystic, CT. Works are held by the Gannet Corporation, Washington, DC; LeStage Manufacturing,

GORDON MORRISON

MA; Advest Corporation, CT; Wildcat Inn, NH; White Flower Farm, CT; Massachusetts Audubon Society, MA; Sudbury Valley Trustees, MA; New England Wildflower Society, MA; Kendall Corporation, MA, and numerous private collections.

■ Illustrator

Lawrence Newcomb, *Newcomb's Wildflower Guide: An Ingenious New Key System for Quick, Positive Field Identification of Wildflowers, Flowering Shrubs and Vines,* Little, Brown, 1977.

John H. Mitchell, *The Curious Naturalist,* Prentice-Hall, 1980.

Edited by Mitchell and Wayne Hawley, *The Energy Book* (Massachusetts Audubon Society Man and Nature Series), Stephen Greene Press, 1980.

Christopher Leahy, *The Birdwatcher's Companion,* Hill & Wang, 1982.

Mitchell, *A Guide to the Seasons,* Massachusetts Audubon Society, 1982.

Leahy, *An Introduction to Insects of Massachusetts,* Massachusetts Audubon Society, 1983.

Fred Powledge, *A Forgiving Wind,* Sierra Club Books, 1983.

Mitchell, *Ceremonial Times,* Doubleday, 1984.

Edward W. Cronin, *Getting Started in Birdwatching,* Houghton, 1986.

John Kricher, *A Field Guide to Eastern Forests,* 1988.

Gordon Hayward, *Designing Your Own Landscape: Gardening Techniques, Tools & Plants,* Whetstone Publishing, 1989.

Ron McAdow, *The Concord, Sudbury and Assabet Rivers: A Guide to Canoeing, Wildlife, & History,* Bliss, 1990.

McAdow, *The Charles River: Exploring Nature and History on Foot and By Canoe,* Bliss, 1992.

Margaret Hensel, *English Cottage Gardening,* Norton, 1992.

Alex Wilson, *Quiet Water Canoe Guide,* Appalachian Mountain Club Books, 1993.

Kricher, *A Field Guide to Ecology of Western Forests,* 1993.

Illustrator of cover art for *Cape Cod Pilot,* by Josef Berger (Jeremiah Digges), MIT Press, 1969. Also designer and illustrator of the Massachusetts Audubon Society's *Curious Naturalist* magazine, 1976-82; contributing artist, Roger Tory Peterson, *Peterson First Guide to Wildflowers,* 1986; illustrator of the "Curious Naturalist" series in the Massachusetts Audubon Society's magazine, *Sanctuary,* 1982—; illustrator of "Native Americans" plant series, *Horticulture,* 1987—; author and illustrator of "Birds in the Garden" series, *Horticulture: The Magazine of American Gardening,* 1991—. Contributor to *Country Journal, Ranger Rick, Organic Gardening, Backpacker, Habitat, Bird Watcher's Digest, New York Conservationist, Yankee Magazine, Bird Observer of New England, Family Food Garden, Design News, Fortune, Playboy,* and *Seventeen.*

PETERSON FIRST GUIDE SERIES FOR CHILDREN, PUBLISHED BY HOUGHTON MIFFLIN

John Kricher, *Peterson First Guide to Dinosaurs,* 1990.

Kricher, *Peterson First Guide to Seashores,* 1992.

Kricher, *Peterson First Guide to Forests,* 1995.

PETERSON FIELD GUIDE COLORING BOOKS, PUBLISHED BY HOUGHTON MIFFLIN

Kricher, *A Field Guide to Dinosaurs Coloring Book,* 1989.

Kricher, *A Field Guide to Seashores Coloring Book,* 1989.

Richard Walton, *A Field Guide to Endangered Wildlife Coloring Book,* 1991.

Kricher, *A Field Guide to Tropical Rainforests Coloring Book,* 1991.

■ Work in Progress

"Presently developing several book ideas, including some children's books on cycles and connections in nature; developing illustrations of plant and animal associations for Missouri Botanical Gardens temperate forest and tropical rainforest exhibits."

■ Sidelights

Gordon Morrison has worked as an illustrator for twenty-eight years. He told *SATA* that he has "illustrated two dozen books, numerous articles, done diora-

PETERSON FIELD GUIDE COLORING BOOKS

ENDANGERED WILDLIFE

RICHARD K. WALTON and **GORDON MORRISON**
Sponsored by the National Wildlife Federation and the National Audubon Society

Morrison, who is primarily a nature artist, has had his art exhibited in galleries across the country, and he has done illustrations for dozens of children's works like this 1991 coloring book.

mas and exhibition work, as well as murals and, of course, countless paintings, primarily on nature or some aspect of it." Morrison's work is available for young children in the Peterson Field Guide Coloring Books, which are sponsored by the National Wildlife Federation and the National Audubon Society, and the Peterson First Guide books.

Morrison explained that he has been drawing since he was a child growing up near Boston. "My father had a great influence on my early artistic development, encouraging and critiquing my work. I am certain that, as a young boy growing up in a family of ten children, the attention I was given at those times was sufficient reason to continue drawing, but as I grew and improved I found this was not only something I did well, but something I loved doing.

"I recall how in junior high school, I became enthralled with the great masters of art, and how I scrimped and saved to send away for a book—*100 of the World's Greatest Paintings,* the pages of which I pored over again and again. Norman Rockwell may have been my favorite artist at that time, but some of these artists spoke to me from hundreds of years ago and left me speechless. Even at that young age I knew that art was going to be the manner in which I would make my living."

As an adult, Morrison focused on painting and attended art school. It was in art school that Morrison "became aware of, and concerned for, the world of nature and the part that man plays in it." Although he spent some time working as a commercial illustrator, he felt that this work was "not very worthwhile." "So, out of a concern for the environment and a personal need to do something meaningful with my talent, I decided to include nature in my fine art paintings. As I did field studies and research for my paintings, contacts with various wildlife organizations and individuals developed, which led to my wildlife studies becoming a part of my illustration work.

"In the beginning I was a city boy who needed hands on experience, so my field sketches became a tool for learning and experiencing, and the perfect excuse for getting out of the studio and into nature. Through those field studies I came to know wildlife more and more, and came to appreciate and understand my relationship to it."

Morrison related his feelings about art and illustration to *SATA:* "As a young artist I recall hearing that an artist should never settle for being 'just' an illustrator. That to be an artist is to answer to a higher calling. I don't know that I can disagree with the higher calling aspect of the comment but I do know that there is no such thing as being 'just' an illustrator. As one who does both there is nothing like the joy and exhilaration of painting. Whatever the subject or for whatever reason it is being done, the act itself can be its own reward. As for illustrating, it can be far more demanding. I have worked twelve to fourteen hour days, seven days a week for months on end. Doing research, compiling material, developing drawings, and all the while trying to bring into the final illustrations a little bit of myself and a little bit of art. And when I succeed at that, the feeling of accomplishment is as great as having just finished a work of art.

"If I were to give one bit of advice to young artists/ illustrators it would be to have as much contact with their subjects as possible. Sketch, study, observe, and come to know them. Absorb as much as you can from the real thing so when the time comes for you to illustrate you will respond from what you know, and even how you feel, while filling in the details with your research. Thoreau said 'How vain it is to sit down to write when one has not stood up to live.' This to me is doubly true for an artist/illustrator."

Morrison hopes that those exposed to his illustrations will be able to see beyond "the details and the visual information.... I believe it is important for an illustration to be a joy to look at and to understand as well as a means to learn." Morrison intends to "depict the unique beauty, character and details of a subject" as well as to "share a sense for it and the place where it's found." Finally, he wants to "help educate readers, giving them a better understanding of the natural world and their connection to it."

N

NELSON, Catherine Chadwick 1926-

■ Personal

Born January 2, 1926, in Detroit Lakes, MN; daughter of Harold H. (a publicity director) and Frances Shirley (a teacher; maiden name, Green) Chadwick; married Daniel A. Nelson (a teacher), June 22, 1947; children: Dianne A. Vandergon, Deborah A. Badalich, Susan K. Nelson. *Education:* University of Minnesota, B.A., 1949.

■ Addresses

Home—2836 Cornelia Tr., Woodbury, MN 55125.

■ Career

Children's book writer. Has held a variety of clerical jobs.

■ Writings

Mary's Invisible Friend, Winston-Derek, 1995.

■ Work in Progress

Two sequels, "Mary's Secret Flight" and "Mary's Vacation," and an adult novel, as yet untitled, complete but undergoing revisions.

■ Sidelights

Catherine Chadwick Nelson told *SATA:* "I have been writing since childhood, but only recently for publication. After graduating from college, I held a series of clerical jobs, first to help my husband get through college, and later to pad the family budget.

"After my husband and I retired, I began to write seriously."

NEWMAN, Robert (Howard) 1909-1988

■ Personal

Born June 3, 1909, in New York, NY; died of a brain tumor, December 7, 1988, in Branford, CT; son of Samuel Jerome and Nance (Ortman) Newman; married Dorothy Crayder (a writer), 1936; children: Hila Feil. *Education:* Attended Brown University, 1927-28. *Hobbies and other interests:* Field archery, sailing.

■ Career

Freelance writer. Office of War Information, overseas branch, New York, chief of Radio Outpost Division, 1942-44. *Member:* Radio Writers Guild (council member, 1942-49; vice president of Eastern region, 1945), Authors Guild, Authors League of America, PEN, Writers Guild East.

■ Awards, Honors

Edgar Allan Poe Award nomination, 1978, for *Night Spell;* eight Junior Literary Guild selections, 1978-1987 for the "Inspector Wyatt" series.

■ Writings

JUVENILE FICTION AND FANTASY

The Boy Who Could Fly, illustrated by Paul Sagsoorian, Atheneum, 1967.
Merlin's Mistake, illustrated by Richard Lebenson, Atheneum, 1970.
The Testing of Tertius, illustrated by Richard Cuffari, Atheneum, 1973.
The Shattered Stone, illustrated by John Gretzer, Atheneum, 1975.
Night Spell, illustrated by Peter Burchard, Atheneum, 1977.

"INSPECTOR WYATT" SERIES; ALL PUBLISHED BY ATHENEUM

The Case of the Baker Street Irregular, 1978.

The Case of the Vanishing Corpse, 1980.
The Case of the Somerville Secret, 1981.
The Case of the Threatened King, 1982.
The Case of the Etruscan Treasure, 1983.
The Case of the Frightened Friend, 1984.
The Case of the Murdered Players, 1985.
The Case of the Indian Curse, 1986.
The Case of the Watching Boy, 1987.

OTHER

The Enchanter, Houghton, 1962.
The Japanese: People of the Three Treasures (nonfiction), illustrated by Mamoru Funai, Atheneum, 1964.
Corbie (adult fiction), Harcourt, 1966.
Grettir the Strong (a retelling), illustrated by John Gretzer, Crowell, 1968.
The Twelve Labors of Hercules (a retelling), illustrated by Charles Keeping, Crowell, 1972.

Also author of radio, television, and movie scripts. Contributor of verse and short stories to periodicals.

■ Sidelights

Robert Newman began writing children's books after a successful career in radio. His credits included not only adult fiction, but juvenile fantasy and an acclaimed series of detective novels for young readers set in Victorian England. "I began writing books for young people fairly late," Newman once told *Something about the Author (SATA).* "I think I first became interested in it when my daughter was quite young and I used to read aloud to her." Newman never forgot his daughter's response to and involvement in the books they read together, and this memory inspired and guided him in the writing of his own books.

Raised in New York, Newman studied for two years at Brown University and then went into construction. But he was already writing poetry and soon turned his hand to short stories and radio scripts as well. In 1936 he married and in that same year became a full-time freelance writer. Newman's radio credits included two daytime programs and five mystery shows, including "Inner Sanctum" and "Adventures of the Thin Man." He also created a hospital show which long predated similar popular television series based in hospitals. For television, Newman wrote episodes for the soap opera *Search for Life* and for the popular *Peyton Place.* His first adult novel appeared in the 1960s, and by the time of the publication of his second he had determined that he would rather write books—children's books in particular—than anything else.

Newman's first children's book was a nonfiction title, *The Japanese: People of the Three Treasures,* which appeared in 1964. A history of the Japanese people from ancient times to the seventeenth century, the book employs the three treasures of the imperial family—the mirror, the sword, and the jewel—to explore the Japanese. Newman discusses religious life as symbolized in the mirror; the cult of samurai and Japanese philosophy

Mark faces unique challenges in trying to protect his younger brother, Joey, who he fears will be exploited for his telepathic and other special powers. (Illustration by Paul Sagsoorian from *The Boy Who Could Fly.*)

are examined in the sword; and the reverence for nature is explored in the jewel motif. With its innovative organization and strong narrative line, *The Japanese: People of the Three Treasures* was dubbed "a distinguished book," by a critic in *Horn Book.*

With *The Boy Who Could Fly,* Newman branched out into juvenile fiction for the first time. The story is told by Mark, the older brother of a pair of orphans. Mark is protective of his younger brother Joey and of his special powers: Joey can read minds and fly. Yet Mark is goaded into bragging about his brother's special abilities and is challenged to provide a public display of Joey's flying powers. Realizing that Joey's special talents must be kept from the public eye if Joey is to lead a normal life, Mark is faced with hard choices in what *Horn Book* reviewer Ruth Hill Viguers calls a "convincing, suspenseful story." Jean Fritz, in *New York Times Book Review,* interpreted the book along biblical lines with Joey being a potential new Messiah and concluded that the questions raised by Newman's book were "even more haunting than the story itself."

Newman moved on to two retellings: an Icelandic saga in *Grettir the Strong* and a recounting of a Greek myth in *The Twelve Labors of Hercules.* Grettir is the archetypal tragic hero of Norse legend, cursed by his own strong will, tormented by a ghost, and racked by his enemies. But he never loses his determination to create his own fate; the strongest boy on the island, he eventually grows up to be the bravest after passing through adventures and tests that would humble a weaker youth. Newman's writing style "characterizes very well the life of this legendary hero," noted Nancy Farrar in *Library Journal,* and a critic in *Kirkus Reviews* commented that Newman's was a "firm, concise retelling of the Icelandic saga." For *The Twelve Labors of Hercules,* Newman teamed up with illustrator Charles Keeping, recreating the mythic story of strongman Hercules and his violent atonement for murder, and giving it a romantic twist that the fatalistic Greek legend did not have in the original. According to Flo Morse in *New York Times Book Review,* "Each episode—in fact the entire book—is well staged," while a critic in *Kirkus Reviews* thought it "a smooth and lively version of the hero's life and labors."

Fantasy was Newman's next literary test, with tales of Merlin and his unwitting apprentice, Tertius, in companion volumes that compress and play with history and provide Camelot with future knowledge: of nuclear reactors and other such twentieth-century science. In *Merlin's Mistake,* Brian joins Tertius in his adventurous quest to find the sorcerer Merlin. Tertius has super powers since he is a godchild of Merlin, but he has mistakenly been given only future knowledge. He knows all about computers but has no clue about curing the common wart. He needs a new blessing from Merlin, but there are dragons, witches, and evil empires to vanquish first. Newman intentionally presents an outrageously anachronistic history in this Merlin tale and tells it with "wit and ingenuity and grace," according to Ethel L. Heins, writing in *Horn Book.* "Reaching far beyond mere cleverness, the book has been conceived and executed with care, imagination, and skill," Heins concluded. In the sequel, *The Testing of Tertius,* the young apprentice and his friends travel to France in an attempt to stop an evil magician, Urlik, who plans to ultimately capture England. Less convincing than the first Merlin book, "nevertheless, interest runs high," noted Ethel L. Heins in *Horn Book,* as Tertius uses such twentieth-century contrivances as tanks and airplanes to try to rout the evil Urlik. Newman continued with fantasy in *The Shattered Stone,* staged in an enchanted forest and featuring another quest story. This time Ivo and Neva, two children who have no conception of who they are or where they came from, set out to find a shattered ancient stone that promises to reveal how peace can be brought to rival warring kingdoms. A rich and complex book with a cast of characters that grows as the children move from one kingdom to the next, *The Shattered Stone* creates a coherent and believable imaginary world with its own myths and history. "The deft handling of the undeclared love between Neva and Ivo and the tidy resolution . . . are enjoyable," noted a reviewer in *Horn Book.*

Newman blended fantasy with mystery in *Night Spell,* a transitional book for him and a nominee for an Edgar Allan Poe Award. In this work, orphaned 14-year-old Tad Harper is sent to spend the summer at a New England coastal community and be the guest of an edgy and disabled recluse, Mr. Gorham. Left to his own

Brian journeys with Tertius to find the sorcerer Merlin, who has mistakenly endowed his godchild Tertius with only *future* knowledge in Newman's 1970 novel. (Illustration by Richard Lebenson from *Merlin's Mistake.*)

devices, Tad befriends the daughter of the lighthouse keeper and together they investigate the drowning death of Gorham's granddaughter the year before and the subsequent disappearance of the girl's mother, Gorham's own daughter. Led on by the dream appearance of the ghost of the drowned girl, the two ultimately find the missing woman. A reviewer in *School Library Journal* concluded that the "supernatural element is well handled," while a *Kirkus Reviews* critic noted that Newman created "a pleasantly sunlit Gothic."

Mystery and history were blended with *The Case of the Baker Street Irregular,* and Newman never looked back. He wrote nine books in what became known as the "Inspector Wyatt" series, though Wyatt—the upper-class constable and then inspector at Scotland Yard who is resented by his fellow officers because of his privileged background—did not come to the fore until the second book in the series. Set in Victorian London, the books all feature young Andrew Tillett, another of Newman's orphan protagonists, Sara Wiggins, and Wyatt. The first book in the series came about through Newman's daughter's interest in the Sherlock Holmes stories and Newman's own love for London. He realized that, although many books had been written about Holmes, none had been done from the perspective of a child. Holmes's helpmates, the Baker Street Irregulars, street kids whom the famous detective from time to time employed, would serve as a perfect vehicle for such a story, Newman decided. Andrew, whose father is dead and who has not seen his mother in years, arrives in London only to have his new guardian abducted and to narrowly escape abduction himself. Accidentally drawn into the gang of youthful assistants to Holmes, Andrew helps Holmes to solve a complex mystery. In the process, he discovers the secret of his own identity and his missing actress mother. Ethel L. Heins, writing in *Horn Book,* commented that Newman is "as urbane and fluent as the legendary Mr. Holmes," and that his story moves along with "unflagging energy," while Drew Stevenson concluded in *School Library Journal* that this Holmesian take-off provided the "perfect opportunity for young readers to become acquainted with the famed detective."

Newman followed this initial success with eight further titles between 1980 and 1987. With the second book in the series, *The Case of the Vanishing Corpse,* he introduced the young constable Wyatt who essentially replaced the Holmes character; as Holmes is still covered by copyright, a large sum of royalty had to be given to use the famous fictional detective. This new investigator works with the younger protagonists, An-

drew and Sara, to solve a series of baffling jewel thefts. Newman provides period atmosphere in everything from locations of shops to street slang. Ann A. Flowers in *Horn Book* found that this book had a "plausible plot, solid characterization, and fascinating London background." *The Case of the Somerville Secret,* the next title in the series, was inspired by an offhand comment in one of Conan Doyle's original stories about how the retarded heir of an ancient dukedom was sequestered in a London suburb. *The Case of the Threatened King* has Sara kidnapped in a tale that is, according to Denise M. Wilms in *Booklist,* both "audacious and disarming" in its credibility. New York provides the venue for the fifth book in the series, *The Case of the Etruscan Treasure,* and once again Andrew, Sara, and Wyatt team up to solve the central mystery—in this case two: stolen diamonds and a missing file cabinet. *School Library Journal* reviewer Drew Stevenson noted Newman's talent for "creating colorful characters and his eye for recreating historic detail"—in this case, New York City in the 1890s.

Back in London for *The Case of the Frightened Friend,* Andrew goes to Wyatt when a school friend mysterious-

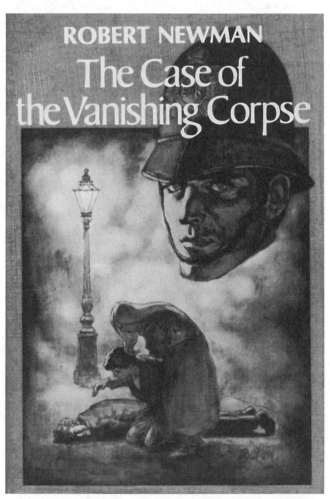

Andrew finds London terrifying, until he meets renowned detective Sherlock Holmes, in this introduction to Newman's popular "Inspector Wyatt" series.

Young Constable Wyatt, assistant to Inspector Finch of Scotland Yard, helps Andrew and Sara solve a series of baffling jewel thefts. (Cover illustration by David L. Stone.)

ly requests that Andrew should check up on him if he does not return to school after vacation. In the course of their investigations, Andrew and Inspector Wyatt uncover a German spy ring in a story that has "enough twists and turns to keep it interesting," according to Drew Stevenson in *School Library Journal. The Case of the Murdered Players* is an investigation of a series of murders of actresses. Wyatt, now engaged to Andrew's actress mother, is more than a little concerned, and once again Sara, Andrew, and Wyatt set out to solve the mystery—this time before the murderer strikes close to home. A reviewer in *Bulletin of the Center for Children's Books* noted that this book has "a brisk style, sound structure, and good period details."

Inspector Wyatt is away on his honeymoon with Andrew's mother in the eighth book in the series when an old friend, Beasley the antiques dealer, comes into mortal danger. The complex plot involves the Indian cult gang known as the Thuggees and a mysterious curse which has been put on Beasley. Once again Sara and Andrew are pressed into service to solve the mystery in a book whose pacing, characters, and British setting are, according to Ilene Cooper in *Booklist*, "delightfully on target." Margaret Porter, writing in *Voice of Youth Advocates*, described the latest book in the series as a "pleasant British counterpart" to such perennial favorites as Nancy Drew and the Hardy Boys. With the ninth and final book in the series, *The Case of the Watching Boy*, Andrew unwittingly aids in the kidnapping of a young child. What begins as a good deed gone awry has dire international consequences, and Inspector Wyatt, along with Sara and Andrew's mother, are soon unraveling the complex set of events which could lead to a revolution in Romania. Ellen Fader said in *School Library Journal* that "this above average mystery" maintains the quality of the previous books in the series, and a reviewer in *Publishers Weekly* wrote that the adventure will have "strong appeal for fans of the previous tales."

Newman died only four months after the publication of this last "Inspector Wyatt" book, but left behind a legacy of writing. His was a writing family: at one time he, his wife, and his daughter were all creating children's books. As he once told *SATA*, "I cannot speak for anyone but myself, but I suspect that all three of us are concentrating on books for young people for the same reason. Because we feel that it is the most rewarding kind of writing one can do today." In that same *SATA* entry, he summed up his career: "I tell stories: stories which I hope will stimulate the imagination by introducing children to places that no longer exist or never existed and to characters and situations that they are not likely to meet in real life but which have some qualities that are recognizable and timeless."

■ Works Cited

Review of *The Case of the Murdered Players, Bulletin of the Center for Children's Books,* March, 1986, p. 134.

Review of *The Case of the Watching Boy, Publishers Weekly,* July 10, 1987, p. 70.

Cooper, Ilene, review of *The Case of the Indian Curse, Booklist,* September 1, 1986, p. 66.

Fader, Ellen, review of *The Case of the Watching Boy, School Library Journal,* September, 1987, p. 182.

Farrar, Nancy, review of *Grettir the Strong, Library Journal,* January 15, 1969, p. 314.

Flowers, Ann A., review of *The Case of the Vanishing Corpse, Horn Book,* June, 1980, p. 302.

Fritz, Jean, review of *The Boy Who Could Fly, New York Times Book Review,* May 7, 1967, pp. 39-40.

Review of *Grettir the Strong, Kirkus Reviews,* October 15, 1968, p. 1170.

Heins, Ethel L., review of *Merlin's Mistake, Horn Book,* June, 1970, pp. 298-99.

Heins, Ethel L., review of *The Testing of Tertius, Horn Book,* June 6, 1973, pp. 381-82.

Heins, Ethel L., review of *The Case of the Baker Street Irregular, Horn Book,* August, 1978, p. 397.

Review of *The Japanese: People of the Three Treasures, Horn Book,* June, 1964.

Morse, Flo, review of *The Twelve Labors of Hercules, New York Times Book Review,* August 27, 1972, p. 24.

Review of *Night Spell, Kirkus Reviews,* April 15, 1977, p. 427.

Review of *Night Spell, School Library Journal,* May, 1977, p. 78.

Porter, Margaret, review of *The Case of the Indian Curse, Voice of Youth Advocates,* February, 1987, p. 286.

Review of *The Shattered Stone, Horn Book,* October, 1975, p. 465.

Stevenson, Drew, review of *The Case of the Baker Street Irregular, School Library Journal,* May, 1978, p. 85.

Stevenson, Drew, review of *The Case of the Etruscan Treasure, School Library Journal,* December, 1983, p. 86.

Stevenson, Drew, review of *The Case of the Frightened Friend, School Library Journal,* May, 1984, p. 102.

Review of *The Twelve Labors of Hercules, Kirkus Reviews,* May 15, 1972, p. 585.

Viguers, Ruth Hill, review of *The Boy Who Could Fly, Horn Book,* April, 1967, p. 208.

Wilms, Denise M., review of *The Case of the Threatened King, Booklist,* April 15, 1982, p. 1097.

■ For More Information See

BOOKS

Sixth Book of Junior Authors and Illustrators, edited by Sally Holmes Holtze, H. W. Wilson, 1989, pp. 206-08.

PERIODICALS

Booklist, February 1, 1969, p. 594; May 15, 1970, p. 1162; October 15, 1975, p. 305; March 15, 1978, p. 1193; March 15, 1980, p. 1060; March 15, 1981, p. 1032; September 1, 1983, p. 88; April 1, 1984, p. 1118; August, 1987, p. 1751.

Horn Book, August, 1977, p. 443; June, 1981, p. 303; June, 1982, p. 291; October, 1983, p. 577; April, 1984, p. 223; March, 1985, p. 204.

New York Times Book Review, November 5, 1967, p. 66; April 30, 1978, p. 44; January 25, 1981, p. 31.

School Library Journal, November, 1975, p. 81; May, 1980, p. 86; November, 1980, p. 47; May, 1981, p. 86; May, 1982, p. 84; October, 1985, p. 185.

Times Literary Supplement, October 3, 1968, p. 1110; April 2, 1971, p. 390; November 23, 1973, p. 1435.

■ Obituaries

PERIODICALS

New York Times, December 9, 1988, p. D18.*

—Sketch by J. Sydney Jones

*   *   *

NICOLL, Helen 1937-

■ Personal

Born October 10, 1937, in Natland, Westmorland, England; married Robert Kime (an antiquarian), 1970; children: Hannah, Tom. *Education:* Attended schools in Bristol, Dartington Hall, Froebel, and Education Institute.

■ Addresses

Home & Office—Dene House, Lockeridge, Marlborough, Wiltshire, England. *Agent*—c/o Heinemann Ltd., Michelin House, 81 Fulham Road, London SW3 6RB, England.

■ Career

British Broadcasting Corp. (BBC-TV), London, England, producer and director of children's programs, 1967-71; *Puffin* and *The Egg* magazines, London, editor, 1977-79; Cover to Cover Cassettes, Wiltshire, England, producer, 1983—; writer of children's books.

■ Writings

"MEG AND MOG" SERIES; ILLUSTRATIONS BY JAN PIENKOWSKI

Meg and Mog, Heinemann, 1972, Atheneum, 1973.
Meg's Eggs, Heinemann, 1973, Atheneum, 1973.
Meg at Sea, Heinemann, 1973, Harvey House, 1976.
Meg on the Moon, Heinemann, 1973, Harvey House, 1976.
Meg's Car, Heinemann, 1975.
Meg's Castle, Heinemann, 1975.
Meg's Veg, Heinemann, 1976.
Mog's Mumps, Heinemann, 1976, Penguin, 1982.
Meg and Mog Birthday Book, Heinemann, 1979, Puffin 1991.
Mog at the Zoo, Heinemann, 1982, Penguin, 1984.
Mog in the Fog, Heinemann, 1984.
Owl at School, Heinemann, 1984, Penguin, 1985.

Mog's Box, Heinemann, 1987.
Owl at the Vet, Heinemann, 1992, Penguin, 1992.

POETRY

Compiler, *Poems for Seven-Year-Olds and Under,* Kestrel, 1983.

OTHER

Quest for the Gloop: The Exploits of Murfy and PHIX, illustrations by Pienkowski, Heinemann, 1980.

Author of *Tom's Home,* 1987.

■ Adaptations

David Wood has created four plays (published by Puffin, 1984) for children based on the "Meg and Mog" series.

■ Sidelights

The enormously creative Helen Nicoll is best known by children as the creator of the witch Meg, her cat Mog, and Snowy the Owl. Nicoll's language is simple enough for the youngest beginning reader, and it rhymes. The bumptious trio of witch, cat, and owl is simply illustrated by Jan Pienkowski in the fourteen-book series. Nicoll has also produced and directed television and radio broadcasts for children for the British Broadcasting Corporation (BBC) and for a very popular series of audio cassettes for Cover to Cover Cassettes that accompany her books in the United Kingdom.

Nicoll uses a witty, minimal text, which is suitable for the very young and for beginning readers in her series. While Meg, Mog, and their sidekick Owl are creatures of darkness, there is nothing dark about their adventures or the pages they flit across, thanks to Pienkowski's

and she flew up the chimney with Mog

Nicoll's popular duo first appeared in 1972's *Meg and Mog.* (Illustration by Jan Pienkowski.)

Meg and Mog travel in space in Nicoll's *Meg on the Moon.* (Illustration by Jan Pienkowski.)

cartoon bright drawings. Meg is the proper, tattered modern witch with pointed hat, scraggly hair, and a tentative hold on her magic powers. They are quite effective when they work but totally unpredictable when they don't. Often when she casts a spell it goes terribly awry; fortunately, Meg is just as quick to resort to practical solutions as she is to magic.

Times Literary Supplement contributor William Feaver, describing Nicoll's two main characters, writes: "Meg the wiry witch and Mog her familiar, a black-and-white-striped cat with a tail like a frayed bootlace, are the perfect couple. Meg and Mog stories seize hold. Meg works her magic, Mog reacts and the audience joins in." In short, they are the perfect pair to charm beginning readers.

Nicoll's plots for Meg and Mog are simple: problem, solution plus catastrophe equals ... lots of laughs. In *Meg and Mog,* Meg turns her peers into mice, although Robert Melville confessed in a review of *Meg's Eggs* in *New Statesman* that he suspected Meg of a "double cross because Mog is on hand to chase [the mice]." In *Meg's Eggs* dinosaurs hatch from the eggs Meg created for dinner.

There's a Meg and Mog for almost every occasion. The books contain about a line of text per page, "encouraging early reading attempts," wrote a reviewer in *Times Literary Supplement.* If you think life is always simple for someone who jets around by broomstick, try *Meg's Car.* Mumps? Mog's got them (and how!) in *Mog's Mumps.* Gardening? In *Meg's Veg* the stalwart trio plant a garden and are overwhelmed with produce. Mog is mistaken for a rare tiger in *Mog at the Zoo.* Meg casts a spell to free him from his cage, but it puts her in his place. Another spell frees her, along with all the other

animals. A reviewer in *School Librarian* stated that *Mog at the Zoo* is a "wealth of fun and language learning." Even jealousy rears its ugly head in the "Meg and Mog" series. Mog is envious of the goodies Meg has prepared for Owl's lunch box, so Meg makes a magic potion to create a lunchbox for Mog.

Since magic is used warily by the scrawny witch, Meg often has practical solutions to life's problems too. When Snowy the Owl's lack of dexterity leaves him in a heap in a tree, Meg enrolls him in flight school in *Owl at School.* But occasionally magic spells *do* come in handy. In *Mog in the Fog,* the cat and witch climb the highest mountain in the world. After Mog gets lost in the fog, Meg whisks it away with a spell that also reveals a yeti standing in the snow. Reviewer Jill Bennett's advice about *Mog in the Fog* in *Books for Keeps* was succinct: "Multiple copies advised."

Nicoll and Pienkowski have collaborated on a science fiction book for older children. According to a reviewer in *British Book News, Quest for the Gloop: The Exploits of Murfy and PHIX* "will no doubt please young science fiction addicts" who enjoy puns.

Nicoll is currently producing a series of audio cassettes in England that accompany books for children, under the label Cover to Cover Cassettes. Like her "Meg and Mog" series, these audio cassettes have received rave reviews. Chris Powling, reviewing the cassettes in *Books for Keeps,* recommended, "My own best buy for tinies is *Meg at Sea* and *Meg on the Moon.*"

■ Works Cited

Bennett, Jill, review of *Mog in the Fog, Books for Keeps,* May, 1986, p. 19.
Feaver, William, "Fantastic Diagrams," *Times Literary Supplement,* July 27, 1984, p. 854.
Reviews of *Meg on the Moon* and *Meg at Sea,* "In Safe Surroundings," *Times Literary Supplement,* March 29, 1974, p. 331.
Melville, Robert, "Grandad's Choice," *New Statesman,* May 21, 1976, pp. 689-90.
Review of *Mog at the Zoo, School Librarian,* September, 1983, p. 235.
Powling, Chris, review of Cover to Cover audiocassettes, *Books for Keeps,* November, 1987, p. 10.
Review of *Quest for the Gloop: The Exploits of Murfy and PHIX, British Book News,* spring, 1981, p. 23.

■ For More Information See

PERIODICALS

Books for Keeps, January, 1986, p. 12.
British Book News, March, 1988, p. 7.
Growing Point, May, 1982, p. 3908.
Observer Review, April 19, 1987, p. 23.
Publishers Weekly, February 18, 1983, pp. 129-130.
Times Educational Supplement, March 15, 1985, p. 24.
Times Literary Supplement, November 3, 1972, p. 1334.*

NIMMO, Jenny 1942-

■ Personal

Born January 15, 1942 (some sources say 1944), in Windsor, Berkshire, England; married David Wynn Millward (an artist and illustrator), 1974; children: two daughters, one son. *Education:* Private boarding schools, 1950-60.

■ Addresses

Home—Henllan Mill, Llangynyw, Welshpool, Powys SY21 9EN, Wales. *Agent*—Murray Pollinger, 4 Garrick St., London WC2E 9BH, England.

■ Career

Theatre Southeast, Sussex and Kent, England, actress and assistant stage manager, 1960-63; governess in Amalfi, Italy, 1963; British Broadcasting Corp. Television, London, England, photographic researcher, 1964-66, assistant floor manager, 1966-68, 1971-74, director and writer of children's programs for "Jackanory," 1970; full-time writer, 1975—.

■ Awards, Honors

Smarties Prize in ages 7-11 category, Rowntree Mackintosh Co., 1986, and Tir Na n'Og Award, Welsh Arts Council, 1987, both for *The Snow Spider.*

■ Writings

FOR CHILDREN; FICTION

The Bronze Trumpeter, illustrated by Caroline Scrace, Angus & Robertson (London), 1975.
Tatty Apple, illustrated by Priscilla Lamont, Methuen (London), 1984.
The Snow Spider (first book in the "Snow Spider" trilogy), illustrated by Joanna Carey, Methuen, 1986, Dutton, 1987.
Emlyn's Moon (second book in the "Snow Spider" trilogy), illustrated by Carey, Methuen, 1987, published as *Orchard of the Crescent Moon,* Dutton, 1989.
The Red Secret, illustrated by Maureen Bradley, Hamish Hamilton, 1989.
The Chestnut Soldier (third book in the "Snow Spider" trilogy), Methuen, 1989.
The Bears Will Get You!, Methuen, 1990.
Jupiter Boots, Heinemann, 1990.
Ultramarine, Methuen, 1990.
Delilah and the Dogspell, Methuen, 1991.
Rainbow and Mr. Zed (sequel to *Ultramarine*), Methuen, 1992, Dutton, 1994.
(Reteller) *The Witches and the Singing Mice,* illustrated by Angela Barrett, Dial, 1993.
The Stone Mouse, illustrated by Helen Craig, Walker (London), 1993.
(Reteller) *The Starlight Cloak,* illustrated by Justin Todd, Dial, 1993.
Griffin's Castle, Methuen, 1994.

Wilfred's Wolf, illustrated by husband, David Wynn Millward, Bodley Head, 1994.
Granny Grimm's Gruesome Glasses, illustrated by Millward, A. & C. Black, 1995.
Ronnie and the Giant Millipede, illustrated by David Parkins, Walker, 1995.

■ Adaptations

The three books of the "Snow Spider" trilogy, *The Snow Spider, Emlyn's Moon,* and *The Chestnut Soldier,* have all been adapted as children's programs for British television. Several of Nimmo's works have been recorded.

■ Sidelights

Jenny Nimmo began to receive much notice as a children's author in the 1980s. Her first book, *The Bronze Trumpeter,* was published in 1975, and led *Times Literary Supplement* contributor Ann Thwaite to call her "a new writer of considerable imagination and skill." The responsibility of raising her three children kept her from publishing another book until 1984, and Nimmo related in *Twentieth-Century Children's Writers:* "I live and work in a rural community in Wales where my three bilingual children are growing into an old but vigorous culture. Here place names hark back to legend and it seems to me that the past is still part of the rhythm of everyday life. My books are concerned with the very real problem of growing children, and most of them are set in a landscape which is undeniably magical; they are described as fantasies." *School Librarian* contributor Donna White affirmed that "Wales has a powerful hold on [the] imagination" of this "relative newcomer to children's fantasy."

Crediting part of her vivid imagination to the influence of the Welsh countryside, Nimmo has received accolades for her faithful renditions of this history-filled landscape. To win the Tir Na n'Og Award, one must present a Welsh language book, or, for an English language book, depict an authentic Welsh setting while raising the standard of writing for children and young people. Nimmo's *The Snow Spider* earned this honor for doing just that. Ten-year-old Gwyn Griffiths, the protagonist of *The Snow Spider,* is having a tough time adjusting to his sister's death, his mother's inability to control her grieving, and his father's accusations that Gwyn is to blame for their loss. In an effort to help, Gwyn is given five strange birthday gifts from his mystic grandmother. He must use these oddities to look inside himself to find the magical powers that have long resided in his bloodline. Throughout the journey, Gwyn is taken aback when he sees his dead sister's ghostly image appear in a spider's sorcerous web. As any ten-year-old might, he disobeys his grandmother and reveals his secret while experimenting with powers greater than his ability to control. His newfound magic creates a dichotomy, for now he must choose either to join his sister in a different world, or to go back home. According to *Horn Book* critic Mary M. Burns, "Gwyn is a very real ten-year-old . . . conscious that he is different from his classmates, touchingly anxious to belong and to be loved." Zena Sutherland, writing for the *Bulletin of the Center for Children's Books,* found *The Snow Spider* a "cohesive and compelling" story that has "depth and nuance."

The mysterious alternate world of Gwyn's Welsh home returns in *Orchard of the Crescent Moon* (published in England as *Emlyn's Moon*); this time Gwyn's neighbor Nia is the person seeking a special talent, which she must then use to rescue her friend Emlyn. Like its predecessor, *Orchard of the Crescent Moon* demonstrates "the 'realness' of the child characters, despite their close access to ancient magical powers," David Bennett noted in *Books for Keeps.* A *Publishers Weekly* critic similarly observed that while the story has fantasy elements, it is "rooted in the miseries of family misunderstandings and sorrows." "*Emlyn's Moon* confirms all our hopes" about Nimmo's "unusual talents," Marcus Crouch asserted in *Junior Bookshelf.* "This is a rich, moving and amusing story, one which demands and receives the reader's total capitulation."

The trilogy concludes with *The Chestnut Soldier,* in which Gwyn is approaching his fourteenth birthday and still exercising his magical powers. This time his irresponsibility causes him to lose control of one of the powers he received on his tenth birthday. His carelessness endangers a weak-spirited, wounded soldier resting at a home in the village. Since the power can thwart Gwyn, he must call on his grandmother and uncle Gwydion to exorcise the evil force from the soldier's abducted spirit. *The Chestnut Soldier* contains many parallels to the ancient Welsh legends known as the Mabinogion, but was favored least by critic Beth E. Andersen. In *Voice of Youth Advocates,* the reviewer faulted the "relentlessly oppressive moodiness" of the characters and the "disappointingly anti-climactic finish." *School Library Journal* contributor Virginia Golodetz, however, applauded the book and stated that "Nimmo has skillfully woven the ancient story into the modern one, making it accessible to those who do not know the legend." White also praised the concluding volume, calling it "Nimmo's best book to date."

"As her major work grows in scale and complexity, Nimmo has turned to the creation of small, simpler worlds," Crouch observed in *Twentieth-Century Children's Writers. The Red Secret,* for instance, is a simple tale of Tom, a city boy whose family moves to the country, and how he rescues a wounded fox cub and makes friends in the process. *Growing Point*'s Margery Fisher praised the "concise, pictorial and energetic prose" of Nimmo's book, which she predicted would enliven the easy-to-read format for the reader. Similarly told with "quiet assurance and [Nimmo's] instinct for the right turn of phrase," according to Crouch in *Junior Bookshelf,* is *Jupiter Boots,* the story of young Timothy's encounter with a pair of fancy footwear. 1993's *The Stone Mouse* also demonstrates the author's "special kind of mastery in the little book," Crouch stated in another *Junior Bookshelf* review. The relationship between Ted, his sister Elly, and a talking stone mouse

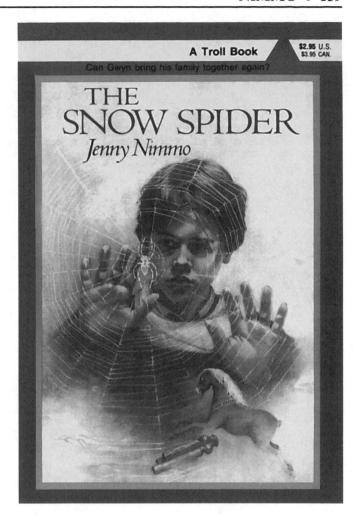

In this Tir Na n'Og Award-winning tale, lonely young Gwyn Griffiths is given five strange birthday gifts by his mystic grandmother.

makes for "a strangely engaging read" in which "the reader is invited to consider many themes," Sue Smedley concluded in *School Librarian.*

Nimmo has also turned her talents to more comic effect, as in two stories about a cat with magical powers. Readers are first introduced to the gifted feline in *Delilah and the Dogspell,* when Delilah begins to shrink all the dogs who annoy her down to mouse size. After one of the miniaturized dogs befriends a lonely girl and Delilah goes too far by shrinking the Prime Minister's favorite pet, peace and order are finally restored. "The book is a romp, splendidly done," David Churchill wrote in *School Librarian,* recommending the story for both reading aloud or alone, while Fisher noted that this "racy bit of nonsense [is] based on a sturdy recognition of the relationship of dogs and cats." The troublemaking witch-cat returns in *Delilah and the Dishwasher Dogs,* in which Delilah is kidnapped by an evil fortune teller and must be rescued by the neighborhood cats. "The story is well delivered, with interesting and stretching vocabulary," stated Janet Sims in *School Librarian,* making for a book that is "exciting, funny, and extremely readable."

In this suspenseful sequel to *Ultramarine*, Nell is sent to the island estate of the mysterious Mr. Zed, who seems to know all about her and her secret heritage. (Cover illustration by Forest Rogers.)

Nimmo returned to a supernatural setting for *Ultramarine*, in which she "again combines fantasy elements with the psychological growth of her protagonists to weave solid entertainment," according to a *Publishers Weekly* critic. Ned and Nell are uneasy when they are scheduled to spend a week alone with an aunt and grandmother they've never met; during their unsettling stay, they learn that their real mother actually drowned when they were young and that their father may have been a sea creature known as a kelpie. This discovery leads them to aid a mysterious stranger in rescuing sea creatures, creating a "tantalizing blend" of elements where the children's "realities are every bit as fascinating as their fantasies," Jody McCoy remarked in *Voice of Youth Advocates*. "The dream-like, secretive quality of the narrative mesmerizes the reader until the children's mystery is fully revealed," Kathryn Jennings wrote in *Bulletin of the Center for Children's Books* in recommending this "haunting story."

Rainbow and Mr. Zed continues the story of Nell, who is adjusting to life without Ned, who has joined their father at sea. Remaining with distant relatives, Nell—whose true name is Rainbow—has been sent to the estate of the mysterious Mr. Zed, who seems to know all about her secret heritage. Nell soon discovers that Mr. Zed is actually her late mother's evil brother, and he wants to use Nell to gain power and revenge against her father. "In a chilling and eerie story that weaves back and forth between fantasy and reality," as *Booklist* writer Kay Weisman described it, "Nell comes to terms with her uniqueness" and thwarts her uncle's sinister plans. *Rainbow and Mr. Zed* "is exciting, moving, and deeply committed to the preservation of the world," Crouch asserted in *Junior Bookshelf,* and concluded: "Great stuff this, with much fun to match the terrors, an exciting adventure worked out in terms of vividly realised characters, all confirmation—if such were needed—that here is an important writer at the height of her powers."

In an assessment of the author's career in *Twentieth-Century Children's Writers,* Marcus Crouch further lauded Nimmo, stating that she "is a living example of the basic formula for success in an author: write what you know. She works in big ideas on a small canvas, which she fills with the figures of her own rural community. Magic or no magic, hers is a real world, viewed with a keen and understanding eye and with rich appreciation of its fun and its folly."

■ Works Cited

Andersen, Beth E., review of *The Chestnut Soldier, Voice of Youth Advocates,* October, 1991, p. 248.

Bennett, David, review of *The Snow Spider* and *Emlyn's Moon, Books for Keeps,* March, 1989, p. 19.

Burns, Mary M., review of *The Snow Spider, Horn Book,* September-October, 1987, p. 613.

Churchill, David, review of *Delilah and the Dogspell, School Librarian,* February, 1992, p. 21.

Crouch, Marcus, review of *Emlyn's Moon, Junior Bookshelf,* February, 1988, p. 51.

Crouch, Marcus, review of *Jupiter Boots, Junior Bookshelf,* February, 1991, p. 26.

Crouch, Marcus, review of *Rainbow and Mr. Zed, Junior Bookshelf,* August, 1992, pp. 158-59.

Crouch, Marcus, review of *The Stone Mouse, Junior Bookshelf,* December, 1993, p. 235.

Crouch, Marcus, "Jenny Nimmo," *Twentieth-Century Children's Writers,* 4th edition, St. James Press, 1995, pp. 706-7.

Fisher, Margery, review of *The Red Secret, Growing Point,* May, 1989, p. 5172.

Fisher, Margery, review of *Delilah and the Dogspell, Growing Point,* November, 1991, p. 5602.

Golodetz, Virginia, review of *The Chestnut Soldier, School Library Journal,* July, 1991, p. 74.

Jennings, Kathryn, review of *Ultramarine, Bulletin of the Center for Children's Books,* July/August, 1992, p. 301.

McCoy, Jody, review of *Ultramarine, Voice of Youth Advocates,* June, 1992, p. 113.

Review of *Orchard of the Crescent Moon, Publishers Weekly,* June 9, 1989, p. 68.

Sims, Janet, review of *Delilah and the Dishwater Dogs, School Librarian,* May, 1994, p. 62.

Smedley, Sue, review of *The Stone Mouse, School Librarian,* November, 1993, p. 157.

Sutherland, Zena, review of *The Snow Spider, Bulletin of the Center for Children's Books,* July-August, 1987, p. 216.

Thwaite, Ann, "Time and Again," *Times Literary Supplement,* April 4, 1975, p. 362.

Review of *Ultramarine, Publishers Weekly,* March 9, 1992, p. 58.

Weisman, Kay, review of *Rainbow and Mr. Zed, Booklist,* February 15, 1995.

White, Donna, "Welsh Legends through English Eyes: An American Viewpoint," *School Librarian,* November, 1991, pp. 130-31.

■ **For More Information See**

PERIODICALS

Booklist, May 1, 1993, p. 1605; August, 1994, p. 2064.

Books for Keeps, September, 1986, p. 25.

Horn Book, September, 1993, p. 611.

Junior Bookshelf, February, 1985, p. 28; April, 1989, pp. 65-66; December, 1995, pp. 214-15.

Publishers Weekly, August 2, 1993, p. 81.

School Librarian, February, 1988, p. 21.

School Library Journal, November, 1992, p. 74; February, 1995.*

*   *   *

NYBERG, (Everett Wayne) Morgan 1944-

■ **Personal**

Born March 16, 1944, in Thunder Bay, Ontario, Canada; son of Carl Gunnar (a carpenter) and Frida Kristin (a homemaker; maiden name, Bolin) Nyberg; children: Lawrence, Meredith. *Education:* University of British Columbia, B.A., 1966, graduate study, 1976-77, teacher's certificate, 1978. *Religion:* "Member of the spiritual organization Subud."

■ **Addresses**

Home—2085 176th St., Surrey, British Columbia, Canada V3S 5J9.

■ **Career**

Writer and educator. Douglas College, New Westminster, British Columbia, Canada, instructor in creative writing, 1974-75; Vancouver Community College, Vancouver, British Columbia, instructor in English as a second language, 1982-84 and 1986-87; University of Aveiro, Aveiro, Portugal, instructor in English as a second language, 1988—. Substitute teacher at high schools in Vancouver, 1978-82; high school English teacher at American school in Quinto, Ecuador, 1984-86; private tutor in English, 1987—; instructor at University of British Columbia, summer 1988.

Young Galahad forms an unusual army of cockroaches, pigeons, and fleas to help him combat evil in this adventure for middle graders. (Cover illustration by VictoR GAD.)

■ **Awards, Honors**

Canada Council grants, 1975, 1977, 1978, 1980; second prize from Canadian Broadcasting Corporation literary competition, 1979, for "Mark, a Memoir"; Governor General's Award, 1987, for *Galahad Schwartz and the Cockroach Army.*

■ **Writings**

The Crazy Horse Suite (poems), Intermedia, 1979.

Galahad Schwartz and the Cockroach Army (young adult novel), Groundwood Books, 1987.

■ **Adaptations**

The Crazy Horse Suite was produced as a stageplay in New York City, 1977, as a radio drama by the Canadian Broadcasting Corporation, 1982, and as music theater by the Banff School of Fine Arts, with music by Stephen Chatman, 1985.

■ **Sidelights**

Morgan Nyberg grew up in Canada. After graduating from the University of British Columbia with a teaching degree, he went on to teach English as a second language in Canada, Portugal, and Ecuador. He published a book of poetry in 1979, then in 1987 published his next work—a novel for young adults. "At first glance one might wonder if *The Crazy Horse Suite* and *Galahad Schwartz and the Cockroach Army* were written by the same Morgan Nyberg," the author once commented. "*The Crazy Horse Suite* is a series of poems for four voices: Crazy Horse, Little Big Man, Black Buffalo Woman, and Custer. It examines the effects upon each of them of the Indian Wars of the 1870s. *Galahad Schwartz and the Cockroach Army* is a novel for nine- to twelve-year-olds, concerning the adventures of an eleven-year-old boy who is uprooted from his home in the South American jungle to live with his grandfather in a North American slum. But there are common threads between the two books: rich imagery, irony, and a concern with magic. In *The Crazy Horse Suite* they blend in an often surrealistic poetry; in *Galahad Schwartz and the Cockroach Army* they contribute to a whimsical novel of adventure."

In *Galahad Schwartz and the Cockroach Army,* young Galahad is sent to the fictional city of Glitterville, where Grandpa Schwartz and his two friends live in a rundown apartment building. Times are hard, and the old men must put on street performances and beg for handouts in order to make money. To make matters worse, Galahad soon learns that an evil exterminator named Creech has developed a spray that can make people disappear, and that he is using it to systematically rid the city of all its old people. Galahad forms an unusual army consisting of cockroaches, pigeons, and fleas to combat Creech and put an end to his plan. In a review for *Books for Young People,* Callie Israel called *Galahad Schwartz and the Cockroach Army* a "light-hearted fantasy-adventure" populated by "some of the most bizarre characters ever to be found in a children's book," adding that Nyberg's "easy-to-read style will entice reluctant readers."

Nyberg once commented, "I believe that, ideally, a human being is a creature with one foot in this world and the other in eternity. This can lead to both magic and pratfalls. Yet my themes do not illustrate this transcendental outlook as much as my voice does, determined as I am to imbue my writing with a personal, yet elusive, energy."

■ Works Cited

Israel, Callie, review of *Galahad Schwartz and the Cockroach Army, Books for Young People,* February 1988, p. 7.*

O-P

PAT O'SHEA

O'SHEA, (Catherine) Pat(ricia Shiels) 1931-

■ Personal

Born January 22, 1931, in Galway, Ireland; daughter of Patrick Joseph (a carpenter) and Bridget Cloonan (a homemaker) Shiels; married John Joseph O'Shea (a chemist), September 12, 1953 (separated, 1960); children: James. *Education:* Attended Presentation Con-

vent, Galway, Ireland, and Convent of Mercy, Galway, Ireland.

■ Addresses

Home—19 Chandos Rd., Chorlton-cum-Hardy, Manchester M21 1SS, England.

■ Career

Writer. Worked variously as a bookstore assistant, doctor's receptionist, and wages clerk. *Member:* Society of Authors.

■ Awards, Honors

British Arts Council Drama bursary, 1967; *The Hounds of the Morrigan* was cited on the *Horn Book* magazine honor list, 1987.

■ Writings

The Hounds of the Morrigan, Oxford University Press, 1985, Holiday House, 1986.
Finn MacCool and the Small Men of Deeds (retelling), illustrated by Stephen Lavis, Holiday House, 1987.

Also author of a drama entitled *The King's Ears* for BBC's Northern Ireland Radio Schools Programme. *The Hounds of the Morrigan* has been translated into Danish, French, German, Italian, and Spanish.

■ Work in Progress

The Wizard of the Wheels, a sequel to *The Hounds of the Morrigan.*

■ Sidelights

A teller and reteller of Irish and Celtic tales, Pat O'Shea is considered a master of rich, humorous language interwoven with magic and mystery. O'Shea worked on her first book, *The Hounds of the Morrigan,* a fantasy/comedy saga about two children who save the world

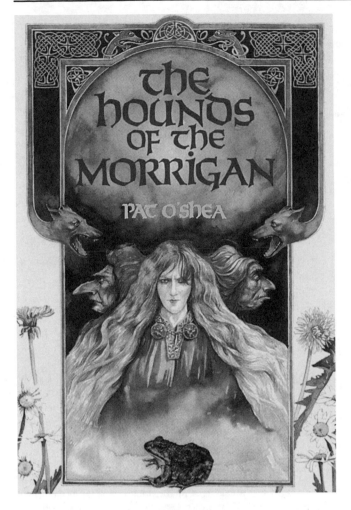

Young brother and sister Pidge and Brigit are chosen to thwart the evil designs of the Morrigan, Irish goddess of war, in this acclaimed comic fantasy. (Cover illustration by Stephen Lavis.)

from destruction, for parts of ten years. Assessing the book in *Twentieth Century Children's Writers,* Pat Donlon declared that "it is rare that an author emerges with a first novel with such style and assurance."

The Hounds of the Morrigan tells the story of a young brother and sister who must search for a stone containing a drop of blood from the evil Morrigan, the Irish goddess of war, who seeks to destroy the Earth. The hounds of the title are the slave dogs Morrigan has at her command. The idea for the story, O'Shea explained, came from a dream she had when her son was six years old: "A fearful giant was terrorising a whole country and nothing could stop him, because he couldn't be killed."

Although the book is over 450 pages long, O'Shea recaps important events in the children's adventures and divides the book into self-contained episodes so readers do not get lost. Several critics deemed the work a classic in children's literature. Among these was Emma Letley, who wrote in the *Times Literary Supplement* that the volume "should take its place alongside such established nineteenth-century works as George MacDonald's fairy-tales."

The Hounds of the Morrigan was the result of the author's life-long exposure to Ireland and its lore, she explained to *Twentieth Century Children's Writers.* "As a backdrop I drew on my knowledge of the countryside and folk customs that I absorbed as a child during summer holidays at Cregmore and Kilbannon in County Galway. I grew up knowing a good deal of the mythology from fireside stories and my school primers. Further mythological background material I garnered from books collected over the years and from the reference section in Manchester Central Library."

In O'Shea's comic retelling of the tall tale of *Finn MacCool and the Small Men of Deeds,* Finn is called upon by a giant to stop a series of kidnappings and retrieve the missing children from an evil witch. Initially immobilized by a headache, MacCool is aided by an outrageous octet of tiny, bumbling men, each with a special magical power. O'Shea's version "is both funny and spirited while still in keeping with the folkloric quality of the tale," wrote Kay McPherson in the *School Library Journal.* A *Bulletin of the Center for Children's Books* contributor commented that the work "takes a bit too long to get started but moves well once it's under way." And *Publishers Weekly* reported that "Finn will suit fans of folklore quite nicely."

O'Shea commented: "I have always written, rejecting chances of further education in favour of self-teaching. The masters are already there on bookshelves—we can learn by reading good writers and valuing excellence and by teaching ourselves to be self-critical."

■ Works Cited

Donlon, Pat, *Twentieth Century Children's Writers,* St. James Press, 1989, p. 725.

Review of *Finn MacCool and the Small Men of Deeds, Bulletin of the Center for Children's Books,* November, 1987.

Review of *Finn MacCool and the Small Men of Deeds, Publishers Weekly,* September 25, 1987, p. 110.

Letley, Emma, "Three Drops of Blood," *Times Literary Supplement,* November 29, 1985, p. 1358.

McPherson, Kay, review of *Finn MacCool and the Small Men of Deeds, School Library Journal,* November, 1987, p. 111.

■ For More Information See

BOOKS

Children's Literature Review, Volume 18, Gale, 1989, pp. 167-170.

PERIODICALS

Booklist, April 1, 1986, pp. 1144-45.
Books for Your Children, spring, 1986, p. 22.
Horn Book, July-August, 1986, p. 451; March-April, 1988, pp. 219-20.
Junior Bookshelf, February, 1986, pp. 44-6.
Language Arts, April, 1988.
Times Literary Supplement, March 11-17, 1988, p. 289.*

Finn, the tallest, wisest, and bravest man in Ireland, helps stop a series of kidnappings with the help of an octet of magical midgets in O'Shea's comic retelling of a popular folktale. (Illustration by Stephen Lavis from *Finn MacCool and the Small Men of Deeds.*)

PAINE, Penelope Colville 1946-

■ Personal

Born October 23, 1946, in London, England; daughter of Donald (an accountant) and Joan (a legal cashier) Wallington; married John H. Paine (a social worker), 1974; children: Dan, John, Diane, Oliver, Miles. *Education:* University of London, B.A. in fine arts.

■ Addresses

Home and office—817 Vincente Way, Santa Barbara, CA 93105.

■ Career

Has worked as a vocational gender equity contract consultant, a community-based organization executive director, a national trainer for vocational, career, and life training programs, and a classroom teacher, under contract with organizations including the California Department of Education Office of Gender Equity, the California Community Colleges Chancellor's Office, the Girls Incorporated Region 1 Service Center, and Business and Professional Women USA, 1975—. Women Helping Girls with Choices, national co-coordinator and publisher of newsletter, 1989—; Focus on Equity, conference coordinator and publisher of newsletter, 1991; "Children's Book Insider" newsletter, contribut-

ing editor; presenter of papers at national conferences; certified trainer in teen career programs. *Member:* Chapel Court Housing (member of board), Women's Economic Ventures (member of board).

■ Awards, Honors

Benjamin Franklin Award for Best Children's Picture Book, 1989, for *My Way Sally;* Eleanor Roosevelt Research and Development Award, American Association of University Women, 1991.

■ Writings

PICTURE BOOKS

(With Mindy Bingham) *My Way Sally,* illustrated by Itoko Maeno, Advocacy Press, 1989.
Time for Horatio, illustrated by Maeno, Advocacy Press, 1990.
(Editor with Sandra Stryker and translator) Agnes Rosentheil, *Mimi Makes a Splash,* Advocacy Press, 1991.
(Editor with Stryker and translator) Rosentheil, *Mimi Takes Charge,* Advocacy Press, 1991.
Molly's Magic, illustrated by Maeno, MarshMedia, 1995.

FOR ADULTS

(Editor with Stryker and Barbara Greene) Mindy Bingham, *More Choices: A Strategic Planning Guide for*

PENELOPE COLVILLE PAINE

Mixing Career and Family, illustrated by Maeno, Advocacy Press, 1993.

OTHER

Also author/creator of the picture books *Flossie Flies Home, Clarissa,* and *Papa Piccolo,* and of the adult nonfiction work *Ensuring a Place for Girls and Women in School-to-Work and Tech Prep.* Contributing Editor of the adult nonfiction works *Choices and Challenges Instructor's Guide, Mother Daughter Choices,* and *Things Will Be Different for My Daughter.* Editor and art director of *Mother Nature Nursery Rhymes.*

■ **Work in Progress**

A special project called *In the Beginning: Early Childhood Traditions from Around the World,* 1997.

■ **Sidelights**

Penelope Colville Paine told *SATA:* "I began my writing career when my good friend, author/publisher Mindy Bingham, was looking for a manuscript for the children's self-esteem series launched with her title *Minou.* Inspired by the format, I pulled ideas from my own childhood spent in England. It has become a wonderful pastime and I tell everyone I am an accidental author.

"I work through an idea visually to start with and then I tell the story to a few friends. I pin up pictures as inspiration and I do research on names, places, animal behaviors, etc. The hardest part is not to compromise one concept to illustrate another and not to use negative messages. I have fun with the stories and there is a little

of my family in all of them—my dog, my father's feet, one of my mother's sayings, my children, and my husband, who models for the illustrations. The books would be nothing without the beautiful illustrations of Itoko Maeno and we work very well as a team.

"Now, I have a special project in the early stages which I hope will bring together my extensive work with gender equity, my desire for the world to have improved cultural awareness and sharing, and my fine art qualifications."

■ **For More Information See**

PERIODICALS

School Library Journal, October 1990, p. 98.

*   *   *

PERNU, Dennis 1970-
 (James Koons)

■ **Personal**

Born January 10, 1970; son of Dennis Sr. (a welder) and Sharon (a mother and homemaker; maiden name, Drajna) Pernu; married Emily Lankton (a photographer), September 16, 1995. *Education:* Hamline University, B.A. in English, 1992; attended Mesabi Community College, one year.

■ **Addresses**

Home—3225 Aldrich Ave. S. #2, Minneapolis, MN 55408.

■ **Career**

Children's book writer, bookseller, editor. Borders, Inc., Minnetonka, MN, bookseller, 1992-95; Callan Publishing, Minneapolis, MN, editor, 1995—. Graywolf Press, St. Paul, MN, editorial intern, 1992, New Rivers Press, Minneapolis, editorial intern, 1994.

■ **Writings**

(Under name James Koons) *Army Rangers,* Capstone Press, 1995.
Hot Rods, Capstone Press, 1995.
Monster Trucks, Capstone Press, 1996.
Pick-Up Trucks, Capstone Press, 1996.

■ **Sidelights**

Dennis Pernu told *SATA:* "My objective in creating books for young readers is not to instill any lofty ideals or 'correct' morals, but rather to simply encourage the act of reading. Capstone Press allows me to do this through their agenda of publishing informative books for young readers on a variety of topics likely to be embraced by that audience.

DENNIS PERNU

"Many times, young people are not encouraged to read by their parents, peers, and yes, their teachers. My own objective in writing can be traced to miserable experiences with a long procession of English teachers with grammar-ridden lesson plans and frequent 'there-is-only-one-correct-reading-of-this' forays into literature. If not for my mother's weekly excursions with me to the library (a habit she thankfully continues with my younger brothers) and the encouragement of one truly inspiring pre-college English instructor (thank you, Mrs. Schley), I may not have followed the path I did.

"Adults sometimes fail to realize that kids are free-thinking individuals. Encourage them to read on their own, and don't mire them down with didactic reading lists and lectures on authorial intent. Let them find an escape in books. This is not to suggest that teachers shouldn't assign texts, but let your students discover some of their own interests."

*   *   *

POLESE, James 1914-

■ Personal

Born September 23, 1914, in Richmond, CA; son of Luigi Natale and Florinda (Caporin) Polese; married Esther M. Holman (a social worker and teacher), February 23, 1941; children: Richard L. Polese, Lia Suzan Cook, Carolyn Polese Lehman, Katherine Louise Galvin. *Education:* Attended Mare Island Apprentice School, journeyman machinist; University of California, vocational teaching credentials; Coast Guard officer training, junior engineer license. *Politics:* Moderate. *Religion:* Christian. *Hobbies and other interests:* Story writing, sailing.

■ Addresses

Home—P.O. Box 130, Inverness, CA 94937. *Agent*—Ocean Tree Books, P.O. Box 1295, Santa Fe, NM 87504.

■ Career

Retired engineer and teacher. Mare Island Navy Shipyard, 1935-41; Ventura Junior College, teacher, 1941-45; U.S. Maritime Service, engineer, 1945; University of California, senior mechanic, 1946-51; Eitel McCollough, project engineer, 1951-55; Varian Associates, project engineer, 1955-60; General Electric, project engineer, 1961-77.

General volunteer work for parks, such as bridge building and trailwork. *Member:* Inverness Yacht Club.

■ Awards, Honors

More than ten U.S. patents awarded related to high-power electron tubes.

JAMES POLESE

Writings

Tales from the Iron Triangle: Boyhood Days in the San Francisco Bay Area of the 1920's, illustrated by Elizabeth Morales, Ocean Tree Books, 1995.

Also published profiles of fellow employees in the company magazine at Varian Associates, circa 1977.

Sidelights

James Polese told *SATA:* "Before the radio was in common use, my father entertained his friends and us children by telling stories. I, in turn, carried on the tradition by telling stories to my children.

"When one of my daughters became a professional story writer she encouraged me to write about my childhood days in story form. These stories lay dormant for several years until one of my granddaughters, Tamsin, asked me what it was like in my early years. Her father upon reading them thought they repesented an important part of our American history and that they should be published. The result was *Tales from the Iron Triangle.*"

* * *

PRATT, Kristin Joy 1976-

Personal

Born March 21, 1976, at Clark Air Base, the Philippines; daughter of Ken (an airline and Air National Guard pilot) and Kathy (a homemaker; maiden name, Groener) Pratt. *Education:* Attended Principia College, Elsah, IL, beginning 1994. *Religion:* Christian Scientist.

Addresses

Home—c/o Principia College, Elsah, IL 62028. *Agent*—Kathy Pratt, 901 Parkview Valley Dr., Manchester, MO 63011.

Career

Freelance illustrator/author, Dawn Publications, Nevada City, CA, 1991—.

Writings

SELF-ILLUSTRATED PICTURE BOOKS

A Walk in the Rainforest, Dawn Publications, 1992.
A Swim through the Sea, Dawn Publications, 1994.
A Fly in the Sky, Dawn Publications, 1996.

Sidelights

Kristin Joy Pratt wrote and illustrated *A Walk in the Rainforest,* an illustrated, ecological alphabet book for children, during her freshman and sophomore years in a Saint Louis, Missouri, high school. Published in 1992, *A Walk in the Rainforest* connects each letter of the alphabet with a creature from the rainforest, and

KRISTIN JOY PRATT

includes a brief description of the plant or animal as well. Placed throughout are information about endangered species and other environmental concerns. Reviewing *A Walk in the Rainforest* for *School Library Journal,* Eva Elisabeth Von Ancken noted that "Pratt presents her viewpoint without didacticism," and praised the illustrations as showing "talent and concern."

Two years after publishing her first book, during her senior year in high school, Pratt completed *A Swim through the Sea,* at the same time earning good enough grades to be named to her high school's honor society. In a similar fashion to Pratt's first book, *A Swim through the Sea* uses the alphabet to introduce readers to a variety of ocean plants, animals, and fish, emphasizing the importance of the sea to earth's environment. In the *Horn Book Guide,* reviewer Kelly A. Ault found Pratt's text "knowledgeable" and her artwork "quite apt." While *School Library Journal* contributor Frances E. Millhouser hailed the "dramatic point of view" of the artwork, explaining that "all of the flowing, fluid pictures are full of action and detail," she faulted the vocabulary as too complex for young children. Frank M. Truesdale, on the other hand, admired Pratt's "clever alliteration" and inclusion of helpful facts. He concluded in *Science Books and Films* that "children will love this book, the more so when parents and teachers emphasize that it was written by a young person who wants them to know that they too can make a difference."

Pratt told *SATA:* "Environmental education at an early age is the key to preserving our natural world for the generations of all species to come. This is why I began writing children's books, and I hope to continue this profession long into the future."

■ **Works Cited**

Ault, Kelly A., review of *A Swim through the Sea, Horn Book Guide,* January-June, 1994, p. 356.

Millhouser, Frances E., review of *A Swim through the Sea, School Library Journal,* August, 1994, p. 151.

Truesdale, Frank M., review of *A Swim through the Sea, Science Books and Films,* November, 1994, p. 240.

Von Ancken, Eva Elisabeth, review of *A Walk in the Rainforest, School Library Journal,* July, 1992, p. 70.

■ **For More Information See**

PERIODICALS

Bloomsbury Review, September, 1992, p. 21.

R

RALSTON, Jan
See DUNLOP, Agnes M(ary) R(obertson)

* * *

RAYNER, Mary 1933-

■ Personal

Born December 30, 1933, in Mandalay, Burma; daughter of A. H. and Yoma Grigson; married E. H. Rayner, 1960 (divorced, 1982); married Adrian Hawksley, 1985; children: Sarah, William, Benjamin. *Education:* University of St. Andrews, M.A. (with second class honors), 1956.

■ Addresses

Home—Wiltshire, England. *Office*—c/o Macmillan Children's Books, 25 Eccleston Place, London SW1W 9NF, England. *Agent*—Laura Cecil, 17 Alwyne Villas, London N1 2HG, England.

■ Career

Freelance writer and book illustrator. Former production assistant at Hammond, Hammond Ltd. (publisher), London, England; Longmans, Green & Co. Ltd. (publisher), London, copywriter, 1959-62. *Member:* Society of Authors.

■ Awards, Honors

Horn Book Honor List citations, 1977, for *Mr. and Mrs. Pig's Evening Out,* 1978, for *Garth Pig and the Ice Cream Lady,* and 1986, for *Babe: The Gallant Pig;* Parents' Choice Award, 1987, for *Mrs. Pig Gets Cross and Other Stories.*

■ Writings

FOR CHILDREN; SELF-ILLUSTRATED

The Witch-Finder, Macmillan, 1975, Morrow, 1976.

MARY RAYNER

Mr. and Mrs. Pig's Evening Out, Atheneum, 1976.
Garth Pig and the Ice Cream Lady, Atheneum, 1977.
The Rain Cloud, Atheneum, 1980.
Mrs. Pig's Bulk Buy, Atheneum, 1981.
Crocodarling, Collins, 1985, Bradbury Press, 1986.
Mrs. Pig Gets Cross and Other Stories, Collins, 1986, Dutton, 1987.
Reilly, Gollancz, 1987.
Oh Paul!, Heinemann, 1988, Barron, 1989.
Bathtime for Garth Pig, Picture Lions, 1989.
Marathon and Steve, Dutton, 1989.

Rug, Collins/Forest House, 1989.
Garth Pig Steals the Show, Dutton, 1993.
One by One: Garth Pig's Rain Song, Dutton, 1994.
Ten Pink Piglets: Garth Pig's Wall Song, Dutton, 1994.

FOR CHILDREN

Open Wide, illustrated by Kate Simpson, Longman, 1990.
The Echoing Green, illustrated by Michael Foreman, Viking, 1992.

Contributor to anthologies, including *Allsorts Six,* edited by Ann Thwaite, Methuen, 1974; *Allsorts Seven,* edited by Thwaite, Methuen, 1975; *Young Winters' Tales Seven,* edited by M. R. Hodgkin, Macmillan, 1976; *Hidden Turnings,* edited by Diana Wynne-Jones, Methuen, 1989; *Stories for the Very Young,* edited by Sally Grindley, Kingfisher, 1989; *Animal Stories for the Very Young,* edited by Grindley, Kingfisher, 1994; and *Best Stories for Six Year Olds,* Hodder, 1995. Contributor of stories to *Cricket.*

ILLUSTRATOR

Daphne Ghose, *Harry,* Lutterworth, 1973.
Stella Nowell, *The White Rabbit,* Lutterworth, 1975.
Griselda Gifford, *Because of Blunder,* Gollancz, 1977.
Gifford, *Cass the Brave,* Gollancz, 1978.
Partap Sharma, *Dog Detective Ranjha,* Macmillan, 1978.
Dick King-Smith, *Daggie Dogfoot,* 1980, published in the U.S. as *Pigs Might Fly,* Viking, 1982.
King-Smith, *Magnus Powermouse,* Gollancz, 1982, Harper, 1984.
King-Smith, *The Sheep-Pig,* 1983, published in the U.S. as *Babe: The Gallant Pig,* Crown, 1985.

Also illustrator of *Silver's Day,* 1980, and *Revenge of the Wildcat,* both by Gifford; *The Boggart,* by Emma Tennant, 1980; *The Dead Letter Box,* by Jan Mark, 1982; *Mr. Weller's Long March,* by Anthea Colbert, 1983; *Lost and Found,* by Jill Paton Walsh, 1984; and *Thank You for the Tadpole,* by Pat Thomson, 1987.

■ Sidelights

A large family of pigs, which includes Mr. and Mrs. Pig and ten lively little piglets, is brought to life in several picture books by author and illustrator Mary Rayner. Often finding themselves in life-threatening situations involving a wolf, the ten youngsters manage to wriggle their way out of trouble in such stories as *Mr. and Mrs. Pig's Evening Out, Garth Pig and the Ice Cream Lady,* and *Garth Pig Steals the Show.* "There are numerous outstanding children's books featuring pigs," maintains Karen Jameyson in *Horn Book,* "but when it comes to stories about families of them, Mary Rayner has practically cornered the market."

The beginnings of the Pig family can be traced back to Rayner's own children. She once told *SATA:* "The pig stories began as stories invented for my children and, although they have now grown beyond picture books, their comments and criticisms are a great help to me

still." The first Pig book was published in 1976. *Mr. and Mrs. Pig's Evening Out* begins with Mother and Father Pig announcing that they are going out and that a baby sitter is coming to watch the ten piglets. When this baby sitter arrives, Mr. and Mrs. Pig fail to realize that she is really a wolf in disguise. As the evening wears on, the wolf gets hungry and attempts to eat Garth Pig for a snack, but his nine brothers and sisters quickly formulate a plan and come to his rescue.

"How lucky children are now!," exclaims Liz Waterland in her *Books for Keeps* review of *Mr. and Mrs. Pig's Evening Out.* "Who could fail to want to read when there are books like this about?" A *Bulletin of the Center for Children's Books* reviewer also praises Rayner's story, pointing out that it "has a felicitous blend of familiar situation, drastic crisis, and resourceful solution by a team of children." *Garth Pig and the Ice Cream Lady* features a similar plot: Young Garth is sent by his brothers and sisters to get treats from the ice cream truck, which turns out to be driven by a wolf who kidnaps him. When Garth's return seems to be taking too long, his siblings once again come to his rescue just in the nick of time. Writing in *Books for Keeps,* Moira Small concludes that *Garth Pig and the Ice Cream Lady* "is a lovely romp with plenty of pace and adventure."

Mrs. Pig's Bulk Buy, published in 1981, provides a more domestic view of the Pig family. The endless activity of the piglets is portrayed as is their habit of pouring ketchup on all their food. Leaving her children with Mr. Pig, Mrs. Pig goes shopping and buys six large jars of ketchup. She then serves the piglets nothing but ketchup for days until they are begging for real food and have learned their lesson. While missing the wolf character

In Rayner's self-illustrated *Mr. and Mrs. Pig's Evening Out,* ten piglets prove their ingenuity when the babysitter "from the agency" turns out to be a sneaky wolf.

from the earlier stories, a *Horn Book* contributor does maintain that "one would not like to miss Mr. Pig reading *The New Porker* or the piglets grumpily stamping upstairs after a supper of ketchup." *Mrs. Pig's Bulk Buy* is a "zesty story that almost surely will be another of Rayner's big successes," asserts a *Publishers Weekly* reviewer.

Seven different stories about the Pig family can be found in Rayner's *Mrs. Pig Gets Cross and Other Stories.* During the course of these tales, the piglets manage to lock themselves in the bathroom, fight over the chores they are assigned, leave a messy trail throughout the house, disrupt their parents' sleep, and cause more damage than good while "helping" with household projects. "These are very much family read-aloud stories, true to the humorous experiences of everyday life and embellished with imaginative flourishes of phrase and watercolor illustration," comments a *Bulletin of the Center for Children's Books* reviewer. *New York Times Book Review* contributor Merri Rosenberg similarly contends: "Once again Mrs. Rayner amusingly, and honestly, deals with the ordinary experiences of family life in a manner that is entertaining to the small fry—and blessedly comforting to the parent." Rosenberg goes on to add: "*Mrs. Pig Gets Cross* is one of those rare finds that are as much fun for a parent to read as they are for a child to hear."

The return of the wolf can be found in Rayner's 1993 Pig story, *Garth Pig Steals the Show.* Having formed a band, the Pig family needs a larger animal to play the sousaphone; but none of them recognize their new band member as a wolf until the day of their first performance. Noticing that Garth has abandoned his piccolo, little William sees his brother's legs sticking out of the sousaphone and is able to save him by getting the wolf to blow into his instrument. Garth goes flying out of the horn into center stage and the show is a success. *Garth Pig Steals the Show* is "told with Rayner's usual brisk good humor and nicely illustrated with deftly drawn, lively, and cheerfully resourceful pigs," according to a *Kirkus Reviews* contributor. And Marianne Saccardi concludes in *School Library Journal:* "This performance definitely deserves an encore!"

In addition to her popular Pig books, Rayner has written and illustrated several other stories, including *The Rain Cloud, Reilly,* and *Marathon and Steve. The Rain Cloud* follows the cloud of the title as it moves across the sky on a nice summer day, holding in its rain so it does not ruin anyone's day. The rain is finally released where it is needed and wanted—over a farmer's crops. During its travels, the cloud passes over the beach, a picnic in the country, and villagers doing their wash, all of which are depicted in Rayner's watercolors. Paul Heins, writing in *Horn Book,* relates that *The Rain Cloud* is "a quiet picture book extolling a fanciful interplay between man and nature."

A precocious cat who has already lost eight of his nine lives is the title character of *Reilly.* Almost drowning as a kitten, Reilly is now leading the life of a stray cat, until

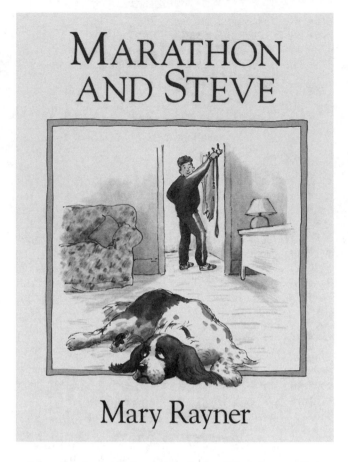

Marathon's owner loves to run, but Marathon prefers lying by a cozy fire watching television in Rayner's self-illustrated tale of comic reversal.

he manages to find a home with Betty and Joyce Braithwaite and wins over the affection of most of their neighbors, much to the dismay of the other cats on the street. "This hilarious and touching story shows an intimate and unsentimental knowledge of cats and their humans," observes Julie Blaisdale in *British Book News.* Richard Brown, writing in the *School Librarian,* also praises Rayner's insights into cats, concluding: "This book deserves to be loved not just by cat-lovers, but by any child who enjoys a good read."

More animal and human interaction is presented in *Marathon and Steve,* the tale of Steve the jogger and his dog Marathon, who does not like to exert himself. In fact, Marathon dreads being forced to run alongside his master through car exhaust fumes on the hard cement. And so it is a relief when Steve strains a tendon and changes his sport of choice to swimming, leaving Marathon at home with the television. "Gentle fun is poked at the trendy human tendency to exhaust one's self exercising while the sensible dog knows how to combine enjoyable activity with leisure," notes *School Library Journal* reviewer Patricia Pearl. "With her delightful, fresh humor," writes Jameyson in *Horn Book,* "Rayner is sure to collect herself a new crowd of fans."

■ Works Cited

Blaisdale, Julie, review of *Reilly, British Book News,* June, 1987, p. 30.

Brown, Richard, review of *Reilly, School Librarian,* August, 1987, pp. 234, 237.

Review of *Garth Pig Steals the Show, Kirkus Reviews,* May 15, 1993.

Heins, Paul, review of *The Rain Cloud, Horn Book,* October, 1980, pp. 514-15.

Jameyson, Karen, review of *Mrs. Pig Gets Cross and Other Stories, Horn Book,* May/June, 1987, pp. 338-39.

Jameyson, Karen, review of *Marathon and Steve, Horn Book,* March/April, 1989, p. 203.

Review of *Mr. and Mrs. Pig's Evening Out, Bulletin of the Center for Children's Books,* January, 1977.

Review of *Mrs. Pig Gets Cross and Other Stories, Bulletin of the Center for Children's Books,* April, 1987.

Review of *Mrs. Pig's Bulk Buy, Horn Book,* February, 1982.

Review of *Mrs. Pig's Bulk Buy, Publishers Weekly,* November 6, 1981, p. 79.

Pearl, Patricia, review of *Marathon and Steve, School Library Journal,* April, 1989, p. 90.

Rosenberg, Merri, "All Pigged Out," *New York Times Book Review,* May 17, 1987.

Saccardi, Marianne, review of *Garth Pig Steals the Show, School Library Journal,* May, 1993.

Small, Moira, review of *Garth Pig and the Ice Cream Lady, Books for Keeps,* January, 1989, p. 18.

Waterland, Liz, review of *Mr. and Mrs. Pig's Evening Out, Books for Keeps,* September, 1988, p. 9.

■ For More Information See

BOOKS

Twentieth-Century Children's Writers, 4th edition, St. James Press, 1995.

PERIODICALS

Bulletin of the Center for Children's Books, May, 1981, p. 179; June, 1986; March, 1989, p. 179.

Growing Point, May, 1989, p. 5172.

Horn Book, February, 1978; October, 1987, pp. 240-41.

Junior Bookshelf, October, 1991, p. 217; February, 1993, p. 34.

Kirkus Reviews, August 15, 1976, p. 906.

School Librarian, November, 1988, p. 135; May, 1993, p. 63.

School Library Journal, December, 1976, p. 68; November, 1980, p. 66; September, 1981, p. 114; March, 1985, p. 137; May, 1986, p. 84; August, 1994, p. 144.

*   *   *

REEVES, James
See REEVES, John Morris

REEVES, John Morris 1909-1978
(James Reeves)

■ Personal

Born July 1, 1909, in London, England; died May 1, 1978; son of Albert John and Ethel Mary (Blench) Reeves; married Mary Phillips, 1936 (died, 1966); children: Stella, Juliet Mary, Gareth Edward. *Education:* Cambridge University, M.A. (honours), 1931.

■ Career

Writer and editor. Teacher in state schools and teacher training college, 1933-52; William Heinemann Ltd., London, England, general editor of "Poetry Bookshelf" series, 1951-78; Unicorn Books, London, general editor, 1960-78. *Member:* Royal Society of Literature (fellow).

■ Writings

FICTION; FOR CHILDREN; UNDER NAME JAMES REEVES

Pigeons and Princesses, illustrated by Edward Ardizzone, Heinemann, 1956.

Mulbridge Manor, illustrated by Geraldine Spence, Heinemann, 1958, Penguin, 1963.

Titus in Trouble, illustrated by Ardizzone, Bodley Head, 1959, Walck, 1960.

Sailor Rumbelow and Britannia, illustrated by Ardizzone, Heinemann, 1962.

Sailor Rumbelow and Other Stories (includes *Pigeons and Princesses* and *Sailor Rumbelow and Britannia*), illustrated by Ardizzone, Dutton, 1962.

The Strange Light, illustrated by Lynton Lamb, Heinemann, 1964, Rand McNally, 1966.

The Story of Jackie Thimble, Dutton, 1964.

The Pillar-Box Thieves, illustrated by Dick Hart, Nelson, 1965.

Rhyming Will, illustrated by Ardizzone, Hamish Hamilton, 1967, McGraw Hill, 1968.

Mr. Horrox and the Gratch, illustrated by Quentin Blake, Abelard Schuman, 1969, Wellington, 1991.

The Path of Gold, illustrated by Krystyna Turska, Hamish Hamilton, 1972.

The Lion That Flew, illustrated by Ardizzone, Chatto & Windus, 1974.

The Clever Mouse, illustrated by Barbara Swiderska, Chatto & Windus, 1976.

Eggtime Stories, illustrated by Colin McNaughton, Blackie, 1978.

The James Reeves Storybook, illustrated by Ardizzone, Heinemann, 1978, published as *The Gnome Factory and Other Stories,* Penguin, 1986.

A Prince in Danger, illustrated by Gareth Floyd, Kaye & Ward, 1979.

RETELLINGS; FOR CHILDREN; UNDER NAME JAMES REEVES

English Fables and Fairy Stories, Retold, illustrated by Joan Kiddell-Monroe, Oxford University Press, 1954, Walck, 1960.

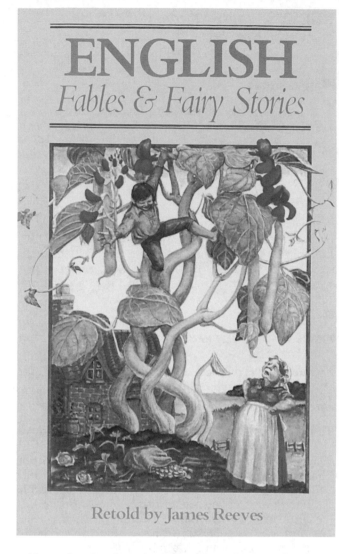

ENGLISH
Fables & Fairy Stories

Retold by James Reeves

Reeves's collection of retellings of popular and lesser-known English tales includes "Tom Thumb," "Jack and the Beanstalk," and "Tattercoats." (Cover illustration by Joan Kiddell-Monroe.)

Jules Verne, *Twenty Thousand Leagues under the Sea,* Chatto & Windus, 1956.

Miguel de Cervantes, *Exploits of Don Quixote, Retold,* illustrated by Ardizzone, Blackie, 1959, Walck, 1960.

Aesop, *Fables from Aesop, Retold,* illustrated by Maurice Wilson, Blackie, 1961, Walck, 1962.

Three Tall Tales, Chosen from Traditional Sources, illustrated by Ardizzone, Abelard Schuman, 1964.

The Road to a Kingdom: Stories from the Old and New Testaments, illustrated by Richard Kennedy, Heinemann, 1965.

The Secret Shoemakers and Other Stories, illustrated by Ardizzone, Abelard Schuman, 1966.

The Cold Flame, Based on a Tale from the Collection of the Brothers Grimm, illustrated by Charles Keeping, Hamish Hamilton, 1967, Meredith Press, 1969.

The Trojan Horse, illustrated by Turska, Hamish Hamilton, 1968, Watts, 1969.

Heroes and Monsters: Legends of Ancient Greece Retold, illustrated by Sarah Nechamkin, Volume 1: *Gods*

and Voyagers, Blackie, 1969, Two Continents, 1978, Volume 2: *Islands and Palaces,* Blackie, 1971, published as *Giants and Warriors,* Blackie, 1977, Two Continents, 1978.

The Angel and the Donkey, illustrated by Ardizzone, Hamish Hamilton, 1969, McGraw Hill, 1970.

Maildun the Voyager, illustrated by John Lawrence, Hamish Hamilton, 1971, Walck, 1972.

How the Moon Began, illustrated by Ardizzone, Abelard Schuman, 1971.

The Forbidden Forest and Other Stories, illustrated by Raymond Briggs, Heinemann, 1973.

The Voyage of Odysseus: Homer's Odyssey Retold, Blackie, 1973.

Two Greedy Bears (a Persian folktale), illustrated by Floyd, Hamish Hamilton, 1974.

Quest and Conquest: Pilgrim's Progress Retold, illustrated by Joanna Troughton, Blackie, 1976.

Snow-White and Rose-Red, illustrated by Jenny Rodwell, Andersen Press, 1979.

POETRY; FOR CHILDREN

The Wandering Moon, illustrated by Evadne Rowan, Heinemann, 1950, 2nd edition, 1957, Dutton, 1960.

The Blackbird in the Lilac: Verses, illustrated by Ardizzone, Oxford University Press, 1952, Dutton, 1959.

Prefabulous Animiles, illustrated by Ardizzone, Heinemann, 1957, Dutton, 1960.

(With others) *A Puffin Quartet of Poets,* edited by Eleanor Graham, illustrated by Diana Bloomfield, Penguin, 1958.

Ragged Robin, illustrated by Jane Paton, Heinemann, Dutton, 1961.

Hurdy-Gurdy: Selected Poems for Children, illustrated by Ardizzone, Heinemann, 1961.

Complete Poems for Children, illustrated by Ardizzone, Heinemann, 1973.

More Prefabulous Animiles, illustrated by Ardizzone, Heinemann, 1975.

PLAYS; FOR CHILDREN

Mulcaster Market: Three Plays for Young People (includes the plays *Mulcaster Market, The Peddler's Dream,* and *The Stolen Boy*), illustrated by Dudley Cutler, Heinemann, 1951, published as *The Peddler's Dream and Other Plays,* Dutton, 1963.

The King Who Took Sunshine, Heinemann, 1954.

A Health to John Patch: A Ballad Operetta, Boosey, 1957.

EDITOR; FOR CHILDREN

Orpheus: A Junior Anthology of English Poetry (two volumes), Heinemann, 1949-50.

Strawberry Fair, Heinemann, 1954.

Green Broom, Heinemann, 1954.

Yellow Wheels, Heinemann, 1954.

Grey Goose and Gander, Heinemann, 1954.

Heinemann Junior Poetry Books (four volumes), Heinemann, 1954.

The Merry-Go-Round: A Collection of Rhymes and Poems for Children, illustrated by John Mackay, Heinemann, 1955.

A Golden Land: Stories, Poems, Songs New and Old, illustrated by Gillian Conway and others, Constable, Hastings House, 1958.

A First Bible: An Abridgement for Young Readers, illustrated by Geoffrey Fraser, Heinemann, 1962.

(Translator) Frantisek Hrubin, *Primrose and the Winter Witch,* illustrated by Jiri Timka, Hamlyn, 1964.

The Christmas Book, illustrated by Briggs, Heinemann, Dutton, 1968.

One's None: Old Rhymes for New Tongues, illustrated by Bernadette Watts, Heinemann, 1968, Watts, 1969.

(Translator) Alexander Pushkin, *The Golden Cockerel and Other Stories,* illustrated by Jan Lebis, Dent, Watts, 1969.

(Translator) Marie de France, *The Shadow of the Hawk and Other Stories,* illustrated by Anne Dalton, Collins, 1975, Seabury Press, 1977.

The Springtime Book: A Collection of Prose and Poetry, illustrated by Colin McNaughton, Heinemann, 1976.

The Autumn Book: A Collection of Prose and Poetry, illustrated by McNaughton, Heinemann, 1977.

POETRY; FOR ADULTS

The Natural Need, Seizin Press, Constable, 1935.

The Imprisoned Sea, Editions Poetry London, 1949.

The Password and Other Poems, Heinemann, 1952.

The Talking Skull, Heinemann, 1958.

Collected Poems, 1929-59, Heinemann, 1960.

The Questioning Tiger, Heinemann, 1964.

Selected Poems, Allison & Busby, 1967, revised edition, 1977.

Subsong, Heinemann, 1969.

Poems and Paraphrases, Heinemann, 1972.

Collected Poems, 1929-74, Heinemann, 1974.

Arcadian Ballads, illustrated by Ardizzone, Whittington Press, 1977.

The Closed Door, Gruffyground Press, Twinrocker, 1977.

EDITOR; FOR ADULTS

(With Denys Thompson) *The Quality of Education: Methods and Purposes in the Secondary Curriculum,* Muller, 1947.

The Poets' World: An Anthology of English Poetry, Heinemann, 1948, revised edition published as *The Modern Poets' World,* 1957.

The Writer's Way: An Anthology of English Prose, Christophers, 1948.

(With Norman Culpan) *Dialogue and Drama,* Heinemann, 1950, Plays, Inc., 1968.

D. H. Lawrence, *Selected Poems,* Heinemann, 1951.

The Speaking Oak: English Poetry and Prose: A Selection, Heinemann, 1951.

John Donne, *Selected Poems,* Heinemann, 1952, Macmillan, 1958.

The Bible in Brief: Selections from the Text of the Authorised Version of 1611, Wingate, 1954, published as *The Holy Bible in Brief,* Messner, 1954.

John Clare, *Selected Poems,* Heinemann, 1954, Macmillan, 1957.

Jonathan Swift, *Gulliver's Travels: The First Three Parts,* Heinemann, 1955.

Gerard Manley Hopkins, *Selected Poems,* Heinemann, 1956, Macmillan, 1957.

Robert Browning, *Selected Poems,* Heinemann, 1956, Macmillan, 1957.

The Idiom of the People: English Traditional Verse from the Manuscripts of Cecil J. Sharp, Heinemann, Macmillan, 1958.

Selected Poems of Emily Dickinson, Heinemann, 1959, Barnes & Noble, 1966.

Samuel Taylor Coleridge, *Selected Poems,* Heinemann, 1959.

The Personal Vision ..., Poetry Book Supplement, 1959.

The Rhyming River: An Anthology of Verse (four volumes), Heinemann, 1959.

(With William Vincent Aughterson) *Over the Ranges,* Heinemann, 1959.

(And author of introduction and notes) *The Everlasting Circle: English Traditional Verse,* Heinemann, Macmillan, 1960.

(With Desmond Flower) *The War 1939-1945,* Cassell, 1960, published as *The Taste of Courage,* Harper, 1960.

Stephen Leacock, *The Unicorn Leacock,* Heinemann, 1960.

Great English Essays, Cassell, 1961.

Selected Poetry and Prose of Robert Graves, Hutchinson, 1961.

Georgian Poetry, Penguin, 1962.

Gulliver's Travels: Parts I-IV, Heinemann, 1964.

The Cassell Book of English Poetry, Cassell, Harper, 1965.

Jonathan Swift, *Selected Poems,* Heinemann, 1966, Barnes & Noble, 1967.

(With Seymour-Smith) *A New Canon of English Poetry,* Barnes & Noble, 1967.

An Anthology of Free Verse, Blackwell, 1968.

The Reader's Bible, Tandem, 1968.

The Sayings of Dr. Johnson, Baker, 1968.

(With Sean Haldane) *Homage to Trumbull Stickney: Poems,* Heinemann, 1968.

Poets and their Critics 3: Arnold to Auden, Hutchinson, 1969.

(With Seymour-Smith) Andrew Marvell, *The Poems of Andrew Marvell,* Barnes & Noble, 1969.

Chaucer: Lyric and Allegory, Heinemann, 1970.

A Vein of Mockery: Twentieth-Century Verse Satire, Heinemann, 1973.

Thomas Gray, *Selected Poems,* Heinemann, 1973, published as *The Complete English Poems of Thomas Gray,* Barnes & Noble, 1973.

Five Late Romantic Poets, Heinemann, 1974.

(With Seymour-Smith) *Selected Poems of Walt Whitman,* Heinemann, 1976.

(With Robert Gittings) *Selected Poems of Thomas Hardy,* Heinemann, 1981.

OTHER; FOR ADULTS

Man Friday: A Primer of English Composition and Grammar, Heinemann, 1953.

The Critical Sense: Practical Criticism of Prose and Poetry, Heinemann, 1956.

Teaching Poetry: Poetry in Class Five to Fifteen, Heinemann, 1956.

A Short History of English Poetry 1340-1940, Heinemann, 1961, Dutton, 1962.

Understanding Poetry, Heinemann, 1965, Barnes & Noble, 1968.

Commitment to Poetry, Barnes & Noble, 1969.

(With Martin Seymour-Smith) *Inside Poetry,* Barnes & Noble, 1970.

How to Write Poems for Children, Heinemann, 1971.

The Reputation and Writings of Alexander Pope, Barnes & Noble, 1976.

The Writer's Approach to the Ballad, Harrap, 1976.

Also author of *XIII Poems,* 1950, and *A.D. One: A Masque for Christmas* (a play), 1974, both privately printed.

■ Sidelights

During his long career, John Morris Reeves functioned as a literary critic, poet, and children's writer. While Reeves' work as a critic was not highly lauded and his poetry for adults has yet to receive great acclaim, his work in children's literature is most appreciated. Reeves was a prolific writer of children's stories and poems, and

his eloquent, often rhythmic style and his broad knowledge of literature found its way into other projects. His retold folktales, fairy tales, Bible stories, classic stories, and translated stories from the Czech and Russian were praised for their characters and style. His edited children's anthologies like *The Springtime Book: A Collection of Prose and Poetry, The Autumn Book: A Collection of Prose and Poetry,* and *The Christmas Book* reflected seasonal themes as they introduced children to the works of well-known authors. Critics have noted that, whether performing in humorous prose or nonsensical poetry, Reeves wrote clearly and crisply, with a child's perspective in mind.

Reeves' fertile and playful imagination often produced works that reviewers considered appropriate for both adults and children. Janet Malcolm reviewed *Rhyming Will* in *New Yorker,* calling it "an adult entertainment that just might amuse children, too." The book tells the story of Will, a young boy of the eighteenth century who does not speak until he is almost seven, and then only in rhyme. Will runs away to London and becomes famous as a poet—until one day, requested to give a speech in verse at a banquet, he is so nervous that he speaks in prose. Although Will fears he is in disgrace, the man he was supposed to honor with his versifying is greatly

In Reeves's tale set in eighteenth-century England, young Will does not speak until the age of seven—and then only in rhyme. (Cover illustration by Edward Ardizzone.)

relieved at not having to hear any more poetry. He gratefully presents Will with five gold coins.

Mr. Horrox and the Gratch, accompanied by the pictures of the celebrated illustrator Quentin Blake, provides another example of Reeves' talent for creating his own stories. Mr. Horrox, an artist, paints what he sees in a realistic fashion. When an art dealer refuses to buy his paintings of farmyards and cottages, Mr. Horrox travels to Scotland to paint what he sees there. Yet something, or someone, keeps stirring up his paintings and ruining them. After Mr. Horrox's art critic declares the adjusted paintings to be marketable as abstracts, the artist realizes that the Gratch, a sprite, has been decorating his paintings. He takes up the Gratch's tool—a bit of string—and revises his style to match that of the Gratch. The message of this "droll, slyly moralistic tale," according to a critic in *Publishers Weekly,* is "about conformity and artistic perception."

Reeves' poems for children were quite popular with readers and critics alike. A reviewer in *New Statesman* described Reeves as a "consistently good performer and . . . his intentionally child-aimed poems are of a piece with his adult ones—both have the same clarity and feeling for clean structure." In his book *How to Write Poems for Children,* Reeves explained how he went about creating verse for a young audience by giving examples of his own work, telling the stories behind the poems, and speculating on the child who might read and appreciate the poem. "My interests and upbringing," Reeves once commented, "are reflected in my poems for children."

In *Mr. Horrox and the Gratch,* **a landscape artist travels to Scotland searching for an inspirational change of scenery, but instead a sprite called the Gratch leads him into the world of abstract art.** (Illustration by Quentin Blake.)

■ Works Cited

Malcolm, Janet, review of *Rhyming Will, New Yorker,* December 14, 1968.
Review of *Mr. Horrox and the Gratch, Publishers Weekly,* October 25, 1991.
New Statesman, November, 1968.

■ For More Information See

PERIODICALS

Book World, November 5, 1967, pp. 23-24; May 5, 1968; February 9, 1986.
Books & Bookmen, February, 1968, pp. 34-35; November, 1979, p. 59.
Christian Science Monitor, November 29, 1968.
Guardian Weekly, November 22, 1969, p. 18.
Poetry, May, 1969.
Times Literary Supplement, December 25, 1969, p. 1467; April 23, 1970, p. 450; February 7, 1971, p. 773; August 4, 1972, p. 910; September 28, 1973; November 23, 1973; July 5, 1974; September 29, 1978.*

*   *   *

REID JENKINS, Debra 1955-

■ Personal

Born March 24, 1955, in Grand Rapids, MI; daughter of Russell E. and Peggy (Roberts) Reid; married Garth Jenkins (a computer programmer), October 14, 1978. *Education:* Attended Kendall School of Design, 1973-75, and Aquinas College, 1975-78, 1988, and 1991. *Hobbies and other interests:* Tai Chi, raising dogs, canoeing, macrobiotic cooking.

■ Addresses

Home—1284 Lancaster N.W., Grand Rapids, MI 49504. *Office*—940 Monroe N.W., Grand Rapids, MI 49504.

■ Career

Hekman Furniture and John Widdicomb Furniture Co., Grand Rapids, MI, hand decorator, 1975-80; LaBarge Mirrors, Holland, MI, hand decorator, 1980-90; freelance artist, 1990—. *Member:* Pastel Society of America, Society of Gilders, American Portrait Society, National Museum of Women in the Arts, Knickerbocker Artists of New York, Ann Arbor (Michigan) Art Association.

■ Awards, Honors

"Emerging Artist" award, *American Artist* magazine, 1995.

DEBRA REID JENKINS

■ Illustrator

Virginia Kroll, *I Wanted to Know All about God,* Eerdman's, 1994.

Also illustrator of book covers for *A Time to Be Silent,* by Gloria Whelan, Eerdman's, 1993, and *That Wild Berries Should Grow,* by Gloria Whelan, Eerdman's, 1994.

■ Work in Progress

Illustrating a ten-stanza poem by Kathi Appelt.

■ Sidelights

After receiving training in illustration and painting, Debra Reid Jenkins spent several years as a hand decorator of furniture, specializing in Chinoiserie (raised and gilded oriental decorations). She was first approached about illustrating a children's book during one of her art exhibitions. About the work she did for Virginia Kroll's *I Wanted to Know All about God,* Reid Jenkins told *SATA* that it was "especially important to me because I felt I accomplished my goal, as an illustrator, of providing a view of God that was accessible to all, regardless of sex, race, or religious beliefs. I

was very pleased to find that people of various faiths, both Christian and non-Christian, purchased this book for their libraries."

■ For More Information See

PERIODICALS

Booklist, February 15, 1994.
Kirkus Reviews, February 15, 1994.
Publishers Weekly, January 3, 1994.
School Library Journal, August, 1994.

* * *

RHODES, Donna McKee 1962-

■ Personal

Born October 12, 1962, in Lewistown, PA; daughter of Stanley Edward (a farmer) and Evelyn Daryl (in health care; maiden name, Glace) McKee; married Loren Kinsel Rhodes (a professor), June 26, 1982; children: Erica, Aaron, Joel. *Education:* Attended Messiah College, 1980-82; Juniata College, B.S., 1984; ongoing study at a seminary. *Religion:* Church of the Brethren. *Hobbies and other interests:* Crafts, music.

DONNA McKEE RHODES

■ Addresses

Home—2722 Warm Springs Rd., Huntingdon, PA 16652. *Office*—Stone Church of the Brethren, 1701 Moore St., Huntingdon, PA 16652.

■ Career

Minister of Nurture, Huntingdon, PA, 1989—. *Member:* Church of Brethren Association of Christian Educators, Juniata College Women's League.

■ Writings

Little Stories for Little Children: A Worship Resource, Herald Press, 1995.

■ Sidelights

Donna McKee Rhodes told *SATA:* "So often a worship service is thought to be only for adults. However, children are an integral part of each church—not only for the future, but also for the present. Having a special time for children within a worship service is an excellent way to include children in worship, as well as teach them scriptural truths and invite them to have a relationship with God. The stories in *Little Stories for Little Children* are short, concise, almost always using an easy-to-find object to teach the scripture theme. I have found using an object familiar to the children to be quite helpful. The object moves the children from what is known to them to the unknown (the scripture concept). Not only can this book be used in worship services, but it can also be used in camp settings, church school, vacation Bible school, home settings, and in classes in colleges and seminaries studying worship and preaching topics.

"I'm a firm believer that children should be taught early. They are capable of learning and being a productive member of society in their own way at an early age."

* * *

ROBLES, Harold E. 1948-

■ Personal

Born October 8, 1948, in Paramaribo, Surinam; emigrated to the Netherlands as a child, and to the United States in 1981; son of Edgar Robles and Carmen Robles del Castilho; married Ruth D'Agostino (an opera singer); children: Martin, Alexander, Julie. *Education:* University of Rotterdam, B.A. (German and Dutch), M.B.A.

■ Addresses

Home—427 Williams Rd., Wallingford, CT 06492. *Office*—Albert Schweitzer Institute for the Humanities, Wallingford, CT 06492.

HAROLD E. ROBLES

■ Career

Albert Schweitzer Institute for the Humanities, Wallingford, CT, founder and president, 1984—. Also founder and president of the Albert Schweitzer Center in the Netherlands, 1973-1981; secretary general, International Albert Schweitzer Organization, 1975-1981; president and founder of the Albert Schweitzer Institute Press, 1994—; president, International Trust for Children's Health Care (founded by former president Mikhail Gorbachev), 1995—; member of board of advisors, Green Cross; member of the council, Temple of Understanding; member of board of advisors, Global Children's Foundation; member of advisory council, Global Kids.

■ Awards, Honors

Medal of the City of Krakow, Poland, 1978; Swedish Albert Schweitzer Award, 1980; Pro Merito Order (Gold), Austria, 1986; United Way Gold Award, 1987; Ehrenzeichen fuer Wissenschaft und Kust, Austrian Albert Schweitzer Society, 1988; Knight Commander, Order of Saint Andrew, England, 1988; Cordon Bleu du Saint-Esprit, Landau, Germany, 1990; Tiffany Apple of New York, 1993; commendation from Rosa L. DeLauro of Connecticut in the House of Representatives, Congressional Record, 104th Congress, Second Session, 1995; honorary D.H.L., Albertus Magnus College, 1996.

■ Writings

FOR CHILDREN

Albert Schweitzer, J. H. Kok (Kampen, Holland), 1978. *Albert Schweitzer: An Adventurer for Humanity,* Millbrook Press, 1994.

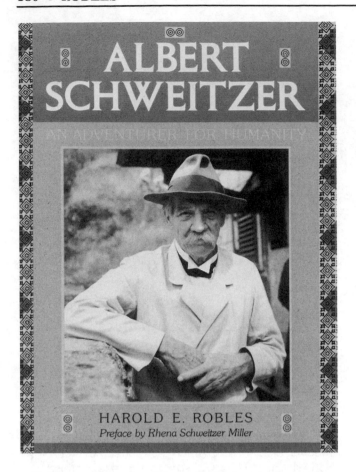

Robles makes the life and work of the great humanitarian Albert Schweitzer accessible to young people in his 1994 book.

FOR ADULTS

(With J. M. van Veen) *Albert Schweitzer,* Bosch & Keuning (Baarn, Holland), 1975.

(Compiler) *Reverence for Life: The Words of Albert Schweitzer,* foreword by Rhena Schweitzer Miller, HarperCollins, 1993.

OTHER

(Editor) *International Albert Schweitzer Symposium,* Van Loghum Slaterus (Deventer, Holland), 1979.

Editor of *Eerbied voor het leven en nieuws uit lambarene* (Dutch magazine), 1976-81; *A.I.S.L. Bulletin* (international newsletter), 1977-81. Contributor of articles to journals in the United States and Holland.

■ Sidelights

Harold E. Robles has been a devotee of the Nobel Prize laureate and humanitarian, Dr. Albert Schweitzer, since he was eight years old. Dedicating himself to the same causes that Schweitzer was interested in, including health care, world peace, arms reduction, and human rights, Robles has played a leading role in creating a number of organizations and educational forums in Schweitzer's name, including the Albert Schweitzer Institute for the Humanities, of which he has been the president since 1984. Robles' children's book, *Albert Schweitzer: Adventurer for Humanity,* is aimed at making the life and works of this famous humanitarian accessible to grade school readers.

■ For More Information See

PERIODICALS

Horn Book Guide, fall, 1994, p. 385.
Kirkus Reviews, February 15, 1994, p. 233.
School Library Journal, May, 1994, p. 126.

S–T

GAIL SAKURAI

SAKURAI, Gail 1952-

■ Personal

Born February 9, 1952, in Detroit, MI; daughter of Peter Robert (an automotive parts inspector) and Virginia Evelyn (a homemaker; maiden name, Jackson) Kwentus; married Eric Sakurai (an executive), July 31, 1971; children: Nicholas, Cameron. *Education:* Oakland University, B.A., 1979. *Hobbies and other interests:* Spending time with family, listening to classical music, reading.

■ Addresses

Office—P.O. Box 1532, West Chester, OH 45071.

■ Career

Children's book author. *Member:* Society of Children's Book Writers and Illustrators.

■ Writings

Peach Boy: A Japanese Legend, Troll, 1994.
Mae Jemison: Space Scientist, Children's Press, 1995.
The Liberty Bell, Children's Press, 1996.
Stephen Hawking, Children's Press, 1996.

Also author of "Why the Sea is Salty" (a retold Japanese folktale), *Jack and Jill* magazine, March, 1995.

■ Work in Progress

Paul Revere's Ride and *The Jamestown Colony,* both for Children's Press; retold folktales from several countries.

■ Sidelights

Gail Sakurai told *SATA* that she "always wanted to be a writer, ever since I learned to read as a child. I planned to have my first book published by the time I was thirteen! Things didn't quite work out that way, however. For many years, other interests and needs interfered with writing, but I never lost my love of books. After getting married, holding a variety of jobs, graduating from college, and having two children, I finally returned to writing. My childhood dream came true with the publication of my first book in 1994—only twenty-nine years later than originally planned."

Sakurai described her first book, *Peach Boy: A Japanese Legend,* as a retelling of a Japanese folktale. "I learned the tale years ago from my Japanese husband, who told it to our two sons as a bedtime story. When I decided to write for children, it just seemed natural to choose

Peach Boy for my first story. I wanted American children to be able to enjoy it as much as Japanese children have for centuries.

"My second book, a biography of Dr. Mae Jemison, the first African-American woman astronaut, grew out of my lifelong interest in space exploration. I get the ideas from my books from everywhere—from things I read, from my children, and even from television. I have more ideas than I'll ever have time to use.

"I specialize in writing nonfiction and retelling folktales from many lands. Through reading I developed an interest in other countries and cultures at an early age. I have studied French, Spanish, Italian, and Japanese, and have traveled widely.

"The hardest parts of writing are finding the time to write in a busy schedule full of family obligations, and getting started. Once I start, the words usually come quickly, because I have planned them in my head before my fingers ever touch the keyboard.

"The best parts of writing are the sense of accomplishment I feel when I have finished a story to my satisfaction, and when I sell that story to a publisher. I also enjoy meeting my readers and giving presentations at schools and libraries. My advice to aspiring writers is to read. Read everything you can get your hands on!"

* * *

SCHLEIN, Miriam 1926-
(Susan Dorritt)

■ Personal

Born in 1926; children: Elizabeth, John. *Education:* Brooklyn College (now of the City University of New York), received degree.

■ Addresses

Home—19 East 95th St., New York, NY 10128.

■ Career

Writer. *Member:* Authors Guild, Authors League of America, PEN American Center, National Writers Union.

■ Awards, Honors

Junior Book Award Medal, Boys' Clubs of America, 1953, for *Fast Is Not a Ladybug; Herald Tribune* Honor Book, 1954, for *Elephant Herd;* Children's Spring Book Festival Honor Book, 1955, for *Little Red Nose; Kirkus Reviews* 100 Best citation, 1974, and Westchester Library Best books citation, 1974-75, both for *What's Wrong with Being a Skunk?;* Outstanding Science Trade Book for Children citation, National Science Teachers Association/Children's Book Council, 1976, and Showcase Title selection, Children's Book Council, 1977, for

MIRIAM SCHLEIN

Giraffe, the Silent Giant; Outstanding Science Trade Book for Children citations, 1979, for *Snake Fights, Rabbit Fights, and More,* 1980, for *Lucky Porcupine!,* 1982, for *Billions of Bats,* 1986, for *The Dangerous Life of the Sea Horse,* and 1991, for *Discovering Dinosaur Babies;* Honor Book citation, New York Academy of Sciences, 1984, for *Project Panda Watch;* Children's Books of the Year citation, Child Study Association, 1989, for *Pigeons;* Outstanding Science Trade Book for Children citation, 1990, and Sunshine State Young Readers Award list and Nebraska Golden Sower Award nominee, both 1992-93, all for *The Year of the Panda;* "Pick of the Lists" citation, American Booksellers Association, 1991, for *I Sailed with Columbus.* Several of Schlein's books have been selections of the Junior Library Guild and other book clubs.

■ Writings

PICTURE BOOKS

A Day at the Playground, illustrated by Eloise Wilkin, Little Golden Books, 1951.
Tony's Pony, illustrated by Van Kaufman, Simon & Schuster, 1952.
Go with the Sun, illustrated by Symeon Shimin, W. R. Scott, 1952.
The Four Little Foxes, illustrated by Luis Quintanilla, W. R. Scott, 1953.
When Will the World Be Mine?, illustrated by Jean Charlot, W. R. Scott, 1953, published as *The Rabbit's World,* illustrated by Peter Parnall, Four Winds Press, 1973.
Elephant Herd, illustrated by Shimin, W. R. Scott, 1954.

The Sun Looks Down, illustrated by Abner Graboff, Abelard Schuman, 1954.

How Do You Travel?, illustrated by Paul Galdone, Abingdon Press, 1954.

Little Red Nose, illustrated by Roger Duvoisin, Abelard Schuman, 1955.

Puppy's House, illustrated by Katherine Evans, Albert Whitman, 1955.

Big Talk, illustrated by Harvey Weiss, W. R. Scott, 1955, illustrated by Joan Auclair, Bradbury, 1990.

Lazy Day, illustrated by Weiss, W. R. Scott, 1955.

City Boy, Country Boy, illustrated by Katherine Evans, Children's Press, 1955.

Henry's Ride, illustrated by Vana Earle, Abingdon Press, 1956.

Deer in the Snow, illustrated by Leonard Kessler, Abelard Schuman, 1956.

A Bunny, a Bird, a Funny Cat, illustrated by Graboff, 1957.

Little Rabbit, the High Jumper, illustrated by Theresa Sherman, W. R. Scott, 1957, published as *Just Like Me,* illustrated by Marilyn Janovitz, Hyperion, 1993.

Amazing Mr. Pelgrew, illustrated by Weiss, Abelard Schuman, 1957.

Here Comes Night, illustrated by Weiss, Albert Whitman, 1957.

The Bumblebee's Secret, illustrated by Weiss, Abelard Schuman, 1958.

Home, The Tale of a Mouse, illustrated by E. Harper Johnson, Abelard Schuman, 1958.

Herman McGregor's World, illustrated by Weiss, Albert Whitman, 1958.

Kittens, Cubs, and Babies, illustrated by Charlot, W. R. Scott, 1959, published as *Big Lion, Little Lion,* illustrated by Joe Lasker, Albert Whitman, 1964.

The Fisherman's Day, illustrated by Weiss, Albert Whitman, 1959.

The Sun, the Wind, the Sea, and the Rain, illustrated by Lasker, Abelard Schuman, 1960.

(Under pseudonym Susan Dorritt) *Laurie's New Brother,* illustrated by Elizabeth Donald, Abelard Schuman, 1961.

The Pile of Junk, illustrated by Weiss, Abelard Schuman, 1962.

Snow Time, illustrated by Lasker, Albert Whitman, 1962.

The Way Mothers Are, illustrated by Lasker, Albert Whitman, 1963, revised edition, 1993.

Who?, illustrated by Weiss, Walck, 1963.

The Big Green Thing, illustrated by Elizabeth Dauber, Grosset & Dunlap, 1963.

Billy, The Littlest One, illustrated by Lucy Hawkinson, Albert Whitman, 1966.

The Best Place, illustrated by Erica Merkling, Albert Whitman, 1968.

My House, illustrated by Lasker, Albert Whitman, 1971.

The Girl Who Would Rather Climb Trees, illustrated by Judith Gwyn Brown, Harcourt, 1975.

I Hate It, illustrated by Brown, Albert Whitman, 1978.

That's Not Goldie!, illustrated by Susan Gough Magurn, Simon & Schuster, 1990.

More Than One, illustrated by Donald Crew, Greenwillow, 1996.

FICTION FOR CHILDREN

Oomi, the New Hunter, illustrated by George Mason, Abelard Schuman, 1955.

Something for Now, Something for Later, illustrated by Leonard Weisgard, Harper, 1956.

The Big Cheese, illustrated by Joseph Low, W. R. Scott, 1958.

The Raggle Taggle Fellow, illustrated by Weiss, Abelard Schuman, 1959.

Little Dog Little, illustrated by Hertha Depper, Abelard Schuman, 1959.

Amuny, Boy of Old Egypt, illustrated by Thea Dupays, Abelard Schuman, 1961.

The Snake in the Carpool, illustrated by N. M. Bodecker, Abelard Schuman, 1963.

Bobo the Troublemaker, illustrated by Ray Cruz, Four Winds Press, 1976.

I, Tut: The Boy Who Became Pharaoh (historical), illustrated by Erik Hilgerdt, Four Winds Press, 1979.

The Year of the Panda, illustrated by Kim Mak, Crowell, 1990.

I Sailed with Columbus (historical), illustrated by Tom Newsom, Harper, 1991.

Secret Land of the Past, illustrated by Kees de Kiefte, Scholastic, 1992.

CONCEPT BOOKS

Shapes, illustrated by Sam Berman, W. R. Scott, 1952.

Fast Is Not a Ladybug: A Book about Fast and Slow Things, illustrated by Kessler, W. R. Scott, 1953 (published in England as *Fast Is Not a Ladybird,* World's Work, 1961).

Heavy Is a Hippopotamus, illustrated by Kessler, W. R. Scott, 1954.

It's about Time, illustrated by Kessler, W. R. Scott, 1955.

My Family, illustrated by Weiss, Abelard Schuman, 1960.

NATURAL SCIENCE FOR CHILDREN

What's Wrong with Being a Skunk?, illustrated by Cruz, Four Winds Press, 1974.

Giraffe: The Silent Giant, illustrated by Betty Fraser, Four Winds Press, 1976.

On the Track of the Mystery Animal: The Story of the Discovery of the Okapi, illustrated by Ruth Sanderson, Four Winds Press, 1978.

Snake Fights, Rabbit Fights, and More: A Book about Animal Fighting, illustrated by Sue Thompson, Crown, 1979.

Antarctica, The Great White Continent, Hastings House, 1980.

Lucky Porcupine!, illustrated by Martha Weston, Four Winds Press, 1980.

Billions of Bats, illustrated by Walter Kessell, Lippincott, 1982.

Project Panda Watch, illustrated by Robert Shetterly, Atheneum, 1984.

What the Elephant Was: Strange Prehistoric Elephants, Atheneum, 1985.

The Dangerous Life of the Sea Horse, illustrated by Gwen Cole, Atheneum, 1986.

Pigeons, photographs by Margaret Miller, Crowell, 1989.

Hippos ("Jane Goodall's Animal World" series), Atheneum, 1989.

Pandas ("Jane Goodall's Animal World" series), Atheneum, 1989.

Elephants ("Jane Goodall's Animal World" series), Atheneum, 1990.

Gorillas ("Jane Goodall's Animal World" series), Atheneum, 1990.

Discovering Dinosaur Babies, illustrated by Margaret Colbert, Four Winds, 1991.

Let's Go Dinosaur Tracking!, illustrated by Kate Duke, Harper, 1991.

Squirrel Watching, photographs by Marjorie Pillar, Harper, 1992.

The Dino Quiz Book, illustrated by Nate Evans, Scholastic, 1995.

Before the Dinosaurs, illustrated by Michael Rothman, Scholastic, 1996.

The Puzzle of the Dinosaur-Bird: The Story of Archaeopteryx, illustrated by Mark Hallett, Dial, 1996.

NONFICTION FOR CHILDREN

Metric: The Modern Way to Measure, illustrated by Jan Pyk, Harcourt, 1975.

Rosh Hashanah and Yom Kippur, illustrated by Erika Weihs, Behrman House, 1983.

Hanukkah, illustrated by Katherine Kahn, Behrman House, 1983.

Shavuot, illustrated by Weihs, Behrman House, 1983.

Shabbat, illustrated by Amy Blake, Behrman House, 1983.

Prayers and Blessings, illustrated by Amye Rosenberg, Behrman House, 1983.

Passover, illustrated by Kahn, Behrman House, 1983.

Sukkot and Simhat Torah, illustrated by Rosenberg, Behrman House, 1983.

Purim, illustrated by Ruth Heller, Behrman House, 1983.

OTHER

Moon-Months and Sun-Days (folktales), illustrated by Shelly Sacks, W. R. Scott, 1972.

Juju-Sheep and the Python's Moonstone, and Other Moon Stories from Different Times and Different Places (folktales), illustrated by Lasker, Albert Whitman, 1973.

Also author of additional books under pseudonym Susan Dorritt, including *Wait Till Sunday,* illustrated by Duvoisin, *Jason's Lucky Day,* illustrated by John Strickland Goodall, and *Jellybean, the Puppy Who Was Born in the Time of the Snow,* illustrated by Pat Marriott, all for Abelard-Schuman. Several of Schlein's books have been translated into Danish, Dutch, French, German, Italian, Norwegian, Russian, and Swedish, or are available in Braille editions.

■ Adaptations

Fast Is Not a Ladybug and *Shapes* were made into short films; other books have been included in school readers and on phonograph records for children.

■ Work in Progress

Sleep Safe, Little Whale, illustrated by Peter Sis, a picture book for Greenwillow, expected 1997.

■ Sidelights

For more than forty years, Miriam Schlein has been providing young children with simple, easy to read books that introduce concepts ranging from shapes and sizes to scientific methods to the special relationship between parents and children. She is best known for her many books which acquaint readers with animals and their behaviors, dispelling myths about creatures such as bats, skunks, and porcupines. In addition to her inviting writing style, Schlein often approaches her subject from a fresh angle so that her readers are entertained as well as educated. As Joan McGrath remarks in *Twentieth-Century Children's Writers,* "Schlein is an extremely important and influential writer for the beginner, for she has made the difficult explication of concepts for the beginning reader her province."

Schlein published her first book, *A Day at the Playground,* in 1951, and for the next ten years her output was divided equally between fiction and nonfiction picture books. Her early concept books covered shapes, speed, weight, and time, while many of her stories were about animals—including pandas, foxes, elephants, dogs, kangaroos, deer, rabbits, mice, and even bumblebees. Schlein's concept books, particularly those illustrated by Leonard Kessler, were pioneers in the field, according to Barbara Bader in *American Picturebooks from Noah's Ark to the Beast Within.* "Her rackety-packety manner of writing for kids . . . , the bounce, the sunshine the two together brought to a book, their blithe young way with ideas, ordinary ideas—these were picked up in turn by many others." *Heavy Is a Hippopotamus,* for instance, has "a quirky kind of humor that fixes a point indelibly in the mind," *New York Times Book Review* writer Ellen Lewis Buell remarks; the critic observes that *Shapes* similarly uses "a deceptively light touch" to explain ideas of round and square, making for "a brilliant little book which will help to train a youngster's eye."

Many of Schlein's fictional picture books also contain more complex concepts—such as family relationships and ownership—along with a pleasant story. The 1953 title *When Will the World Be Mine?,* for instance, tells of a young snowshoe hare whose mother teaches him how to enjoy the things of the forest which "belong" to him—the stream, the snow, the trees. Schlein's "experimental, imaginative" work is reminiscent of that of Margaret Wise Brown's "at its best," Buell asserts in the *New York Times Book Review,* "yet it has its own individuality." The story is "gentle in tone [and] unobtrusively informative," a *Bulletin of the Center for Children's Books* reviewer notes of the book's 1974 reissue as *The Rabbit's World;* the critic also praises the "warm" portrayal of the mother-child relationship. *The Four Little Foxes* likewise focuses on an animal family with which children can identify. Lois Palmer comments in the *New York Times Book Review* that "the just-like-us quality of the story helps children to sense the parallel to their own progress from small to big," among other family interactions.

In her first natural science book, 1974's *What's Wrong with Being a Skunk?*, Schlein uses an informal, conversational approach to provide readers with "a wealth of information" that refutes the animal's negative reputation, according to a *Publishers Weekly* critic. While the "simply worded text" is "conversational in style and makes use of analogies to human behavior," Mary M. Burns observes in *Horn Book,* the skunk is never portrayed as anything other than an animal. Similarly, in *Lucky Porcupine!* (1980) "Schlein has created an anecdotal narrative of another misunderstood animal," Rebecca Keese remarks in *School Library Journal.* The myth that porcupines can "shoot" their quills is dismissed, and the creatures' behaviors "are depicted in an informative, thoughtful, and personalized manner," *Booklist*'s Barbara Elleman states. "Lucky readers," concludes a *Kirkus Reviews* critic, "who have Schlein to introduce them to this interesting creature."

Schlein traces the perilous journey of the sea horse from its birth in the seaweed beds to coral reefs and coastal waters in this nonfiction work. (Cover illustration by Gwen Cole.)

Another misunderstood animal is featured in 1982's *Billions of Bats,* which Timothy C. Williams calls "a very impressive book" in *Science Books and Films.* Looking at the anatomy, behavior, and feeding habits of bats—which *don't* include sucking people's blood or flying into their hair—Schlein shows how these flying mammals are an important part of environments all over the world. Williams also praises the author for conveying "mature zoological concepts without watering down the information." A less well-known creature is the focus of *The Dangerous Life of the Sea Horse,* a 1986 study that demonstrates Schlein's "usual care and thorough attention to facts," Elleman notes in *Booklist.* Beginning with the birth of baby sea horses—who are carried by their father, not their mother—the author traces the life cycle of these unusual fish, providing "extensive information about this small creature's struggle for survival, its means of propelling itself, and different types of sea horses," Peggy Ellen Leahy explains in *School Library Journal.* Not only is Schlein's text "easy to read," Susan D. Chapnick writes in *Appraisal,* but her style "flows well and keeps the interest of the reader even when introducing difficult biological facts" and terms.

While Schlein often writes about animals that are unfamiliar or misunderstood, she has also provided readers with information on creatures they can see every day. 1989's *Pigeons* is "a much-needed look at our cities' most common bird," Elizabeth S. Watson claims in *Horn Book.* Although the "interesting, factual text ... is pared down to essentials," Watson continues, it also includes Schlein's own journal of the time she spent observing two new pigeon chicks. Containing "lots of facts," according to Betsy Hearne of the *Bulletin of the Center for Children's Books,* *Pigeons* is "a must for urban nature study." *Squirrel Watching* similarly "introduces the joy of wildlife observation to children," Susan Oliver comments in *School Library Journal,* with Schlein's style making the book "engaging and personable." *Bulletin of the Center for Children's Books* reviewer Roger Sutton also hails the writing, terming it "conversational, with short sentences that are easy to read and occasionally funny," and concludes that the book's emphasis "encourages readers to participate in the investigation."

Schlein has also written books that examine animal behavior as well as ones that look at how human behavior can affect animals and their surroundings. In *Snake Fights, Rabbit Fights, and More,* the author covers the many reasons animals might battle another of their species, including gaining rank, territory, or mates. This "succinct, authoritative, and smoothly written" book makes clear that animals "fight for a clearly defined purpose," a *Bulletin of the Center for Children's Books* critic states. Calling Schlein "an accomplished hand at science books for the young," an *Appraisal* reviewer adds that *Snake Fights* is an "intriguing book" that will "make fascinating reading as well as being useful." The efforts of people to study and save the giant panda of China are profiled in *Project Panda Watch.* The author presents information on the panda's behav-

Chinese farmboy Lu Yi rescues an orphaned panda cub in Schlein's *Year of the Panda*, illustrated by Kam Mak.

ior—as well as what is being done to prevent its extinction—all in "an informative manner that instills concern," Karen Jameyson observes in *Horn Book*.

The Year of the Panda provides much of the same information about saving the panda as *Project Panda Watch*, but this time Schlein tells the story through a ten-year-old Chinese farm boy who rescues an orphaned panda cub. Lu Yi takes his new friend to the Panda Rescue Center, where he (and the reader) learn about the conditions endangering the panda; while "the essence of the story is factual," Watson observes in *Horn Book*, Lu Yi's story develops "with enough suspense ... to carry the reader along swiftly." "This is a well-crafted, absorbing story," Susan Middleton declares in the *School Library Journal*, and its efforts to inform readers about the panda are "an added bonus." *Let's Go Dinosaur Tracking!* similarly explores paleontology, or how scientists use fossils to learn about prehistoric creatures, in "a format that's more appealing to younger children," Cathryn A. Camper says in *School Library Journal*. As a scientist takes some children around the world to learn from fossilized dinosaur tracks, "the text's conversational style and liberal use of questions convey a sense of discovery, making it interesting,

informative, and quite readable," *Appraisal* writer Ann M. Glannon states. The result, concludes Donna A. Robertson in the same review, is "a funny, informative, and easy to digest dinosaur book."

Schlein has also taken a fictional approach to communicating historical information to her readers. In *I, Tut: The Boy Who Became Pharaoh*, Schlein uses Tutankhamen himself to narrate the story of how he came to rule his ancient Egyptian kingdom at the age nine. "By selecting such an inviting narrator," Jacqueline van Zanten explains in the *New York Times Book Review*, Schlein "manages to pack her text with glimpses of what life was like in Egypt 3,000 years ago without making her reader feel overwhelmed." Tut describes his role as head of ancient Egypt's government and religion, and after his early death at eighteen, his friend Hekenefer relates how the king was mourned and buried, leaving behind the treasure trove we know today as "King Tut's Tomb." "Simple and dignified, the story should appeal to the many children who know of [Tut's] tomb," Zena Sutherland observes in the *Bulletin of the Center for Children's Books*, also praising Schlein's "carefully factual" writing.

Similarly, in *I Sailed with Columbus* the author's portrayal of Christopher Columbus's journey to the New World "is notable for its bits of navigational information eagerly revealed by its likable protagonist," Sylvia V. Meisner writes in *School Library Journal*. This

Tyrannosaurus tracks show us that these big flesh-eaters traveled alone, or in pairs.

A scientist takes a group of children around the world to learn from fossilized dinosaur tracks in Schlein's *Let's Go Dinosaur Tracking!* (Illustration by Kate Duke.)

Mother Rabbit tells her son the story of a little cottontale rabbit and his remarkable powers and adventures in Schlein's classic picture book, *Just Like Me*. (Illustration by Marilyn Janovitz.)

time a fictional character, the ship's boy Julio, writes down in his journal all of the notable events he sees during Columbus's pioneering voyage to America. Schlein used details she found from Columbus's own diaries, and the facts that Julio "reports with refreshing simplicity and candor" make for a story that is "compelling as well as accurate," a *Publishers Weekly* critic states.

While she may be better known for her nonfiction works, Schlein has written distinctive stories as well, some of which have remained in print more than thirty years after they first appeared. *Big Talk,* for instance,

was reprinted with new illustrations in 1990, providing a new generation of readers with this story of a boastful baby kangaroo. As the baby joey brags about his bravery and his ability to run fast and jump high, his mother calmly accepts his inventions and then tells him he will be able to do all these things when he grows up. *Big Talk*'s "exotic" Australian background and gentle story make it "a natural for toddler storytimes," Jeanette Larson remarks in *School Library Journal,* while a *Publishers Weekly* critic praises Schlein's "straightforward, 'less is more' approach" in presenting "an appealingly offbeat look at mother-child relationships."

Two more of Schlein's classic stories of motherly love have been reissued in new editions during the 1990s. In *The Way Mothers Are,* a mother cat reassures her offspring she will love it no matter what it does, good or bad. While the 1993 version contains a few changes from the original 1963 text, "the story still captures the interaction between" mother and child, Ilene Cooper states in *Booklist. Just Like Me* similarly shows a parent's love as a mother rabbit relates the legend of a great jumper while her child adds a "just like me" to all its adventures; the storyteller echoes these words when she relates the joy of the jumper's mother at its return. *School Library Journal* contributor Beth Tegart finds *Just Like Me* "a delightful reissue," adding that "this lovely story belongs on the shelf" with classics by Margaret Wise Brown and Ann Tompert.

Whether in gentle stories of the mother-child bond, fictionalized histories, or straight nonfiction, "Schlein's especial talent lies in her ability to explain while entertaining," McGrath declares. In a book such as *Antarctica: The Great White Continent,* for example, "the writing is easy enough" for beginning readers, "yet has a verve and humor that older children will appreciate," Ellen D. Warwick observes in *School Library Journal.* In addition, Schlein rarely talks down to her readers; in books like *Giraffe: The Silent Giant* the author has "stuck to the facts and let the unusualness of [her] subject come through clearly without resort[ing] to a gee-whiz factor," an *Appraisal* critic remarks. As McGrath concludes, Schlein's books "are works of charm and simplicity that have stood the tests of time."

■ Works Cited

Bader, Barbara, *American Picturebooks from Noah's Ark to the Best Within,* Macmillan, 1976, pp. 394-97.

Review of *Big Talk, Publishers Weekly,* August 31, 1990, p. 62.

Buell, Ellen Lewis, "Round and Square," *New York Times Book Review,* November 16, 1952, p. 41.

Buell, Ellen Lewis, "A World for a Rabbit," *New York Times Book Review,* January 17, 1954, p. 18.

Buell, Ellen Lewis, "Triad," *New York Times Book Review,* October 31, 1954, p. 36.

Burns, Mary M., review of *What's Wrong with Being a Skunk?, Horn Book,* August, 1974, p. 392.

Camper, Cathryn A., review of *Let's Go Dinosaur Tracking!, School Library Journal,* January, 1992, p. 106.

Chapnick, Susan D., review of *The Dangerous Life of the Sea Horse, Appraisal,* summer, 1987, pp. 79-80.

Cooper, Ilene, review of *The Way Mothers Are, Booklist,* April 1, 1993, p. 1442.

Elleman, Barbara, review of *Lucky Porcupine!, Booklist,* May 1, 1980, p. 1299.

Elleman, Barbara, review of *The Dangerous Life of the Sea Horse, Booklist,* September 1, 1986, p. 67.

Review of *Giraffe: The Silent Giant, Appraisal,* winter, 1977, p. 36.

Glannon, Ann M., review of *Let's Go Dinosaur Tracking!, Appraisal,* summer, 1992, pp. 50-51.

Hearne, Betsy, review of *Pigeons, Bulletin of the Center for Children's Books,* September, 1989, pp. 18-19.

Review of *I Sailed with Columbus, Publishers Weekly,* October 25, 1991, p. 69.

Jameyson, Karen, review of *Project Panda Watch, Horn Book,* March/April, 1985, p. 199.

Keese, Rebecca, review of *Lucky Porcupine!, School Library Journal,* August, 1980, p. 56.

Larson, Jeanette, review of *Big Talk, School Library Journal,* November, 1990, p. 98.

Leahy, Peggy Ellen, review of *The Dangerous Life of the Sea Horse, School Library Journal,* January, 1987, pp. 78-79.

Review of *Lucky Porcupine!, Kirkus Reviews,* April 1, 1980, p. 442.

McGrath, Joan, "Miriam Schlein," *Twentieth-Century Children's Writers,* 4th edition, St. James Press, 1995.

Meisner, Sylvia V., review of *I Sailed with Columbus, School Library Journal,* October, 1991, p. 128.

Middleton, Susan, review of *The Year of the Panda, School Library Journal,* October, 1990, p. 119.

Oliver, Susan, review of *Squirrel Watching, School Library Journal,* March, 1992, p. 252.

Palmer, Lois, "Growing Up," *New York Times Book Review,* August 9, 1953, p. 14.

Review of *The Rabbit's World, Bulletin of the Center for Children's Books,* May, 1974, pp. 148-49.

Robertson, Donna A., review of *Let's Go Dinosaur Tracking!, Appraisal,* summer, 1992, p. 51.

Review of *Snake Fights, Rabbit Fights, and More, Appraisal,* spring, 1980, p. 72.

Review of *Snake Fights, Rabbit Fights, and More, Bulletin of the Center for Children's Books,* September, 1980, p. 21.

Sutherland, Zena, review of *I, Tut: The Boy Who Became Pharaoh, Bulletin of the Center for Children's Books,* March, 1979, p. 126.

Sutton, Roger, review of *Squirrel Watching, Bulletin of the Center for Children's Books,* March, 1992, p. 193.

Tegart, Beth, review of *Just Like Me, School Library Journal,* July, 1993, p. 71.

van Zanten, Jacqueline, review of *I, Tut: The Boy Who Became Pharaoh, New York Times Book Review,* May 6, 1979, p. 20.

Warwick, Ellen D., review of *Antarctica: The Great White Continent, School Library Journal,* August, 1980, p. 70.

Watson, Elizabeth S., review of *Pigeons, Horn Book,* November/December, 1989, p. 793.

Watson, Elizabeth S., review of *The Year of the Panda, Horn Book,* November/December, 1990, p. 745.

Review of *What's Wrong with Being a Skunk?, Publishers Weekly,* May 20, 1974, p. 64.

Williams, Timothy C., review of *Billions of Bats, Science Books and Films,* November/December, 1982, p. 93.

■ For More Information See

PERIODICALS

Booklist, December 15, 1978, p. 689; December 1, 1990, p. 752.

Bulletin of the Center for Children's Books, February, 1967, pp. 97-98; September, 1974, p. 16; March, 1977, p. 113; February, 1985, p. 116; November, 1990, p. 69; October, 1991, pp. 28-29.

Kirkus Reviews, November 15, 1976, p. 1219; October 15, 1978, p. 1141.

Publishers Weekly, October 2, 1972, p. 54.

School Library Journal, September, 1975, p. 111; March, 1976, p. 97; November, 1976, p. 63; November, 1978, p. 79; January, 1980, p. 60; March, 1985, p. 171; December, 1989, p. 116; January, 1991, p. 80; July, 1991, p. 86.

—Sketch by Diane Telgen

* * *

SCOTT, Bill
See SCOTT, William N(eville)

* * *

SCOTT, W. N.
See SCOTT, William N(eville)

* * *

SCOTT, William N(eville) 1923-
(Bill Scott, W. N. Scott)

■ Personal

Born October 4, 1923, in Bundaberg, Queensland, Australia; son of William (a railwayman) and Elizabeth Florence (a homemaker; maiden name, Christie) Scott; married Mavis Richards (a writer), 1949; children: Harry Alan. *Hobbies and other interests:* Woodcarving, prospecting for gold and precious stones, playing the tin whistle, telling tall stories.

■ Addresses

Home—157 Pratten St., Warwick, Queensland, 4370, Australia.

■ Career

Worked as a bookseller, publisher, and editor during the 1950s and 1960s; full-time writer, 1974—. *Military service:* Royal Australian Navy, 1942-46; served in Pacific theater. *Member:* Australian Folklore Society, ISCLR Australian Folklore Association, Order of Australia Association, Queensland Folk Federation.

WILLIAM N. SCOTT

■ Awards, Honors

Mary Gilmore National Award, 1964, for the story, "One Is Enough"; Australian Council fellowships, 1977, 1980, 1981; runner-up for Book of the Year Award, Children's Book Council of Australia, 1979 and 1982; Medal of the Order of Australia, 1992.

■ Writings

FOR CHILDREN

(Under name Bill Scott) *Boori,* illustrated by A. M. Hicks, Oxford University Press, 1978.

(Under name Bill Scott) *Darkness under the Hills,* illustrated by A. M. Hicks, Oxford University Press, 1980.

Shadows among the Leaves, illustrated by Bill Farr, Heinemann, 1984.

Many Kinds of Magic: Tales of Mystery, Myth and Enchantment, illustrated by Lisa Herriman, Penguin, 1988.

Following the Gold (poetry), Omnibus, 1989.

Hey Rain (recordings), Restless Music, 1992.

Songbird in Your Pocket (recordings), Restless Music, 1994.

The Currency Lad, illustrated by Annmarie Scott, Walter McVitty, 1994.

FOR ADULTS

Focus on Judith Wright, University of Queensland Press, 1967.

Some People (stories), Jacaranda Press, 1968.

(Under name W. N. Scott) *Brother and Brother* (poems), Jacaranda Press, 1972.

(Under name Bill Scott) *Portrait of Brisbane,* illustrated by Cedric Emanuel, Rigby, 1976.

My Uncle Arch and Other People (stories), Rigby, 1977.

(Under name Bill Scott) *Tough in the Old Days* (autobiography), Rigby, 1979.

Australian Bushrangers (originally published as *The Child and Henry Book of Bushrangers*), Child & Henry, 1983.

The Long and the Short and the Tall: Australian Yarns, Western Plains Publishing, 1985.

Brisbane Sketchbook, Herron, 1988.

EDITOR

The Continual Singing: An Anthology of World Poetry, Jacaranda Press, 1973.

(Under name Bill Scott) *The Complete Book of Australian Folklore,* Ure Smith, 1976.

(Under name Bill Scott; with Pro Hart) *Bushranger Ballads,* Ure Smith, 1976.

The Second Penguin Australian Songbook, Penguin Australia, 1980.

(Under name Bill Scott; with John Meredith) *Ned Kelly after a Century of Acrimony,* Lansdowne Press, 1980.

Impressions on a Continent (stories), Heinemann, 1983.

The Penguin Book of Australian Humorous Verse, Penguin Australia, 1984.

OTHER

Editor of series "Australian Content Readers," 1981—. Work represented in anthologies, including *More Australian Poetry for Fun,* Hamlyn, 1975. Author of narration for documentary film *Explorer Safari,* 1984. Contributor to folktale journals, including *Stringybark and Greenhide, Folklore Round Table,* and *Folklines.*

■ Sidelights

William N. Scott is an Australian writer and poet who has written extensively (and often sings) about the Australian aborigines' myths, customs, and "Dreamtime," as well as Australia's folklore, songs, and tall tales. His writing style has been described as heroic, especially when dealing with the themes of aboriginal life, their ties to their homeland, spiritualism, and their strict code of interpersonal and intertribal relationships.

Scott's path to becoming a writer and poet was quite unexpected. He once commented that "I was brought up in a small country town during the bitter days of the Depression. I left school at age fourteen and worked at various jobs, mainly as a storeman [stock boy or salesperson], until I was old enough to enlist in the navy during World War II. I served on a minelayer and later in the small wooden ships of the Coastal Forces as a seaman and antiaircraft gunner. From 1946 to 1948, I traveled around eastern Australia, working as a gold prospector, miner, sugar cane cutter, and locomotive driver; this part of my life is recorded in the book *Tough in the Old Days.* After my marriage in 1949, I worked as a seaman on the ship which supplied the lighthouses along the Great Barrier Reef, and as a steam engine driver in various industries. Following an industrial accident in 1954, I began work as a bookseller, and later I became one of the people who founded the publishing house of what is now Jacaranda/Wiley Press in Bris-

Australian author Scott retells folklore stories from around the world in this 1988 collection. (Cover illustration by Lisa Herriman.)

bane, Australia. I resigned my position as trade manager in 1974 to write fulltime.

"I began writing poetry in the late 1940s," Scott continued, "and some of it was published in newspapers and magazines. In the mid-1950s I began writing short stories with some success and became involved in the investigation and collection of Australian folklore. I wrote, and sometimes presented, scripts for radio.

"I have written and lectured widely on aspects of Australian folklore and poetry," Scott explained. "I've acted as a tutor at workshops for children's writers, mainly for the University of New England. As a folklorist, my interest is in the field of 'contemporary urban legends,' and I carry on a vigorous correspondence with fellow enthusiasts in England and the United States."

Two of Scott's most popular children's books, *Boori* and its sequel, *Darkness under the Hills,* are about Boori, an aboriginal man of magical powers, not born as a human, but created out of clay by one of his tribe's most powerful elders. Since the elders cannot teach Boori all the skills and magic a person must have, Boori has to learn this knowledge for himself by serving his community, the aboriginal law, and the spirits that govern both. Though alone on his quest, Boori does not have to endure all these trials and tests alone, for he is provided with a quick-witted spirit friend, Jaree, who lives in a leather pouch hanging from his neck. Together these two battle the forces of evil. According to the complex Australian aboriginal law, a code of belief and honor that governs every facet of aboriginal life, all people are responsible for their actions in nature, the spiritual world, and their human community. According to aboriginal belief, anyone who breaks this law—whether they are aboriginal or not—must try to restore the delicate balance of harmony. Both of these myth-rich novels tell the heroic story of Boori and his spirit-friend/sidekick Jaree battling horrifyingly evil spirits and forces in the outback to return their land to harmony. Woven into these stories are snatches of songs, legends, dances, and dramas that form the basis of the incredibly complex Australian aboriginal culture.

Writing in *Booklist,* reviewer Betsy Hearne stated that those who study mythology might be interested in comparing [*Boori*] with "the more familiar exploits of Greco-Roman hero figures." However, modern readers may not be as comfortable in Australian aboriginal Dreamtime as they are in terms of sound-bite television time. A reviewer in *Kirkus Reviews* cautioned about the initial slow pace of *Boori,* stating that "stories drawn from the Australian aboriginal past have a fatal tendency to seem at once dense and aimless, and for some way into the book, [*Boori*] is no exception."

Patricia A. Morgans said in *Best Sellers* that *Darkness under the Hills* is "a beautifully, sometimes poetically, written book that will appeal to fantasy lovers in junior high school." But, she warned, "Some may find it a trifle wordy." That concern was echoed by George Shannon's review of this same book in *School Library Journal* when he wrote, "Dialogue falls into speechmaking, and so many facts are deposited that narrative flow is impeded."

In the aboriginal equivalent of an ecology thriller, Scott's *Shadows among the Leaves* tells the frightening story of the Shadows, terrifying, formless animated "things" or spirit forces which tear through the Australian rain forest with the fury of an invisible storm, destroying anyone or anything that tries to harm their jungle habitat. These are the forces young Jo Brady must contend with as she travels regularly each week from her father's farm through the rain forest to help an elderly, part-aboriginal neighbor woman. A *Junior Bookshelf* reviewer commented that "here are the makings of a strong story. It is enriched, and made more credible, by the space devoted to the ordinary life of a country settlement." Whether or not the reader believes in the spirit world of the Australian aborigines, books by Bill Scott are a good introduction to the complexities of these original Australians' complex belief systems and the mysterious land they once roamed.

■ **Works Cited**

Review of *Boori, Kirkus Reviews,* March 1, 1979, pp. 267-68.
Hearne, Betsy, review of *Boori, Booklist,* May 1, 1979, p. 1366.
Morgans, Patricia A., review of *Darkness under the Hills, Best Sellers,* April, 1981, p. 39.
Review of *Shadows among the Leaves, Junior Bookshelf,* February, 1986, p. 40.
Shannon, George, review of *Darkness under the Hills, School Library Journal,* April, 1981, p. 131.

■ **For More Information See**

PERIODICALS

Growing Point, September, 1979, p. 3563.
School Library Journal, September, 1987, p. 133.
Voice of Youth Advocates, June, 1981, p. 55.

*   *   *

SCRIBNER, Charles, Jr. 1921-1995

OBITUARY NOTICE—See index for *SATA* sketch: Born July 13, 1921, in Quogue, NY; died of pneumonia after suffering from a lengthy bout with a degenerative neurological disorder, November 11, 1995, in Manhattan, NY. Publisher, author. Scribner gained prominence as the heir to the Charles Scribner's Sons Publishing Company, serving as its president from 1952 to 1977. For the next two years he was chairman of the firm, which was founded in 1846. He remained chairman with the firm through a number of mergers and slight name changes, retiring from Scribner Book Companies in 1986, shortly after the house was acquired by Macmillan. Scribner began his career with the family business in 1946 as its advertising manager. Within two years he was promoted to production manager and vice president. While at Scribner, he served as the personal editor and publisher for Ernest Hemingway. In 1951, he began an eleven year stint as president of Princeton University Press. A trustee of Princeton University for ten years beginning in 1969, he was also trustee for Blair Academy and Skidmore College. From 1966 to 1968 he was president of the American Book Publishers Council. In addition to his work in publishing, Scribner penned several volumes, including a translation of *Hansel and Gretel* for children, a book of memoirs called *In the Company of Writers: A Life in Publishing,* and a volume of writings entitled *In the Web of Ideas: The Education of a Publisher.* He also edited *The Enduring Hemingway: An Anthology of a Lifetime in Literature.*

OBITUARIES AND OTHER SOURCES:

BOOKS

Who's Who in America, Marquis, 1992.

PERIODICALS

Los Angeles Times, November 14, 1995, p. A18.
New York Times, November 13, 1995, p. B8.
Washington Post, November 14, 1995, p. B7.

SHEDD, Warner 1934-

■ Personal

Born March 11, 1934, in Burlington, VT; son of Emerson W. and Eleanor F. (Folsom) Shedd; married Edith Wheeler (a registered hospice nurse), August 4, 1956; children: Susan Dorothy, Mark Emerson, David Robert. *Education:* University of Maine, B.S. (forestry; summa cum laude), 1956, M.S. (plant physiology), 1958. *Hobbies and other interests:* Hunting, fishing, birding, camping, cross-country skiing, canoeing, nature photography, golf, wine, gourmet cooking, classical music, choral singing, oriental rugs, reading (particularly history—especially the Civil War—and mysteries).

■ Addresses

Home and office—Shedd Rd., East Calais, VT 05650.

■ Career

Vermont Department of Forests and Parks, Northern District, municipal forester, 1958-66; Vermont Extension Service, Lamoille, Washington, and Orange Counties, VT, area resource specialist, 1966-69; New England Regional Executive, National Wildlife Federation, 1969-89; freelance writer, 1990—. Part-time farmer, raising Beefalos. Chairman, Vermont Non-game Advisory Committee; member, board of directors, Vermont Green Up. Has served as Boy Scout troop leader and Little League and Babe Ruth baseball coach. *Member:* Vermont Alliance of Conservation Voters (former chair), Vermont Sportsmen's Coalition (secretary), New Hampshire Wildlife Federation (board of directors), Xi Sigma Chi.

■ Awards, Honors

Distinguished Service Award, New Hampshire Wildlife Federation, 1984; Community Resource Award, Vermont Association for Learning Disabilities, 1985.

■ Writings

The Kids' Wildlife Book: Exploring Animal Worlds through Indoor/Outdoor Experiences, illustrated by Loretta Trezzo Braren, Williamson Publishing, 1994.
The Kids' Bug Book, Williamson Publishing, 1996.

Contributor to *Outdoor Life's 1991 Deer Hunting Annual;* contributor of articles to magazines, including *Diversion, Field & Stream, Harrowsmith Country Life, Outdoor Life, Shooting Sportsman, Sports Afield, Vermont Life,* and *Vermont* magazine.

■ Work in Progress

A murder mystery set in Scotland, expected to be complete by 1996; research on "comfortable camping," prehistoric extinct creatures (prior to latter part of present interglacial period), and the American Civil War.

■ Sidelights

"The path to my writing career was lengthy, with numerous twists and turns along the way," Warner Shedd told *SATA.* "It had its genesis, however, when I was quite young.

"My parents lived on my grandparents' Vermont dairy farm while I was growing up, and, when I was five or six, my grandfather took me fishing in the creek which flowed through our farm. I was enthralled, at least as much by the forested setting and the sight and sound of clear, rushing water as by actually catching fish!

"Several years later I also began to hunt, bringing back squirrels and an occasional grouse for the family table. As a result, the woods and streams became my natural habitat, which I haunted at every opportunity. I came to treasure glimpses of every sort of wildlife, as well as the incredible peace and beauty of unspoiled forests and waters.

"When I was in the eighth grade, my parents moved to a little town in western Maine. There, I vividly remember giving the eighth-grade graduation address (I think there were three or four of us graduating from the town's two one-room schools!) on the subject 'Keeping Maine Clean.' I had become incensed at the slobs who threw bottles, papers, and trash along the roadsides and into streams, and this anger fostered my debut as a conservation activist.

"When it came time to choose a career, I studied forestry and plant physiology at the University of Maine because I wanted work which had an orientation toward natural resources. After several years as a forester, however, I found that I wanted a broader relationship to natural resources. This led me first into extension service work and then into the position of New England Regional Executive with the National Wildlife Federation—a post which I held for twenty years.

"Writing had always come easily to me, and I viewed it as something which was fun to do whenever I had the chance. At some point, though, fairly late in my career with the National Wildlife Federation, it dawned on me that writing was something greater than mere fun. I found that I had a real passion for the English language, and that words were my playthings—my building blocks, Tinkertoys, erector sets. At that moment, I began to contemplate early retirement in order to become a writer, and the occasion of my twentieth anniversary with National Wildlife Federation provided that opportunity.

"My entry into the world of children's literature was completely serendipitous—an overworked word, but completely appropriate in this case! It began when I went to see publishers Susan and Jack Williamson about

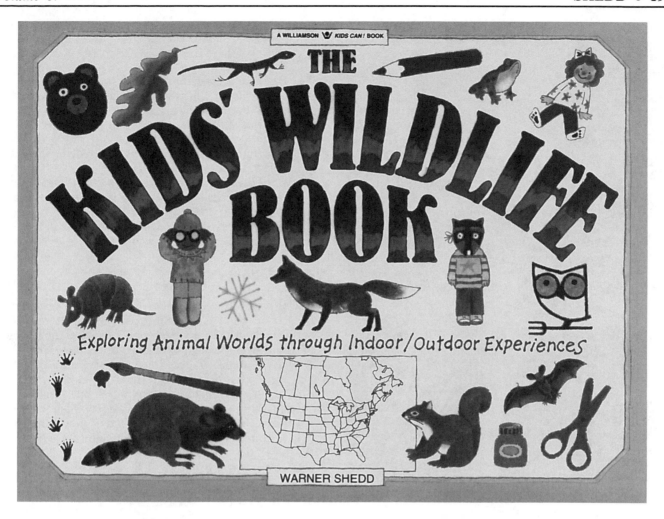

A WILLIAMSON KIDS CAN! BOOK

THE KIDS' WILDLIFE BOOK

Exploring Animal Worlds through Indoor/Outdoor Experiences

WARNER SHEDD

Shedd describes scores of practical ways for children to explore animal lives and their natural habitats in this 1994 nonfiction work. (Cover illustration by Loretta Trezzo Braren.)

a couple of ideas for adult books of the type which they publish.

"I had long been concerned with the erroneous ideas which many people have about wildlife; this problem arises partly from a largely urban/suburban culture which has lost contact with the land and its wild inhabitants and partly from pop culture misinformation such as that fostered by *Gentle Ben* and its ilk. As a partial antidote, I envisioned a book for adults which would portray wild creatures as they really are.

"In the course of my conversation with Jack Williamson, I mentioned this adult book (tentatively titled *Wildlife Myths and Misunderstandings*) as one which I thought would NOT fit into their publishing house format. In passing, I offered several examples of common misunderstandings about wildlife.

"Jack listened attentively and suddenly said, 'You know, children's books are our biggest sellers, and I think this would make a great children's book. Susan edits our children's books, so let's talk with her.' As he spoke a great light seemed to dawn over my head, and I thought, 'Of course!'

"The rest is history. Although the title of the book was changed, it still provides a wealth of accurate information about wildlife and demolishes many common misperceptions. Now I'm in the process of writing a similar children's book about insects; it has the same goal—accurate information presented in a manner which children can enjoy.

"Because of my love for the natural world and my concern for what we are doing to it, I can think of nothing finer than helping educate future generations to understand and appreciate the world as it is, not as sentiment or ignorance dictate that it ought to be. As a corollary, I hope to instill a deep and lasting conservation ethic in children, so that they will do a better job of caring for this planet and its natural resources than their elders have."

■ For More Information See

PERIODICALS

American Forests, September/October, 1994, p. 57.
School Library Journal, August, 1994, p. 152.

LISA SITA

SITA, Lisa 1962-

■ Personal

Born April 30, 1962, in Far Rockaway, NY; daughter of Anthony (a carpenter) and Margaret (Margioni) Sita. *Education:* New York University, B.A. (anthropology), 1984; New School for Social Research, M.A. (anthropology), 1988.

■ Addresses

Office—American Museum of Natural History, Education Department, Central Park West at 79th St., New York, NY 10024.

■ Career

Museum of the American Indian/Heye Foundation, New York City, assistant educator, 1987-88; American Museum of Natural History, New York City, senior museum educator in anthropology, 1988—.

■ Writings

FOR CHILDREN

The Rattle and the Drum: Native American Rituals and Celebrations, illustrated by James Watling, Millbrook Press, 1994.
Rocks, Gems, and Minerals ("Exploring Science" series), Thomson Learning, 1995.
Human Biology and Evolution ("Exploring Science" series), Thomson Learning, 1995.
Worlds of Belief: Religion and Spirituality ("Our Human Family" series), edited by Bruce Glassman, Blackbirch Press, 1995.
Search for Beauty: Art and Music ("Our Human Family" series), Blackbirch Press, 1996.

■ Sidelights

"I was about nine years old when I decided I wanted to become a writer," Lisa Sita told *SATA.* "It seemed a natural response to my passion for reading: the flip side of discovering through books was to create on paper. In college, I took several courses in literature and creative writing. My major, though, was anthropology, which has offered me so much to explore about people and customs around the globe. Now, expressing these discoveries in children's books, I find it gratifying to be able to communicate the beauty of cultural traditions in the hope that young people will take an interest in celebrating the world's diversity."

■ For More Information See

PERIODICALS

School Library Journal, March, 1995, p. 219.

*   *   *

SPOHN, Kate 1962-

■ Personal

Born September 15, 1962, in Geneva, NY; daughter of Robert F. (a teacher) and Barbara (a teacher; maiden name, Kortweg) Spohn. *Education:* Cooper Union, B.F.A., 1985. *Politics:* None. *Religion:* None.

■ Addresses

Home—110 East First St., Apt. 20, New York, NY 10009.

■ Career

Author and illustrator of children's books. *Exhibitions:* Works exhibited at the Eastman-Wahmendorf Gallery and Civilization Gallery, both New York City, 1986, and the Society of Illustrators Museum of American Illustration, 1993 and 1994; works held in the collection of the Weatherspoon Museum, North Carolina.

KATE SPOHN

■ Writings

FOR CHILDREN; SELF-ILLUSTRATED

Clementine's Winter Wardrobe, Orchard Books, 1989.
Ruth's Bake Shop, Orchard Books, 1990.
Introducing Fanny, Orchard Books, 1991.
Fanny and Margarita: Five Stories about Two Best Friends, Viking, 1993.
Christmas at Anna's, Viking, 1993.
Broken Umbrellas, Viking, 1994.
Night Goes By, Macmillan, 1995.

ILLUSTRATOR

Agatha Rose, *Hide and Seek in the Yellow House,* Viking, 1992.
Bill Staines, *River,* Viking, 1994.

■ Work in Progress

An "Easy-to-Read" book for Viking titled *Dog and Cat Shake a Leg.*

■ Sidelights

Combining simple texts with illustrations that range from simple colored pencil drawings to impressionistic oils, Kate Spohn has created several well-received picture books for children. In her first book, *Clementine's Winter Wardrobe,* Spohn shows a cat preparing for the cold season by picking out articles of clothing she will need, one by one. The author's soft pencil illustrations include hints of items to come, providing readers with a puzzle of sorts. "Children will love poring over the array of garments," a *Publishers Weekly* reviewer remarks, adding that Spohn's drawings "are chock-full of charm and detail." Karen Litton similarly praises the artwork in her *School Library Journal* review, noting that the "spareness and the soft colored-pencil hues

sustain a quiet mood and balance the modest excitement of problem-solving."

Spohn also uses colored-pencil drawings to illustrate her books about a special friendship between a self-conscious pear and a supportive banana. *Introducing Fanny* contains four brief stories about Fanny, who worries about her plump, green figure, and her best friend Margarita, who joins Fanny in activities such as doll-making and a sleepover. While a story starring two fruits may sound absurd, "readers will believe in the characters ... easily," Anna Biagioni Hart writes in *School Library Journal,* praising *Introducing Fanny* as "unusual and different." A *Publishers Weekly* critic likewise calls the book "engaging" and explains that Spohn's illustrations "successfully echo the text's tender, quirky tones and draw the reader" into the story.

The two fruit pals return in *Fanny and Margarita: Five Stories about Two Best Friends,* where they are shown learning to "fly," dealing with Fanny's first crush, and telling jokes in the rain. While another *Publishers Weekly* writer notes the "idiosyncratic look" of Spohn's "delicate, whispery pencil outlines and muted hues," the critic faults the book for its "preoccupation with Fanny's inferred flaws," such as her weight and shape. *Booklist* contributor Hazel Rochman, however, finds both text and artwork "quiet and expressive," concluding that "the story of the outsider who finds she's not alone will touch kids where it hurts."

A self-conscious pear finds needed support in her friendship with a banana in Spohn's self-illustrated *Introducing Fanny.*

For her next work, Spohn used oil paints and a more sophisticated, impressionistic style for her artwork. *Christmas at Anna's* tells of Sam and Thea's visit to spend the holiday with their favorite cousin. Anna is an artist, and her activities with Sam and Thea include choosing a Christmas tree, making wreaths, and drinking eggnog before they open presents on Christmas morning. "The pared-down text glows with quiet exuberance," a *Publishers Weekly* reviewer states, but it is Spohn's artwork that is most memorable, according to Carolyn Phelan of *Booklist*. With their "simplified forms and unusual color combinations," the critic writes, Spohn's paintings "express the happiness stated in the text with energy and conviction."

In *Broken Umbrellas* Spohn addresses a subject unusual for younger readers: the situation of the homeless. The author shows a homeless woman from her early days as a girl interested in nature to her career as a university professor to her life on the street. "Spohn's text neither judges nor explains ...," a *Publishers Weekly* writer notes. "Instead, its quiet strength illuminates the heroine's character, with sadness but without pity." Noting that Spohn's "evocative" oils "work particularly well," Ilene Cooper of *Booklist* finds the book "a spare, sensitive offering that can spark discussion or contemplation." Spohn's "warm oil paintings are luminous," a *Kirkus Reviews* critic remarks, and although the book doesn't fully address the issues of homelessness, the reviewer concludes that this "gem of book" contains "an elemental lesson in humanity."

A gentle story of how the sun, the moon, and stars spend their time, *Night Goes By* is a "simple, lively, but at the same time calming and dreamy story," Ruth K. MacDonald writes in *School Library Journal*. After a cloudless day when he has not had a chance for a nap, Sun is happy to see Moon appear in the sky so he can get some rest. Moon, in turn, welcomes her friend Star, who keeps her company until Sun returns the next morning, refreshed and ready to light the world. In his *Bulletin of the Center for Children's Books* review recommending the book, Roger Sutton observes that readers, particularly younger children, "will enjoy the sweetly symmetrical story and Spohn's bravely naive oil paintings." A *Kirkus Reviews* critic similarly praises the artwork—filled with bold shapes among pink, aqua, green, and gray backgrounds—as "finger-paint simple but radiantly expressive," concluding that *Night Goes By* is "a serenely happy fantasy."

Kate Spohn told *SATA:* "I recently read a book where a mother put flowers in her grown daughter's room to prepare for her daughter's visit. My mother does that. Things like this make me happy. In books you can find a kindred spirit. Also, you can learn about worlds that are foreign to you. I like being an artist that makes books because books are so important to me. I wish to encourage beginning readers by telling them that I got off to a slow start learning to read, and that my spelling was terrible and it still is."

■ Works Cited

Review of *Broken Umbrellas, Kirkus Reviews,* September 15, 1995, pp. 1282-83.

Review of *Broken Umbrellas, Publishers Weekly,* September 19, 1994, p. 69.

Review of *Christmas at Anna's, Publishers Weekly,* September 20, 1993, p. 37.

Review of *Clementine's Winter Wardrobe, Publishers Weekly,* August 11, 1989, pp. 455-56.

Cooper, Ilene, review of *Broken Umbrellas, Booklist,* September 15, 1994, p. 145.

Review of *Fanny and Margarita: Five Stories about Two Best Friends, Publishers Weekly,* March 1, 1993, p. 56.

Hart, Anna Biagioni, review of *Introducing Fanny, School Library Journal,* April, 1991, pp. 102, 104.

Review of *Introducing Fanny, Publishers Weekly,* January 11, 1991, pp. 100-101.

Litton, Karen, review of *Clementine's Winter Wardrobe, School Library Journal,* November, 1989, p. 95.

MacDonald, Ruth K., review of *Night Goes By, School Library Journal,* June, 1995.

Review of *Night Goes By, Kirkus Reviews,* April 1, 1995.

Phelan, Carolyn, review of *Christmas at Anna's, Booklist,* August, 1993, p. 2071.

Rochman, Hazel, review of *Fanny and Margarita: Five Stories about Two Best Friends, Booklist,* January 15, 1993, p. 924.

Sutton, Roger, review of *Night Goes By, Bulletin of the Center for Children's Books,* June, 1995.

■ For More Information See

PERIODICALS

Booklist, September 15, 1989, p. 190; August, 1990, p. 2180.

Bulletin of the Center for Children's Books, September, 1994, pp. 3-4.

Kirkus Reviews, April 1, 1992.

Publishers Weekly, November 22, 1993.

School Library Journal, October, 1990, p. 102; March, 1992; March, 1993, p. 186; October, 1993, p. 48; June, 1994; October, 1994.

*   *   *

STORR, Catherine (Cole) 1913-
(Irene Adler, Helen Lourie)

■ Personal

Born July 21, 1913, in London, England; daughter of Arthur Frederick (a lawyer) and Margaret (Gaselee) Cole; married Anthony Storr (a psychiatrist and writer), February 6, 1942; married Lord Balogh (an economist), 1970; children: (first marriage) Sophia, Cecilia, Emma. *Education:* Newnham College, Cambridge, 1932-36 and 1939-41, B.A. (honors) in English, 1935; West London Hospital, 1941-44, qualified medical practitioner, 1944. *Religion:* Agnostic.

■ Addresses

Home—12 Frognal Gardens, London NW3 6UX, England. *Agent*—Peters, Fraser, & Dunlop, 5th Floor, The Chambers, Chelsea Harbour, Lots Road, London SW10 0XF, England.

■ Career

West London Hospital, London, England, assistant psychiatrist, 1948-50; Middlesex Hospital, London, England, assistant psychiatrist, 1950-62; Penguin Books Ltd., London, assistant editor, 1966-70. Writer, 1952—. *Member:* Royal College of Physicians (Licensee), Royal College of Surgeons.

■ Writings

FICTION FOR CHILDREN

Ingeborg and Ruthy, Harrap, 1940.
Clever Polly and Other Stories, illustrated by Dorothy Craigie, Faber, 1952.
Stories for Jane, illustrated by Peggy Jeremy, Faber, 1952.
Clever Polly and the Stupid Wolf, illustrated by Marjorie-Ann Watts, Faber, 1955.
Polly, the Giant's Bride, illustrated by Marjorie-Ann Watts, Faber, 1956.
The Adventures of Polly and the Wolf, illustrated by Marjorie-Ann Watts, Faber, 1957, Macrae Smith, 1970.
Marianne Dreams, illustrated by Marjorie-Ann Watts, Faber, 1958, revised edition, Penguin, 1964, published as *The Magic Drawing Pencil,* A. S. Barnes, 1960.
Marianne and Mark, illustrated by Marjorie-Ann Watts, Faber, 1960.
Lucy, illustrated by Dick Hart, Bodley Head, 1961, Prentice Hall, 1968.
Lucy Runs Away, illustrated by Dick Hart, Bodley Head, 1962, Prentice Hall, 1969.
Robin, illustrated by Peggy Fortnum, Faber, 1962, published as *The Freedom of the Seas,* Duell, 1965.
The Catchpole Story, Faber, 1965.
Rufus, illustrated by Peggy Fortnum, Faber, 1969, Gambit, 1969.
Puss and Cat, illustrated by Carolyn Dinan, Faber, 1969.
Thursday, Faber, 1971, Harper, 1972.
Kate and the Island, illustrated by Gareth Floyd, Faber, 1972.
The Painter and the Fish, illustrated by Alan Howard, Faber, 1975.
The Chinese Egg, Faber, 1975, McGraw Hill, 1975.
The Story of the Terrible Scar, illustrated by Gerald Rose, Faber, 1976.
Who's Bill?, Macmillan, 1976.
Hugo and His Grandma, illustrated by Nita Sowter, Dinosaur, 1977.
Hugo and His Grandma's Washing Day, illustrated by Nita Sowter, Dinosaur, 1978.
Winter's End, Macmillan, 1978, Harper, 1979.

Tales of Polly and the Hungry Wolf, illustrated by Jill Bennett, Faber, 1980.
Vicky, Faber, 1981.
The Bugbear, illustrated by Elaine McGregor Turney, Hamish Hamilton, 1981.
It Couldn't Happen to Me, Dinosaur, 1982.
February Yowler, illustrated by Gareth Floyd, Faber, 1982.
The Castle Boy, Faber, 1983.
Two's Company, Hardy, 1984.
It Shouldn't Happen to a Frog, Macmillan, 1984.
Enter Wagga ("Wagga Storybooks"), illustrated by Colin Caket, Hamlyn, 1984.
Lost and Found Wagga ("Wagga Storybooks"), illustrated by Colin Caket, Hamlyn, 1984.
Wagga's Magic Ears ("Wagga Storybooks"), illustrated by Colin Caket, Hamlyn, 1984.
Watchdog Wagga ("Wagga Storybooks"), illustrated by Colin Caket, Hamlyn, 1984.
Cold Marble and Other Ghost Stories, Faber, 1985.
The Underground Conspiracy, Faber, 1987.
The Boy and the Swan, illustrated by Laszlo Acs, Deutsch, 1987.
(With Griselda Gifford and Jill Kent) *Not Too Young and Other Stories,* Macmillan, 1987.
Mrs. Circumference, Deutsch, 1989.
Daljit and the Unqualified Wizard, Heinemann, 1989.
The Spy before Yesterday, Hamish Hamilton, 1990.
We Didn't Think of Ostriches, Longman, 1990.
Last Stories of Polly and the Wolf, illustrated by Jill Bennett, Puffin, 1992.
Babybug, illustrated by Fiona Dunbar, Simon & Schuster, 1992.
Finn's Animal, illustrated by Paul Howard, Heinemann, 1992.
The Mirror Image Ghost, Faber, 1994.
Watcher at the Window, illustrated by Judith Lawton, Longman, 1995.
Stephen and the Family Nose, Ginn, 1995.

NONFICTION FOR CHILDREN

Pebble (reader), Macmillan, 1979.
Pen Friends (reader), illustrated by Charles Front, Macmillan, 1980.
Feasts and Festivals, illustrated by Jenny Rhodes, Hardy, 1983.
Competitions and Ponies, Macmillan, 1987.

"PEOPLE OF THE BIBLE" SERIES; RETELLER

Noah and His Ark, Watts, 1982, Raintree, 1982.
Joseph and His Brothers, Watts, 1982, Raintree, 1982.
The Birth of Jesus, Watts, 1982, Raintree, 1982.
Jesus Begins His Work, Watts, 1982, Raintree, 1982.
Adam and Eve, Watts, 1983, Raintree, 1983.
Jonah and the Whale, Watts, 1983, Raintree, 1983.
The Prodigal Son, Watts, 1983, Raintree, 1983.
Miracles by the Sea, Watts, 1983, Raintree, 1983.
The First Easter, Watts, 1984, Raintree, 1984.
Moses of the Bulrushes, Watts, c. 1984, Raintree, c. 1984.
Joseph the Dreamteller, Watts, c. 1984, Raintree, c. 1984.
The Good Samaritan, Watts, c. 1984, Raintree, c. 1984.

Abraham and Isaac, Watts, 1985, Raintree, 1985.
Moses and the Plagues of Egypt, Watts, 1985, Raintree, 1985.
David and Goliath, Watts, 1985, Raintree, 1985.
St. Peter and St. Paul, Watts, 1985, Raintree, 1985.
Jesus and John the Baptist, Watts, 1985, Raintree, 1985.
The Trials of Daniel, Watts, 1985, Raintree, 1985.
King David, Watts, 1985, Raintree, 1985.
Sampson and Delilah, Watts, 1985, Raintree, 1985.
Ruth's Story, Watts, 1985, Raintree, 1985.
Jesus the Healer, Watts, 1985, Raintree, 1985.
Joseph the Long Lost Brother, Watts, c. 1986, Raintree, c. 1986.
Moses Leads His People, Watts, c. 1986, Raintree, c. 1986.

"GREAT TALES FROM LONG AGO" SERIES; RETELLER

Robin Hood, Methuen, 1984, Raintree, 1984.
Rip Van Winkle, Methuen, 1984, Raintree, 1984.
Hiawatha, Methuen, 1984, Raintree, 1984.
The Pied Piper of Hamelin, Methuen, 1984, Raintree, 1984.
Joan of Arc, Methuen, 1985, Raintree, 1985.
King Midas and His Gold, Methuen, 1985, Raintree, 1985.
Odysseus and the Enchanters, Methuen, 1985, Raintree, 1985.
Theseus and the Minotaur, Methuen, 1985, Raintree, 1985.
Dick Whittington, Methuen, 1985, Raintree, 1985.
The Wooden Horse, Methuen, 1985, published as *The Trojan Horse,* Raintree, 1985.
King Arthur's Sword, Methuen, c. 1986, Raintree, c. 1986.
Androcles and the Lion, Methuen, c. 1986, Raintree, c. 1986.
Richard the Lionheart, Methuen, c. 1986, Raintree, c. 1986.

"EASY PIANO PICTURE BOOKS"; RETELLER

(With Dianne Jackson) *Swan Lake,* Faber, 1987.
The Nutcracker, Faber, 1987.
The Sleeping Beauty, Faber, 1987.
Hansel and Gretel, Faber, 1987.
Peter & the Wolf, Faber, 1991.

"LET'S READ TOGETHER" SERIES; ILLUSTRATED BY TONI GOFFE

A Fast Move, Macdonald, 1987, Silver Burdett, 1987.
Find the Specs, Macdonald, 1987, Silver Burdett, 1987.
Grandpa's Birthday, Macdonald, 1987, Silver Burdett, 1987.
Gran Builds a House, Macdonald, 1987, published as *Building a House,* Silver Burdett, 1987.

ADULT FICTION

(Under pseudonym Helen Lourie) *A Question of Abortion,* Bodley Head, 1962.
(Under pseudonym Irene Adler) *Freud for the Jung; Or, Three Hundred and Sixty-Six Hours on the Couch,* Cresset Press, 1963.
The Merciful Jew, Barrie & Rockliff, 1968.
Black God, White God, Barrie & Jenkins, 1972.

Unnatural Fathers, Quartet, 1976.
Tales from the Psychiatrist's Couch, Quartet, 1977.

ADULT NONFICTION

Cook's Quick Reference: Essential Information on Cards, Penguin, 1971.
(Editor) Isabelle Jan, *On Children's Literature,* Allen Lane, 1973, Schocken, 1974.
Growing Up: A Practical Guide to Adolescence for Parents and Children, Arrow, 1975.

OTHER

Author of *Flax into Gold: The Story of Rumpelstiltskin,* a children's libretto with music by Hugo Cole, Chappell, 1964; also author of the children's television plays in the *Starting Out* series, 1973-78, and the adult radio play, *Bevil,* 1984. Contributor of reviews to *Times Literary Supplement* and of articles to *Nova* and *Cosmopolitan.* Manuscript collection at Kerlan Collection, University of Minnesota, Minneapolis.

■ Sidelights

Trained as a psychiatrist, the English writer Catherine Storr has found her most effective form of personal therapy in writing. "I started writing when I was ten years old," she once told *SATA,* "and it has become an addiction.... I think in story form and my dreams often take the form of stories, though hardly ever useful as plots.... I don't write with a child readership in mind, I write for the childish side of myself, and find it often acts as psychotherapy."

Psychotherapy, compulsion, or pure enjoyment, Storr's writings have spanned more than five decades, several genres, and include some one hundred picture books, retellings, and novels for both children and adults. Exploring such themes as the power of dreams and adolescent sexuality, Storr's books often employ elements of myth and folktale, blending realism with fantasy. On the whole, her work has been better received in her own country than in the United States, where some reviewers have tended to take her empowering stories for children a bit too literally: her encouragement to understand one's dream life has been criticized as not facing up to real-life problems; a gift of love to a troubled youth from his young girlfriend was interpreted as misguided and base sexuality. Perhaps best known for her children's books about clever Polly and the stupid Wolf who is forever trying to eat her up and for the Lucy books about the young tomboy protagonist, Storr has also produced an impressive array of young adult novels, including *Rufus, Thursday,* and *Marianne Dreams,* which Fred Inglis, writing in *Twentieth-Century Children's Writers,* called Storr's "best book."

Storr had a lengthy apprenticeship, however, before the writing of such books. The ten-year-old child who suddenly and impulsively began writing a poem to the moon had almost twenty years to go before the publication of her first children's book, thirty before publishing with any regularity. Meanwhile, she wrote poetry and stories incessantly, often forcing her younger brother to listen to her creations. Beginning as a teenager, she regularly sent her stories and poems to magazines, and just as regularly had them returned. Graduating with a degree in English, Storr began to wonder about the wisdom of being an unpublished writer, but did not give up writing. Instead she chose medicine as a career, partly, as she wrote in *The Thorny Paradise,* because "I thought that as a doctor I would get that experience of life which was wanted in my writing." Of course the inevitable happened: just before embarking on her medical studies, she sold her first children's book, *Ingeborg and Ruthy,* a fantasy about a doll she'd had as a child. There followed another decade of studies and qualifying as a medical doctor and then as a practicing psychiatrist. She also married and had three children. Plenty of real-life experiences for Storr, plenty of story material. When she began writing again, it was only natural to continue with children's books, as she had her own children now to whom she was telling stories.

Some of Storr's earliest children's books, the Polly stories, were also among her most popular. *Clever Polly and the Stupid Wolf* and *The Adventures of Polly and the Wolf* appeared in the mid-1950s and found an eager readership. Storr returned to the Polly stories 25 years later with *Tales of Polly and the Hungry Wolf* and finished out the series in 1990 with *Last Stories of Polly and the Wolf.* Employing the big bad wolf motif, Storr stands this primal myth on its head by making the young girl incredibly clever and almost indifferent to the machinations of the clumsy and gullible wolf who marauds around a suburban landscape in hopes of gobbling Polly up. "Catherine Storr pits Polly against the wolf in round after round of this contest," noted Dick King-Smith in *Books for Keeps.* Reviewing Storr's *Last Stories of Polly and the Wolf,* Angela Redfern noted in the *School Librarian* that "the usual winning ingredients are in evidence again," the primary ingredient being the resourcefulness of young Polly, who is walking and talking proof of the old adage about brains winning out over brawn.

Survival and empowerment are also themes explored in the Lucy books, including *Lucy,* in which the little tomboy tries to be accepted by the neighborhood boys by pretending to be Lew the detective, and *Lucy Runs Away,* in which Lucy does in fact go off on an adventure on a train all the way to the sea, where she helps to save an old man from drowning. While *Kirkus Reviews* thought the latter book was "bouncy and brash enough" to probably content other little girls who had Lucy's craving for adventure, and *Bulletin of the Center for Children's Books* noted that it had "good dialogue, and a satisfying plot," Marguerite M. Murray, writing in *Library Journal,* took the story rather more literally: "A pedestrian adventure that should not be allowed to circulate," commented Murray, who felt the book might incite children to run away from home.

With *Marianne Dreams* and *Marianne and Mark,* Storr moved into the realms of juvenile and young adult fiction, where she has continued to make a name for herself. *Marianne Dreams* is the story of a long conva-

lescence which gives Marianne the chance to explore her dream world. The book becomes, in effect, a discourse on the power of dreams, and at the same time is an effective suspense novel involving the invalid Mark and Marianne's care of him. Inglis, in *Twentieth-Century Children's Writers,* calls the book "a metaphor for nursing.... [It] has gravity and power ... [and is] unquestionably a classic." *Marianne and Mark* is a bit lighter in tone, with Marianne on vacation at the seashore, where a fortuneteller's prophecy about someone special coming into her life makes her accept a date from a total stranger and leads her to ignore Mark, who is the only person of real quality around. C. Nordhielm Wooldridge, writing in *School Library Journal,* noted that the book deals with "universal growing-up problems."

Such problems were further investigated in *Rufus* and *Thursday,* both realistic novels tinged with an element of fantasy. In *Rufus,* the friendless protagonist is an orphan who leaves the world of bullies behind for his dreamscape of ancient Britain. Finally his dream world gives Rufus the power to deal with his real-life problems, as well, making a reviewer for *Kirkus Reviews* wonder if there is "any reader with a sensibility so corrugated to resist Rufus' appeal." Other reviewers, including Susan Rowe in *New York Times Book Review,*

Storr's 1969 tale describes the efforts of a little tomboy who must prove her courage to win the acceptance of the neighborhood boys. (Cover illustration by Victoria de Larrea.)

again took a more literal view, criticizing the book for encouraging the notion that difficult situations can be resolved by "retreating into the world of dreams," as Rowe characterized the story.

Thursday looks at another outsider, a London teenager who disappears from school only to be found by his young girlfriend, Bee. Thursday, the boy, seems to have had a mental breakdown, but Bee subscribes to the notion that his spirit has been stolen by the wee folk, and restores it to him by an all-night vigil on Midsummer Eve. A *Publishers Weekly* critic thought it was an "unusual and suspenseful book and one that young girls especially should enjoy," and Mary M. Burns in *Horn Book* noted that the "narrative is filled with an unusual blend of common sense and something beyond sense.... A provocative and moving study." Once again, however, other reviewers took a more literal view of the story: According to a *Kirkus Reviews* contributor who understood the all-night vigil to be a love tryst, "Bee's solution is nothing more than a crock of fool's gold."

Sometimes criticized for her use of the dream world and the unconscious in her stories, and sometimes applauded for it, Storr also employs such forces in the very

Young Stephen, Vicky, and Chris become involved in a desperate search for a kidnapped baby in Storr's suspenseful tale of mystery and magic. (Cover illustration by Andrew Rhodes.)

process of writing. "As a writer I rely enormously on the unconscious," she commented in *The Thorny Paradise.* But Storr was also quick to point out that "however rich the material and great the impetus given by the dynamic unconscious, there must always be the more objective attitude, the power to judge, evaluate and shape into coherence, provided by the conscious intelligence." It is this blending that makes not only her writing effective, but that informs her themes and plots, as well. In *The Chinese Egg,* for example, Storr blends a realistic story of suspense and kidnapping with an element of magic when Stephen loses some of the pieces to his interlocking wooden puzzle. Vicky, finding one of the pieces, suddenly discovers that, with Stephen, she is endowed with the power to foresee events. With the aid of her sister Chris, the three help the initially skeptical police to find kidnappers who have taken a baby, a plot that results in an "utterly absorbing story of suspense," according to a *Horn Book* critic. "With its well done characterizations, it is definitely absorbing enough to hold most good junior high and average high school readers," concluded Christine Milana in *School Library Journal.*

Vicky makes another appearance in a later book of the same name in which she uses the remnants of her telepathic powers to discover the identity of her biological father. In this book the reader learns that Vicky has been adopted at birth: she and sister Chris came home from the hospital together, in fact, after Vicky's mother had died in the hospital. Now with the death sixteen years later of her adoptive mother, Vicky desperately wants to find out who her real father is, and enlists the aid of a police inspector from *The Chinese Egg* to help her. Yet when she finally discovers her father, she decides not to let him know of her identity. In *Times Literary Supplement,* Jennifer Moody reflected on the "distinguished series of books for the younger reader" that Storr had thus far written, and concluded that *Vicky* was "the best of them all." A *Junior Bookshelf* writer noted that the book has well drawn characters and in particular a climax that is "clearly and cleverly plotted and excellently written."

Storr deals head-on with adolescent and teenage sexuality in two novels, *Winter's End* and *Two's Company.* In the former she blends elements of Gothic romance in the form of a mysterious house, together with realism and fantasy. Two young undergraduate couples take a study holiday at a country house one of them has inherited. Philip, the owner of the house, is troubled, and not just by his flirtatious girlfriend Cary, who finally coaxes him into bed with her. Another pair arrives, a fellow student and his younger sister, and just in time for this younger sister to help the brooding Philip recover his wits. "Catherine Storr has the ability to capture the stark misty atmosphere of the countryside," noted Drew Stevenson in *School Library Journal,* and a *Bulletin of the Center for Children's Books* reviewer concluded that while the element of fantasy gave the story color and driving force, "it is the realistic problems and relationships that give it substance ... presented with depth and perception."

In *Two's Company,* the theme of love and relationships leads two sisters on holiday in France into the realms of homosexuality and bisexuality. When the sisters meet two young boys, a natural pairing up seems to occur. The younger sister/narrator, however, soon realizes that her love for Val, a homosexual, is hopeless, while her sister is exploited by the more predatory Steve. This action resonates with the predicament of their mother, who is coming to terms with the father's infidelity. Nicholas Tucker in *Times Literary Supplement* found *Two's Company* to be "a moving story, its heart in the right place," while Margaret Meek in *The School Librarian* commented that the book avoided prurient traps and told a universal story: "A more grown-up book than many books for grown-ups," Meek concluded.

An experimenter in genre forms, Storr has also ventured into ghost stories with *Cold Marble and Other Stories* and *The Mirror Image Ghost,* as well as suspense novels with *The Castle Boy* and *The Underground Conspiracy.* Additionally, she has an impressive list of retellings of both Biblical stories and favorite tales such as *Robin Hood* and *Rip Van Winkle.* Yet whatever genre Storr works in, whatever subtexts of psychological inflection, myth and fable, or sexual awakenings she is exploring thematically, her work is first and foremost a simple old-fashioned matter of storytelling. And she is "one of the best story-tellers in the business," according to a *Junior Bookshelf* critic. "I've continued to write for the young," Storr wrote in *The Thorny Paradise,* "not only long after I should have ceased to be childish, but also after my own children were grown up, because of my lasting need for the story form." It is this reliance on story that is, according to Storr, so unique to children's literature. As the author summed up her career for *SATA,* she once said, "I'm basically a storyteller."

■ Works Cited

Burns, Mary M., review of *Thursday, Horn Book,* April, 1973, p. 148.

Review of *The Chinese Egg, Horn Book,* February, 1976, p. 58.

Inglis, Fred, "Storr, Catherine," in *Twentieth-Century Children's Writers,* St. James Press, 1995, pp. 909-12.

King-Smith, Dick, review of *Clever Polly and the Stupid Wolf, Books for Keeps,* November, 1988, pp. 29-30.

Review of *Lucy Runs Away, Bulletin of the Center for Children's Books,* May, 1970, p. 152.

Review of *Lucy Runs Away, Kirkus Reviews,* December 15, 1969, p. 1317.

Meek, Margaret, review of *Two's Company, School Librarian,* March, 1985, pp. 62-63.

Milana, Christine, review of *The Chinese Egg, School Library Journal,* January, 1976, pp. 56-57.

Moody, Jennifer, review of *Vicky, Times Literary Supplement,* November 20, 1981, p. 1355.

Murray, Marguerite M., review of *Lucy Runs Away, Library Journal,* April 15, 1970, p. 1630.

Redfern, Angela, review of *Last Stories of Polly and the Wolf, School Librarian,* February, 1991, p. 25.

Rowe, Susan, review of *Rufus, New York Times Book Review,* November 9, 1969, p. 38.

Review of *Rufus, Kirkus Reviews,* October 1, 1969, pp. 1065-66.

Stevenson, Drew, review of *Winter's End, School Library Journal,* May, 1979, p. 83.

Storr, Catherine, "Why Write? Why Write for Children?," in *The Thorny Paradise,* edited by Edward Blishen, Kestrel Books, 1975, pp. 25-33.

Review of *Thursday, Kirkus Reviews,* July 1, 1972, p. 730.

Review of *Thursday, Publishers Weekly,* August 14, 1972, p. 46.

Tucker, Nicholas, review of *Two's Company, Times Literary Supplement,* July 13, 1984, p. 794.

Review of *The Underground Conspiracy, Junior Bookshelf,* December, 1987, p. 289.

Review of *Vicky, Junior Bookshelf,* April, 1982, p. 76.

Review of *Winter's End, Bulletin of the Center for Children's Books,* July-August, 1979, p. 202.

Wooldridge, C. Nordhielm, review of *Marianne and Mark, School Library Journal,* March, 1980, p. 137.

■ For More Information See

PERIODICALS

Booklist, January 1, 1969, p. 500; November 15, 1972, p. 303; December 15, 1975, pp. 574, 581; December 15, 1976, p. 615; August 1, 1982, p. 1529; February 1, 1985, p. 791; February 15, 1996, p. 861.

Bulletin of the Center for Children's Books, January, 1969, p. 85; March, 1976, p. 119; May, 1979, p. 164; April, 1983, p. 143; April, 1985, p. 150.

Junior Bookshelf, April, 1977, p. 101; February, 1979, p. 61; April, 1981, p. 73; June, 1982, p. 101; April, 1983, p. 79; August, 1983, p. 174; December, 1983, p. 250; February, 1985, p. 31; June, 1985, p. 135; April, 1986, pp. 61, 72; April, 1987, p. 95; October, 1990, p. 213; December, 1990, p. 284; December, 1991, p. 255; June, 1994, p. 111.

Library Journal, September 15, 1970, p. 3054; October 15, 1972, p. 3465.

School Library Journal, January, 1980, p. 62; April, 1981, p. 117; October, 1981, p. 136; November, 1982, p. 91; April, 1985, p. 89; March, 1986, p. 179.

Times Educational Supplement, November 15, 1985, p. 49; November 6, 1987, p. 46; March 18, 1988, p. 32; October 6, 1989, p. 32; April 1, 1994, p. 22.

Times Literary Supplement, November 30, 1967, p. 1137; August 8, 1968, p. 841; April 3, 1969, p. 355; December 4, 1969, p. 1384; December 8, 1972, p. 1491; October 1, 1976, p. 1248; December 1, 1978, p. 1394; March 26, 1982, p. 344; July 23, 1982, p. 797; May 29, 1987, p. 589; January 1, 1988, p. 21.*

—Sketch by J. Sydney Jones

SYME, (Neville) Ronald 1913-1992

■ Personal

Born March 13, 1913 (some sources say 1910), in Lancashire, England; died December 19, 1992; son of David Godfrey and Ida Florence (Kerr) Syme; married Ngamarama Heiarii Feena Amoa, February 12, 1960; children: Florence Tia te Pa Tua. *Education:* Attended Durham School, England, 1924-26, and Collegiate School, Wanganui, New Zealand, 1926-29. *Politics:* Conservative.

■ Career

Freelance writer, 1946-1992. British Merchant Service, cadet and officer, 1930-34, gunner, 1939-50; reporter and foreign correspondent, 1934-39; John Westhouse & Peter Lunn Ltd., London, England, assistant editor, 1946-48; British Road Federation, London, public relations officer, 1948-50; public relations officer and parliamentary correspondent, Cook Islands Government, 1979-83. *Military service:* British Army, Intelligence Corps, 1940-45; became major. *Member:* Authors Society (England).

■ Awards, Honors

Boys' Clubs of America medalist award, 1951, for *Bay of the North.*

■ Writings

JUVENILE FICTION

That Must Be Julian, illustrated by William Stobbs, Lunn, 1947.
Julian's River War, illustrated by John Harris, Heinemann, 1949.
Ben of the Barrier, illustrated by J. Nicholson, Evans, 1949.
I, Mungo Park, illustrated by Stobbs, Burke, 1951.
I, Captain Anson: My Voyage around the World, illustrated by Stobbs, Burke, 1952.
I, Gordon of Khartoum, illustrated by Stobbs, Burke, 1953.
The Settlers of Carriacou, Hodder & Stoughton, 1953.
Gipsy Michael, illustrated by Stobbs, Hodder & Stoughton, 1954.
They Came to an Island, illustrated by Stobbs, Hodder & Stoughton, 1955.
Isle of Revolt, illustrated by Stobbs, Hodder & Stoughton, 1956.
Ice Fighter, illustrated by Stobbs, Hodder & Stoughton, 1956.
The Amateur Company, Hodder & Stoughton, 1957.
The Great Canoe, Hodder & Stoughton, 1957.
The Forest Fighters, illustrated by Stobbs, Hodder & Stoughton, 1958.
River of No Return, illustrated by Stobbs, Hodder & Stoughton, 1958.
The Spaniards Came at Dawn, illustrated by Stobbs, Hodder & Stoughton, 1959.

Thunder Knoll, illustrated by Stobbs, Hodder & Stoughton, 1960.
The Buccaneer Explorer, illustrated by Stobbs, 1960.
The Mountainy Men, illustrated by Richard Payne, Hodder & Stoughton, 1961.
Coast of Danger, illustrated by Payne, Hodder & Stoughton, 1961.
Nose-Cap Astray, illustrated by Payne, Hodder & Stoughton, 1962.
Two Passengers for Spanish Fork, illustrated by Brian Keogh, Hodder & Stoughton, 1963.
Switch Points at Kamlin, illustrated by Keogh, Hodder & Stoughton, 1964.
The Dunes and the Diamonds, illustrated by Keogh, Hodder & Stoughton, 1964.
The Missing Witness, Hodder & Stoughton, 1965.
The Saving of the Fair East Wind, illustrated by A. R. Whitear, Dent, 1967.

JUVENILE NONFICTION

Full Fathom Five, Lunn, 1946.
Hakluyt's Sea Stories, illustrated by Stobbs, Heinemann, 1948.
Bay of the North: The Story of Pierre Radisson, illustrated by Ralph Ray, Morrow, 1950, Hodder & Stoughton, 1951.
Cortes of Mexico, illustrated by Stobbs, Morrow, 1951 (published in England as *Cortez, Conqueror of Mexico,* Hodder & Stoughton, 1952).
Champlain of the St. Lawrence, illustrated by Stobbs, Morrow, 1952, Hodder & Stoughton, 1953.
Columbus, Finder of the New World, illustrated by Stobbs, Morrow, 1952.
The Story of Britain's Highways, Pitman, 1952.
La Salle of the Mississippi, illustrated by Stobbs, Morrow, 1953, Hodder & Stoughton, 1953.
Magellan, First around the World, illustrated by Stobbs, Morrow, 1953.
John Smith of Virginia, illustrated by Stobbs, Morrow, 1954, Hodder & Stoughton, 1954, new edition, University of London Press, 1965.
Henry Hudson, illustrated by Stobbs, Morrow, 1955 (published in England as *Hudson of the Bay,* Hodder & Stoughton, 1955).
Balboa, Finder of the Pacific, illustrated by Stobbs, Morrow, 1956.
De Soto, Finder of the Mississippi, illustrated by Stobbs, Morrow, 1957.
The Man Who Discovered the Amazon (on Pizarro), illustrated by Stobbs, Morrow, 1958.
Cartier, Finder of the St. Lawrence, illustrated by Stobbs, Morrow, 1958.
On Foot to the Arctic: The Story of Samuel Hearne, illustrated by Stobbs, Morrow, 1959 (published in England as *Trail to the North,* Hodder & Stoughton, 1959).
Vasco Da Gama, Sailor towards the Sunrise, illustrated by Stobbs, Morrow, 1959.
Captain Cook, Pacific Explorer, illustrated by Stobbs, Morrow, 1960.
Francis Drake, Sailor of the Unknown Seas, illustrated by Stobbs, Morrow, 1961.

First Man to Cross America: The Story of Cabeza de Vaca, illustrated by Stobbs, Morrow, 1961.

Walter Raleigh, illustrated by Stobbs, Morrow, 1962.

The Young Nelson, illustrated by Susan Groom and Trevor Parkin, Parrish, 1962, Roy, 1963.

African Traveler: The Story of Mary Kingsley, illustrated by Jacqueline Tomes, Morrow, 1962.

Francisco Pizarro, Finder of Peru, illustrated by Stobbs, Morrow, 1963.

Invaders and Invasions, illustrated by Stobbs, Batsford, 1964, Norton, 1965.

The Invasions of Britain: A Historical Record, Batsford, 1964.

Nigerian Pioneer: The Story of Mary Slessor, illustrated by Jacqueline Tomes, Morrow, 1964.

Alexander Mackenzie, Canadian Explorer, illustrated by Stobbs, Morrow, 1964.

Sir Henry Morgan, Buccaneer, illustrated by Stobbs, Morrow, 1965.

Francisco Coronado and the Seven Cities of Gold, illustrated by Stobbs, Morrow, 1965.

Quesada of Colombia, illustrated by Stobbs, Morrow, 1966.

William Penn, Founder of Pennsylvania, illustrated by Stobbs, Morrow, 1966.

Garibaldi, the Man Who Made a Nation, illustrated by Stobbs, Morrow, 1967.

Bolivar, the Liberator, illustrated by Stobbs, Morrow, 1968.

Captain John Paul Jones, America's Fighting Seaman, illustrated by Stobbs, Morrow, 1968.

Amerigo Vespucci, Scientist and Sailor, illustrated by Stobbs, Morrow, 1969.

Frontenac of New France, illustrated by Stobbs, Morrow, 1969.

Benedict Arnold, Traitor of the Revolution, illustrated by Stobbs, Morrow, 1970.

Vancouver, Explorer of the Pacific Coast, illustrated by Stobbs, Morrow, 1970.

Toussaint, the Black Liberator, illustrated by Stobbs, Morrow, 1971.

Zapata, Mexican Rebel, illustrated by Stobbs, Morrow, 1971.

John Cabot and His Son Sebastian, illustrated by Stobbs, Morrow, 1972.

Juarez, the Founder of Modern Mexico, illustrated by Richard Cuffari, Morrow, 1972.

Verrazano, Explorer of the Atlantic Coast, illustrated by Stobbs, Morrow, 1973.

Fur Trader of the North: The Story of Pierre de la Verendrye, illustrated by Cuffari, Morrow, 1973.

John Charles Fremont, the Last American Explorer, illustrated by Cuffari, Morrow, 1974.

Marquette and Joliet, Voyagers on the Mississippi, illustrated by Stobbs, Morrow, 1974.

Geronimo, the Fighting Apache, illustrated by Ben Stahl, Morrow, 1975.

Osceola, Seminole Leader, illustrated by Stahl, Morrow, 1976.

ADULT NONFICTION

The Story of British Roads, British Road Federation, 1951.

The Windward Islands (Frontiers of the Caribbean, Islands of the Sun, A Schooner Voyage in the West Indies), photographs by the author, Pitman, 3 vols., 1953.

The Story of New Zealand (We Dip Into the Past, Life in New Zealand Today, A Tour of New Zealand), Pitman, 3 vols., 1954.

The Cook Islands (The Coming of Man, Life in the Islands Today, A Tour of the Islands), Pitman, 3 vols., 1955.

The Travels of Captain Cook, photographs by Werner Forman, McGraw Hill, 1971, Joseph, 1972.

Isles of the Frigate Bird (autobiography), Joseph, 1975.

The Lagoon Is Lonely Now (autobiography), Millwood Press, 1979.

■ Sidelights

Ronald Syme was a prolific writer of adventure stories for young readers as well as the creator of a series of nonfiction books on explorers and leaders worldwide, all marked by an easy and engaging style. English by birth, Irish by nationality and temperament, New Zealander by education, Syme lived a nomadic and wandering existence—as a merchant seaman and freelance reporter—until he settled on Rarotonga in the Cook Islands in the early 1950s. Here, in his late forties, Syme married a young and beautiful Polynesian girl, began a family, and settled into a routine of writing that endured for well over a quarter of a century. "Six mornings a week, I sit on my verandah overlooking a subtropical garden of flowers and distant mountains," Syme once related. "While drinking a strong mug of tea, I turn over in my mind the part of the story I will be writing on that particular day. After breakfast, I start work at nine a.m. and go right through until twelve noon. If the story has been running well, another thousand words of manuscript are generally completed by then. During the afternoons, I usually take myself off to fish on the nearby reef and review in my mind what I have written that morning. If a sudden weakness or *non sequitur* occurs to me, I correct my pages in the evening. If all has gone well, I never touch them again until the next morning."

It was a recipe for success, or as much success as Syme needed to support a simple life in paradise. Producing about two books per year, both fiction and nonfiction, Syme had plenty of time for fishing and family, and his adventure tales especially echo his experiences at sea and his life on what was at the time an unspoiled South Sea island. None of Syme's fiction was published in the United States, but in England his name—when not confused for that of the scholar and historian of ancient Rome, Sir Ronald Syme—is associated with his fast moving and exciting tales for boys set in exotic parts of the world. The South Seas was often the setting for his stories, as in *Nose-Cap Astray,* which tells of the recovery of a missing space rocket by a young white boy and a Polynesian boy, and *The Saving of the Fair East Wind,* which dealt with the salvaging of a cargo ship. Both of these stories also feature Prince Oro of Manapoa.

They Came to an Island, also set in the South Pacific, is a cautionary tale of how a developed culture can negatively impact on a primitive one. This message, however, is gift-wrapped in Syme's typical packaging: an action-packed tale of mutiny and shipwreck blended with exploring and treasure hunting. *The Amateur Company* also explores this theme of intrusion, when Joe and his Uncle Ben come to the island of Arorangi in the South Seas to develop its natural resources. But after doing so, the doubt exists whether the island is truly better off now than it was before the two came. *The Great Canoe* tells of fishing life in the Cook Islands. "I've paddled outrigger canoes into deep water beyond the reef," Syme once told *SATA,* "and caught fish which were so large that they towed the canoe for a considerable distance." Syme noted that "being a wanderer in the South Pacific" enabled him to get material for such books as *They Came to an Island* and *The Great Canoe.*

Syme's tales of adventures are also set in the Caribbean, and in historical times as well as the modern day. *Isle of Revolt* deals with an eighteenth-century black uprising against white planters as told through the eyes of the teenage son of one of the planters. *The Settlers of Carriacou,* set on Dominica, concerns the battle for survival of a small group of English settlers set upon by the French. By turns thematically light or serious, Syme's fiction is always incident-packed. In fact it is this very quality, according to Alan Edwin Day in *Twentieth-Century Children's Writers,* that constitutes Syme's major fault as a writer of fiction. Piling up incident upon incident, climax upon climax, "there is no time for reflection, and the story jerks along, breathless and impatient," Day commented. On the other hand, it was a style that kept Syme's young readers turning pages and was, according to Day, an impressive display of the author's inventiveness. Employing essentially stock characters and easily defined situations, Syme appealed

Syme's juvenile biography of Giuseppe Garibaldi, called the father of modern Italy, was his first such study of the life of a political figure. (Illustration by William Stobbs from *Garibaldi, the Man Who Made a Nation.*)

Syme explores the life of the sixteenth-century founder of New Granada (now Colombia) in his biography, *Quesada of Colombia.* (Illustration by William Stobbs.)

to a young readership for whom such recognition was welcome. "At this stage reading should essentially be full of fun and excitement, and these Syme provides in plenty," Day concluded.

Better known in the United States is Syme's nonfiction for juvenile readers. His own background provided valuable grist for this mill, for Syme had travelled over most of the world and spoke several languages. A cosmopolitan by nature, Syme found subjects for his narrative histories in explorers of the golden age of discovery, in political leaders from Italy to South America, in colonists in Africa. Some fifty such men and women became the subjects for Syme's biographies, all told with something of the same reliance on incident that made his adventure stories so popular. Life on peaceful Rarotonga allowed for such an effort. "I think too many authors make the mistake of living ... where a high cost of living necessitates a high rate of literary productivity," Syme told *SATA.* "Nowadays I write a couple of books a year—more or less—and go fishing the rest of the time. Moreover, I now have infinitely more leisure for historical study, on which my books (U.S.A.) are largely based." A fair amount of study there had to be, for Syme writes as knowledgeably of the founding of Mexico as he does of Italy; of the travails of the Seminole Indians of Florida as of a slave revolt in Haiti.

With *Magellan, First around the World,* one of the earliest titles in what became a series for his U.S. publisher, Morrow, Syme set the workmanlike tone for the books to come. His biography of the Portuguese explorer Ferdinand Magellan was a "clear and simple account," according to a *Booklist* reviewer, enhanced by the "bold" pen-and-ink drawings of William Stobbs, who would illustrate most of Syme's titles. A *Kirkus Reviews* critic noted the hallmarks of the series in a review of *Sir Henry Morgan, Buccaneer:* "lively" use of historical documents and enriching vocabulary, as well as a "wholesome respect for the younger reader's capacity to know and enjoy the truth." Virginia Haviland, writing in *Horn Book,* concurred with this assessment, dubbing *Sir Henry Morgan, Buccaneer* an "action-filled biography."

Syme was fascinated by explorers, and focused on many who came to the New World: Christopher Columbus, Rene de La Salle, Samuel de Champlain, Vasco Balboa, Hernando De Soto, Francisco Pizarro, Jacques Cartier, Vasco da Gama, Captain Cook, Francis Drake, and Alvar Cabeza de Vaca all found their way onto the pages of Syme's many books. *Francisco Coronado and the Seven Cities of Gold* followed in this line and was, according to *Kirkus Reviews,* "another excellent biography" that "draws heavily on direct quotations." Nor did Syme only deal with the famous. A less well-known explorer was examined in *Quesada of Colombia;* Gonzalo Quesada was a Spanish lawyer and adventurer who founded the sixteenth-century South American kingdom of New Granada, later to become Colombia. A *Booklist* reviewer called the book a "dispassionate, graphic account" of Quesada's exploits, while Mary Jo Klinger-

man noted in *Library Journal* that Syme's use of actual diary excerpts "lend authenticity and a sense of reality to the text."

With *Garibaldi, the Man Who Made a Nation,* Syme branched out into a study of leaders, political organizers, and national heroes. Garibaldi, called the founder of modern Italy, was a tough sell to young American readers for whom knowledge of even American history was spotty at best. But by using incident and adventure, Syme made his story "exciting, explicit reading," as a *Kirkus Reviews* critic observed. *Horn Book*'s Haviland called it a "competent, easily read account of an important figure" and added that Syme's text "has color and substance." More books on political and social leaders followed. *Bolivar the Liberator,* about the enigmatic spoiled aristocrat turned South American revolutionary, was written "succinctly and smoothly," according to a *Bulletin of the Center for Children's Books* reviewer. Arthur Orrmont, writing in *New York Times Book Review,* thought it was "successful in portraying Bolivar's complex personality." Syme took on another controversial historical personage in *Benedict Arnold, Traitor of the Revolution* and created what a *Horn Book*

Syme's account of the life of the controversial Benedict Arnold has been commended as a balanced, objective portrait. (Illustration by William Stobbs from *Benedict Arnold, Traitor of the Revolution.*)

writer termed a "balanced account" of this American general. Lavinia Russ, in *Publishers Weekly*, felt the book was a "sympathetic, yet objective biography," that presented a rounded picture of the American Revolution, with all its sights and sounds.

Syme continued this series of biographies with studies of what might be called underdogs: about the one-time Haitian slave Toussaint Louverture, who defied both the British and Napoleon's French; about Benito Juarez and the fight for Mexican independence and Emiliano Zapata, who fought for land reform in that same country; and about two native North Americans—Geronimo of the Apaches and Osceola of the Seminoles. *Toussaint, the Black Liberator* was "objective in tone, candid in approach, and written with authoritative informality," according to a *Bulletin of the Center for Children's Books* critic. With *Juarez, the Founder of Modern Mexico*, Syme found another subject who rose from lowly station to become a national hero. Born with the double disadvantage of facing poverty and prejudice against Indians, Juarez became a lawyer and a battler of corruption and ultimately helped found the modern nation of Mexico. Jack Forman, writing in *Library*

Syme's sympathetic biography, *Osceola: Seminole Leader*, recounts the Seminoles' fight to keep their Florida homeland. (Illustration by Ben F. Stahl.)

Journal, found the biography to be "objective and accurate," while a *Bulletin of the Center for Children's Books* reviewer noted that it was also an "excellent survey of Mexican history in the 19th century."

Syme's last juvenile biography was *Osceola, Seminole Leader*, a study of the native American leader—son of an English trader and a Creek Indian woman—who found refuge with the Seminoles and led a guerilla movement with his adopted tribe against the United States removal plan that would have deported the Seminoles to Oklahoma. Finally captured under a flag of truce, Osceola became a symbol of the betrayal of Native Americans by U.S. policy. A *Kirkus Reviews* writer termed the biography an "energetic, fairly straightforward reconstruction," while a critic for *Booklist* concluded that it was a "sympathetic presentation of a complex series of tragic events."

It was ironic that while Syme wrote of such historical injustices, similar events were also occurring under his very nose. During the last years of Syme's life, he witnessed the gradual and then quite rapid destruction of traditional ways on his South Sea island. The advent of tourism on Rarotonga changed forever the peaceful lives of the islanders. Immigration to New Zealand also diluted the native population, and Syme wrote about

Syme's biography traces the life of Toussaint, the eighteenth-century slave and plantation overseer who gained freedom and struggled against Napoleon to liberate Haiti from French control. (Cover illustration by William Stobbs.)

these changes in autobiographical accounts intended for adult readership: *Isles of the Frigate Bird* and *The Lagoon Is Lonely Now.* Yet he stayed on, writing in the morning and fishing in the afternoon. In the final analysis, writing was a good friend to him. "The thought has never occurred to me as to what I may/may not achieve by my writing," he once remarked. "I was utterly content with the pleasure of being able to move in and out of the lives of others for a brief time while I was recreating their invariably remarkable careers.... Once a book of mine is off to the printing presses, I have lost all interest in it.... Authorship has provided me with a good and carefree life in my own unambitious way."

■ Works Cited

Review of *Benedict Arnold, Traitor of the Revolution, Horn Book,* June, 1971, p. 301.

Review of *Bolivar the Liberator, Bulletin of the Center for Children's Books,* December, 1969, p. 67.

Day, Alan Edwin, "Ronald Syme," in *Twentieth-Century Children's Writers,* 4th edition, St. James Press, 1995, pp. 926-28.

Forman, Jack, review of *Juarez, the Founder of Modern Mexico, Library Journal,* February 15, 1973, p. 648.

Review of *Francisco Coronado and the Seven Cities of Gold, Kirkus Reviews,* September 15, 1965, p. 986.

Review of *Garibaldi, the Man Who Made a Nation, Kirkus Reviews,* September 1, 1967, p. 1053.

Haviland, Virginia, review of *Sir Henry Morgan, Buccaneer, Horn Book,* June, 1965, p. 293.

Haviland, Virginia, review of *Garibaldi, the Man Who Made a Nation, Horn Book,* April, 1968, pp. 190-91.

Review of *Juarez, the Founder of Modern Mexico, Bulletin of the Center for Children's Books,* May, 1973, p. 146.

Klingerman, Mary Jo, review of *Quesada of Colombia, Library Journal,* March 15, 1967, p. 1321.

Review of *Magellan, First around the World, Booklist,* September 15, 1985, p. 144.

Orrmont, Arthur, review of *Bolivar the Liberator, New York Times Book Review,* March 16, 1969, p. 56.

Review of *Osceola, Seminole Leader, Booklist,* September 1, 1976, p. 43.

Review of *Osceola, Seminole Leader, Kirkus Reviews,* May 15, 1976, p. 599.

Review of *Quesada of Colombia, Booklist,* February 15, 1967, p. 640.

Russ, Lavinia, review of *Benedict Arnold, Traitor of the Revolution, Publishers Weekly,* August 31, 1970, p. 280.

Review of *Sir Henry Morgan, Buccaneer, Kirkus Reviews,* January 1, 1965, p. 7.

Review of *Toussaint, the Black Liberator, Bulletin of the Center for Children's Books,* May, 1972, p. 147.

■ For More Information See

PERIODICALS

Booklist, October 1, 1965, p. 163; June 1, 1968, p. 1145; October 1, 1968, p. 192; June 1, 1969, p. 1128; October 15, 1970, p. 197; December 1, 1971, p. 335; June 15, 1972, p. 910; February 15, 1973, p. 574; September 1, 1973, p. 53; May 1, 1974, p. 1007.

Kirkus Reviews, February 1, 1968, p. 120; March 1, 1969, p. 244; August 1, 1974, p. 808.

Library Journal, April 15, 1965, p. 2026; January 15, 1968, p. 296; January 15, 1969, p. 305; April 15, 1969, p. 1786; February 15, 1970, p. 782; November 15, 1970, p. 4064; February 15, 1971, p. 745; September 15, 1971, p. 2937; November 15, 1971, p. 3904; March 15, 1972, p. 1014; September 15, 1972, p. 2955; November 15, 1973, p. 3458.

New York Times Book Review, January 10, 1965, p. 20; November 7, 1965, p. 44; May 5, 1968, p. 40.

Publishers Weekly, November 15, 1971, p. 73.

Times Literary Supplement, September 22, 1972, p. 1124.*

—Sketch by J. Sydney Jones

*   *   *

SYMYNKYWICZ, Jeffrey B(ruce) 1954-

■ Personal

Born September 13, 1954, in Woonsocket, RI; son of Anthony and Margaret (Linder) Symynkywicz; married Elizabeth Fontaine (in religious studies), September 9, 1978; children: Micah, Sarah, Noah. *Education:* Rhode Island College, B.A., 1977; Harvard University, M.Div., 1981. *Politics:* Progressive. *Religion:* Unitarian Universalist.

■ Addresses

Home—98 Bassick Circle, Stoughton, MA 02072. *Office*—P.O. Box 284, Stoughton, MA 02072.

■ Career

First Universalist Society, Hartland, VT, minister, 1982-85; First Universalist Church, Rockland, ME, minister, 1985-93; First Parish Universalist Church, Stoughton, MA, minister, 1993—.

■ Writings

Germany, United Again, Silver Burdett, 1995.

1989: The Year the World Changed, Silver Burdett, 1995.

Vaclav Havel and the Velvet Revolution, Silver Burdett, 1995.

The Soviet Collapse, Silver Burdett, 1996.

*   *   *

TAYLOR, Gage 1942-

■ Personal

Born January 20, 1942, in Texas; married Uriel Dana (an artist), 1986. *Education:* University of Texas,

GAGE TAYLOR

B.F.A.; Michigan State University, M.F.A. *Hobbies and other interests:* Composing, playing, and recording music.

■ Addresses

Office—P.O. Box 2163, Sausalito, CA 94966.

■ Career

Fine artist, 1972—; writer, 1988—.

■ Writings

FOR CHILDREN

(Self-illustrated) *Bears at Work: An A to Z of Bearable Jobs,* Chronicle Books, 1995.

FOR ADULTS

The Book of the Elders, Bibliobytes, 1995.
The Akbar Manuscript, Bibliobytes, 1995.
The Pillars of Fire, Bibliobytes, 1995.

■ Work in Progress

An animated movie, CD-ROM, music album, and series of children's books, all based on *Adventures from Raccoon Hollow;* a children's CD-ROM of *Bears at Work: An A to Z of Bearable Jobs,* for Palladium Interactive, 1996.

■ Sidelights

Gage Taylor has been a professional fine artist for twenty-four years. His work has been shown in galleries and museums throughout the United States and in eleven other countries, and has also appeared in national publications, including *Omni* and *Newsweek.* Since 1984, Gage has painted in collaboration with his wife, Uriel Dana. "Several years ago, I realized I wanted to tell more about the scenes we painted than a still picture could convey: Why is the cheetah sitting in the window of an old temple? Does he sit there every day? Who built the temple? It was then I began my first novel," Taylor told *SATA.*

Taylor began his writing career with a trilogy of metaphysical adventure novels for adults, to be published on the internet by Bibliobytes in 1996. He followed quickly with his first book for children, *Bears at Work: An A to Z of Bearable Jobs.* "It came about as a result of a poster I was commissioned to do for the 'Music from Bear Valley' classical music festival of 1986. It depicted four bears playing music in the mountains ('Quartet in D Meadow') and was a great success," Taylor explained to *SATA.* Over the next few years, Taylor discussed his desire to do "something more with bears" with his wife, artist Uriel Dana. "One day, I was struck by a National Public Radio piece in which a reporter surveyed hundreds of graduating high school seniors and found that many of them had no idea what they wanted to *be,* only what they wanted to *have.* I felt inspired to address this problem, remembered the discussions about 'doing something with bears,' and *Bears at Work* was born," he continued. *Bears at Work* provides children with a lighthearted look at various occupations. It is told in verse and includes detailed paintings of bears doing the jobs described.

*   *   *

TORRES, Laura 1967-

■ Personal

Born March 21, 1967, in Yakima, WA; daughter of James R. (a data technician) and Shirley (a loan officer; maiden name, Gray) Hofmann; married John C. Torres (an assistant professor of sociology), December 19, 1987; children: Brennyn, John Andrew. *Education:* Brigham Young University, A.A., 1987. *Religion:* Church of Jesus Christ of Latter Day Saints (Mormon).

■ Addresses

Home—1643 North 1100 W., Mapleton, UT 84664.

■ Career

Freelance writer, 1990—; creative consultant, 1995—.

LAURA TORRES

■ Awards, Honors

National Parenting Publications Award and Cuffie Award, both 1994, both for *The Incredible Clay Book: How to Make and Bake a Million and One Clay Creations.*

■ Writings

(With Sherri Haab) *The Incredible Clay Book: How to Make and Bake a Million and One Clay Creations,* Klutz Press, 1994.
Beads: A Book of Ideas and Instruction, Klutz Press, 1996.
Friendship Bracelets, Klutz Press, 1996.
The Sticker Book, Klutz Press, 1996.

Contributor to periodicals, including *Children's Digest* and *Jack and Jill.*

■ Work in Progress

A sewing book and a book about pipecleaner crafts, both for Klutz Books, 1997; *The Student Spouse Survival Guide;* children's books; stories for periodicals.

■ Sidelights

"I knew I wanted to be a writer since the second grade," Laura Torres told *SATA.* "When I was a child, I was painfully shy and had a soft voice and was often overlooked. I felt like the invisible girl. When I had to read a story I had written out loud in front of my second-grade class, I thought I would rather die. I read the story. It was about a monster called the Oobla Goobla. The other children listened, laughed, and really seemed to like it. That was an epiphany. I felt, for the first time, I was heard. My most prolific period was in grade school.

"When I was a teenager, after learning the odds of actually making it as a freelance writer, my confidence wavered and my studies and career took a different route, but always centered around books. In high school I worked in a library, in college I studied literature, after college I worked in a print shop, then finally at a publishing company for six years, where I did everything from marketing to purchasing. I sent in stories to children's periodicals here and there and had modest success. I persuaded the publisher I worked for to let my sister and me develop a book on polymer clay projects for kids, which went on to be a best-seller. I found children's nonfiction very satisfying and began selling a few articles on various craft-related subjects.

"My second child was born prematurely and I quit my job to be home with him. My husband was in school, a few years from completing his Ph.D., and we had mounting medical bills. This was the best thing that ever happened to me, career-wise. I dove into freelancing to make ends meet, with jobs from my former employer at first, and my career exploded from there.

"At any given moment I have four projects on the burner and two preschoolers underfoot. I have learned the value of a quiet, concentrated twenty minutes. In less than a year and a half, I will have three books written, all done in these twenty-minute spurts. My goal is to expand into fiction and other genres by the time I'm thirty. (The kids will be in school and my husband will be out!)"

*   *   *

TRAHERNE, Michael
See WATKINS-PITCHFORD, Denys James

V–W

VAUGHAN, Richard 1947-

■ Personal

Born October 19, 1947; married Marcia Pearson (a librarian and writer), November 14, 1984; children: Sam.

■ Addresses

Home and office—P.O. Box 13351, Burton Station, Vashon Island, WA 98013.

■ Career

Writer and songwriter. Has worked as a counselor for children with learning disabilities.

■ Writings

(With wife, Marcia Vaughan) *Who?*, Ashton Scholastic (Australia), 1985.
(With M. Vaughan) *Ships and Boats and Things That Float*, Harcourt (Australia), 1989.
(With M. Vaughan) *Adam's Apple*, illustrated by Coral Tulloch, Five Mile Press (Australia), 1989.
Charlie, Shortland/Rigby (Australia), 1990.
The Magic of Marvin, Rigby (Australia), 1992.
A Skirt for Susan, illustrated by Lesley Boston, Random House (Australia), 1992.
Zoo Babies, Scott, Foresman, 1993.
Trees, Shortland/Rigby, 1994.
Apple Seeds, Scott, Foresman, 1994.
Two Gardens, Scott, Foresman, 1994.
Bon Voyage, HarperCollins (Toronto), 1994.
Looking Up, HarperCollins, 1995.
Lift up the Sky, illustrated by Robin Moore, HarperCollins, 1995.
Going to the Doctor, Harcourt, 1996.
Wildlife of the Tundra, ScottForesman, 1996.
Ten Tortillas, Shortland/Rigby, 1996.
Going Up, Scott, Foresman, 1996.
Wild Baby Animals, Scott, Foresman, 1996.
Rashee and the Elephants, Scott, Foresman, 1996.

RICHARD VAUGHAN

■ Sidelights

Remembering his own childhood, and what it was like to be labeled "learning disabled," writer Richard Vaughan told *SATA* that he "found reading and writing incredibly difficult, and those strange buildings called libraries downright scary." But Vaughan didn't let his difficulty with learning stand in the way of accomplishing his goals. After completing his education, he began a career as a counselor, working with children with learning difficulties similar to his own. "I also married a librarian. Surprise, surprise!" Vaughan quipped.

His first professional writing assignment was a magazine article about his counseling work: "I had to relive the terror of self-expression and rejection. Yet," he added, "overcoming those fears and achieving acceptance opened for me the mysterious world of the written word."

After publishing several more articles, Vaughan felt he had gained the confidence to tackle writing a children's book. "Easy, right? Wrong!," he exclaimed. "It was five years of rejection letters before I had my first book published." That first book was *Who?*, which Vaughan published in 1985. Even with a successful career as a children's writer underway—he has written nineteen books—Vaughan remains humble: "I am still learning how to write."

As a writer, Vaughan continues to encourage children to give reading a try. "Giving author presentations to schools and organizations, I endeavor to convey how facing weaknesses builds strength and overcoming fears can open the door to the magical world of literature."

■ For More Information See

PERIODICALS

Magpies, March, 1992, p. 26.

* * *

WATKINS-PITCHFORD, Denys James 1905-1990 (BB, Michael Traherne)

■ Personal

Born July 25, 1905, in Lamport, Northamptonshire, England; died September 8, 1990; son of Walter (a clergyman) and Edith Elizabeth (Wilson) Watkins-Pitchford; married Cecily Mary Adnitt, August 10, 1939 (died, 1974); children: Angela June, Robin John (deceased). *Education:* Studied art in Paris, 1924; graduated from Royal College of Art; Royal College of Art Painting School associate, 1926-28.

■ Addresses

Agent—David Higham Associates Ltd., 5-8 Lower John St., Golden Square, London W1R 4HA, England.

■ Career

Writer and illustrator. Assistant art master at Rugby School, Warwickshire, England, 1934-49. Broadcaster on natural history subjects. *Military service:* City of London Yeomanry Royal Horse Artillery, territorial army, 1925-29; King's Prize, 1928; captain in the Home Guard during World War II, 1940-46. *Member:* Royal Society of Arts (fellow).

Denys James Watkins-Pitchford with daughter, Angela.

■ Awards, Honors

Carnegie Medal, British Library Association, 1942, for *The Little Grey Men: A Story for the Young in Heart;* M.A., Leicester University, 1986; member of the Order of the British Empire, 1989.

■ Writings

SELF-ILLUSTRATED FICTION FOR CHILDREN; UNDER PSEUDONYM BB

Wild Lone: The Story of a Pytchley Fox, Scribner, 1938.
Manka, the Sky Gipsy: The Story of a Wild Goose, Scribner, 1939, published in England as *Sky Gipsy: The Story of a Wild Goose,* Eyre & Spottiswoode, 1939.
The Little Grey Men: A Story for the Young in Heart, Eyre & Spottiswoode, 1942, Scribner, 1949.
Brendon Chase, Hollis & Carter, 1944, Scribner, 1945.
Down the Bright Stream, Eyre & Spottiswoode, 1948, published as *The Little Grey Men Go Down the Bright Stream,* Methuen, 1977.
The Forest of Boland Light Railway, Eyre & Spottiswoode, 1955, published as *The Forest of the Railway,* Dodd, 1957.
Monty Woodpig's Caravan, Edmund Ward, 1957.
Ben the Bullfinch, Hamish Hamilton, 1957.
Wandering Wind, Hamish Hamilton, 1957, published as *Bill Badger and the Wandering Wind,* Methuen, 1981.
Alexander, Basil Blackwell, 1957.

Monty Woodpig and His Bubblebuzz Car, Edmund Ward, 1958.

Mr. Bumstead, Eyre & Spottiswoode, 1958.

The Wizard of Boland, Edmund Ward, 1959.

Bill Badger's Winter Cruise, Hamish Hamilton, 1959.

Bill Badger and the Pirates, Hamish Hamilton, 1960.

Bill Badger's Finest Hour, Hamish Hamilton, 1961, published as *Bill Badger and the Secret Weapon,* Methuen, 1983.

Bill Badger's Whispering Reeds Adventure, Hamish Hamilton, 1962.

Lepus, the Brown Hare, Benn, 1962.

Bill Badger's Big Mistake, Hamish Hamilton, 1963.

Bill Badger and the Big Store Robbery, Hamish Hamilton, 1967.

The Whopper, Benn, 1967, published as *The Monster Fish,* Scholastic, 1972.

At the Back o'Ben Dee, Benn, 1968.

Bill Badger's Voyage to the World's End, Kaye & Ward, 1969.

The Tyger Tray, Methuen, 1971.

The Pool of the Black Witch, Methuen, 1974.

Lord of the Forest, Methuen, 1975.

Contributor with A. L. E. Fenton and A. Windsor-Richards to *Stories of the Wild,* Benn, 1975, and with Windsor-Richards to *More Stories of the Wild,* Benn, 1977.

SELF-ILLUSTRATED NONFICTION FOR CHILDREN; UNDER PSEUDONYM BB

Meeting Hill: BB's Fairy Book, Hollis & Carter, 1948.

The Wind in the Wood, Hollis & Carter, 1952.

The Badgers of Bearshanks, Benn, 1961.

The Pegasus Book of the Countryside, Dobson, 1964.

SELF-ILLUSTRATED NONFICTION FOR ADULTS; UNDER PSEUDONYM BB

The Idle Countryman, Eyre & Spottiswoode, 1943.

The Wayfaring Tree, Hollis & Carter, 1946.

A Stream in Your Garden: How the Amateur May Install Running Water in Rock Gardens, and the Construction of Pools, Eyre & Spottiswoode, 1948.

Confessions of a Carp Fisher, Eyre & Spottiswoode, 1950, revised edition, Witherby, 1970.

Tide's Ending, Scribner, 1950.

Letters from Compton Deverell, Eyre & Spottiswoode, 1950.

Dark Estuary, Hollis & Carter, 1953, revised edition, Boydell Press, 1984.

A Carp Water (Wood Pool) and How to Fish It, Putnam (London), 1958.

The Autumn Road to the Isles, Nicholas Kaye, 1959.

The White Road Westwards, Nicholas Kaye, 1961.

September Road to Caithness and the Western Sea, Nicholas Kaye, 1962.

The Summer Road to Wales, Nicholas Kaye, 1964.

A Summer on the Nene, Kaye & Ward, 1967.

Recollections of a 'longshore Gunner, Boydell Press, 1976.

A Child Alone: The Memoirs of "BB", M. Joseph, 1978.

Ramblings of a Sportsman-Naturalist, M. Joseph, 1979.

The Naturalist's Bedside Book, M. Joseph, 1980.

The Quiet Fields, M. Joseph, 1981.

Indian Summer, M. Joseph, 1984.

The Best of "BB", M. Joseph, 1985.

Fisherman's Folly, Boydell and Brewer, 1987.

EDITOR; UNDER PSEUDONYM BB

The Sportsman's Bedside Book, illustrated by G. D. Armour, Eyre & Spottiswoode, 1937.

(Self-illustrated) *The Countryman's Bedside Book,* Eyre & Spottiswoode, 1941.

(Self-illustrated) *The Fisherman's Bedside Book,* Eyre & Spottiswoode, 1945, Scribner, 1946.

(Self-illustrated) *The Shooting Man's Bedside Book,* Scribner, 1948.

ILLUSTRATOR

Hesketh V. Prichard, *Sport in Wildest Britain,* Philip Allan, 1936.

Robert G. Walmsley, *Winged Company: Studies in Birdwatching,* Eyre & Spottiswoode, 1940.

Clarence H. Warren, *England Is a Village,* Eyre & Spottiswoode, 1940, Dutton, 1941.

Eric Benfield, *Southern English,* Eyre & Spottiswoode, 1942.

L. T. C. Rolt, *Narrow Boat,* Eyre & Spottiswoode, 1944.

Brian Vesey-Fitzgerald, *It's My Delight,* Eyre & Spottiswoode, 1947.

Arthur Applin, *Philandering Angler,* Hurst & Blackett, 1948.

J. B. Drought, *A Sportsman Looks at Eire,* Hutchinson, 1949.

Arthur G. Street, *Landmarks,* Eyre & Spottiswoode, 1949.

Gerald D. Adams, *Red Vagabond: The Story of a Fox,* Batchworth, 1951.

Mabel C. Carey, editor, *Fairy Tales of Long Ago,* Dutton, 1952.

Henry S. Tegner, *The White Foxes of Gorfenletch,* Hollis & Carter, 1954.

William Mayne, *The Long Night,* Basil Blackwell, 1957.

Elfrida Vipont, *The Secret of Orra,* Basil Blackwell, 1957.

Mayne, *Thirteen O'Clock,* Basil Blackwell, 1959.

Arthur B. W. Richards, *Vix: The Story of a Fox Cub,* Benn, 1960.

Tegner, *Beasts of the North Country: From Whales to Shrews,* Galley Press, 1961.

Andrew Lang, *Prince Prigio and Prince Ricardo,* Dent, 1961.

Richards, *Birds of the Lonely Lake,* Benn, 1961.

Richards, *The Cabin in the Woods,* Friday Press, 1963.

A. R. Channel, *Rogue Elephant,* Macrae-Smith, 1963.

Norah A. Burke, *King Todd: The True Story of a Wild Badger,* Putnam (London), 1963.

Frances Browne, *Granny's Wonderful Chair,* Dutton, 1963.

Richards, *The Wild White Swan,* Friday Press, 1965.

Tegner, *To Do with Birds,* Jenkins, 1965.

George Macdonald, *The Lost Princess: A Double Story,* Dutton, 1965.

Channel, *Jungle Rescue,* S. G. Phillips, 1968.

Gerald Summers, *Where Vultures Fly,* Collins, 1974.

OTHER

(Under pseudonym Michael Traherne) *Be Quiet and Go A-Angling* (adult nonfiction), Lutterworth Press, 1949.

Contributor under the pseudonym BB of adult fiction to *Five More Stories,* Basil Blackwell, 1958. Regular contributor to periodicals, including *Country Life, Field,* and *Shooting Times.* Watkins-Pitchford's books have been translated for publication in Germany, Holland, Yugoslavia, Israel, and Switzerland.

■ Adaptations

The Little Grey Men was adapted for a television series by the BBC, 1975, and has been optioned for a film in the United States; *Brendon Chase* was adapted for a radio series, and for a fifteen-episode television series by Southern TV, 1981.

■ Sidelights

British author and illustrator Denys James Watkins-Pitchford filled his children's tales with descriptions and characters that reflected his lifelong fascination with and appreciation of nature. The adventures of the three gnomes in his Carnegie Medal-winning *The Little Grey Men* are set in the natural landscape of Watkins-Pitchford's childhood home, and other popular books such as *Wild Lone: The Story of a Pytchley Fox* and *Brendon Chase* use the English woods as their backdrop. The author's adult books similarly draw on his knowledge as a natural historian and sportsman in order to provide detailed descriptions of nature and all its wonders. "In all of D. J. Watkins-Pitchford's books," observed Ann G. Hay in *Twentieth-Century Children's Writers,* "the English countryside is not merely supportive but a leading character, making them pleasurable reading for all ages."

Watkins-Pitchford was born just shortly before his larger twin brother on July 25, 1905. "So precarious appeared my hold on life that I had to be christened at once by my father who was fortunately a clergyman—rector of a country parish in the middle of England, a village called Lamport—for to die unchristened in those days was supposed to consign one to limbo, whatever that means," related Watkins-Pitchford in an essay for *Something about the Author Autobiography Series* (*SAAS*). "So delicate was I, there was no thought of sending me away to school like my twin, Roger, and elder brother, Engel."

As a child, Watkins-Pitchford found himself alone for many hours, and it was during this period that he became an ardent naturalist. Much of his time was spent fishing and hunting near his home. "There was not a tree or hedgerow, wood, stream, or pool, within five miles of our home with which I was unfamiliar," recalled Watkins-Pitchford in *SAAS.* "I knew my country as intimately as a wild fox knows his territory." This country surrounded the rectory where the author was born, a large home built during the reign of Queen Anne

for clergymen of the parish. Watkins-Pitchford added: "The view from the lawns to the north was breathtaking—the valley falling away in gentle folds to where the lakes glimmered between oak trees and tall rustling poplars."

In 1926 Watkins-Pitchford left his family's country home to study art in London. "I had always liked drawing and painting; both my parents were good at it and I had inherited the gift of drawing," he noted in *SAAS.* The noisy streets and crowds of people in London seemed worlds away from the quiet woodlands and rolling fields of Northamptonshire, and Watkins-Pitchford longed for home. "What an impact [London] made after my wild woodland life!" he exclaimed in *SAAS,* adding: "Streets and houses, crowds of people—the smell of the underground (it had a peculiar odour I do not notice now) and living in a great city made me quite sick for the sight of green fields."

Completing his schooling at the Royal College of Art, Watkins-Pitchford "had to look round for a job which suggested teaching, for to live by one's art in my day was definitely dodgy." He accepted a position as assistant art master at Rugby School in Warwickshire, where he remained for sixteen years. While at Rugby in 1938, Watkins-Pitchford published his first children's book—*Wild Lone: The Story of a Pytchley Fox.* "My early life, the boy roaming the fields, knowing so intimately each copse and field, gave me the idea of writing the story of a wild fox called Rufus and the writing of this story, which turned out to be *Wild Lone,* a best-seller too, coincided with my losing my heart to a girl I had known since childhood," he recalled in *SAAS.* Watkins-Pitchford married Cecily Mary Adnitt in 1939.

Following the publication of *Wild Lone* and his first adult book, *The Idle Countryman,* Watkins-Pitchford wrote the story that won him the Carnegie Medal—*The Little Grey Men.* "Again I wrote this at speed without any previous plan on how the story was to develop, but it seemed to write itself," he related in *SAAS.* "I illustrated it too, as I do with all my books and I write under the nom de plume 'BB' as my own name was so unwieldy being doubled barrelled." It was only after receiving the recognition of such an award that Watkins-Pitchford realized he might be able to make his living as a freelance author and illustrator. "So I cut my anchor rope after sixteen years at Rugby and moved to a house in the country," he recalled.

It was in this new home, Woodford Lodge, that Watkins-Pitchford's son Robin died, and for a year thereafter the author could not write. "Whether it was the loss of my son, or because the years of teaching had 'drained' me, I did no work for a year but returned to my childhood loves—rambling in the woods and shooting over the estate," related Watkins-Pitchford in *SAAS.* This absence of work eventually depleted his finances, however, and Watkins-Pitchford had to give up his country estate for a small village home, fittingly named the Round House. "I designed an iron wild-goose with wings stretched for a weather vane and this made a famous landmark for the villagers, telling them which way the wind was blowing," he explained.

Once settled in his new home, Watkins-Pitchford made four tours of Britain with his wife and daughter, writing and illustrating each one. "We were away from home for six to eight weeks at a time," he pointed out in *SAAS,* adding: "So I was able to enjoy a wild wandering life as well as to write about it, which was a very pleasant state of affairs." While home, Watkins-Pitchford explored the large forest nearby, which was part of the ancient Forest of Rockingham. This was also the forest into which he introduced the purple emperor, considered by many to be the finest of British butterflies. Previously glimpsing the rare butterfly in a forest in Oxfordshire, he collected a number of eggs and placed them in an outdoor muslin cage, bringing them through the winter until they turned into butterflies in late July. By repeating this process annually, Watkins-Pitchford managed to establish the purple emperor in a natural habitat. "One sunny day I released over forty males and females in a forest ride. The flew onto the sallow bush and there they displayed in the sun—a wondrous sight indeed, so many gleaming jewels."

Many books followed the move to the Round House, with nature and its "gleaming jewels" often providing the main focus. Watkins-Pitchford's personal favorites, *Brendon Chase* and *Wild Lone,* involve characters who must fend for themselves in the English woods and countryside. *Brendon Chase* is the story of three boys who run away from home and spend eight months in a nearby ancient forest. During this time they obtain their food and clothing from Brendon Chase, the forest, which sustains them until they return home. Ellen Lewis Buell wrote in a *New York Times* review that "this curious mixture of moods and styles binds the reader of ten and up in a leisurely unique enchantment." Rufus, the fox in *Wild Lone,* is also alone in the forest, his parents having died when he was a pup. This book tells the story of his life, during which he becomes an almost legendary figure to farmers, hunters, and many others. A *Saturday Review of Literature* contributor, who found Rufus "very close to a poet," added that "the whole volume is an unusually fine piece of bookmaking."

Although not his personal favorite of the more than fifty books written during his long career, *The Little Grey Men* remains Watkins-Pitchford's best selling work. This story of three gnomes recounts the adventures of Baldmoney, Sneezewort, and Dodder as they journey up Folly Brook looking for their lost brother Cloudberry. Many small animals and birds help them along the way, and the book includes three songs. Folly Brook actually ran down the valley near Watkins-Pitchford's childhood home, and in *SAAS* he explained that "one fine spring day my brother and I traced the Folly Brook to its source and this gave me the idea for my story." A reviewer in the *New Yorker* maintained that *The Little Grey Men* is "a sylvan fairy story, with a rich, sombre flavor ... that will probably make a permanent place for itself among imaginative readers."

These same readers can sample the extensive writings of Watkins-Pitchford's career in *The Best of "BB",* an anthology that contains selected passages from a number of his works. "Here is a book not to be gobbled down at a sitting but one for leisurely reading and re-reading over half a lifetime and more, for it is the record of the thoughts and observations of a most rarely gifted and clear-sighted man, one in whom the two talents of writing and painting are combined at a very high level," asserted Marcus Crouch in *Junior Bookshelf.* Writing of Watkins-Pitchford's contribution to children's literature, Crouch concluded: "The motto that has appeared on every one of BB's books from the beginning briefly sums up the nature of his vision and the motivation of his art: 'The wonder of the world, the beauty and the power, the shapes of things, their colours, lights and shades....' This is the essence of his achievement and the explanation of his enduring power to delight and move his readers."

■ Works Cited

Buell, Ellen Lewis, review of *Brendon Chase, New York Times,* November 11, 1945.

Crouch, Marcus, "'BB' at Eighty," *Junior Bookshelf,* August, 1985, pp. 165-68.

Hay, Ann G., "Denys James Watkins-Pitchford," *Twentieth-Century Children's Writers,* 4th edition, St. James Press, 1995, pp. 1000-02.

Review of *The Little Grey Men, New Yorker,* December 3, 1949.

Watkins-Pitchford, Denys James, essay in *Something about the Author Autobiography Series,* Volume 4, Gale Research, 1987.

Review of *Wild Lone: The Story of a Pytchley Fox, Saturday Review of Literature,* December 31, 1938.

■ For More Information See

PERIODICALS

Children's Literature in Education, autumn, 1990, pp. 145-54.

Growing Point, October, 1975, pp. 2714-15; November, 1978, pp. 3429-30; March, 1981, pp. 3839-40; September, 1981, pp. 3954-56.

Times Literary Supplement, May 25, 1967, p. 443; March 29, 1974, p. 326.

■ Obituaries

PERIODICALS

Times (London), September 12, 1990.*

—Sketch by Susan M. Reicha

*   *   *

WEBER, Michael 1945-

■ Personal

Born September 25, 1945, in New York, NY; son of David (a musician) and Dorothy (a teacher; maiden

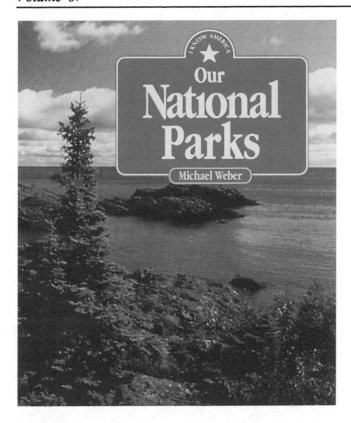

One of Weber's nonfiction titles is this entrant in the "I Know America" series.

name, Silverberg) Weber. *Education:* Hunter College, B.A. (magna cum laude), 1966; University of Wisconsin, graduate studies, 1966-67; New York University, M.A., 1968. *Politics:* "Enrolled Democrat."

■ Addresses

Home—6 Peter Cooper Rd., #2D, New York, NY 10010. *Electronic mail*—m1756w@aol.com (America Online).

■ Career

Nonfiction writer and acquisitions and development editor in humanities and social science publishing. Macmillan Publishing Company, New York City, assistant editor, 1970-71; Columbia University Press, New York City, associate editor, 1971-74; McGraw-Hill Book Company, New York City, editing supervisor, 1974-76; Harcourt Brace Jovanovich, New York City, associate editor, 1976-79; St. Martin's Press, New York City, project editor, 1979-81, acquisitions editor and development editor, 1981-89; M. E. Sharpe, Inc. (publisher), Armonk, NY, executive editor, 1989-95.

■ Writings

Our National Parks, Millbrook Press (Connecticut), 1994.
Our Congress, Millbrook Press, 1994.
Library of Presidents, volumes 1, 2, and 3, Rourke, in press.

Associate editor and contributor, *The New Columbia Encyclopedia,* Columbia University Press, 1975, and various materials in political science and history to the College Division of St. Martin's Press.

■ Sidelights

Michael Weber told *SATA:* "American students are sadly deficient in historical knowledge. I hope through my writing to help in some small way in remedying that deficiency. Educators and publishers bear a heavy responsibility for improving the population's historical literacy. Without some understanding of our past, we have little hope of coping with the problems of the present and preparing for the challenges of the future."

■ For More Information See

PERIODICALS
School Library Journal, June, 1994; January, 1995.

*   *   *

WERLIN, Nancy 1961-

■ Personal

Born October 29, 1961, in Salem, MA; daughter of Arnold (a computer engineer) and Elaine (a homemaker; maiden name, Romotsky) Werlin. *Education:* Yale

NANCY WERLIN

University, B.A., 1983. *Politics:* Liberal Democrat. *Religion:* Jewish.

■ Addresses

Home—22 Pearson Ave., Somerville, MA 02144. *Electronic mail*—nwerlin@ix.netcom.com. *Agent*—Shelley Roth, 138 Bay State Rd., Rehoboth, MA 02769.

■ Career

Software technical writer for various companies, 1983-87; Thomson Investment Software, Boston, MA, part-time software technical writer, 1987—. Member of board of directors, Shriver Clinical Services, Inc. *Member:* Authors Guild, Authors League of America, Society of Children's Book Writers and Illustrators.

■ Writings

Are You Alone on Purpose?, Houghton, 1994.

■ Work in Progress

Elena, a young adult fantasy novel; *Cambridge Gothic,* an adult novel; *Are You Alone on Purpose?* will be published in Germany by Loewe.

■ Sidelights

As Nancy Werlin told interviewer Kit Alderdice in a profile of the first-time novelist in *Publishers Weekly,* Werlin decided to become a writer when she was ten years old. "I just read all the time and it occurred to me that somebody had to write these things—and why shouldn't it be me?" Two decades, three drafts and a couple of rejections later, Werlin's first novel, *Are You Alone on Purpose?,* proves that she can do what she set out to do as a child—and with acclaim. She writes about issues she knows about first hand, including autism—which afflicts a member of her family—and its effects on the loved ones of an autistic child.

In *Are You Alone on Purpose?* Werlin tells the story of two Jewish teenagers locked in struggles with their families, with each other, and with their own identities. Thirteen-year-old Alison Shandling, a well-behaved high achiever, resents her tormentor, Harry Roth, who's just her opposite: a loud, crude, trouble-making bully who is also the town's widowed rabbi's only child. Alison's sweetness and drive to succeed are based on her need to compensate for her family's most draining problem, her autistic twin brother, Adam. Much of Harry's behavior seems to be an attempt just to get his bereaved father's attention, even if his father's only response is to reprimand him. Harry has taunted Alison openly for years about her autistic brother and her brilliance in the classroom.

It is not until the two teenagers are forced to spend time together under tragic circumstances that Alison and Harry come to terms with their problems—and their budding sexuality. After a diving accident Harry is left a paraplegic, confined to a wheelchair. Alison fears that this tragedy may have befallen Harry because of her mother's wish that Rabbi Roth's son might become even more handicapped than Adam, her autistic son. The girl tries to make amends for this by becoming friends with Harry, only to find as they are thrown together in Jewish studies that they become more than friends.

"Despite an ending a little too neatly resolved, this is a wonderful first novel," a reviewer for *Voice of Youth Advocates* noted. Writing in *School Library Journal,* Sharon Grover commented that although Alison's confrontation with her parents through letters misses the force of "Werlin's wonderfully strong dialogue, this first novel is a moving portrayal of two remarkable teenagers ably coming to grips with their unhappy circumstances." And a *Horn Book* contributor called *Are You Alone on Purpose?* "a promising debut."

Werlin told *SATA* that the scene in which Alison's enraged mother shouts her horrifying wish at Rabbi Roth is the one that inspired her to write *Are You Alone on Purpose?* "For me, a novel begins with a scene that takes up residence in my mind and will not go away," she explained. "In *Are You Alone on Purpose,* that scene was the one in which Betsy Shandling screams at her rabbi while her daughter Alison looks on. It haunted me for over a year, and while it did, characters and scenes formed around it, and finally—frightening though it was because I had never done it before—I began to write a novel. And now I've written one, and most of another, and can honestly say: I still don't know how to do it."

Werlin described her approach to writing a novel to *SATA* this way: "I fumble through writing a book the same way I read one: begin on page one, and go forward a sentence at a time. If I don't know the next sentence, I stop dead—sometimes for months—until I do. I think this is a stinky method and hope to find a better one a book or two down the road. On the other hand, it's worked so far."

■ Works Cited

Alderdice, Kit, "Nancy Werlin," *Publishers Weekly,* December 19, 1994, p. 34.
Review of *Are You Alone on Purpose?, Horn Book,* January/February, 1995, p. 13.
Review of *Are You Alone on Purpose?, Voice of Youth Advocates,* October, 1994.
Grover, Sharon, review of *Are You Alone on Purpose?, School Library Journal,* August, 1994, p. 204.

■ For More Information See

PERIODICALS

Booklist, August, 1994, p. 2039.
Publishers Weekly, November 14, 1994.

WOOD, David 1944-

■ Personal

Born February 21, 1944, in Sutton, Surrey, England; son of Richard Edwin and Audrey Adele (Fincham) Wood; married Sheila Ruskin, 1966 (marriage dissolved, 1970); married Jacqueline Stanbury (an actress), January 17, 1975; children: Katherine, Rebecca. *Education:* Worcester College, Oxford, B.A. (with honors), 1966. *Hobbies and other interests:* Writing, conjuring, collecting old books.

■ Addresses

Agent—(for plays) Casarotto Ramsay Ltd., National House, 60-66 Wardour St., London W1V 3HP, England; (for children's books) Eunice McMullen, 38 Clewer Hill Rd., Windsor, Berkshire SL4 4BW, England.

■ Career

Actor, composer, producer, director, playwright and author. W.S.G. Productions Ltd., director, 1966—; Whirligig Theatre (touring children's theatre company), co-founder and director, 1979—; Verronmead Limited (television production company), founder and director, 1983—; Westwood Theatre Productions, founder and director, 1986-95; W2 Productions Ltd., 1995—. Member of drama advisory panel, Arts Council of Great Britain, 1978-80. *Member:* BASCA, British Actors Equity Association, Society of Authors, Green Room Club.

■ Awards, Honors

Nottinghamshire Children's Book of the Year Award, 1990, for *Sidney the Monster*.

■ Writings

CHILDREN'S PLAYS

The Tinder Box (two-act; adaptation of a story by Hans Christian Andersen), produced in Worcester, England, 1967.

(Author of lyrics) *Cinderella*, book by Sid Collin, music by John Gould, produced in Glasgow, Scotland, 1968.

(With Sheila Ruskin) *The Owl and the Pussycat Went to See...* (two-act musical; adaptation of works by Edward Lear; produced in Worcester, 1968, and in London, 1969), Samuel French, 1970.

(With Ruskin) *Larry the Lamb in Toytown* (two-act musical; adaptation of stories by S. G. Hulme Beaman; produced in Worcester, 1969, and in London, 1973), French, 1977.

The Plotters of Cabbage Patch Corner (two-act musical; produced in Worcester, 1970, and in London, 1971), French, 1972.

Flibberty and the Penguin (two-act musical; produced in Worcester, 1971, and in London, 1977), French, 1974.

Tickle (produced on tour in England, 1972, and in London, 1977), French, 1978.

DAVID WOOD

The Papertown Paperchase (two-act musical; produced in Worcester, 1972, and in London, 1973), French, 1976.

Hijack over Hygenia (two-act musical; produced in Worcester, 1973), French, 1974.

Old Mother Hubbard (two-act musical; produced in Hornchurch, Essex, England, 1975), French, 1976.

Old Father Time (two-act musical; produced in Hornchurch, Essex, 1976), French, 1977.

The Gingerbread Man (two-act musical; produced in Basildon, Essex, England, 1976, and in London, 1977), French, 1977.

Mother Goose's Golden Christmas (two-act; produced in Hornchurch, Essex, 1977), French, 1978.

Nutcracker Sweet (two-act; produced in Farnham, Surrey, England, 1977, and in London, 1980), French, 1981.

Babes in the Magic Wood (two-act; produced in Hornchurch, Essex, 1978), French, 1979.

There Was an Old Woman ... (two-act; produced in Leicester, England, 1979), French, 1980.

Cinderella (produced in Hornchurch, Essex, 1979), French, 1980.

The Ideal Gnome Expedition (produced as *Chish and Fips,* Liverpool, England, 1980; produced as *The Ideal Gnome Expedition,* on tour and in London, 1981), French, 1982.

Aladdin (produced in Hornchurch, Essex, 1980), French, 1981.

(With Dave and Toni Arthur) *Robin Hood* (produced in Nottingham, England, 1981, and in London, 1982), French, 1985.

Meg and Mog Show (adaptation of stories by Helen Nicoll and Jan Pienkowski; produced in London, 1981), French, 1984.

Dick Whittington and Wondercat (produced in Hornchurch, Essex, 1981), French, 1982.

Jack and the Giant (produced in Hornchurch, Essex, 1982), French, 1987.

Magic and Music Show (one-man show), produced in London, 1983.

The Selfish Shellfish (produced in Farnham, Surrey, England, and in London, 1983), Amber Lane Press, 1983, French, 1986.

(With Dave and Toni Arthur) *Jack the Lad,* produced in Manchester, England, 1984.

The Old Man of Lochnagar (adaptation of the story by Prince Charles; produced in Aberdeen and London, 1986), Amber Lane Press, 1986.

Dinosaurs and All That Rubbish (music by Peter Pontzen; adaptation of the story by Michael Foreman; produced in Denbigh, Wales, 1986, and in London, 1988), Amber Lane Press, 1986, French, 1990.

The See-Saw Tree (produced in Farnham, Surrey, 1986, and in London, 1987), Amber Lane Press, 1987, French, 1987.

(With Dave and Toni Arthur) *The Pied Piper* (based on the tale by Robert Browning; produced at Yeovil, England and on tour, 1988), French, 1991.

Save the Human (adapted from the story by Toni Husband and David Wood; produced in Cambridge and London, 1990), French, 1990.

(Adaptor) *The BFG (Big Friendly Giant)* (adapted from the book by Roald Dahl; produced in London, 1991), French, 1991.

(Adaptor) *The Witches* (adapted from the book by Dahl; produced at Sheffield, England, and in London, 1992), French, 1994.

Noddy (adapted from stories by Enid Blyton; produced in London, 1993), French, 1995.

Rupert and the Green Dragon (adaptation of the *Rupert Bear* stories; produced in Leatherhead and on tour, 1993) French, 1996.

The BFG: Plays for Children, illustrated by Jane Walmsley, Puffin, 1993.

Meg and Mog: Four Plays for Children (adaption of stories by Helen Nicoll and Jan Pienkowski), Puffin, 1994.

More Adventures of Noddy (adapted from stories by Enid Blyton; produced in Wimbledon, England, and on tour, 1995-96), French, 1996.

Contributor of plays to books, including *Robin Hood and Friar Tuck* and *Marian and the Witches' Charm,* in *Playstages,* edited by John Alcock, Methuen, 1987.

CHILDREN'S FICTION

The Operats of Rodent Garden, illustrated by Geoffrey Beitz, Methuen, 1984.

The Gingerbread Man (from Wood's play), illustrated by Sally Anne Lambert, Pavilion, 1985.

The Discorats, illustrated by Beitz, Methuen, 1985.

(With Don Seed) *Chish 'n' Fips,* Boxtree, 1987.

Play Theatre (includes *Nativity Play* and *Jack and the Beanstalk*), two volumes, illustrated by Richard Fowler, Pavilion, 1987.

Sidney the Monster, illustrated by Clive Scruton, Walker, 1988.

Happy Birthday, Mouse! A First Counting Book, illustrated by Richard Fowler, Hodder & Stoughton, 1990.

Save the Human! (from Wood's play), illustrated by Toni Husband, Hamish Hamilton, 1991.

Baby Bear's Buggy Ride (To the Shops/To the Park), illustrated by Fowler, Hazar, 1993.

Kingfisher Pop-up Theatre: Cinderella, illustrated by Fowler, Kingfisher, 1994.

Bedtime Story: A Slip-in-the-Slot Book, illustrated by Fowler, Doubleday, 1995.

The Magic Show, illustrated by Fowler, Hazar, 1995.

ADULT PLAYS

(With David Wright) *Hang Down Your Head and Die* (two-act), produced in Oxford, England, in London, and in New York City, 1964.

(With John Gould) *Four Degrees Over* (two-act), produced in Edinburgh, Scotland, and in London, 1966.

(With Mick Sadler and Gould) *And Was Jerusalem,* produced in Oxford, 1966; produced as *A Present from the Corporation* in Worcester, England, and in London, 1967.

(With David Wright) *A Life in Bedrooms* (two-act), produced in Edinburgh, 1967; produced as *The Stiffkey Scandals of 1932* in London, 1968.

(With Gould) *Three to One On* (two-act), produced in Edinburgh at Edinburgh Festival, 1968.

(With Gould) *Postscripts* (two-act), produced in London, 1969.

(With Gould) *Down Upper Street* (two-act), produced in London, 1971.

(With Gould) *Just the Ticket* (two-act), produced in Leatherhead, Surrey, England, 1973.

Rock Nativity (two-act musical; music by Tony Hatch and Jackie Trent; produced in Newcastle-upon-Tyne, England, 1974; produced as *A New Tomorrow* in Wimbledon, England, 1976), Weinberger, 1977.

(With Iwan Williams) *Maudie* (two-act), produced in Leatherhead, Surrey, 1974.

(With Bernard Price and Julian Sluggett) *Chi-Chestnuts* (two-act), produced in Chichester, England, 1975.

(With Gould) *Think of a Number* (two-act), produced in Peterborough, England, 1975.

(Co-author) *More Chi-Chestnuts* (two-act), produced in Chichester, 1976.

(With Gould) *Bars of Gould* (two-act revue), produced in Exeter, England, 1977.

(With Gould) *The Luck of the Bodkins* (two-act; adaptation of a work by P. G. Wodehouse), produced in Windsor, 1978.

Abbacadabra (music by Bjorn Ulvaeus and Benny Andersson, lyrics by Don Black, Mike Batt, and Ulvaeus), produced in London, 1983.

OTHER

Swallows and Amazons (screenplay), Anglo EMI Ltd., 1974.

Also writer for television, including the series *Playaway,* 1973-77, *Emu's Christmas Adventure,* 1977, *Chish 'n' Fips,* 1984, *Chips' Comic,* 1984, *Seeing and Doing,*

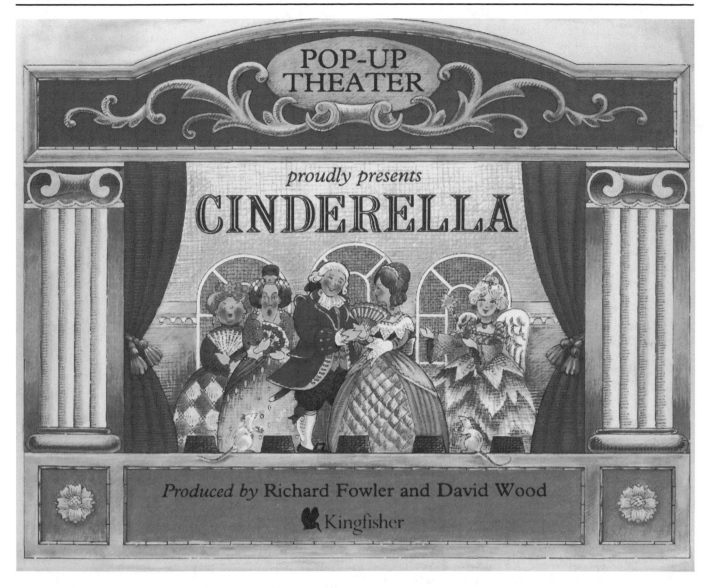

This pop-up book features one of playwright and author Wood's popular adaptations for children. (Cover illustration by Richard Fowler.)

1986, and *Back Home* (adaptation of the story by Michelle Magorian), 1989. Author of the screenplay *Tide Race,* 1989. Contributor of articles to *Drama* and *London Drama.*

■ Adaptations

Wood's stage adaptation of Enid Blyton's books was adapted into the video production *Noddy,* BBC Video, 1994.

■ Sidelights

David Wood's popular, successful plays focus on the often overlooked audience of children. An actor, director, and writer, Wood is the co-founder of the Whirligig Theatre, a touring company devoted entirely to bringing his plays, as well as the works of others, to children throughout England. Among these plays are those that give a new spin to old tales, including *The Gingerbread Man* and *The Owl and the Pussycat Went to See ...,* and

those that bring original, new stories to audiences, such as *Flibberty and the Penguin* and *The See-Saw Tree.* Wood's "musical plays appeal to children's love of action, movement, colour, and spectacle," asserts Colin Mills in *Twentieth-Century Children's Writers.* And a *Plays and Players* contributor adds: "It might be said, now that he has cornered the market, that Wood is our first, and only children's dramatist."

Wood first began to write seriously while a student at Oxford University; his first play as a cowriter, *Hang Down Your Head and Die,* was produced at the Comedy Theatre in 1964 while he was still a student. From that point on, he has written, directed, and acted in several plays, both for children and adults. In addition, Wood writes for television and for films, and has also recently broken into the children's book market. It is his children's plays, however, for which he is best known. Mills writes that among the reasons for the success of these plays is that "they all have an actor's instinct for their impact, as well as a gifted storyteller's feel for character, plot, and theme."

The plays that are based on well-known stories, such as *Robin Hood* and *Old Mother Hubbard,* are familiar to children, offering a level of comfort. At the same time, though, they "have imaginative and convoluted fun with their sources—and celebrate minor characters," points out Mills. Wood's original plays utilize traditional stock characters like those found in his adaptations— friendly dragons, well-intentioned but bumbling characters, and evil villains—and place them in action-filled adventures that incorporate audience participation. "The original plays are vital and unflagging," maintains Mills, adding that Wood "is a superb creator of names that capitalise upon children's love of word play: Blotch and Carbon, Kernel Walnut, Herr Von Cuckoo. In his dialogue and songs, he exploits the fun to be had from the topsy-turvy and the illogical."

Wood's imaginative children's plays and his work with Whirligig make theatre much more accessible to his young patrons. "The dream was to form a company to tour the shows, one that was not four actors and a hamper, that would sit upon the set that happened to be there," he explains in his *Plays and Players* interview. "We give a fully staged show, with 60 or 70 lighting cues. My belief is that we've short-changed children over the years—we've only given them theatre where it has been convenient. The mere phrase 'children's theatre,' in this country, has always had a second division tag on it. But these are tomorrow's theatregoers: they deserve more."

■ Works Cited

Mills, Colin, "David Wood," *Twentieth-Century Children's Writers,* 4th edition, St. James Press, 1995, pp. 1038-40.
Wood, David, interview "Child's Play," *Plays and Players,* December, 1987, pp. 8-9.

■ For More Information See

PERIODICALS

Books for Keeps, March, 1988, p. 17.
British Book News, December, 1987, p. 27.
Junior Bookshelf, February, 1986, p. 30.
Plays and Players, December, 1992, pp. 84-85.
School Librarian, February, 1992, p. 22; May, 1994, p. 69.

*   *   *

WRIGHT, Kit 1944-

■ Personal

Born in 1944, in Kent, England. *Education:* Attended Berkhamsted School, Hertfordshire, and New College, Oxford.

KIT WRIGHT

■ Addresses

Agent—c/o Viking Kestrel, 27 Wrights Lane, London W8 5TZ, England.

■ Career

Teacher in a comprehensive school, London, England; Brock University, St. Catharines, Ontario, lecturer in English, 3 years; Trinity College, Cambridge, England, fellow-commoner in Creative Arts, 1977-79; writer. *Member:* Poetry Society (education secretary, 1970-75).

■ Awards, Honors

Geoffrey Faber Memorial prize, 1978; Alice Hunt Bartlett prize, Poetry Society, 1978; Arts Council bursary, 1985.

■ Writings

POETRY FOR CHILDREN

(Editor) *Soundings: A Selection of Poems for Speaking Aloud,* Heinemann, 1975.
Arthur's Father, illustrated by Eileen Browne, Methuen, 1978.
Arthur's Granny, illustrated by Browne, Methuen, 1978.
Arthur's Sister, illustrated by Browne, Methuen, 1978.
Arthur's Uncle, illustrated by Browne, Methuen, 1978.
Rabbiting on and Other Poems, illustrated by Posy Simmonds, Fontana, 1978.
Hot Dog and Other Poems, illustrated by Simmonds, Viking Kestrel, 1981.
Professor Potts Meets the Animals of Africa, illustrated by Gillian Chapman, Watts, 1981.
(Editor) *Poems for 9-Year-Olds and Under,* illustrated by Michael Foreman, Viking Kestrel, 1984.

(Editor) *Poems for Over 10-Year-Olds,* illustrated by Foreman, Viking Kestrel, 1984.

Cat among the Pigeons, illustrated by Simmonds, Viking Kestrel, 1987.

(Editor) *Funny Bunch,* illustrated by Foreman, Viking, 1993.

Tigerella, illustrated by Peter Bailey, Scholastic, 1993.

Great Snakes!, illustrated by Simmonds, Viking, 1994.

POETRY FOR ADULTS

(With Stephen Miller and Elizabeth Maslen) *Treble Poets 1,* Chatto & Windus, 1974.

The Bear Looked over the Mountain, Salamander Imprint, 1977.

Bump-Starting the Hearse, Hutchinson, 1983.

From the Day Room, Windows Press (Liverpool), 1983.

Real Rags and Red, Hutchinson, 1988.

Poems 1974-1983, Hutchinson, 1988.

Short Afternoons, Hutchinson, 1989.

■ Sidelights

"Kit Wright's poetry for children has an exuberance, a vitality, and a technical virtuosity that works equally well on the page or when read aloud," Michael Glover asserts in *Twentieth-Century Children's Writers.* Author of verse for both adults and children, Wright is probably best-known in his native England for humorous, pun-filled poems that include subjects from family situations to school matters, and characters like the infamously mischievous Dave Dirt. Placing the author in the tradition of Lewis Carroll and Stevie Smith, *Times Literary Supplement* critic Tim Dooley calls Wright's work "striking for the versatility and inventiveness of its rhythms [and] its play with light-verse forms, free-verse improvisation, hymn tunes and blues. It is notable also for a comedy that is innocent of accepted notions of decorum or outrage and a clarity of vision that keeps a cool unflinching eye on madness, misery and mortality." According to Gavin Ewart in *British Book News,* Wright is "undoubtedly" the "best light verse writer" of his generation.

Following his first collection of children's verse, 1978's *Rabbiting on and Other Poems,* Wright published the highly-praised *Hot Dog and Other Poems* in 1981. Marcus Crouch, for instance, observes in *School Librarian* that *Hot Dog* "confirms earlier impressions that this is a poet of individual quality." The book includes poems about a boy who wants to avoid his aunt's hugs and kisses; a rabbit whose Christmas is spoiled by a lost carrot; and Dave Dirt's dog, who inspires an assortment of ridiculous descriptions. Many of these pieces are "just fun and the wit is always perceptive rather than malicious," A. R. Williams writes in *Junior Bookshelf.* Wright has "a playful—but sharp and witty—grasp of what drives people up the wall and how merciless children's observation of adult silliness can be," Alan Jenkins explains in *Times Literary Supplement.* "The tone of the eye of these poems may be innocent, but not as innocent as all that. There is room for the absurd, the grotesque and the egomaniacal." *Hot Dogs* also contains several more serious poems, such as "Cathedral Gardens," an evocative description of a graveyard at sunset, and "Useful Person," about an encounter between a family waiting for a train and a mentally impaired girl.

Cat among the Pigeons similarly demonstrates that Wright is a "versatile poet" who "appeals to a wide range of moods and tastes," Brian Merrick notes in *Children's Literature in Education.* The quieter pieces of the collection "slip easily in among the humorous, which are frequently as pointed as they are entertaining," *Times Literary Supplement* contributor Alan Brownjohn remarks. While acknowledging the collection's humor, Margery Fisher of *Growing Point* hails

And then she was gathering pace through the whispering hay fields,
Running, racing, the beat of her heart in tune
With the earth and the night and the creatures ~ until she coiled
And LEAPT and bit a piece from the rolling moon!

In Wright's whimsical poetic tale *Tigerella,* quiet, well-behaved young Ella turns into a giant jungle cat at the stroke of midnight. (Illustration by Peter Bailey.)

Wright's use of rhyme and other poetic techniques, writing that the poems "suggest that the manipulation of words and rhythms can be fun." As Brownjohn concludes, Wright "is a dexterous craftsman as well as a comedian, and his poems consistently ask children to stretch both their imaginations and their sympathies."

In 1994's *Tigerella*, Wright uses verse to tell a single story, that of a little girl who is well-behaved by day but at night turns into a ferocious flying tiger. Wright relates Ella's adventures chasing the moons and playing among the stars in "lyrical language," Lucinda Snyder Whitehurst relates in *School Library Journal*, adding that the story "maintains a playful mood and therefore can be mysterious without being frightening." Wright's use of "sophisticated meters ... mostly adds to the fantasy element," creating an "atmospheric tale," a *Publishers Weekly* critic comments. With language that is "both straightforward and soaring," as a *Kirkus Reviews* writer describes it, Wright "delivers an imaginative and beautifully told tale here."

In addition to producing his own verse, Wright has attempted to bring poetry to a wider audience by performing his work and by compiling several anthologies of poetry by other authors. In the collection *Poems for 9-Year-Olds and Under*, for instance, Wright "could hardly have chosen a better set of rhymes," Crouch declares in *Junior Bookshelf*. Similarly, the poems Wright selected for *Funny Bunch* "are all humorous in a way—some seem to be ridiculous, others are witty and clever," B. Clark observes in another *Junior Bookshelf* article. I. Anne Rowe likewise remarks in *School Librarian* that the poems in *Funny Bunch* will "hit the right spot.... Once this book is loose in the classroom, teachers will have to stand in line to get their hands on it." Providing an insight into Wright's ability to find and create poems that entertain children, Glover concludes: "There is an infectiously joyful quality about his attitude to his subject matter that is likely to serve as an inspiration to all aspiring writers, whether they be young or old."

■ Works Cited

Brownjohn, Alan, "Left out and Back In: Poetry for Children," *Times Literary Supplement*, April 1-7, 1988, p. 368.

Clark, B., review of *Funny Bunch, Junior Bookshelf*, April, 1994, p. 61.

Crouch, Marcus, review of *Hot Dog and Other Poems, School Librarian*, September, 1981, p. 246.

Crouch, Marcus, review of *Poems for 9-Year-Olds and Under, Junior Bookshelf*, August, 1984, p. 172.

Dooley, Tim, "Beyond a Joke," *Times Literary Supplement*, February 17-23, 1989, p. 169.

Ewart, Gavin, "Poetry in Britain 1978-81," *British Book News*, June, 1982, pp. 336-40.

Fisher, Margery, review of *Cat among the Pigeons, Growing Point*, May, 1988, pp. 4970-71.

Glover, Michael, "Kit Wright," *Twentieth-Century Children's Writers*, 4th edition, St. James Press, 1995, pp. 1044-45.

Jenkins, Alan, review of *Hot Dog and Other Poems, Times Literary Supplement*, July 24, 1981, p. 843.

Merrick, Brian, review of *Cat among the Pigeons, Children's Literature in Education*, March, 1991, p. 32.

Rowe, I. Anne, review of *Funny Bunch, School Librarian*, February, 1994, p. 30.

Review of *Tigerella, Kirkus Reviews*, August 15, 1994, p. 1141.

Review of *Tigerella, Publishers Weekly*, July 25, 1994, p. 54.

Whitehurst, Lucinda Snyder, review of *Tigerella, School Library Journal*, December, 1994, pp. 90-91.

Williams, A. R., review of *Hot Dog and Other Poems, Junior Bookshelf*, October, 1981, p. 204.

■ For More Information See

BOOKS

Contemporary Poets, 3rd edition, St. James Press, 1991, pp. 1084-85.

PERIODICALS

Booklist, September 15, 1994, p. 146.

Books for Your Children, spring, 1990, p. 19.

Junior Bookshelf, February, 1985, pp. 47-48; December, 1993, pp. 228-29.

Listener, November 19, 1987, p. 40.

School Librarian, March, 1979, p. 50; December, 1984, p. 370; March, 1985, p. 53; February, 1994, p. 18.

Times Educational Supplement, September 22, 1978, p. 23; February 5, 1988, p. 55; November 12, 1993, p. R6; November 11, 1994, p. R7.*

Cumulative Indexes

Illustrations Index

In the following index, the number of the volume in which an illustrator's work appears is given *before* the colon, and the page number on which it appears is given *after* the colon. For example, a drawing by Adams, Adrienne appears in Volume 2 on page 6, another drawing by her appears in Volume 3 on page 80, another drawing in Volume 8 on page 1, another drawing in Volume 15 on page 107, and so on.

YABC

Index citations including this abbreviation refer to listings appearing in *Yesterday's Authors of Books for Children,* also published by Gale Research Inc., which covers authors who died prior to 1960.

Author Index

The following index gives the number of the volume in which an author's biographical sketch, Brief Entry, or Obituary appears.

This index includes references to all entries in the following series, which are also published by Gale Research Inc.

YABC—*Yesterday's Authors of Books for Children: Facts and Pictures about Authors and Illustrators of Books for Young People from Early Times to 1960*

CLR—*Children's Literature Review: Excerpts from Reviews Criticism, and Commentary on Books for Children*

SAAS—*Something about the Author Autobiography Series*

Andrew, Prudence (Hastings) 1924- *87*
Andrews, Benny 1930- *31*
Andrews, F(rank) Emerson
  1902-1978 ....*22*
Andrews, J(ames) S(ydney) 1934- *4*
Andrews, Jan 1942- *58*
  Brief entry *49*
Andrews, Julie 1935- *7*
Andrews, Laura
  See Coury, Louise Andree
Andrews, Roy Chapman 1884-1960 ......*19*
Andrews, V(irginia) C(leo) (?)-1986
  Obituary *50*
Andrews, Wendy
  See Sharmat, Marjorie Weinman
Andrews, William G. 1930- *74*
Andrezel, Pierre
  See Blixen, Karen (Christentze Dinesen)
Andriola, Alfred J. 1912-1983
  Obituary *34*
Andrist, Ralph K. 1914- *45*
Anfousse, Ginette 1944-
  Brief entry *48*
Angel, Marie (Felicity) 1923- *47*
Angeles, Peter A. 1931- *40*
Angell, Judie 1937- *78*
  Earlier sketch in SATA *22*
  See also CLR *33*
Angell, Madeline 1919- *18*
Angelo, Valenti 1897- *14*
Angelou, Maya 1928- *49*
Angier, Bradford *12*
Angle, Paul M(cClelland) 1900-1975
  Obituary *20*
Anglund, Joan Walsh 1926- *2*
  See also CLR *1*
Angrist, Stanley W(olff) 1933- *4*
Anholt, Catherine 1958- *74*
Anholt, Laurence 1959- *74*
Anita
  See Daniel, Anita
Annett, Cora
  See Scott, Cora Annett (Pipitone)
Annixter, Jane
  See Sturtzel, Jane Levington
Annixter, Paul
  See Sturtzel, Howard A(llison)
Anno, Mitsumasa 1926- *77*
  Earlier sketches in SATA *5, 38*
  See also CLR *14*
Anrooy, Frans van
  See Van Anrooy, Francine
Anstey, Caroline 1958- *81*
Antell, Will D. 1935- *31*
Anthony, Barbara 1932- *29*
Anthony, C. L.
  See Smith, Dorothy Gladys
Anthony, Edward 1895-1971 ....*21*
Anthony, John
  See Ciardi, John (Anthony)
Anthony, Piers 1934- *84*
  See also SAAS *22*
Anthony, Susan C(arol) 1953- *87*
Anticaglia, Elizabeth 1939- *12*
Antolini, Margaret Fishback 1904-1985
  Obituary *45*
Anton, Michael (James) 1940- *12*
Antonacci, Robert J(oseph) 1916- *45*
  Brief entry *37*
Aoki, Hisako 1942- *45*
Apfel, Necia H(alpern) 1930- *51*
  Brief entry *41*
Aphrodite, J.
  See Livingston, Carole
Apostolou, Christine Hale 1955- *82*
Appel, Benjamin 1907-1977 ....*39*
  Obituary *21*
Appel, Martin E(liot) 1948- *45*
Appel, Marty
  See Appel, Martin E(liot)
Appelt, Kathi 1954- *83*
Appiah, Peggy 1921- *84*
  Earlier sketch in SATA *15*
  See also SAAS *19*
Apple, Margot *64*
  Brief entry *42*
Applebaum, Stan 1929- *45*

Appleton, Victor
  See Macdonald, James D.
Appleton, Victor [Collective
  pseudonym] *67*
  Earlier sketch in SATA *1*
Appleton, Victor II [Collective
  pseudonym] *67*
  Earlier sketch in SATA *1*
Apsler, Alfred 1907- *10*
Aquillo, Don
  See Prince, J(ack) H(arvey)
Aragones, Sergio 1937- *48*
  Brief entry *39*
Araujo, Frank P. 1937- *86*
Arbuckle, Dorothy Fry 1910-1982
  Obituary *33*
Arbuthnot, May Hill 1884-1969 ....*2*
Archambault, John *67*
Archer, Frank
  See O'Connor, Richard
Archer, Jules 1915- *85*
  Earlier sketch in SATA *4*
  See also SAAS *5*
Archer, Marion Fuller 1917- *11*
Archibald, Joe
  See Archibald, Joseph S(topford)
Archibald, Joseph S(topford)
  1898-1986 ....*3*
  Obituary *47*
Ardai, Charles 1969- *85*
Arden, Barbie
  See Stoutenburg, Adrien
Arden, William
  See Lynds, Dennis
Ardizzone, Edward 1900-1979 ....*28*
  Obituary *21*
  Earlier sketch in SATA *1*
  See also CLR *3*
Ardley, Neil (Richard) 1937- *43*
Arehart-Treichel, Joan 1942- *22*
Arenella, Roy 1939- *14*
Arkin, Alan (Wolf) 1934- *59*
  Brief entry *32*
Armer, Alberta (Roller) 1904- *9*
Armer, Laura Adams 1874-1963 ....*13*
Armitage, David 1943-
  Brief entry *38*
Armitage, Ronda (Jacqueline)
  1943- *47*
  Brief entry *38*
Armour, Richard (Willard)
  1906-1989 ....*14*
  Obituary *61*
Armstrong, George D. 1927- *10*
Armstrong, Gerry (Breen) 1929- *10*
Armstrong, Jennifer 1961- *77*
Armstrong, Louise *43*
  Brief entry *33*
Armstrong, Richard 1903- *11*
Armstrong, William H. 1914- *4*
  See also CLR *1*
  See also SAAS *7*
Arndt, Ursula (Martha H.) *56*
  Brief entry *39*
Arneson, D(on) J(on) 1935- *37*
Arnett, Carolyn
  See Cole, Lois Dwight
Arno, Enrico 1913-1981 ....*43*
  Obituary *28*
Arnold, Caroline 1944- *85*
  Brief entry *34*
  Earlier sketch in SATA *36*
Arnold, Elliott 1912-1980 ....*5*
  Obituary *22*
Arnold, Emily 1939- *76*
  Earlier sketch in SATA *50*
Arnold, Katya 1947- *82*
Arnold, Oren 1900- *4*
Arnold, Susan (Riser) 1951- *58*
Arnold, Tedd 1949- *69*
Arnoldy, Julie
  See Bischoff, Julia Bristol
Arnosky, Jim 1946- *70*
  Earlier sketch in SATA *22*
  See also CLR *15*
Arnott, Kathleen 1914- *20*
Arnov, Boris, Jr. 1926- *12*

Arnow, Harriette (Louisa) Simpson
  1908-1986 ....*42*
  Obituary *47*
Arnsteen, Katy Keck 1934- *68*
Arnstein, Helene S(olomon) 1915- *12*
Arntson, Herbert E(dward) 1911- *12*
Aroner, Miriam *82*
Aronin, Ben 1904-1980
  Obituary *25*
Arora, Shirley (Lease) 1930- *2*
Arquette, Lois S(teinmetz) 1934- *1*
  See Duncan, Lois S(teinmetz)
Arrick, Fran
  See Angell, Judie
Arrowood, (McKendrick Lee) Clinton
  1939- *19*
Arrowsmith, Pat
  See Barton, Pat
Arthur, Robert
  See Feder, Robert Arthur
Arthur, Ruth M(abel) 1905-1979 ....*7*
  Obituary *26*
Artis, Vicki Kimmel 1945- *12*
Artzybasheff, Boris (Miklailovich)
  1899-1965 ....*14*
Aruego, Ariane
  See Dewey, Ariane
Aruego, Jose 1932- *68*
  Earlier sketch in SATA *6*
  See also CLR *5*
Arundel, Honor (Morfydd)
  1919-1973 ....*4*
  Obituary *24*
  See also CLR *35*
Arundel, Jocelyn
  See Alexander, Jocelyn (Anne) Arundel
Arvey, Michael 1948- *79*
Asare, Meshack (Yaw) 1945- *86*
Asbjoernsen, Peter Christen
  1812-1885 ....*15*
Asch, Frank 1946- *66*
  Earlier sketch in SATA *5*
Ash, Jutta 1942- *38*
Ashabranner, Brent (Kenneth)
  1921- *67*
  Earlier sketch in SATA *1*
  See also CLR *28*
  See also SAAS *14*
Ashby, Gwynneth 1922- *44*
Ashe, Arthur (Robert, Jr.), Jr.
  1943-1993 ....*65*
  Obituary *87*
Ashe, Geoffrey (Thomas) 1923- *17*
Ashe, Mary Ann
  See Lewis, Mary (Christianna)
Asher, Sandy (Fenichel) 1942- *71*
  Brief entry *34*
  Earlier sketch in SATA *36*
  See also SAAS *13*
Ashey, Bella
  See Breinburg, Petronella
Ashford, Daisy
  See Ashford, Margaret Mary
Ashford, Margaret Mary 1881-1972 ......*10*
Ashley, Bernard 1935- *79*
  Brief entry *39*
  Earlier sketch in SATA *47*
  See also CLR *4*
Ashley, Elizabeth
  See Salmon, Annie Elizabeth
Ashley, Ray
  See Abrashkin, Raymond
Ashton, Lorayne
  See Gottfried, Theodore Mark
Ashton, Warren T.
  See Adams, William Taylor
Asimov, Isaac 1920-1992 ....*74*
  Earlier sketches in SATA *1, 26*
  See also CLR *12*
Asimov, Janet (Jeppson) 1926- *54*
Asinof, Eliot 1919- *6*
Aska, Warabe 1944- *56*
Astley, Juliet
  See Lofts, Norah (Robinson)
Aston, James
  See White, T(erence) H(anbury)